I0754588

SENEY'S OHIO CODE.

THE CODE OF CIVIL PROCEDURE, AND THE CODE OF PROCEDURE BEFORE JUSTICES OF THE PEACE, for the State of Ohio. With Notes of the Decisions of the Courts of Ohio, Kentucky, Indiana and New York. By Hon. Geo. E. Seney, Judge of the Tenth Judicial District.

1 Vol. 8vo. $5.00.

NASH'S PLEADINGS AND PRACTICE.

PLEADING AND PRACTICE UNDER THE CIVIL CODES OF OHIO AND KANSAS. By Hon. Simeon Nash. Second edition, thoroughly revised, enlarged and improved.

1 Vol. Royal 8vo. $5.00.

SWAN'S PLEADINGS AND PRECEDENTS.

COMMENTARIES ON PLEADINGS UNDER THE OHIO CODE, with Precedents of Petitions, Answers, Demurrers and Replies. By Hon. Joseph R. Swan.

1 Vol. 8vo. $5.00.

SWAN'S NEW TREATISE FOR JUSTICES IN OHIO.

A TREATISE ON THE LAW RELATING TO THE POWERS AND DUTIES OF JUSTICES OF THE PEACE AND CONSTABLES, in the State of Ohio (and in Kansas), with Practical Forms, etc. By Hon. Joseph R. Swan. Eighth edition corrected and enlarged. Revised to conform to the Statutes, etc., in force May, 1862.

1 Vol. Royal 8vo. $5.00.

RAFF'S GUIDE FOR EXECUTORS AND ADMINISTRATORS IN OHIO.

A GUIDE TO EXECUTORS AND ADMINISTRATORS in the settlement of the Estates of Deceased Persons within the State of Ohio, to which is prefixed a brief Comment upon the Statute of Wills, showing how Wills are Executed and Proved in this State, and their effect in certain cases. By Geo. W. Raff, late Probate Judge of Stark County. Second and thoroughly revised edition.

1 Vol. 8vo. $1.50.

TAYLOR'S OHIO SCHOOL SYSTEM.

A MANUAL OF THE OHIO SCHOOL SYSTEM, consisting of an Historical View of its Progress, and a republication of the School Laws in force. By James W. Taylor.

1 Vol. 8vo. $1.50.

KENTUCKY REPORTS.

Reports of Cases at Common Law and in Equity, argued and decided in the Court of Appeals of the Commonwealth of Kentucky, as follows:

Bibb,	1808 to 1817,	4 vols.	$20.00
A. K. Marshall,	1817 to 1821,	3 vols. in 2,	10.00
Littell,	1822 to 1824,	6 vols. in 3,	20.00
" select cases,	1795 to 1821,		
T. B. Monroe,	1824 to 1828,	7 vols. in 3,	25.00
J. J. Marshall,	1829 to 1832,	7 vols. in 4,	25.00
Dana,	1833 to 1840,	9 vols. in 5,	35.00
Ben Monroe,	1840 to 1858,	18 vols.	90.00
Metcalfe,	1859 to 1862,	3 vols.	15.00

The Set, 57 Vols. in 42. $240.00.

THE REVISED STATUTES OF KENTUCKY.

Approved and adopted by the General Assembly, 1851 and 1852, and in force from July 1, 1852, with all the amendments subsequently enacted, and Notes of the Decisions of the Court of Appeals of Kentucky, by Hon. Richard H. Stanton. With Supplement, embracing the Acts of a General Nature passed by the Legislature of 1859-60.

[*Made authority in all Courts in Kentucky, by Act of General Assembly.*]

2 Vols. Royal 8vo. $10.00.

STANTON'S KENTUCKY CODE OF PRACTICE.

Code of Practice in Civil and Criminal Cases for the State of Kentucky. Originally prepared by M. C. Johnson, James Harlan, and J. W. Stevenson, Commissioners, and adopted by the Legislature; with the subsequent Amendments, and illustrated by Notes of the Decisions of the Court of Appeals of Kentucky and other Courts. (1859.) By Hon. R. H. Stanton.

[*Made authority in all Courts in Kentucky, by Act of General Assembly.*]

1 Vol. Royal 8vo. $5.00.

STANTON'S TREATISE FOR JUSTICES, ETC., IN KENTUCKY.

A Practical Treatise for the Use of Justices of the Peace, Constables, Sheriffs, Jailors and Coroners, of Kentucky, with Forms for these officers. By Hon. Richard H. Stanton, of Maysville, Ky.

1 Vol. 8vo. $4.00.

STANTON'S MANUAL FOR EXECUTORS, ADMINISTRATORS, GUARDIANS AND TRUSTEES IN KENTUCKY.

A Practical Manual for the use of Executors, Administrators, Guardians and Trustees, in Kentucky, with the Law in regard to Wills, and the Probate thereof, and Forms for the use of these Officers. By Hon. Richard H. Stanton, of Maysville, Ky.

1 Vol. 12mo. $1.50.

RAFF'S MANUAL OF PENSIONS AND BOUNTIES.

A Manual of Pensions and Bounties, containing full forms and instructions for obtaining Pensions, Bounty Money and Bounty Lands, under the various Acts of Congress, to August, 1862. By Hon. George W. Raff.

1 Vol. 12mo. $2.00.

MOREHEAD'S KENTUCKY PRACTICE.

The Practice in Civil Actions and Proceedings at Law in Kentucky, together with various Precedents of Declarations, with Practical Notes. By Hon. James T. Morehead.

1 Vol. 8vo. $2.00.

McDONALD'S TREATISE FOR JUSTICES IN INDIANA.

A Treatise on the Law relating to the Powers and Duties of Justices of the Peace and Constables, in the State of Indiana, with Practical Forms and Essays on various Titles of the Common Law. By David McDonald.

1 Vol. Royal 8vo. $5.00.

GWYNNE OF SHERIFFS AND CORONERS.

A Practical Treatise on the Law of Sheriff and Coroner, with Forms and References to the Statutes of Ohio, Indiana and Kentucky. By A. E. Gwynne.

1 Vol. 8vo. $2.00.

HOLCOMBE'S EQUITY JURISPRUDENCE.

An Introduction to Equity Jurisprudence, on the basis of Story's Commentaries, with Notes and References to English and American Cases. Adapted to the use of Students. By James P. Holcombe.

1 Vol. 8vo. $3.00.

BARTON'S SUIT IN EQUITY.

History of a Suit in Equity, from its commencement to its final termination. By Charles Barton, of Middle Temple. Revised and enlarged, with Forms of Bills, Answers, Pleas, Demurrers and Decrees. By James P. Holcombe. With an Appendix, containing the Ordinances of Lord Bacon, Rules of Practice in Equity in the Circuit Courts of the United States, and the English Orders in Chancery. *New Edition*, 1859.

1 Vol. 8vo. $2.25.

McLEAN'S CIRCUIT COURT REPORTS.

Reports of Cases argued and decided in the Circuit Court of the United States, for the Seventh District, from 1829 to 1855. By Hon. John McLean, Circuit Judge.

6 Vols. 8vo. $33.00.

HANDY'S CINCINNATI SUPERIOR COURT REPORTS.

REPORTS OF CASES ARGUED AND ADJUDGED IN THE SUPERIOR COURT OF CINCINNATI, in 1854 and 1855. By R. D. & J. H. Handy.

1 Vol. 8vo. $3.50.

Also, three numbers of Vol. 2, 1855–1856, 96 pages each.

Sewed. Each 50 Cents.

JOHNSON'S CHANCERY REPORTS.

REPORTS OF CASES ADJUDGED IN THE COURT OF CHANCERY OF NEW YORK, from 1814 to 1823. To which is added a General Digested Index of Cases decided in the Court of Chancery and in the Court for the Correction of Errors on Appeal, from 1799 to 1822, with tables, etc. By William Johnson.

7 Vols. in 3. 8vo. $18.00.

GILMAN'S INDIANA AND ILLINOIS DIGEST.

DIGEST OF THE DECISIONS OF THE SUPREME COURTS of the States of Indiana and Illinois, and the Circuit Court of the United States for the Seventh Circuit. By Charles Gilman.

1 Vol. 8vo. $3.00.

LEGAL BLANKS.

The following forms are now ready:

WARRANTY DEED—(With Dower.)
WARRANTY DEED—(Without Dower.)
QUIT CLAIM DEED—(With Dower.)
QUIT CLAIM DEED—(Without Dower.)
MORTGAGE—(With Dower)
MORTGAGE—(Without Dower.)
CHATTEL MORTGAGE.
ASSIGNMENT OF LEASE.
ASSIGNMENT OF JUDGMENT.
LEASE—(Long Term.)
LEASE—(Short Term.)
BOND.
POWER OF ATTORNEY.

The greatest care has been taken to make this series in every way worthy of patronage. The forms have been carefully prepared by an experienced Conveyancer; the Paper, made expressly for them, is of superior quality, a fine, white wove paper, extra tough, not liable to break when folded; the Type is new and appropriate, and the marginal and faint ruling neatly executed.

Price, $1.00 per Quire.

PENSION, PAY AND BOUNTY BLANKS.

Claim of Officer or Soldier for Invalid Pension.
Claim of Widow of Deceased Officer or Soldier for Pension.
Claim of Mother of Deceased Officer or Soldier for Pension.
Claim of Guardian of Minor Sister of Officer or Soldier for Pension.
Claim of Officer or Soldier for Arrears of Pay, Bounty Money, etc.
Claim of Widow of Deceased Officer or Soldier for Arrears of Pay, Bounty Money, etc.
Claim of Father of Deceased Officer or Soldier for Arrears of Pay, Bounty Money, etc.
Claim of Mother of Deceased Officer or Soldier for Arrears of Pay, Bounty Money, etc.
Claim of Adult Children or Guardian of Minor Children, or their Joint Claim for Arrears of Pay, Bounty Money, etc.
Claim of Brother or Sister of Deceased Officer or Soldier for Arrears of Pay, Bounty Money, etc.
Application of Officer or Soldier for Payment of Invalid Pension.
Application of Widow for Payment of Pension.

The above Forms have been prepared with great care, and conform in every respect to the latest regulations of the Pension and Second Auditor's Offices. All the Forms pertaining to an application are printed upon one sheet, embracing the Declaration of the Applicant, Certificates of the Magistrate, Certificate of the Surgeon, Power of Attorney, Clerk's Certificate, etc., etc., with ample blank spaces and full instructions for filling up.

Price, 75 Cents per Quire.

Sent by Mail prepaid on receipt of the price.

A

MANUAL

OF

PENSIONS, BOUNTY AND PAY:

CONTAINING THE

LAWS, FORMS AND REGULATIONS

RELATING TO

PENSIONS, BOUNTY LAND, BOUNTY MONEY, PAY, CLAIMS FOR HORSES AND OTHER PROPERTY DESTROYED, ETC.; WITH NOTES OF OFFICIAL DECISIONS, AND OPINIONS OF THE ATTORNEYS-GENERAL, WITH REFERENCE TO THE SUBJECTS NAMED.

By GEORGE W. RAFF.

SECOND EDITION—REVISED.

CINCINNATI:
ROBERT CLARKE & CO.,
LAW PUBLISHERS AND STATIONERS.
1863.

E. MORGAN & SONS,
Stereotypers, Printers & Binders,
CINCINNATI, O.

PREFACE.

THIS Manual is designed to embrace all that is of most importance pertaining to the subjects to which it relates. While brevity has been aimed at, nothing has been excluded which, in the judgment of the Compiler, would add to its usefulness. Some portions of the Contents may seem to possess no practical value; but, as exhibiting the growth and scope of the Pension System of the United States, their omission would have rendered the book incomplete.

CANTON, O., *October*, 1862.

CONTENTS.

GRATUITOUS PENSIONS.

CHAPTER VII.

CHAPTER VIII.

CHAPTER IX.

CHAPTER X.

CHAPTER XI.

CHAPTER XII.

CHAPTER XIII.

CHAPTER XIV.

MISCELLANEOUS.

CHAPTER XV.

CHAPTER XVI.

CHAPTER XVII.

CHAPTER XVIII.

CHAPTER XIX.

CHAPTER XX.

CHAPTER XXI.

CHAPTER XXII.

CHAPTER XXIII.

CHAPTER XXIV.

CHAPTER XXV.

CHAPTER XXVI.

CHAPTER XXVII.

CHAPTER XXVIII.

MANUAL

OF

PENSIONS, BOUNTY AND PAY.

CHAPTER I.

OF THE CLASSES OF PENSIONS.

The bounty of the Government of the United States towards those who engage in its military service, whether by land or sea, usually assumes one or more of three forms, namely: Invalid Pensions, Gratuitous Pensions, or Land Donations.

Invalid Pensions are grants of money to persons who become disabled in the service, either by wounds or other injuries received, or by sickness contracted, in the line of duty, whereby the sufferer is rendered incapable, in whole or part, of procuring for himself, and those dependent upon him, a livelihood. When promised at or before the time of entering the service, this class of pensions may be regarded as forming a part of the consideration upon which the contract of service is based, and not as a gratuity merely.[1] When granted at the expiration of the term of service, they partake of the nature of gratuitous pensions; but differ from these in this, that the disabled soldier has an equitable claim, or *quasi* right, to be provided for by his countrymen, for whose sake he has

---

[1] Decision of Secretary Stuart, Oct. 29, 1850.

risked and suffered, and become incapable of providing for himself.

Gratuitous Pensions are such as are usually granted at the close of a war or term of service, as a reward for eminent services rendered, or as evidence of a nation's gratitude to its defenders and preservers. In this class of pensions properly belongs the half-pay granted to the widows and orphans of those who die of wounds or sickness incurred in the service.

Land Donations, or bounty lands, are sometimes promised at or before the time of enlistment, as an inducement to enter the service; and in such cases these, too, may be regarded as entering into the consideration leading to the contract of service. At other times these are granted as gratuities, after the close of a war, to surviving officers, soldiers, seamen, etc., and to the widows and orphans of such as have died, from the same motives which characterize the granting of gratuitous pensions.

It is of the first importance that these distinctions between the several forms of governmental bounty should be fully understood and kept in view, in making application for the benefit of any of the numerous acts by which grants have been made.

CHAPTER II.

INVALID PENSIONS.

SECTION I.

WHO ENTITLED.

THE persons entitled to the benefit of the various laws and resolutions of Congress relating to Invalid Pensions are, in general, commissioned and non-commissioned officers of the army (including regulars,[1] volunteers, rangers and militia), and navy (including the navy proper, sea-fencibles, flotilla service, marine corps, and revenue cutters when co-operating with the navy)[2] musicians, privates, marines, seamen, ordinary seamen, and all others, in whatsoever capacity they may have served, who were regularly enlisted or drafted, or who volunteered;[3] and who, while in the line of duty,[4] were disabled, by wounds or sickness, from subsequently procuring a livelihood.

---

1 Cadets at West Point belong to the regular army, and are entitled to pensions for disabilities. *Opinion of Attorney-General Wirt, April* 8, 1820.

2 Act of April 18, 1814, (page 85.)

3 It is not sufficient that a man should be employed in a mechanical occupation by the government to make him an artificer of the army. The law does not contemplate such persons as these; but only those who formed a component part of the army, and were not only *mechanics*, but were *enlisted* also as *soldiers*. *Decision of Secretary Ewing, July* 18, 1849. The widow of a person who served as steward, but appeared upon the ship's books as one of the crew, and amenable to martial law is entitled to a pension. *Opinion of Attorney-General Butler, Nov.* 18, 1837.

4 LINE OF DUTY, WHAT:—Every officer in full commission, and not on furlough, although not at the moment employed; also soldiers kept in pay, with some exceptions. *Opinion of Attorney-General Rush, April* 6, 1815. It extends to all the operations of the ship, whether civil or military; and

Numerous special acts granting pensions to individuals have been passed by Congress; but as these have no immediate relation to the general pension system of the United States, they do not come within the purview of this compilation.

---

takes in the whole of her navigation during the entire cruise. The officer who is killed, or dies by reason of a wound received by the falling of a spar in a tempest, is as entirely within the description of being killed, or dying by reason of a wound received in the line of his duty, as the officer who is killed or dies by a wound in battle. *Attorney-General Wirt, March* 31, 1825. Disability incurred from any cause by a person in the line of his military duty, if not occasioned by his own misconduct, is entitled to a pension. *Attorney-General Butler, Dec.* 20, 1833. The law is understood to embrace only those who have been injured in the service of the United States, while actually employed in duties peculiar to them as soldiers; or from exposure to inclemencies of the weather at the posts or stations at which they may have been put on duty; or while on the march to such stations. *Secretary of War* (*through Surgeon-General*), *July* 15, 1824. The soldier is to be regarded as being always in "the line of his duty," when he is not under arrest, in confinement, on furlough,* or absent without leave, although there may be peculiar circumstances in particular cases which should modify this construction. *Secretary Ewing, April* 10, 1849. Death by drowning, in the line of duty in the naval service, entitles the widow of deceased to a pension. *Secretary Ewing, Feb.* 19, 1850. Disability of a soldier incurred in the line of his duty in removing Indians, entitles him to a pension. *Secretary Ewing, July* 2, 1850. Where the death of a soldier is caused by intemperance, which is an offense against the military laws, he does not die from a disease contracted in the service and in the line of his duty; and therefore is not entitled to a pension. *Secretary Stuart, October* 10, 1850. Insanity, when the effect of injury received, or exposure in the line of duty, and resulting in *suicide*, entitles the widow to the benefit of the pension laws. *Commissioner Waldo, June* 4, 1853.

A seaman was taken prisoner, and attempted to escape, for which he was severely punished by the enemy, and thereby disabled. It was held that the disability was contracted while in "the line of his duty," and for which he was entitled to a pension.

A soldier discharged on account of a disease, under which he was laboring at the time he entered the service, is not entitled to a pension.

See for further decisions, etc., after GRATUITOUS PENSIONS.

---

* A soldier on furlough is considered to be "in the service." *Secretary Stuart, Jan.* 27, 1852.

SECTION II.

INVALIDS OF THE REVOLUTION—ARMY AND NAVY.

Before proceeding to notice the laws still existing for the relief of invalids of the revolution, let us briefly review the acts which have been repealed or rendered entirely obsolete.

The Continental Congress, by a series of resolutions passed August 26, 1776, provided that every commissioned and non-commissioned officer and private soldier in the army, who should lose a limb in any engagement, or be otherwise so disabled in the service of the States, in the war then existing with the mother country, as to be rendered incapable "afterward of getting a livelihood," should receive during life, or the continuance of such disability, one half his monthly pay after his pay as soldier should cease. The same provision was made for the commanders, commissioned officers, marines and seamen, of ships-of-war and armed vessels of the United States, who should lose a limb in an engagement in which no prize should be taken, or should be otherwise so disabled as to be incapable of obtaining a livelihood. In case a prize should be taken, the amount received by the disabled person as prize money should be considered as part of his half-pay. Should the wounds received not cause total disability, it was provided that the invalid should receive such monthly pension as might be deemed adequate by the Legislature of the State in which he resided—not exceeding his half-pay.

To obtain the benefit of these provisions, the invalid was required to produce to the receiving committee or officer appointed in the State of his residence, or to the Legislature of such State, a certificate from the commanding officer in the same engagement in which the wound was received; or, in case of the death of the commanding officer, from some other officer of the corps, and the surgeon who attended him; or a certificate from the commander of the vessel engaged in the action in which the wound was received, and from the attending surgeon, of his name, office, rank, department, regiment, company, ship, the nature of his wound and the action in which such wound was received.

The State Legislatures were recommended to appoint persons to receive and examine the certificates, and keep a record of the same, as well as of the amount adjudged by the several Legislatures for the support of those partially disabled, and of the payments made, and the death of disabled persons. Quarterly reports of the proceedings of the committees were required to be made to the Secretary of Congress, or Board of War. The Legislatures were also recommended to make payment to such disabled persons, in accordance with the foregoing provisions, on account of the United States.

Such of the officers, soldiers, marines and seamen, thus entitled to a pension, as were capable of doing guard or garrison duty, were to be formed into a corps of invalids, and employed accordingly.

By a resolution of the 25th of September, 1778, the provisions of the resolutions of August 26, 1776, were extended to all persons who lost a limb, or were otherwise disabled in the service of the United Colonies or States of America before the passage of the last-mentioned resolutions; and by a resolution of April 23, 1782, all such sick or wounded soldiers as were reported unfit for duty, either in the field or garrison, were entitled to a discharge upon application for the same; and also to receive as a pension five dollars per month, in lieu of all pay and emoluments.

These resolutions lie at the foundation of the pension system of the United States.

By act of Congress of the 29th September, 1789, the payment of the pensions thus provided was assumed by the United States for one year, under regulations to be prescribed by the President; by acts of July 16, 1790, and March 3, 1791, the payment was assumed for two additional years; and by act of March 23, 1792, the pensions were confirmed for life, and their payment assumed by the United States, under regulations prescribed by the act.

Sundry acts were subsequently passed, altering, modifying or repealing the last-named act; and they in their turn submitted to like processes; and, finally, by act of April 10, 1806, all former laws were repealed, and general provision was made for the payment of pensions to invalids of the revolution. This act being deemed to be still in force for some purposes, is here given in full.

AN ACT *to provide for Persons who were Disabled by known Wounds received in the Revolutionary War.*[1]

SECTION 1. *Be it enacted,* That any commissioned or non-commissioned officer, musician, soldier, marine or seaman disabled in the actual service of the United States, while in the line of his duty, by known wounds received during the revolutionary war, and who did not desert the service; or who in consequence of disability as aforesaid, resigned his commission or took a discharge; or who, after incurring disability as aforesaid was taken captive by the enemy, and remained either in captivity or on parol, until the close of said revolutionary war, or who, in consequence of known wounds re-

[1] U. S. Statutes at large, vol. ii, 376. The benefits of this act were by act of April 25, 1808, extended to commissioned and non-commissioned officers, musicians and privates wounded *since* the revolutionary war, while in the line of duty, whether belonging to regulars, volunteers, or militia.

ceived as aforesaid, has, at any period since, become and continued disabled in such manner as to render him unable to procure a subsistence by manual labor, whether such officer, musician, soldier, marine or seaman, served as a volunteer in any proper service against the common enemy, or belonged to a detachment of the militia which served against the common enemy, or to the regular forces of the United States, or of any particular State, he shall, upon substantiating his claim in the manner hereinafter described, be placed on the pension list of the United States, during life, or the continuance of such disability, and be entitled, under the regulations hereinafter mentioned, to receive such sum as shall be found just and proper by the testimony adduced.

SEC. 2. In substantiating such claim, the following rules and regulations shall be complied with, that is to say:

All evidence shall be taken on oath or affirmation, before the judge of the district, or one of the judges of the Territory in which such claimant resides, or before some person especially authorized by commission from said judge.[1]

Decisive disability, the effect of a known wound or wounds received while in the actual service and line of duty, against the common enemy during the revolutionary war, must be proved by the affidavit of the commanding officer of the regiment, corps, company, ship, vessel or craft, in which such claimant served; or of two other credible witnesses to the same effect, setting forth the time when, and the place where such known wound or wounds were received, and particularly describing the same. The nature of such disability and in what degree it prevents the claimant from obtaining his subsistence, must be proved by the affidavit of some reputable physician or surgeon, stating his opinion, either from his own knowledge and acquaintance with the claimant, or from an examination of such claimant, on oath or affirmation; which when necessary for that purpose, shall be administered to said claimant by said judge or commissioner. And the said physician or surgeon, in his affidavit,

1 This was afterward (act of April 18, 1814) so amended as to authorize the testimony to be taken before any judge of any State or Territorial Court.

By an act of March 2, 1829 (U. S. Statutes at Large, vol. iv, 350), it is provided that the testimony, in cases of applications for wounds received in the revolutionary war, may be authenticated in the same manner as in applications for pensions for wounds received in the war of 1812.

shall particularly describe the wound or wounds from whence the disability appears to be derived.

Every claimant must prove, by at least one credible witness, that he continued in service during the whole time for which he was detached, or for which he engaged, unless he was discharged, or left the service in consequence of some derangement of the army, or in consequence of his disability resigned his commission, or was after his disability in captivity, or on parole until the close of the revolutionary war. And in the same manner must prove his mode of life and employment since he left the service, and the place or places where he has since resided, and his place of residence at the time of taking such testimony.

Every claimant shall, by his affidavit, give satisfactory reasons why he did not make application for a pension before, and that he is not on the pension list of any State; and the judge or commissioner shall certify, in writing, his opinion of the credibility of the witnesses whose affidavits he shall take, in all those cases where by this act it is said that the proof shall be made by a credible witness or witnesses; and also, that the examining physician or surgeon is reputable in his profession.

SEC. 4. Every pension or income thereof by virtue of this act, shall commence on the day when the claimant shall have completed his testimony before the authority proper to take the same.[1]

SEC. 5. An increase of pension may be allowed to persons already placed upon the pension list of the United States, for disabilities caused by known wounds received during the revolutionary war, in all cases where justice shall require the same; *Provided*, That the increase when added to the pension formerly received shall in no case exceed a full pension.

SEC. 6. A full pension given by this act to a commissioned officer, shall be one half of the monthly pay legally allowed at the time of incurring said disability, to his grade in the forces raised by the United States; and the proportions less than a full pension, shall be the correspondent proportions of said half-pay; and a full pension to a non-commissioned officer, musician, soldier, marine, or seaman,

1 The rule is revived which declares that the evidence is perfect when no objection whatever exists to the admission of the claim. In future, therefore, the pension will commence at the date of the last certificate which authenticates the papers. *Rule of War Department, January* 30, 1832.

shall be five dollars per month, and the proportions less than a full pension, shall be the like proportions of five dollars a month; but no pension of a commissioned officer shall be calculated at a higher rate than the half-pay of a lieutenant-colonel.[1]

SEC. 7. The pensions, or increase thereof which may be allowed by this act, shall be paid in the same manner as pensions to individuals who have been heretofore placed on the pension list, are now paid, and under such restrictions and regulations, in all respects, as are prescribed by law.

SEC. 8. From and after the passage of this act, no sale, transfer or mortgage of the whole or any part of the pension payable to any non-commissioned officer, musician, soldier, marine or seaman, before the same becomes due, shall be valid. And every person claiming such pension or any part thereof, under power of attorney or substitution, shall, before the same is paid, make oath or affirmation, before some magistrate, legally authorized to take the same, a copy of which, attested by said magistrate, shall be lodged with the person who pays said pension, that such power or substitution is not given by reason of any transfer of such pension or part thereof. And any person who shall swear or affirm falsely in the premises, and be thereof convicted, shall suffer as for willful and corrupt perjury.

SEC. 9. All laws of the United States heretofore passed, so far as they authorize persons to be placed on the pension list of the United States, for and in consequence of disabilities derived from known wounds received in the revolutionary war, shall be, and they are hereby repealed: *Provided*, That nothing in this repealing clause shall injure, or in any way affect, those persons already upon the pension list of the United States; and that the Secretary for the War Department shall proceed upon the testimony which has been transmitted to him by any claimant before the passage of this act, in the same manner as though this act had never passed.

---

1 An act approved April 24, 1816, increased the rates of monthly pensions, as follows: A first lieutenant, to seventeen dollars; a second lieutenant, to fifteen dollars; a third lieutenant, to fourteen dollars; an ensign, to thirteen dollars; a non-commissioned officer, musician, or private, to eight dollars. These rates represent the highest degree of disability: for disabilities of a degree less than the highest it is prescribed by the act that the sum shall be "proportionably less." For further particulars of this act, see "INVALID PENSIONS, REGULAR SERVICE," page 23.

SEC. 10. This act, so far as it authorizes the admission of persons upon the pension list of the United States, shall remain in force for and during the space of six years from the passage thereof, and no longer:[1] *Provided*, That this limitation shall not affect or impair the right of any invalid who may have completed his testimony in the manner prescribed by this act, before this limitation commences its operation, but which has not been transmitted to the Secretary for the Department of War.

In accordance with the provisions of this law a large number of lists containing the names of persons entitled to pensions were transmitted by the District Judges to the Secretary of War, and by him to Congress, to be placed by special acts upon the pension rolls.[2]

The act of 1806 is still in force so far as relates to the *payment* of pensions; although it is presumed that few (if any) persons are drawing pensions under its provisions.

An act of March 18, 1818, grants pensions to such of the surviving officers, musicians, private soldiers, and all officers in the hospital department and medical staff as served in the war of the revolution until the end of the

---

1 This section was revived and kept in force by sundry acts until May 24, 1832. The reason why it was permitted to expire at that time was, evidently, that the liberal provisions of the act of June 7, 1832, rendered the continuance of this section unnecessary.

2 By an act approved April 25, 1808, the Secretary of War was authorized and directed to place on the pension rolls of the United States all persons remaining on the pension lists of the several States, for disability occasioned by known wounds received in the revolutionary war, whether in the land or sea forces of the United States, or of any particular State, in regular corps, volunteers, or militia. Pensions, under this act, were restricted to the amounts prescribed in the sixth section of the act of 1806; and applicants for the benefits of this enactment were required to furnish evidence of their being upon the pension lists of the States, by producing satisfactory documents from the proper officers of the several States. An act of March 3, 1819, authorized the Secretary of War to place upon the pension rolls the names of *all persons* entitled to pensions, without reporting the same to Congress.

same, or for a term of at least nine months at some period of the war,[1] on the continental establishment; and also to the surviving officers, seamen and marines, who served for a like term in the navy of the United States, and who were, or thereafter might be, in reduced circumstances in life, and unable to obtain a livelihood. To such indigents (whether invalids or otherwise) the act allows a pension for life, as follows: commissioned officers, twenty dollars per month; and to non-commissioned officers, musicians, marines, seamen, and private soldiers, eight dollars per month. But to obtain the benefits of this act, an invalid must relinquish any pension he may previously have been receiving;[2] and is precluded from claiming one under any other act.

This act, with the regulations and forms pertaining thereto, will be found under the title "GRATUITOUS PENSIONS—REVOLUTION;" to which the reader is referred.

From the passage of the act of March 18, 1818, invalid pensions for injuries received in the revolution were merged in gratuitous pensions; and no acts specially relating to the former were subsequently passed. Should any applications for pensions remain to be made for services rendered in the revolution, they should be made under the act of May 15, 1828, or the act of June 7, 1832, which will be found in full under "GRATUITOUS PENSIONS—REVOLUTION," pp. 111 to 113.

---

[1] The war of the revolution terminated in April, 1783, upon ratification of the treaty of peace. *Opinion of Attorney-General Wirt, February* 12, 1825.

[2] Should a pension received under the act of April, 1806, be relinquished, in order to obtain the benefits of the act of March 18, 1818, and should the pensioner subsequently be deprived of his pension under the last-named act, he can claim to be restored to the pension which he relinquished. *See act of May* 1, 1820, *sec.* 3, U. S. Statutes at Large, vol. iii, 570.

CHAPTER III.

INVALID PENSIONS.

SECTION I.

MILITARY ESTABLISHMENT OR REGULAR SERVICE SINCE THE REVOLUTION.

By "an act for regulating the military establishment of the United States," approved April 30, 1790,[1] provision is made for the formation of a regiment[2] of infantry, consisting of three battalions, and a battalion of artillery. After prescribing the organization of the several corps, the act proceeds:

SEC. 11. *And be it further enacted*, That if any commissioned officer, non-commissioned officer, private or musician aforesaid, shall be wounded or disabled, while in the line of his duty in public service, he shall be placed on the list of the invalids of the United States, at such rate of pay, and under such regulations as shall be directed by the President of the United States for the time being: *Provided always*, That the rate of compensation for such wounds or disabilities shall never exceed, for the highest disability, half the monthly pay received by any commissioned officer at the time of being so wounded or disabled; and that the rate of compensation to non-commissioned officers, privates and musicians, shall never exceed five dollars per month: *And provided also*, That all inferior disabilities shall entitle the person so disabled to receive only a sum in proportion to the highest disability.

Three regiments were added to the establishment by an act of March 5, 1792, "for making further and more

---

1 U. S. Statutes at Large, vol. i, p. 119.

2 An additional regiment of infantry was attached to the establishment by act of March 3, 1791 (U. S. Stats., vol. i, 222), with the same provisions for wounds or disability in the line of duty as other troops of the United States.

effectual provision for the protection of the frontiers of the United States;"[1] and it is provided:

SEC. 11. *And be it further enacted*, That all the commissioned and non-commissioned officers, privates and musicians of the said three regiments, shall take the same oaths, shall be governed by the same rules and regulations, and in cases of disabilities shall receive the same compensations as are described in the before-mentioned act, entitled "an act for regulating the military establishment of the United States." (April 30, 1790.)

These acts remained in force until they were repealed by act of March 3, 1795. The repeal did not affect any rights acquired under them.[2]

The repealing act of March 3, 1795, just adverted to, is entitled "an act for continuing and regulating the military establishment of the United States, and for repealing sundry acts heretofore passed on that subject."[3] Section thirteen of this act is as follows:

SEC. 13. *And be it further enacted*, That if any officer, non-commissioned officer, private or musician, aforesaid, shall be wounded or disabled, while in the line of his duty in public service, he shall be placed on the list of the invalids of the United States, at such rate of pay, and under such regulations, as shall be directed by the President for the time being: *Provided always*, That the rate of compensation to be allowed for such wounds or disabilities, to a commissioned officer, shall never exceed, for the highest disability, half the monthly pay of such officer, at the time of his being so disabled or wounded; and that the rate of compensation to non-commissioned officers, privates and musicians, shall never exceed five dollars per

[1] U. S. Statutes at Large, vol. i, 241.

[2] In a parallel case Secretary Stuart decided (October 29, 1850), that where inducements were held out for the purpose of filling up the ranks of the army, they "partook of the nature of the consideration of a contract." In other words: that a promise contained in an act, under which a soldier enlists, that he shall be provided for in case of disability incurred in the service, binds the government, and can not be receded from without the consent of the soldier.

[3] U. S. Statutes at Large, vol. i, 430.

month: *And provided also*, that all inferior disabilities shall entitle the person so disabled to receive an allowance proportionate to the highest disability.

This act, although marked "obsolete"[1] in the United States Statutes at Large, is still in force so far as relates to rights acquired under it, whether to the allowance or payment of pensions, or otherwise.

By "an act to ascertain and fix the military establishment of the United States," approved May 30, 1796,[2] all former acts relating to the organization of the military establishment were repealed, except as to the "enlistments or terms of service of any of the troops" then constituting the army. These troops were retained in the new organization. The provision made by this act for invalids is identical, *verbatim*, with that in the act of March 3, 1795.[3] [4]

The aspect of the existing relations between this country and France being threatening, Congress, by act of May 28, 1798, authorized the President to "raise a provisional army"[5] by enlisting a number of troops not exceeding ten thousand, to serve for not more than three years. These forces were provided for as follows:

SEC. 2. *And be it further enacted*, That . . . the commissioned and non-commissioned officers, musicians, and privates, raised in pursuance of this act, shall be subject to the rules and articles of war, and regulations for the government of the army, and be entitled to the same pay, clothing, rations, forage, and all other emoluments, bounty excepted, and in case of wounds or disa-

---

[1] This act is, in fact, *repealed* by act of March 16, 1802, (p. 17.)

[2] U. S. Statutes at Large, vol. i, 483.

[3] See note to act of March 3, 1795, (p. 14.)

[4] Repealed by act of March 16, 1802, U. S. Statutes at Large, vol. ii, 132.

[5] U. S. Statutes at Large, vol. i, 558.

bility received in service, to the same compensation as the troops of the United States are by law entitled.[1]

"An act to augment the army of the United States, and for other purposes," approved July 16, 1798,[2] authorizes the President to enlist, and to add to the military establishment, twelve regiments of infantry, and six troops of dragoons, to serve during the difficulties then existing with the French Republic, unless sooner discharged. The eighth section of the act contains the following provisions:

SEC. 8. *And be it further enacted*, That the officers, non-commissioned officers, musicians and privates, raised by virtue of this act, shall take and subscribe the oath or affirmation prescribed by the law entitled "an act to ascertain and fix the military establishment of the United States;" and they shall be governed by the rules and articles of war, which have been or may be established by law, and shall be entitled to the legal emoluments in case of wounds or disabilities received while in actual service, and in the line of duty.[2] . . . .

The difficulties with France still remaining unsettled, the President was empowered by act of March 2, 1799, entitled "An act giving eventual authority to the President of the United States to augment the army,"[4] in case war should break out with a European power, or there should be imminent danger of a foreign invasion, to add, by enlistment for not more than three years, twenty-four regiments of infantry, a regiment and a battalion of riflemen, a battalion of artillerists and engineers, and three regiments of cavalry. Section three of this act provides for these troops, as follows:

SEC. 3. *And be it further enacted*, That the officers, non-commis-

1 Repealed by act of March 16, 1802, (page 17.)

2 U. S. Statutes at Large, vol. i, 604.

3 Repealed by act of March 16, 1802, (page 17.)

4 U. S. Statutes at Large, vol. i, 725.

sioned officers, and privates, of the troops which may be organized or raised pursuant to this act, shall be entitled to the like pay, clothing, rations, forage, and other emoluments, and to the like compensation in case of disability by wounds, or otherwise, incurred in the service, as the officers, non-commissioned officers, and privates, of other troops of correspondent denominations, composing the army of the United States; and, with them, shall be subject to the rules and articles of war, and to all other regulations for the discipline and government of the army; *Provided*, That no officer, except captains and subalterns who may be employed in the recruiting service, shall be entitled to any pay or other emolument until he shall be called into actual service.

This act, and the four acts immediately preceding, were repealed by an act of March 16, 1802; but they are mentioned in this compilation for the reason that they are still in force in respect to rights acquired under their provisions. [1]

The military establishment was reduced to a peace *status* by an act of March 16, 1802, entitled "an act fixing the military peace establishment of the United States."[2] This act repeals all former acts relating to the subject, except in so far as they appertain to enlistments and terms of service. It directs that one regiment of artillerists and two of infantry, with the necessary officers, and a corps of engineers to be stationed at West Point, in the State of New York, and to form a military academy, shall constitute the military establishment. Provision is made for invalids, as follows.

SEC. 14. *And be it further enacted*, That if any officer, non-commissioned officer, musician, or private in the corps[3] composing the

1 See note to act of March 3, 1795, (page. 14.)

2 U. S. Statutes at Large, vol. ii, 132.

3 In some acts, relating to the several corps of the army, no distinct provision is made for the allowance of pensions for disability incurred in the service; but as *all* the corps of the army form parts of the *entire* establishment, all regularly enlisted persons, whether belonging to the artillery,

peace establishment of the United States, shall be disabled by wounds or otherwise,[1] while in the line of his duty in public service, he shall be placed on the list of invalids of the United States, at such rate of pay, and under such regulations as may be directed by the President, for the time being;[2] *Provided always*, That the compensation to be allowed for such wounds or disabilities to a commissioned officer, shall not exceed for the highest rate of disability, half the monthly pay of such officer at the time of his being disabled or wounded;[3] and no officer shall receive more than the half-pay of a lieutenant-colonel; and the rate of compensation to non-commissioned officers, musicians and privates, shall not exceed five dollars per month; *And provided also*, That all inferior disabilities shall entitle the person so disabled to receive an allowance proportionate to the highest disability.

This act took effect June 1, 1802.

An act of April 12, 1808, entitled "an act to raise for a limited time an additional military force,"[4] adds five regiments of infantry, one regiment of riflemen, one regiment of light artillery, and one regiment of light

ordnance, cavalry, dragoons, infantry, engineers (including cadets at West Point. *See opinion of Attorney-General Wirt, April* 8, 1820), topographical engineers, sappers and miners, rangers, or other corps or branch of the service, are equally entitled, according to grade and pay, to invalid pensions, in case of wounds or sickness, received or contracted in the line of duty.

1 It would not, I think, be going too far to say that, in every case where an officer or private loses his health while in the service, to such a degree as to be disabled from performing his duty any more, he is contemplated, *prima facie*, as an object of this charitable relief from the Legislature. *Opinion of Attorney-General Rush, April* 6, 1815.

2 The claims of civil officers to be placed on the pension rolls, and the rates of pension to be allowed them, depend upon the regulations prescribed by the President, under this act. *Attorney-General Taney, May*, 31, 1832.

3 In a case arising under this act, Attorney-General Cushing held (August 30, 1853), that mere brevet rank, without a command corresponding to the higher grade of office, is but honorary, and does not entitle the party to an increase of pay nor of pension.

4 U. S. Statutes at Large, vol. ii, 481.

dragoons, to the regular army, to serve for five years, unless sooner discharged; and it is provided:

SEC. 5. *Be it further enacted*, That the officers, cadets, non-commissioned officers, musicians, artificers and privates, raised pursuant to this act, shall be entitled to the like compensation, in case of disability by wounds, and otherwise, incurred in the service, as the officers, cadets, non-commissioned officers, musicians, artificers and privates, in the present military establishment.[1] . . . .

The benefits of the act of April 10, 1806, relating to revolutionary invalids, were, by act of April 25, 1808,[2] extended to *all* persons who served after the revolution and before the passage of the last-named act. The sections containing these provisions are as follows:

SEC. 4. *And be it further enacted*, That any officer, non-commissioned officer, musician or private, who has been wounded or disabled since the revolutionary war, while in the line of his duty, in the actual service of the United States, whether he belong to the military establishment or the militia, or any volunteer corps called into service under the authority of the United States, may be placed on the pension list of the United States, at such rate of compensation, and under such regulations, as are prescribed by the act entitled "An act to provide for persons who were disabled by known wounds received in the revolutionary war," passed April the tenth, one thousand eight hundred and six.[3]

SEC. 5. *And be it further enacted*, That the pensioners, becoming such in virtue of this act, shall be paid in the same manner as invalid pensioners are paid who have heretofore been placed on the pension list of the United States, under such restrictions and regulations, in all respects, as are prescribed by the laws of the United States in such cases provided.

In anticipation of a war with Great Britain an act was passed (approved January 11, 1812), entitled "an act to

[1] See act of March 16, 1802, (p.17), for the provisions for disability then existing.

[2] U. S. Statutes at Large, vol. ii, 496.

[3] For act of April 10, 1806, see page 5.

raise an additional military force,"[1] which provided for adding ten regiments of infantry, two regiments of artillery, and one regiment of dragoons, to the regular army, to be enlisted for five years, unless sooner discharged; and—

SEC. 14. *And be it further enacted*, That if any officer,[2] non-commissioned officer, musician or private, shall be disabled by wounds, or otherwise, while in the line of his duty in public service, he shall be placed on the list of invalids of the United States, at such rate of pension, and under such regulations, as are or may be directed by law:[3] *Provided always*, That the compensation to be allowed for such wounds or disabilities, to a commissioned officer shall not exceed, for the highest rate of disability, half the monthly pay of such officer, at the time of his being disabled or wounded; and that no officer shall receive more than the half-pay of a lieutenant-colonel; and that the rate of compensation to non-commissioned officers, musicians, and privates, shall not exceed five dollars per month: *And provided also*, That all inferior disabilities shall entitle the person so disabled to receive an allowance proportionate to the highest disability.[4]

By acts of January 2, 1812;[5] July 1, 1812,[6] and February 25, 1813,[7] the President was authorized to raise

1 U. S. Statutes, vol. ii, 671.

2 An aid-de-camp can not claim a pension according to his pay as aid, but only according to his pay and rank in the line. *Attorney-General Wirt, December* 5, 1820.

3 The regulations directed by law were, at this time, the regulations prescribed by the President, under the act of March 16, 1802; and the claims of civil officers to be placed on the pension rolls, with the rates of pensions which they shall be allowed, depend upon the regulations thus made by the President. *Attorney-General Taney, May* 31, 1832.

4 "An act in addition" to this act, approved April 8, 1812 (U. S. Statutes at Large, vol. ii, 704), authorizes the President to enlist any of the troops specified in this act, and promises them the same provision in case of wounds, etc., as is contained in this section.

5 U. S. Statutes at Large, vol. ii, 670.

6 *Ibid*, vol. ii, 774.

7 *Ibid*, vol. ii, 804.

certain companies of rangers for the defense of the frontiers, who were allowed like pensions, in case of wounds or other disabilities, with other troops of the United States. The acts granting these pensions will be found at large under the title "INVALID PENSIONS—INDIAN WARS."

The first act for augmenting the regular army, passed after the declaration of war with Great Britain, was that of January 29, 1813: it is entitled, "an act in addition to the act entitled 'an act to raise an additional military force.'"[1] It provides for enlisting and adding to the establishment twenty regiments of infantry, to serve for one year, if not sooner discharged; and officers and men are allowed the same pay as persons of like grades in the army as then existing. Also,

SEC. 10. *And be it further enacted*, That if any officer, non-commissioned officer, musician or private, shall be disabled, by wounds or otherwise, while in the line of his duty in public service, he shall be placed on the list of invalids of the United States, at such rate of pension and under such regulations as are or may be directed by law: *Provided, always*, That the compensation to be allowed for such wounds or disabilities, to a commissioned officer,[2] shall not exceed, for the highest rate of disability, half the monthly pay of such officer, at the time of his being disabled or wounded; and that no officer shall receive more than the half-pay of a lieutenant-colonel; and that the rate of compensation to non-commissioned officers, privates and musicians, shall not exceed five dollars per month. *And provided also*, That all inferior disabilities shall entitle the person so disabled to receive an allowance proportionate to the highest disability.

This act was subsequently[3] so amended as to authorize

---

1 U. S. Statutes at Large, vol. ii, 794.

2 A lieutenant and adjutant may receive an invalid pension equal to one half the monthly pay of such rank under the act of January 29, 1813. *Secretary Case, June* 29, 1832.

3 Act of February 25, 1813. (U. S. Statutes at Large, vol. ii, 804).

the President to receive ten companies of rangers in lieu of one of the regiments prescribed by the act—the rangers to be raised under the provisions, restrictions and conditions of "an act authorizing the President of the United States to raise certain companies of rangers for the protection of the frontier of the United States," approved January 2, 1812.[1] [2]

"An act to raise three regiments of riflemen," approved February 10, 1814,[3] provides:

SEC. 4. *And be it further enacted*, That each man recruited under the authority of this act be allowed the same bounty in land and money as is allowed by law to men enlisted for five years or during the war, and that the officers, non-commissioned officers, musicians and privates shall receive the same pay, clothing, subsistence and forage, be entitled to the same provisions for wounds and disabilities, the same benefits and allowances, and be placed in every respect on the same footing as the other regular troops of the United States.

The term of service of these riflemen was fixed at five years, unless sooner discharged.

At the close of the war the army was reduced to a peace *status*, by an act of March 3, 1815, entitled, "an act fixing the military peace establishment of the United

---

[1] See "INVALID PENSIONS—INDIAN WARS," page 217.

[2] The act of January 29, 1813, was also amended by acts of July 5, 1813 (U. S. Statutes at Large, vol. iii, 3), and March 30, 1814 (U. S. Statutes at Large, vol. iii, 113), so as to authorize the enlistment of five of the regiments mentioned therein for five years, to serve for the defense of the sea-board; and the officers and men belonging to the same were placed upon the same footing, in every respect, as regular troops. And by an act of January 28, 1814 (U. S. Statutes at Large, vol. iii, 96), the President was authorized to enlist the remaining fourteen regiments (one having been, as stated in the text, superseded by a corps of rangers) for five years or during the war; and the officers, non-commissioned officers, musicians and privates were also placed upon the same footing, in every respect, as other regular troops.

[3] U. S. Statutes at Large, vol. iii, 96.

States.[1] By the terms of this act the number of men (including officers) was limited at ten thousand, to consist of such proportions of artillery, infantry and riflemen, as the President should deem proper. In addition to these, the corps of engineers, as then by law established, was retained.[2] Invalids, who should become such in the service, were provided for as follows:

SEC. 7. *And be it further enacted*, That the several corps authorized by this act shall be subject to the rules and articles of war, be recruited in the same manner, and with the same limitations; and that officers, non-commissioned officers, musicians and privates shall be entitled to the same provisions for wounds and disabilities, the same provisions for widows and children, and the same benefits and allowances in every respect not inconsistent with the provisions of this act, as are authorized by act of March 16, 1802, entitled "an act fixing the military peace establishment of the United States," and the act of 12th April, 1808, entitled, "an act to raise for a limited time an additional military force." [3] . . . .

"An act to increase the pensions of invalids in certain cases; for the relief of invalids of the militia; and for the appointment of pension agents in those States where there is no commissioner of loans," approved April 24, 1816,[4] provides as follows:

SEC. 1. *Be it enacted by the Senate and House of Representatives of the United States of America in Congress assembled*, That all persons of the ranks hereinafter named, who are now on the military pension roll of the United States, shall, from and after the passage of this act, be entitled to, and receive, for disabilities of the highest degree, the following sums, in lieu of those to which they are now

1 U. S. Statutes at Large, vol. iii, 224.

2 Cadets at West Point belong to the engineer corps, and are entitled to pensions under this act. *Opinion of Attorney-General Wirt, April* 8, 1820.

3 The act of March 2, 1821, to reduce and fix the military establishment, does not repeal the act of March 3, 1815. *Attorney-General Wirt, Nov.* 17, 1828; *and Decision of the Secretary of War, Nov.* 18, 1828.

4 U. S. Statutes at Large, vol. iii, 296.

entitled, to-wit: a first lieutenant, seventeen dollars; a second lieu. tenant, fifteen dollars; a third lieutenant, fourteen dollars; an ensign, thirteen dollars; and a non-commissioned officer,[1] musician or private, eight dollars per month; and for disabilities of a degree less than the highest, a sum proportionably less.

SEC. 2. *And be it further enacted*, That all persons of the aforesaid ranks, who may hereafter be placed on the military pension roll of the United States, shall, according to their ranks and degrees of disability, be placed on (*sic*) at the aforesaid rates of pensions, in lieu of those heretofore established: *Provided*, That nothing herein contained shall be construed to lessen the pension of any person who by special provision, is entitled to a higher pension than is herein provided.

The two remaining sections of the act relate to the placing of officers and soldiers of the militia on the pension roll of the United States upon equal terms with regulars, and to the appointment of pension agents in certain cases.

By an act of March 2, 1821, "to reduce and fix the military peace establishment of the United States,"[2] the regular army was reduced to four regiments of artillery and seven regiments of infantry, with the necessary officers. This act does not provide a pension for invalids; but as it does not repeal existing laws, except in so far as they are at variance with it, those who served under its provisions are entitled to pensions in like manner as other persons engaged in the regular service.[3]

1 This was held to apply to a sergeant of marines who, while serving on land during the war with Mexico, was disabled by wounds received in battle. *Attorney-General Toucey, Nov.* 21, 1848.

A subaltern claiming the benefits of the act of April 24, 1816, is not entitled to any allowance for services as a staff officer. *Secretary of War Poinsett, April,* 1837.

2 U. S. Statutes at Large, vol. iii, 615.

3 The act of March 2, 1821, to reduce and fix the military establishment, does not repeal the act of March 3, 1815. *Opinion of Attorney-General Wirt, Nov.* 17, 1828; *and Decision of the Secretary of War, Nov.* 18, 1828.

A regiment of dragoons was added to the army by an act of March 2, 1833, "for the more perfect defense of the frontiers;"[1] consisting of ten companies, with the necessary officers. These dragoons were provided for as follows:

SEC. 3. *And be it further enacted*, That the said regiment of dragoons shall be liable to serve on horse or foot, as the President may direct; shall be subject to the rules and articles of war, be recruited in the same manner, and with the same limitations; that the officers, non-commissioned officers, musicians, farriers and privates, shall be entitled to the same provisions for wounds and disabilities, the same provisions for widows and children, and the same allowances and benefits in every respect, as are allowed the other troops constituting the present military peace establishment.[2]

"An act making appropriations for the payment of revolutionary and other pensioners of the United States, for the fiscal year ending on the thirtieth of June, one thousand eight hundred and forty-five," approved April 30, 1844,[3] establishes a rule to be observed in the allowance of pensions, as follows:

Be it enacted by the Senate and House of Representatives of the United States of America in Congress assembled, That . . . *Provided*, . . . *And provided, also*, That no person in the army, navy or marine corps shall be allowed to draw both a pension as an invalid and the pay of his rank or station in the service, unless the alleged disability for which the pension was granted be such as to have occasioned his employment in a lower grade, or in some civil branch of the service.[4]

---

1 U. S. Statutes at Large, vol. iv, 652.

2 Another regiment of dragoons, constituted like the one referred to in the text, and placed upon the same footing, in every respect, was authorized by act of May 23, 1836. *U. S. Statutes at Large*, vol. v, 32.

3 U. S. Statutes at Large, vol. v, 656.

4 Commodore Porter was held to be entitled to his salary as Minister at Constantinople and to his pension at the same time. *Attorney-General Legare, May* 26, 1842. An officer, who lost a limb in the war of 1812, was

By an act approved May 15, 1846,[1] a company of sappers, miners and pontoniers was added to the corps of engineers; these, in case of disability, were provided for as follows:

SEC. 3. *And be it further enacted*, That the said engineer company shall be subject to the rules and articles of war, shall be recruited in the same manner and with the same limitation, and shall be entitled to the same provisions, allowances and benefits, in every respect, as are allowed to the other troops constituting the present military establishment.

Provision was made, by an act of May 19, 1846,[2] for raising a regiment of mounted riflemen, to serve along the line of military stations on the way to Oregon. These were promised:

SEC. 3. *And be it further enacted*, That the said regiment of riflemen shall be subject to the rules and articles of war, and shall be recruited in the same manner as other troops in the service of the United States, and with the same conditions and limitations; and the officers, non-commissioned officers, musicians, privates, blacksmiths and farriers shall be entitled to the same provisions for wounds and disabilities, and the same provisions for widows and children, and the same allowances and benefits, in every respect, as are allowed to the other troops composing the army of the United States.

An act of July 10, 1848,[3] extends the benefits of existing pension laws to the ordnance corps, as follows:

---

mustered out of the service upon a captain's commission. He was subsequently appointed battalion paymaster, and it was held that this was a civil branch of the service, and that he was entitled to both pay and pension. *Attorney-General Toucey, November* 1, 1848. *See also notes to act of August* 16, 1841, *under title* "INVALID PENSIONS—NAVAL," page 86.

1 U. S. Statutes at Large, vol. ix, 12.

2 *Ibid.*, vol. ix, 13.

3 *Ibid.*, vol. ix, 246.

AN ACT *to extend the Provisions of existing Pension Laws to Enlisted Men of the Ordnance Corps of the United States Army.*

Be it enacted by the Senate and House of Representatives of the United States in Congress assembled, That the acts of Congress granting pensions to soldiers disabled by wounds or otherwise, while in the line of their duty in public service, shall be construed to apply to the enlisted men of the ordnance department who have been or may be disabled, in the same manner as to non-commissioned officers, artificers,[1] musicians and privates of other corps of the army, subject to the limitation that in no such case shall the rate of pension exceed eight dollars per month.

By a joint resolution of August 10, 1848,[2] Congress placed the officers and men of the marine and ordnance corps, who served with the army in Mexico, upon the same footing, in respect to pensions and bounty land, as persons belonging to the army. That portion of the resolution which makes these provisions is as follows:

Resolved by the Senate and House of Representatives of the United States of America in Congress assembled, That the officers, non-commissioned officers, privates and musicians of the marine corps, who have served with the army in the war with Mexico, and also the artificers[1] and laborers of the ordnance corps serving in said war, be placed, in all respects as to bounty land and other remuneration,[3] in addition to ordinary pay, on a footing with the officers, non-commissioned officers, privates and musicians of the army: *Provided*, That this remuneration shall be in lieu of prize money and all other extra allowances. . . .

The eighth section of an act entitled "an act making appropriations for the support of the army for the year ending the thirtieth day of June, one thousand eight

1 An artificer must be regularly enlisted if he would claim a pension. *Secretary Ewing, July* 18, 1849.

2 U. S. Statutes at Large, vol. ix, 340.

3 The phrase "other remuneration," employed in said resolution, must be understood to refer to pensions. *Attorney-General Toucey, November* 21, 1848.

hundred and fifty-six, and for other purposes," approved March 3, 1855,[1] adds two regiments of infantry and two of cavalry to the army, and provides:

SEC. 8. *And be it further enacted*, That . . . . and that the officers and men authorized by this act shall be entitled to the same provisions for wounds and disabilities, and the same provisions for widows and children, and the same allowances and benefits, in every respect, as are allowed to other troops composing the army of the United States. They shall be subject to the rules and articles of war; and the men shall be recruited in the same manner as other troops, and with the same conditions and limitations.

WAR FOR THE UNION, 1861.

Soon after the commencement of the war of 1861, for the preservation of the Union, the President of the United States, by proclamation of May 3, 1861,[2] directed that the regular army be increased by the addition of eight regiments of infantry, one regiment of cavalry, and one regiment of artillery; the maximum aggregate of increase being twenty-two thousand seven hundred and fourteen—officers and men.

By an act approved July 14, 1862, Congress made general provision for the payment of pensions to invalids of the war for the Union, and also to the widows, orphans, mothers and minor sisters of such as might die or be killed in the line of duty. This being a very important act, it is here given entire:

AN ACT *to Grant Pensions.*

Be it enacted by the Senate and House of Representatives of the United States of America in Congress assembled, That if any officer, non-commissioned officer, musician or private of the army, including

1 U. S. Statutes at Large, vol. x, 639.

2 For this proclamation, see page 57.

regulars, volunteers and militia, or any officer, warrant or petty officer, musician, seaman, ordinary seaman, flotillaman, marine, clerk, landsman, pilot or other person in the navy or marine corps, has been, since the fourth day of March, eighteen hundred and sixty-one, or shall hereafter be disabled by reason of any wound received or disease contracted while in the service of the United States and in the line of duty, he shall, upon making due proof of the fact according to such forms and regulations as are or may be provided by or in pursuance of law, be placed upon the list of invalid pensioners of the United States, and be entitled to receive, for the highest rate of disability, such pension as is hereinafter provided in such cases, and for an inferior disability an amount proportionate to the highest disability, to commence as hereinafter provided, and continue during the existence of such disability. The pension for a total disability for officers, non-commissioned officers, musicians and privates employed in the military service of the United States, whether regulars, volunteers or militia, and in the marine corps, shall be as follows, viz: Lieutenant-colonel and all officers of a higher rank, thirty dollars per month; major, twenty-five dollars per month; captain, twenty dollars per month; first lieutenant, seventeen dollars per month; second lieutenant, fifteen dollars per month; and non-commissioned officers, musicians and privates, eight dollars per month. The pension for total disability for officers, warrant or petty officers, and others employed in the naval service of the United States, shall be as follows, viz: Captain, commander, surgeon, paymaster and chief engineer, respectively, ranking with commander by law, lieutenant commanding and master commanding, thirty dollars per month; lieutenant, surgeon, paymaster and chief engineer, respectively, ranking with lieutenant by law, and passed assistant surgeon, twenty-five dollars per month; professor of mathematics, master, assistant surgeon, assistant paymaster and chaplain, twenty dollars per month; first assistant engineers and pilots, fifteen dollars per month; passed midshipman, midshipman, captains' and paymasters' clerk, second and third assistant engineer, masters' mate and all warrant officers, ten dollars per month; all petty officers and all other persons before named employed in the naval service, eight dollars per month; and all commissioned officers, of either service, shall receive such and only such pension as is herein provided for the rank in which they hold commissions.

SEC. 2. *And be it further enacted*, That if any officer or other person named in the first section of this act has died since the fourth day of March, eighteen hundred and sixty-one, or shall hereafter die, by reason of any wound received or disease contracted while in the service of the United States and in the line of duty, his widow, or, if there be no widow, his child or children under sixteen years of age, shall be entitled to receive the same pension as the husband or father would have been entitled to had he been totally disabled, to commence from the death of the husband or father, and to continue to the widow during her widowhood, or to the child or children until they severally attain to the age of sixteen years, and no longer.

SEC. 3. *And be it further enacted*, That where any officer or other person named in the first section of this act shall have died subsequently to the fourth of March, eighteen hundred and sixty-one, or shall hereafter die, by reason of any wound received or disease contracted while in the service of the United States and in the line of duty, and has not left or shall not leave a widow nor legitimate child, but has left or shall leave a mother who was dependent upon him for support, in whole or in part, the mother shall be entitled to receive the same pension as such officer or other person would have been entitled to had he been totally disabled; which pension shall commence from the death of the officer or other person dying as aforesaid: *Provided, however*, That if such mother shall herself be in receipt of a pension as a widow, in virtue of the provisions of the second section of this act, in that case no pension or allowance shall be granted to her on account of her son, unless she gives up the other pension or allowance: *And provided further*, That the pension given to a mother on account of her son shall terminate on her re-marriage: *And provided further*, That nothing herein shall be so construed as to entitle the mother of an officer or other person dying, as aforesaid, to more than one pension at the same time, under the provisions of this act.

SEC. 4. *And be it further enacted*, That where any officer or other person named in the first section of this act shall have died subsequently to the fourth day of March, eighteen hundred and sixty-one, or shall hereafter die, by reason of any wound received or disease contracted while in the service of the United States and in the line of duty, and has not left or shall not leave a widow, nor legitimate child, nor mother, but has left or may leave an orphan sister or sisters, under sixteen years of age, who were dependent upon him for support, in whole or in part, such sister or sisters shall be entitled to receive the same pension as such officer or other person would have been entitled to had he been totally disabled; which pension to said orphan shall commence from the death of the officer or other person dying as aforesaid, and shall continue to the said orphans until they severally arrive at the age of sixteen years, and no longer: *Provided, however*, That nothing herein shall be so construed as to entitle said orphans to more than one pension at the same time, under the provisions of this act: *And provided, further*, That no moneys shall be paid to the widow or children, or any heirs of any deceased soldier on account of bounty, back pay or pension, who have in any way been engaged in or who have aided or abetted the existing rebellion in the United States; but the right of such disloyal widow or children, heir or heirs of such soldier, shall be vested in the loyal heir or heirs of the deceased, if any there be.

SEC. 5. *And be it further enacted*, That pensions which may be granted, in pursuance of the provisions of this act, to persons who may have been, or shall be, employed in the military or naval service of the United States, shall commence on the day of the discharge of such persons in all cases in which the application for such provisions is filed within one year after the date of said discharge; and in cases in which the application is not filed during said year, pensions granted to persons employed as aforesaid shall commence on the day of the filing of the application.

SEC. 6. *And be it further enacted*, That the fees of agents and attorneys, for making out and causing to be executed the papers necessary to establish a claim for a pension, bounty and other allowance, before the Pension Office under this act, shall not exceed the following rates: For making out and causing to be duly executed a declaration by the applicant, with the necessary affidavits, and forwarding the same to the Pension Office, with the requisite correspondence, five dollars. In cases wherein additional testimony is required by the Commissioner of Pensions, for each affidavit so required and executed and forwarded (except the affidavits of surgeons, for which such agents and attorneys shall not be entitled to any fees), one dollar and fifty cents.

SEC. 7. *And be it further enacted*, That any agent or attorney who shall, directly or indirectly, demand or receive any greater compensation for his services under this act than is prescribed in the preceding section of this act, or who shall contract or agree to prosecute any claim for a pension, bounty or other allowance under this act, on the condition that he shall receive a per centum upon, or any portion of the amount of such claim, or who shall wrongfully withhold from a pensioner or other claimant the whole or any part of the pension or claim allowed and due to such pensioner or claimant, shall be deemed guilty of a high misdemeanor, and upon conviction thereof shall, for every such offense, be fined not exceeding three hundred dollars, or imprisoned at hard labor not exceeding two years, or both, according to the circumstances and aggravations of the offense.

SEC. 8. *And be it further enacted*, That the Commissioner of Pensions be and he is hereby empowered to appoint, at his discretion, civil surgeons to make the biennial examinations of pensioners which are or may be required to be made by law, and to examine applicants for invalid pensions, where he shall deem an examination by a surgeon to be appointed by him necessary; and the fees for each of such examinations, and the requisite certificate thereof, shall be one dollar and fifty cents, which fees shall be paid to the surgeon by the person examined, for which he shall take a receipt, and forward the same to the Pension Office; and upon the allowance of the claim of the person examined, the Commissioner of Pensions shall furnish to such person an order on the Pension Agent of his State for the amount of the surgeon's fees.

SEC. 9. *And be it further enacted*, That the Commissioner of Pensions, on application made to him in person or by letter by any claimants or applicants for pension, bounty or other allowance required by law to be adjusted and paid by the Pension Office, shall furnish such claimants, free of all expense or charge to them, all such printed instructions and forms as may be necessary in establishing and obtaining said claim; and in case such claim is prosecuted by an agent or attorney of such claimant or applicant, on the issue of a certificate of pension or the granting of a bounty or allowance, the Commissioner of Pensions shall forthwith notify the applicant or claimant that such certificate has been issued or allowance made, and the amount thereof.

SEC. 10. *And be it further enacted*, That the pilots, engineers, sailors and crews upon the gunboats and war vessels of the United States, who have not been regularly mustered into the service of the

United States, shall be entitled to the same bounty allowed to persons of corresponding rank in the naval service, provided they continue in service to the close of the present war; and all persons serving as aforesaid, who have been or may be wounded or incapacitated for service, shall be entitled to receive for such disability the pension allowed by the provisions of this act, to those of like rank, and each and every such person shall receive pay according to corresponding rank in the naval service: *Provided*, That no person receiving pension or bounty under the provisions of this act shall receive either pension or bounty for any other service in the present war.

SEC. 11. *And be it further enacted*, That the widows and heirs of all persons described in the last preceding section who have been or may be employed as aforesaid, or who have been or may be killed in battle, or of those who have died or shall die of wounds received while so employed, shall be paid the bounty and pension allowed by the provisions of this act, according to rank, as provided in the last preceding section.

SEC. 12. *And be it further enacted*, That the Secretary of the Interior be and he is hereby authorized to appoint a special agent for the Pension Office, to assist in the detection of frauds against the pension laws, to cause persons committing such frauds to be prosecuted, and to discharge such other duties as said Secretary may require him to perform; which said agent shall receive for his services an annual salary of twelve hundred dollars, and his actual traveling expenses incurred in the discharge of his duties shall be paid by the Government.

SEC. 13. *And be it further enacted*, That all acts and parts of acts inconsistent with the provisions of this act be and the same are hereby repealed.

GENERAL OBSERVATIONS.

The acts of March 16, 1802; January 11, 1812; January 29, 1813; and March 3, 1815, with the act of April 24, 1816, increasing the rate of pensions in certain cases, are those to which all acts establishing the several corps, and providing for the augmentation of the army, relate, in prescribing pensions for disabilities incurred in the regular service. Under the provisions of one of these acts, all pensions for disabilities so incurred, before March, 1861, are allowed and paid. The first named act is the one having the most general application. The benefits of the act of April 10, 1806, granting pensions to invalids of the revolution, were, by act of April 25, 1808, extended to invalids of the regular army, who became disabled after the revolution, and before the passage of the act. This act has, therefore, no relation to cases of disability of recent occurrence.

The act of July 14, 1862, makes general provision for invalids in the war of 1861, and for those dependent upon them.

SECTION II.

REGULATIONS AND FORMS FOR OBTAINING PENSIONS FOR INVALIDS OF THE REGULAR ARMY.

REGULATIONS.

All persons applying for pensions, by reason of disability incurred in the line of duty while in the military service of the United States, must make a declaration, under oath (or affirmation), before some court of record, [1] setting forth the age and residence of the claimant; the service in which he was engaged; the time, place, and manner of incurring the disability alleged, with its precise character; and the date of his discharge; together with a statement of his residence and occupation since leaving the service.

In support of the averments of such declaration, the following rules must be observed in presenting the testimony:

1. The claimant's identity must be proved by two witnesses, certified by a judicial officer to be respectable and credible, who are present and witness the signature of the declaration, and who state, upon oath (or affirmation), their belief, either from personal acquaintance or for other reasons given, that he is the identical person he represents himself to be.

1 Or before a judge or clerk of such court. As to what is a court of record, see "OPINIONS AND DECISIONS," Chapter XV, page 266.

2. The applicant must, if in his power, produce the certificate of the captain, or of some other commissioned officer, under whom he served, distinctly stating the time and place of the said applicant's having been wounded, or otherwise disabled, and the nature of the disability; and that the said disability arose while he was in the service of the United States and in the line of his duty.

3. If it be impracticable to obtain such certificate, by reason of death or removal of said officers, it must be so stated in the declaration of the applicant, and his averment of the fact proved by persons of known respectability, who must state particularly all the knowledge they may possess in relation to such death or removal. Then secondary evidence can be received. In such case the applicant must produce the testimony of at least two credible witnesses (who were in a condition to know the facts about which they testify), whose good character must be vouched for by a judicial officer, or by some one known to the Department. These witnesses must give a minute narrative of the facts in relation to the matter, and must show how they obtained a knowledge of the facts to which they testify.

4. The surgeon's certificate of discharge should show the character and degree of the claimant's disability, but when that is wanting, and when the certificate of an army surgeon is not obtainable, the certificate of two respectable civil surgeons will be received, in accordance with the form. These surgeons must give, in their certificate, a particular description of the wound, injury or disease, and specify how and in what manner his present condition and disability are connected therewith. The degree of disability must also be stated.

5. The habits of the applicant, and his occupation, since he left the service, must be shown by at least two credible witnesses.

6. All evidence should be verified by oath, before a judge of the United States Court, or some judge or justice of the peace, or other officer of a State, having authority to administer oaths for general purposes; and, if verified before an officer of any State, his official character must be duly authenticated; and such officer must, in all cases, certify that he is not interested in the prosecution of the claim.

7. Attorneys for claimants must, in all cases, have proper authority from those in whose behalf they appear. Powers of attorney

must be signed in the presence of two witnesses, and acknowleged before a duly qualified officer, whose official character must be properly shown. JOSEPH H. BARRETT, *Commissioner.*

FORMS.

Form of Application for an Invalid Pension.

STATE OF —— } *Sct.*
County of —— }

On this —— of —— A. D. one thousand eight hundred and —— personally appeared before [*here insert the name of the court, or the official character of the person administering the oath*], within and for the county and State aforesaid, —— aged —— years, a resident of ——, in the State of ——, who, being duly sworn according to law, declares that he is the identical ——, who enlisted in the service of the United States as a —— in the company commanded by ——, in the —— regiment of U. S. infantry (*or* cavalry, *or other corps*), [*here describe what war or other service declarant was engaged in*], and was honorably discharged on the —— day of —— in the year ——, as will appear by his certificate of discharge herewith presented;[1] that, while in the service aforesaid, and in the line of his duty, he received the following wound (*or other disability, as the case may be.*) [*Here give a particular and minute account of the wound or other injury, and state how, when and where it occurred, where the applicant has resided since leaving the service, and what has been his occupation.*]

[*Should the applicant be unable to obtain the certificate of an officer, respecting his disability, insert here the following:* He further says, that Captain —— who commanded said company is dead [*or* has removed to parts unknown; *or*, resides at ——, and the great distance at which he resides from deponent renders it impracticable to obtain his certificate]; that first Lieutenant —— of said company [*here enter into particulars of death, removal, etc., as in the case of captain*]; and second Lieutenant —— [*here give particulars of death, removal, etc.*]; and he is, therefore, unable to procure a certificate of disability from one of them in support of this his declaration.]

He makes this declaration for the purpose of obtaining the benefit of the invalid pension laws of the United States; and hereby appoints —— his attorney, to prosecute this claim, and procure a certificate of pension in accordance herewith.[2]

(*Signature of claimant.*)

---

[1] *If no discharge received, say:* but no certificate of discharge was ever received by deponent. *If discharge lost or destroyed, say:* a certificate of which discharge was at the time received by deponent, but which was afterwards —— [*state particulars of loss or destruction.*]

[2] The power of attorney should be a separate instrument.

Also personally appeared —— and ——, residents of the (*county, city or town*), persons whom I certify to be respectable and entitled to credit, and who, being by me duly sworn, say that they were present and saw —— sign his name (or make his mark) to the foregoing declaration; and they further swear, that they have every reason to believe, from the appearance of the applicant and their acquaintance with him, that he is the identical person he represents himself to be, that they reside as above stated, and are disinterested in this claim for a pension; that since leaving the service of the United States, as aforesaid, his habits have been uniformly good, and his occupation ——.

(*Witnesses' Signatures.*)

Sworn to and subscribed before me; and I certify that I am not interested in this claim or concerned in its prosecution; that I know the affiants to be credible witnesses, and the claimant is the person he represents himself to be.

(*Signature of Judge or Clerk.*)

This declaration must be made before a Court of Record, or a Judge or a Clerk of such Court. Accompanying testimony may be taken before any officer authorized to administer oaths, generally. *See*, as to other FORMS OF CERTIFICATE, etc., Chapter IV, Sec. II.

For REGULATIONS and FORMS relating to POWERS OF ATTORNEY, *see*, Chapter XVI.

Captain's Certificate of Soldier's Disability.

—— —— 18—.

I, ——, captain of company ——, of the —— regiment of regulars, do hereby certify that I am acquainted with ——, who was a member of my company, and as I am informed is an applicant for an invalid pension. That the said —— was mustered into service on or about the —— day of ——, 18—, and discharged for disability about the —— day of —— 18—, having become disabled from doing duty as a soldier, from, on or about the —— day of ——, 18—, while in the service of the United States, and in the line of his duty as a soldier, in the manner and at the place, as follows: [*Here state fully the time, place and manner in which the wound or other injury, or sickness, was incurred.*] That the said soldier was in good health at the time he entered the service, and the disability above referred to affected him while in the service and at his discharge, as follows: [*Here state the nature and effect of the disability.*]

(*Signature.*)

w *Surgeon's Affidavit to Disability of Invalid.*

STATE OF —— }
County of —— } *ss.*

It is hereby certified that ——, late a —— in the company commanded by Captain ——, in the regiment of United States infantry [*or* cavalry *or other corps*], commanded by Col. ——, is rendered incapable of performing the duty of a soldier, by reason of wounds received [*or* disease contracted] while he was actually in the service aforesaid, and in the line of his duty, as follows:

By satisfactory evidence and accurate examination, it appears that on or about the —— day of ——, 18—, being engaged at a place called ——, in the State of ——, he was disabled in the manner following, viz: [*Here state fully the manner in which the disability was incurred, its nature, and how it affects the invalid*]; and he is thereby not only incapacitated for military duty, but, in the opinion of the undersigned, is totally [*or* three fourths; *or* one half; *or* one third; *as the degree of disability may be*] disabled from obtaining his subsistence by manual labor.

(*Signatures of two Surgeons.*)

I certify that, on the —— day of ——, 18—, —— and ——, whom I know to be physicians reputable in their profession, appeared before me, a justice of the peace [*or* other officer] within and for said county of ——, and subscribed the foregoing affidavit, and made oath to the contents of the same, in due form of law. I further certify that I am not interested in the pension claim of the said ——, or concerned in its prosecution.

(*Official Signature.*)

STATE OF —— }
—— *County,* } *ss.*

I, ——, clerk of the —— court, in and for the county and State aforesaid, do hereby certify that ——, before whom the foregoing affidavits were made, and who has thereunto signed his name, was at the time of so doing a —— in and for said county, duly commissioned and sworn, that all his official acts are entitled to full faith and credit, and that his signature thereto is genuine.

[L. S.] In testimony whereof, I have hereunto signed my name and affixed my official seal, this —— day of ——, 18—.

Clerk.

Affidavit of Witnesses, when Certificate of Captain, or other Commissioned Officer, can not be obtained.

THE STATE OF ——, }
—— *County,* } *ss.*

On this — day of —, before the undersigned, a — within and for said county, personally appeared — and —, residents of said county, who being by me first sworn according to law, say, that they are well acquainted with —, whose declaration for the purpose of obtaining an invalid pension is hereto attached, and know him to be the idenitical —— who was a —— in the company commanded by ——, in the regiment of infantry, U. S. A. [*or* cavalry, U. S. A., *or other corps of the army*], commanded by Col. ——; that he entered the service on or about the —— day of ——, 18—, and was honorably discharged on the —— day of ——, 18—. That while in the service of the United States, and in the line of his duty, the said —— became disabled, in manner following: [*Here state the manner in which the disability was incurred, and its nature and extent*], by reason of which the said —— was rendered incapable of discharging the duties of a soldier. That since his discharge, the aforesaid disability affected the said —— [*State the effect of the disease, and how it unfits the applicant for manual labor*]; that the said —— is by occupation a ——; and that his habits now are, and since the time of his discharge aforesaid have been, uniformly good.

They further state that the commissioned officers of said company were the following: Captain ——, first Lieutenant —— and second Lieutenant ——; that the said Captain —— is dead [*or* has removed to parts unknown, *or* lives at ——, too remote from the place of residence of the said invalid to make it practicable to obtain his certificate], that the said [*Here state particulars, relative to the lieutenants, in same manner as in the case of captain.*]

They further state that they obtained knowledge of the facts relating to the service and disability of the said —— by being themselves in the service of the United States, at the same time; as follows: the said [*one of the witnesses*], as a —— in the company commanded by Captain ——; and the said [*the other witness*], as a —— in the same company [*or* company commanded by Captain ——].

They further say that they are disinterested witnesses.

(*Signatures.*)

Sworn to and subscribed before me, the day and year aforesaid. And I certify that I am well acquainted with the said —— and ——, and know them to be respectable and credible persons. I further certify that I am in no manner interested in the claim of —— for a pension.

(*Judge's Signature.*)

[Here should follow the clerk's certificate, under the seal of the court, to the official character of the judge.]

PENSION ACT OF JULY 14, 1862.

GENERAL PROVISIONS.

Under the act of Congress approved July 14, 1862, pensions are granted to the following classes of persons:

1. INVALIDS, disabled since March 4, 1861, in the military or naval service of the United States, in the line of duty.

2. WIDOWS of officers, soldiers or seamen dying of wounds received or of disease contracted in the military or naval service, as above.

3. CHILDREN, under sixteen years of age, of such deceased persons, if there is no widow surviving, or from the time of the widow's re-marriage.

4. MOTHERS (who have no husband living) of officers, soldiers or seamen, deceased as aforesaid, provided the latter have left neither widow nor children under sixteen years of age, and provided, also, that the mother was dependent, wholly or in part, upon the deceased for support.

5. SISTERS, under sixteen years of age, of such deceased persons, dependent on the latter, wholly or in part, for support, provided there are no rightful claimants of either of the three last preceding classes.

The rates of pension to the several classes and grades are distinctly set forth in the first section of the act, a copy of which is herewith published. Only one full pension in any case will be allowed to the relatives of a deceased officer, soldier or seaman, and in order of precedence as set forth above. When more than one minor child or orphan sister thus becomes entitled to pension, the same must be divided equally between them.

Invalid pensions, under this law, will commence from the date of the pensioner's discharge from service, provided application is made within one year thereafter. If the claim is not made until a later date, the pension will commence from the time of the application. Pensions of widows and minors will commence from the death of the officer, soldier or seaman, on whose service the claim is based.

ARMY PENSIONS.

Declarations are required to be made before a court of record, or before some officer of such court duly authorized to administer oaths, and having custody of its seal. *Testimony* may be taken before a justice of the peace or other officer having like authority to administer oaths, but in no case will any evidence be received that is verified before an officer who is concerned in prosecuting the claim or has a manifest interest therein.

The subjoined forms, marked, respectively, A, B, C, D, E and F,[1] will guide applicants for pensions, of the army branch, in the several

[1] A portion of these forms are inserted under other titles.

classes. The forms should be exactly followed in every instance. No attorney will be regarded as having filed the necessary declaration and affidavit, as contemplated by the seventh section of the act, unless the *forms*, as well as the instructions given in this pamphlet, are strictly complied with.

In support of the allegations made in the claimant's declaration, testimony will be required in accordance with the following rules:

1. The claimant's identity must be proved by two witnesses, certified by a judicial officer to be respectable and credible, who are present and witness the signature of the declarant, and who state, upon oath or affirmation, their belief, either from personal acquaintance or for other reasons given, that he or she is the identical person he or she represents himself or herself to be.

2. Every applicant for an invalid pension must, if in his power, produce the certificate of the captain, or of some other commissioned officer under whom he served, distinctly stating the time and place of the said applicant's having been wounded or otherwise disabled, and the nature of the disability; and that the said disability arose while he was in the service of the United States and in the line of his duty.[1]

3. If it be impracticable to obtain such certificate, by reason of the death or removal of said officers, it must be so stated under oath by the applicant, and his averment of the fact proved by persons of known respectability, who must state particularly all the knowledge they may possess in relation to such death or removal; then secondary evidence can be received. In such case the applicant must produce the testimony of at least two credible witnesses (who were in a condition to know the facts about which they testify), whose good character must be vouched for by a judicial officer, or by some one known to the department. The witnesses must give a minute narrative of the facts in relation to the matter, and must show how they obtained a knowledge of the facts to which they testify.

4. The surgeon's certificate for discharge should show the character and degree of the claimant's disability; but when that is wanting, and when the certificate of an army surgeon is not obtainable, the certificate of two respectable civil surgeons will be received, in accordance with form F. These surgeons must give in their certificate a particular description of the wound, injury or disease, and specify how and in what manner his present condition and disabil-

[1] For form of certificate see page 37.

ity are connected therewith. The degree of disability for obtaining subsistence by manual labor must also be stated.

5. The habits of the applicant, and his occupation since he left the service, must be shown by at least two credible witnesses.

If the applicant claim a pension as the widow of a deceased officer or soldier, she must prove the legality of her marriage, the death of her husband, and that she is still a widow. She must also furnish the names and ages of her children under sixteen years of age at her husband's decease, and the place of their residence. On a subsequent marriage her pension will cease, and the minor child or children of the deceased officer or soldier, if any be living, under the age of sixteen years, will be entitled to the same in her stead, from the date of such marriage.

Proof of the marriage of the parents and of the age of claimants will, in like manner, be required in all applications in behalf of minor children.

The legality of the marriage may be ascertained by the certificate of the clergyman who joined them in wedlock, or by the testimony of respectable persons having knowledge of the fact, in default of record evidence. The ages and number of children may be ascertained by the deposition of the mother, accompanied by the testimony of respectable persons having knowledge of them, or by transcripts from the parish or town registers duly authenticated.

Similar proof will be required of the marriage of the claimant, if the mother of a deceased officer or soldier, and that she remains a widow.

If the claimant be a dependent sister, like proof will be required of the marriage of her parents, and of her relationship to the deceased.

Guardians of minor claimants must, in all cases, produce evidence of their authority as such, under the seal of the court from which their appointment is obtained.

Applicants of the last four classes above given, who have in any manner aided or abetted the rebellion against the United States government, are not entitled to the benefits of this act.

Attorneys for claimants must have proper authority from those in whose behalf they appear. Powers of attorney must be signed in the presence of two witnesses, and acknowledged before a duly qualified officer, whose official character must be certified under seal.

In all cases the post office address of the claimant must be distinctly stated.

Applications under this act will be numbered and acknowledged, to be acted on in their turn. In filing additional evidence, correspondents should always give the number of the claim as well as the name of the claimant.

JOSEPH H. BARRETT, *Commissioner.*

PENSION OFFICE, *July* 21, 1862.

"A."

Form of Declaration for an Invalid Pension.

STATE [DISTRICT OR TERRITORY] OF ——
County of —— } *ss.*

On this —— day of —— A. D. one thousand eight hundred and ——, personally appeared before me, —— [*here state the official character of the person administering the oath*] within and for the county and State aforesaid, ——, aged —— years, a resident of ——, in the State of ——, who, being duly sworn according to law, declares that he is the identical —— who enlisted in the service of the United States at ——, on the —— day of ——, in the year ——, as a —— in company ——, commanded by ——, in the —— regiment of ——, in the war of 1861, and was honorably discharged on the —— day of ——, in the year ——; that while in the service aforesaid, and in the line of his duty, he received the following wound (*or other disability as the case may be*): [*Here give a particular and minute account of the wound or other injury, and state how, when and where it occurred, where the applicant has resided since leaving the service, and what has been his occupation.*]

(*Signature of Claimant.*)

Also personally appeared —— and ——, residents of (*county, city or town*), persons whom I certify to be respectable and entitled to credit, and who, being by me duly sworn, say that they were present and saw —— sign his name (*or make his mark*) to the foregoing declaration; and they further swear that they have every reason to believe, from the appearance of the applicant and their acquaintance with him, that he is the identical person he represents himself to be; and they further state that they have no interest in the prosecution of this claim.

(*Signatures of Witnesses.*)

Sworn to and subscribed before me this —— day of ——, A. D., 18—; and I hereby certify that I have no interest, direct or indirect, in the prosecution of this claim.

(*Signature of Judge or other Officer.*)

Applicant's post-office address:

For REGULATIONS and FORMS relating to POWERS OF ATTORNEY in pension cases, see Chapter XVI.

"F."

Form of Surgeon's Affidavit.

If the claimant for a pension has not been examined, and the degree of his disability certified, by an army surgeon, he must produce the affidavit of two surgeons reputable in their profession, and certified as such by the magistrate before whom their statement is sworn to, in accordance with the following form:

(*Date.*)

It is hereby certified that ——, a —— in the company of ——, in the —— regiment of the United States ——, is rendered incapable of performing the duty of a soldier, by reason of wounds [or other injuries] inflicted while he was actually in the service aforesaid, and in the line of his duty, viz:

By satisfactory evidence and accurate examination, it appears that on the —— day of ——, in the year ——, ——, being engaged —— at or near a place called ——, in the State (District or Territory) of ——, he received, (or contracted)[1] —— and he is thereby not only incapacitated for military duty, but, in the opinion of the undersigned, is [2] —— disabled from obtaining his subsistence from manual labor.

Surgeon.
Surgeon.

Sworn to and subscribed before me, this —— day of ——, A. D. 18—; and I hereby certify that the said —— and —— are known to me as surgeons in actual practice, reputable in their profession, and that I have no interest, direct or indirect, in the prosecution of this claim.

(*Magistrate's Signature.*)

The REGULATIONS and FORMS prepared by the Commissioner for invalid cases, arising under the act of July 14,

1 Here give a particular description of the wound, injury or disease, and specify in what manner it has affected the applicant so as to produce disability in the degree stated.

2 The blank in the last line is to be filled up with the proportional "degree" of disability; for example: "three fourths," "one half," "one third," etc., or "totally," as the case may be.

1862, are substantially the same as those provided in cases of a like character under former acts. Claimants may, therefore, obtain aid in the preparation of their papers by referring to the forms hereinbefore given.

SPECIAL INSTRUCTIONS.

In every instance where the certificate of the certifying officer who authenticates the papers is not written on the same sheet of paper which contains the affidavit, or other paper authenticated, the certificate must be attached thereto by a piece of tape or small ribbon, the ends of which must pass under the seal of office of the certifying officer, so as to prevent any paper from being improperly attached to the certificate.

Interlineations or erasures in papers prepared for filing in pension cases, should be noted in the certificate of the magistrate, before signing, in order to show that they were not made after the execution of the papers.

All the "discharge papers" received by the soldier when discharged, should be sent with his declaration. The additional testimony that will be required to establish the claim, depends on the character of these papers.

The officer's certificate required by the rules of the Pension Office, may be given by any commissioned officer under whom the applicant served.

In case the applicant lives within thirty miles of a surgeon of the regular army, his certificate of disability must be obtained; but if he does not, then the affidavit of two respectable surgeons will be sufficient.

CHAPTER IV.

INVALID PENSIONS.

SECTION. I.

VOLUNTEERS AND MILITIA, SINCE THE WAR OF THE REVOLUTION.

BY acts of September 29, 1789,[1] and April 30, 1790,[2] the President was authorized to call into service, from time to time, such portion of the militia of the States as he might deem necessary to protect the people of the frontiers against the hostile incursions of Indians; and "an act for raising and adding another regiment to the military establishment of the United States, and for making further provision for the protection of the frontiers," approved March 3, 1791,[3] authorized the President to call out the militia, in case of exigency, to defend the frontiers, and,

SEC. 10. *And be it further enacted,* That the commissioned and non-commissioned officers, privates and musicians of the militia, or such corps of levies, shall, during the time of their service, be subject to the rules and articles of war; and they shall be entitled to the same pay, rations and forage, and, in case of wounds or disability in the line of their duty, to the same compensation as the troops of the United States.

The benefits of the act of April 10, 1806, granting pensions to invalids of the revolution, were, by act of April 25, 1808,[4] extended to *all* persons who served after

---

[1] U. S. Statutes at Large, vol. i, 95.

[2] *Ibid,* vol. i, 121.

[3] *Ibid,* vol. i, 222.

[4] *Ibid,* vol. ii, 496.

the revolution, and before the passage of the last-named act, as follows:

SEC. 4. *And be it further enacted*, That any officer, non-commissioned officer, musician or private, who has been wounded or disabled since the revolutionary war, while in the line of his duty, in the actual service of the United States, whether he belong to the military establishment or the militia, or any volunteer corps called into service under the authority of the United States, may be placed on the pension list of the United States, under such rate of compensation, and under such regulations, as are prescribed by the act entitled "an act to provide for perons who were disabled by known wounds received in the revolutionary war," passed April the tenth, one thousand eight hundred and six.

SEC. 5. *And be it further enacted*, That the pensioners becoming such in virtue of this act, shall be paid in the same manner as pensioners are paid, who have heretofore been placed on the pension list of the United States, under such restrictions and regulations, in all respects, as are perscribed by the laws of the United States in such cases provided.

The President was empowered, by an act approved, January 2, 1812,[1] whenever satisfactorily advised of an actual or threatened invasion of any State or Territory, by any Indian tribe or tribes, to raise, by enlistment, or the acceptance of volunteers, for one year,[2] six companies of rangers.[3] These were provided for, in cases of disability, as follows:

---

[1] U. S. Statutes at Large, vol. ii, 670.

[2] This was extended, by act of July 24, 1813, for an additional year, and until the close of the next session of Congress thereafter. U. S. Statutes at Large, vol. iii, 39.

[3] An act passed July 1, 1812 (U. S. Statutes at Large, vol. ii, 776), authorized the raising of an additional company, under the same provisions, conditions and restrictions contained in the act of January, 1812; and an act approved February 25, 1813 (U. S. Statutes at Large, vol. ii, 804), added ten more companies, upon same terms. The companies last mentioned were intended for use upon the frontier, to prevent the incursions of the Indian allies of the British, and were authorized for one year; but the

SEC. 4. *And be it further enacted*, That the officers, non-commissioned officers and privates, raised pursuant to this act, shall be entitled to the like compensation in case of disability by wounds and otherwise, incurred in the service, as officers, non-commissioned officers and privates in the present military establishment, and with them shall be subject to the rules and articles of war, which have been established, or may hereafter by law be established; and the provisions of the act entitled "an act fixing the military peace establishment of the United States," so far as they may be applicable, shall be extended to all persons, matters and things within the intent and meaning of this act, in the same manner as if they were inserted at large in the same. . . . .

An act approved February 6, 1812, entitled "an act authorizing the President of the United States to accept and organize certain volunteer military corps,"[1] passed in view of pending difficulties with Great Britain, empowered the President of the United States to accept volunteers, either artillery, cavalry or infantry, to the number of fifty thousand, subject to call at any time within two years after their acceptance, and to serve twelve months from the time of arriving at the place of rendezvous. Section five of this act is as follows:

SEC. 5. *And be it further enacted*, That if any officer, non-commissioned officer, musician or private shall be disabled by wounds or otherwise, while in the line of his duty in public service, he shall be placed on the list of invalid pensioners of the United States, at such rate of pension and under such regulations as are or may be directed by law: *Provided, always*, That the compensation to be allowed for such wounds or disabilities to a commissioned officer shall not exceed, for the highest rate of disability, half the monthly pay of such officer at the time of his being wounded or disabled; and that no officer shall receive more than the half-pay of a lieutenant-colonel; and that the rate of pension to non-commissioned

---

term of service was extended an additional year by act of February 24, 1814 (U. S. Statutes at Large, vol. iii, 98).

[1] U. S. Statutes at Large, vol. ii, 676.

officers, musicians and privates shall not exceed five dollars per month: *And provided, also,* That all inferior disabilities shall entitle the person so disabled to receive an allowance proportionate to the highest disability.

This act was repealed by act of January 29, 1813;[1] but it is expressly provided by the repealing act, that officers and men who entered the service as volunteers should not be deprived "of any rights, immunities or privileges" acquired under the provisions of the act repealed; nor should the United States be deprived of their services until the expiration of the term for which they volunteered.

An act approved August 2, 1813, entitled "an act to provide for the widows and orphans of militia slain and for militia disabled in the service of the United States,"[2] made the same provision for pensions to disabled volunteers and militia as were then allowed by law to regular troops. Section two of this act is as follows:

SEC. 2. *And be it further enacted,* That if any officer, non-commissioned officer, musician or private of the militia or of any volunteer corps, shall be disabled by known wounds received in the actual service of the United States, while in the line of his duty, he shall, upon substantiating his claim, in the manner described by an act entitled "an act to provide for persons who were disabled by known wounds received in the revolutionary war," passed the tenth day of April, eighteen hundred and six, be placed on the list of invalids of the United States, at such rate of pension and under such regulations as are provided by the said act, or as may hereafter be provided by law: *Provided, always,* That the compensation to be allowed for such wounds or disabilities to a commissioned officer shall not exceed, for the highest rate of disability, half the monthly pay of such officer at the time of his being wounded or disabled; and that no officer shall receive more than the half-pay of a lieutenant-

1 U. S. Statutes at Large, vol. ii, 794.

2 *Ibid,* vol. iii, 73.

colonel; and that the rate of compensation to non-commissioned officers, musicians and privates shall not exceed five dollars per month: *And provided also*, That all inferior disabilities shall entitle the persons so disabled to receive an allowance proportionate to the highest disability.

Section three provides that the act shall be construed to take effect from and after the 18th day of June, 1812.

The first section of an act entitled "an act to authorize the President to receive into service certain volunteer corps," approved February 24, 1814,[1] authorizes the President to receive into the service such proportion of the volunteers mentioned in the acts of February 6, 1812, and July 6, 1812, as in his judgment the public service may require, to serve for five years or during the war. The second section allows them:

SEC. 2. *And be it further enacted*, That the volunteers which shall be taken into service under the authority of the preceding section, shall be entitled to the same bounty, pay, rations, clothing, forage and emoluments of every kind, and to the same benefits and allowances, as the regular troops of the United States.

An act approved January 27, 1815,[2] empowered and directed the President to receive into the service of the United States all the troops that had been or might be raised by authority of the several States, not exceeding, (officers and men) forty thousand, to serve not less than twelve months; and promises these troops "the same pay, clothing, rations, forage and emoluments of every kind, and" (bounty excepted) "the same benefits and allowances, as the regular troops of the United States." This act was repealed in one month after its passage; and as hostilities were at that time suspended, it is not

1 U. S. Statutes at Large, vol. iii, 98.

2 *Ibid*, vol. iii, 193

probable that any rights accrued to individuals under its provisions.

"An act making further provision for military services during the late war, and for other purposes," approved April 16, 1816,[1] provides, among other things, as follows:

Be it enacted by the Senate and House of Representatives of the United States of America in Congress assembled, That when any officer or private soldier of the militia, including rangers, sea-fencibles and volunteers, or any non-commissioned officer, musician or private, enlisted for either of the terms of one year or eighteen months, or any commissioned officer of the regular army, shall have died while in the service of the United States during the late war, or in returning to his place of residence after being mustered out of service, or who shall have died at any time thereafter in consequence of wounds received while in the service, and shall have left a widow, or, if no widow, a child or children under sixteen years of age, such widow, or, if no widow, such child or children, shall be entitled to receive . . . *Provided, always,* . . . *Provided also,* That the officers and private soldiers of the militia, as aforesaid, who have been disabled by wounds or otherwise, while in the service of the United States in the discharge of their duty, during the late war, shall be placed on the list of pensioners, in the same manner as the officers and soldiers of the regular army, under such forms of evidence as the President of the United States may prescribe. . . .

The rates of pensions to certain invalids, in cases past and future, were increased by an act of April 24, 1816, entitled "an act to increase the pensions of invalids in certain cases; for the relief of invalids of the militia; and for the appointment of pension agents in those States where there is no commissioner of loans."[2] This act contains several important provisions.

Be it enacted by the Senate and House of Representatives of the United States of America in Congress assembled, That all persons of the ranks

1 U. S. Statutes at Large, vol. iii, 285.

2 *Ibid,* vol. iii, 296.

hereinafter named, who are now on the military pension roll of the United States, shall, from and after the passage of this act, be entitled to and receive, for disabilities of the highest degree, the following sums, in lieu of those to which they are now entitled, to-wit: A first lieutenant, seventeen dollars; a second lieutenant, fifteen dollars; a third lieutenant, fourteen dollars; an ensign, thirteen dollars; and a non-commissioned officer, musician or private, eight dollars per month; and for disabilities of a degree less than the highest, a sum proportionably less.[1]

SEC. 2. *And be it further enacted*, That all persons of the aforesaid ranks, who may hereafter be placed on the military pension roll of the United States, shall, according to their ranks and degrees of disabilities, be placed on at the aforesaid rates of pensions, in lieu of those heretofore established: *Provided*, That nothing herein contained shall be construed to lessen the pension of any person who, by special provision, is entitled to a higher pension than is herein provided.

SEC. 3. *And be it further enacted*, That all laws and regulations relating to the admission of the officers and soldiers of the regular army to be placed on the pension roll of the United States, shall and they are hereby declared to relate equally to the officers and soldiers of the militia, while in the service of the United States.[2]

Section four and last provides for the appointment of pension agents in certain States.

By "an act to authorize the President to raise mounted volunteers for the defense of the frontier," approved June 15, 1832,[3] provision is made for the acceptance, for one year, of six hundred mounted rangers, for the protection

---

1 A subaltern claiming the benefits of the act of April 24, 1816, is not entitled to any allowance for services as a staff officer. *Secretary of War Poinsett, April*, 1837.

2 Militia of the several States are allowed pensions for injuries received while in the service of the United States only under act of April 24, 1816. *Commissioner Waldo, February* 4, 1854. The armed police of a State are not entitled to invalid pensions. *Commissioner Waldo, February* 4, 1854.

3 U. S. Statutes at Large, vol. iv, 533.

and defense of the north-western frontier of the United States, and,

SEC. 4. *And be it further enacted*, That the officers, non-commissioned officers and privates, raised pursuant to this act, shall be entitled to the like compensation, in case of disability, by wounds or otherwise, incurred in the service, as has heretofore been allowed to officers, non-commissioned officers and privates, in the military establishment of the United States; and shall be subject to the rules and articles of war, and such regulations as have been or shall be established according to law for the government of the army of the United States, as far as the same may be applicable to the said rangers, within the intent and meaning of this act, for the protection and defense of the north-western frontier of the United States.

In lieu of this battalion of rangers, a regiment of dragoons was added to the regular army, by act of March 2, 1833;[1] and the President was directed to discharge the rangers on their being relieved by the dragoons. The discharge was probably not effected until the expiration of the term for which the rangers volunteered.

The benefits of the provisions of existing pension laws were, by act of March 19, 1836, entitled, "an act to provide for the payment of volunteers and militia corps in the service of the United States,"[2] extended to the volunteers and militia who had been or might be engaged in subduing the Indians of Florida, as follows:

SEC. 4. *And be it further enacted*, That the volunteers or militia who have been or who may be, received into the service of the United States, to suppress Indian depredations in Florida, shall be entitled to all the benefits which are conferred on persons wounded or otherwise disabled in the service of the United States.

Hostilities being threatened, and actually commenced,

---

[1] U. S. Statutes at Large, vol. iv, 652.

[2] *Ibid*, vol. v, 7.

by the Creek Indians, an act was passed May 23, 1836,[1] authorizing the President to accept volunteers, either cavalry or infantry, to the number of ten thousand, to serve for six or twelve months after arriving at the place of rendezvous, unless sooner discharged. These were liable to be called out only in case of Indian hostilities, or to repel invasions. Invalid pensions are provided for these volunteers as follows:

SEC. 5. *And be it further enacted*, That the volunteers who may be received into the service of the United States by virtue of the provisions of this act, shall be entitled to all the benefits which may be conferred on persons wounded in the service of the United States.

"An act granting pensions to the Cherokee warriors who assisted the United States, in the war of 1812, against Great Britain," was passed April 14, 1842.[2] This act is as follows:

Be it enacted by the Senate and House of Representatives of the United States of America in Congress assembled, That the Secretary of War be, and he hereby is, required to place on the pension roll such warriors of the Cherokee nation as were engaged on the side of the United States in the late war with Great Britain and the Southern Indians, and who were wounded in such service, at the same rates of pensions as are allowed by law to the officers and soldiers of the regular army of the United States, under such rules and regulations as to the proof of disability as the Secretary of War shall prescribe; which pensions shall commence from the period of disability.[3]

It will be observed that only those Cherokee warriors who were *wounded* in the service, are entitled to the benefits of this act.

The first section of a pension appropriation act of April 30, 1844,[4] contains the following proviso:

1 U. S. Statutes at Large, vol. v, 32.

2 *Ibid*, vol. v, 473.

3 For special forms and regulations in making applications under this law, see page 67.

4 U. S. Statutes at Large, vol. v, 656.

And provided also, That no person in the army, navy or marine corps, shall be allowed to draw both a pension as an invalid, and the pay of his rank or station in the service, unless the alleged disability for which the pension was granted be such as to have occasioned his employment in a lower grade or in some civil branch of the service.[1]

For the purpose of providing sufficient military strength to bring the war with Mexico to a speedy and successful termination, Congress, by an act of May 13, 1846,[2] authorized the President to employ the "militia, naval and military forces of the United States, and to call for and accept the service of any number of volunteers, not exceeding fifty thousand, who may offer their services, either as cavalry, artillery, infantry or riflemen, to serve twelve months after they shall have arrived at the place of rendezvous, or to the end of the war, unless sooner discharged, according to the time for which they shall have been mustered into the service." The organization of these volunteers into proper companies, battalions, regiments and divisions is marked out by the act, and it is prescribed,

SEC. 7. *And be it further enacted,* That the volunteers who may be received into the service of the United States by virtue of the provisions of this act, and who shall be wounded or otherwise disabled in the service, shall be entitled to all the benefits which may be conferred on persons wounded in the service of the United States.

WAR FOR THE UNION, 1861.

The proclamations of President Lincoln, and the acts of Congress relating to the calling out of volunteers and militia to suppress the rebellion in certain States of the Union, are so important, that they are here given entire.

[1] See notes to act of April 30, 1844, p. 25, and act of August 16, 1841, p. 86.

[2] U. S. Statutes at Large, vol. ix, 9.

[*Proclamation of the President, April* 15, 1861.]

BY THE PRESIDENT OF THE UNITED STATES OF AMERICA.

A PROCLAMATION.

WHEREAS the laws of the United States have been for some time past, and now are opposed, and the execution thereof obstructed, in the States of South Carolina, Georgia, Alabama, Florida, Mississippi, Louisiana and Texas, by combinations too powerful to be suppressed by the ordinary course of judicial proceedings or by the powers vested in the marshals by law:

Now, therefore, I, ABRAHAM LINCOLN, President of the United States, in virtue of the power in me vested by the constitution and the laws, have thought fit to call forth, and hereby do call forth, the militia of the several States of the Union, to the aggregate number of seventy-five thousand,[1] in order to suppress said combinations, and to cause the laws to be duly executed.[2]

The details for this object will be immediately communicated to the State authorities through the War Department.

I appeal to all loyal citizens to favor, facilitate and aid this effort to maintain the honor, the integrity and the existence of our national Union, and the perpetuity of popular government; and to redress wrongs already long enough endured.

I deem it proper to say that the first service assigned to the forces hereby called forth will probably be to repossess the forts, places and property which have been seized from the Union; and in every event, the utmost care will be observed, consistently with the objects aforesaid, to avoid any devastation, any destruction of, or interference with, property, or any disturbance of peaceful citizens in any part of the country.

1 The Attorney-General has given an opinion on the laws regulating pensions for officers, soldiers, their widows and minor children, in which he says that "the 14th section of the act of March 16, 1802, provides for those *volunteers* who are wounded or otherwise disabled in the service." This provides for the officers and soldiers who entered the service under the act of July 22, 1861, for three years or during the war. The volunteers called into the service for *three months*, by the President's proclamation of April 15, 1861, and disabled by "*known wounds*," are entitled, under the act of August 2, 1813.

2 An act of August 6, 1861 (U. S. Statutes at Large, vol. xii, 326), legalizes the "acts, proclamations and orders of the President," respecting the army and navy, calling out the militia, etc.

And I hereby command the persons composing the combinations aforesaid to disperse, and retire peaceably to their respective abodes within twenty days from this date.

Deeming that the present condition of public affairs presents an extraordinary occasion, I do hereby, in virtue of the power in me vested by the constitution, convene both Houses of Congress. Senators and Representatives are therefore summoned to assemble at their respective chambers, at twelve o'clock, noon, on Thursday, the fourth day of July next, then and there to consider and determine such measures as in their wisdom the public safety and interest may seem to demand.

In witness whereof, I have hereunto set my hand, and caused the seal of the United States to be affixed.

[L. S.] Done at the City of Washington, this 15th day of April, in the year of our Lord one thousand eight hundred and sixty-one, and of the Independence of the United States the eighty-fifth.

ABRAHAM LINCOLN.

By the President:

WILLIAM H. SEWARD, *Secretary of State.*

[*Proclamation of the President, May* 3, 1861.]

BY THE PRESIDENT OF THE UNITED STATES OF AMERICA.

A PROCLAMATION.

WHEREAS existing exigencies demand immediate and adequate measures for the protection of the national constitution and the preservation of the national Union by the suppression of the insurrectionary combinations now existing in several States for opposing the laws of the Union and obstructing the execution thereof, to which end a military force in addition to that called forth by my proclamation of the fifteenth day of April in the present year, appears to be indispensably necessary:

NOW, therefore, I, ABRAHAM LINCOLN, President of the United States, and Commander-in-Chief of the Army and Navy thereof, and of the Militia of the several States when called into actual service, do hereby call into the service of the United States forty-two thousand and thirty-four volunteers,[1] to serve for the period of three years

1 An act of August 6, 1861 (U. S. Statutes at Large, vol. xii, 326), legalizes the "acts, proclamations and orders of the President," respecting the army and navy, calling out the militia, etc.

unless sooner discharged, and to be mustered into service as infantry and cavalry. The proportions of each arm and the details of enrollment and organization will be made known through the Department of War.

And I also direct that the regular army of the United States be increased by the addition of eight regiments of infantry, one regiment of cavalry, and one regiment of artillery, making altogether a maximum aggregate increase of twenty-two thousand seven hundred and fourteen, officers and enlisted men, the details of which increase will also be made known through the Department of War.

And I further direct the enlistment for not less than one or more than three years, of eighteen thousand seamen, in addition to the present force, for the naval service of the United States. The details of the enlistment and organization will be made known through the Department of the Navy.

The call for volunteers, hereby made, and the direction for the increase of the regular army, and for the enlistment of seamen hereby given, together with the plan of organization adopted for the volunteers and for the regular forces hereby authorized, will be submitted to Congress as soon as assembled.

In the meantime, I earnestly invoke the co-operation of all good citizens in the measures hereby adopted, for the effectual suppression of unlawful violence, for the impartial enforcement of constitutional laws, and for the speediest possible restoration of peace and order, and, with these, of happiness and prosperity throughout the country.

In testimony whereof, I have hereunto set my hand and caused the seal of the United States to be affixed.

[L. S.] Done at the City of Washington, this third day of May, in the year of our Lord one thousand eight hundred and sixty-one, and of the Independence of the United States the eightyfifth. ABRAHAM LINCOLN.

By the President:

WILLIAM H. SEWARD, *Secretary of State.*

AN ACT *to authorize the Employment of Volunteers to aid in enforcing the Laws and protecting Public Property, approved July* 22, 1861.

WHEREAS, certain of the forts, arsenals, custom-houses, navy yards, and other property of the United States, have been seized, and other violations of law have been committed and are threatened by organized bodies of men in several of the States, and a conspiracy has been entered into to overthrow the Government of the United States, Therefore,

Be it enacted by the Senate and House of Representatives of the United States of America in Congress assembled, That the President be and is hereby authorized to accept the services of volunteers, either as cavalry, infantry or artillery, in such numbers, not exceeding five hundred thousand, as he may deem necessary, for the purpose of repelling invasion, suppressing insurrection, enforcing the laws, and preserving and protecting the public property: *Provided,* That the services of the volunteers shall be for such time as the President may direct, not exceeding three years, nor less than six months, and they shall be disbanded at the end of the war. And all provisions of law applicable to three years' volunteers, shall apply to two years' volunteers, and to all volunteers who have been or may be accepted into the service of the United States for a period not less than six months, in the same manner as if such volunteers were specially named. Before receiving into service any number of volunteers exceeding those now called for and accepted, the President shall, from time to time, issue his proclamation, stating the number desired, either as cavalry, infantry or artillery, and the States from which they are to be furnished, having reference, in any such requisition, to the number then in service from the several States, and to the exigencies of the service at the time, and equalizing, as far as practicable, the number furnished by the several States, according to federal population.

SEC. 2. *And be it further enacted,* That the said volunteers shall be subject to the rules and regulations governing the army of the United States, and that they shall be formed, by the President, into regiments of infantry, with the exception of such numbers for cavalry and artillery, as he may direct, not to exceed the proportion of one company of each of those arms to every regiment of infantry, and to be organized as in the regular service. Each regiment of infantry shall have one colonel, one lieutenant-colonel, one major, one adjutant (a lieutenant), one quartermaster (a lieutenant), one surgeon, and one assistant-surgeon, one sergeant-major, one regimental quartermaster sergeant, one regimental commissary sergeant, one hospital steward, two principal musicians, and twenty-four musicians for a band; and shall be composed of ten companies, each company to consist of one captain, one first lieutenant, one second lieutenant, one first sergeant, four sergeants, eight corporals, two musicians, and one wagoner, and from sixty-four to eighty-two privates.

SEC. 3. *And be it further enacted*, That those forces, when accepted as herein authorized, shall be organized into divisions of three or more brigades each; and each division shall have a major-general, three aides-de-camp, and one assistant adjutant-general with the rank of major. Each brigade shall be composed of four or more regiments, and shall have one brigadier-general, two aides-de-camp, one assistant adjutant-general with the rank of captain, one surgeon, one assistant quartermaster, and one commissary of subsistence.

SEC. 4. *And be it further enacted*, That the President shall be authorized to appoint, by and with the advice and consent of the senate, for the command of the forces provided for in this act, *a number of major-generals, not exceeding six, and a number of brigadier-generals, not exceeding eighteen*, and the other division and brigade officers required for the organization of these forces, except the aides-de-camp, who shall be selected by their respective generals from the officers of the army or volunteer corps: *Provided*, That the President may select the major-generals and brigadier-generals provided for in this act from the line or staff of the regular army, and the officers so selected shall be permitted to retain their rank therein. The Governors of the States furnishing volunteers under this act, shall commission the field, staff and company officers requisite for the said volunteers; but in cases where the State authorities refuse or omit to furnish volunteers at the call or on the proclamation of the President, and volunteers from such States offer their services under such call or proclamation, the President shall have power to accept such services, and to commission the proper field, staff, and company officers.

SEC. 5. *And be it further enacted*, That the officers, non-commissioned officers and privates, organized as above set forth, shall, in all respects, be placed on the footing, as to pay and allowances, of similar corps of the regular army: *Provided*, That the allowances of non-commissioned officers and privates for clothing, when not furnished in kind, shall be three dollars and fifty cents per month, and that each commissioned officer, non-commissioned officer, private, musician and artificer of cavalry, shall furnish his own horse and horse equipments, and shall receive forty cents per day for their use and risk,[1] except that in case the horse shall become disabled or

[1] Repealed, act of July 17, 1862.

shall die, the allowance shall cease until the disability be removed or another horse be supplied. Every volunteer non-commissioned officer, private, musician and artificer, who enters the service of the United States under this act, shall be paid at the rate of fifty cents in lieu of subsistence, and if a cavalry volunteer, twenty-five cents additional, in lieu of forage, for every twenty miles of travel from his place of enrollment to the place of muster,—the distance to be measured by the shortest usually traveled route; and when honorably discharged, an allowance at the same rate, from the place of his discharge to his place of enrollment, and in addition thereto, if he shall have served for a period of two years, or during the war, if sooner ended, the sum of one hundred dollars: *Provided*, That such of the companies of cavalry herein provided, as may require it, may be furnished with horses and horse equipments in the same manner as in the United States army.

SEC. 6. *And be it further enacted*, That any volunteer who may be received into the service of the United States under this act, and who may be wounded or otherwise disabled in the service, shall be entitled to the benefits which have been or may be conferred on persons disabled in the regular service; and the widow, if there be one, and if not, the legal heirs of such as die, or may be killed in service, in addition to all arrears of pay and allowances, shall receive the sum of one hundred dollars.

SEC. 7. *And be it further enacted*, That the bands of the regiments of infantry, and of the regiments of cavalry, shall be paid as follows: one fourth of each shall receive the pay and allowances of sergeants of engineer soldiers; one fourth, those of corporals of engineer soldiers; and the remaining half, those of privates of engineer soldiers of the first class; and the leaders of the band shall receive the same pay and emoluments as second lieutenants of infantry.[1]

SEC. 8. *And be it further enacted*, That the wagoners and saddlers shall receive the pay and allowances of corporals of cavalry. The regimental commissary-sergeants shall receive the pay and allow ances of regiment sergeant-major, and the regimental quartermaster-serjeant shall receive the pay and allowances of a sergeant of cavalry.

SEC. 9. *And be it further enacted*, That there shall be allowed to each regiment one chaplain, who shall be appointed by the regi-

[1] Repealed and other provision made for bands, act of July 17, 1862.

mental commander on the vote of the field officers and company commanders on duty with the regiment at the time the appointment shall be made. The chaplain so appointed must be a regular ordained minister of a Christian denomination, and shall receive the pay and allowances of a captain of cavalry, and shall be required to report to the colonel commanding the regiment to which he is attached, at the end of each quarter, the moral and religious condition of the regiment, and such suggestions as may conduce to the social happiness and moral improvement of the troops.

SEC. 10. *And be it further enacted*, That the general commanding a separate department or a detached army, is hereby authorized to appoint a military board or commission of not less than three nor more than five officers, whose duty it shall be to examine the capacity, qualifications, propriety of conduct and efficiency of any commissioned officer of volunteers within his department or army, who may be reported to the board or commission, and upon such report, if adverse to such officer, and if approved by the President of the United States, the commission of such officer shall be vacated; *Provided always*, That no officer shall be eligible to sit on such board or commission whose rank or promotion would in any way be affected by its proceedings, and two members at least, if practicable, shall be of equal rank of the officer being examined. And when vacancies occur in any of the companies of volunteers, an election shall be called by the colonel of the regiment, to fill such vacancies, and the men of each company shall vote in their respective companies for all officers as high as captain, and vacancies above captain shall be filled by the votes of the commissioned officers of the regiment, and all officers so elected shall be commissioned by the respective Governors of the States, or by the President of the United States.

SEC. 11. *And be it further enacted*, That all letters written by soldiers in the service of the United States may be transmitted through the mails without pre-payment of postage, under such regulations as the Post-office Department may prescribe, the postage thereon to be paid by the recipients.

SEC. 12. *And be it further enacted*, That the Secretary of War be, and is hereby authorized and directed to introduce among the volunteer forces in the service of the United States, the system of allotment tickets now used in the navy, or some equivalent system, by which the family of the volunteer may draw such portions of his pay as he may request.

[Approved July 22, 1861.]

AN ACT *in addition to the "act to authorize the employment of Volunteers to aid in enforcing the Laws and protecting Public Property," approved July* 25, 1861.

Be it enacted by the Senate and House of Representatives of the United States of America in Congress assembled, That the President of the United States be, and he is hereby authorized to accept the services of volunteers, either as cavalry, infantry or artillery, in such numbers as the exigencies of the public service may, in his opinion, demand, to be organized as authorized by the act of the twenty-second of July, eighteen hundred and sixty-one; *Provided,* That the number of troops hereby authorized shall not exceed five hundred thousand.

SEC. 2. *And be it further enacted,* That the volunteers authorized by this act shall be armed as the President may direct: they shall be subject to the rules and articles of war, and shall be upon the footing, in all respects, with similar corps of the United States army and shall be mustered into the service for "during the war."

SEC. 3. *And be it further enacted,* That the President shall be authorized to appoint, by and with the advice and consent of the senate, for the command of the volunteer forces, such number of major-generals and of brigadier-generals as may, in his judgment, be required for their organization.

[Approved, July 25, 1861.]

AN ACT *to secure to the Officers and Men actually employed in the Western Department, or Department of the Missouri, their Pay, Bounty and Pension, approved March* 25, 1862.

Be it enacted by the Senate and House of Representatives of the United States of America in Congress assembled, That the Secretary of War be, and he is hereby authorized and required to allow and pay to the officers, non-commissioned officers, musicians and privates, who have been heretofore actually employed in the military service of the United States, whether mustered into actual service or not, where their services were accepted and actually employed by the generals who have been in command of the Department in the

West, or the Department of the Missouri, the pay and bounty as in cases of regular enlistment. [1]

SEC. 2. *And be it further enacted*, That the officers and non-commissioned officers, musicians and privates so employed, who may have been wounded or incapacitated for service, shall be entitled to and receive the pension allowed for such disability: *Provided*, That the length and character of their enlistment and service be such as to entitle them, under existing laws, to such pension.

SEC. 3. *And be it further enacted*, That the heirs of those killed in battle, or those who may have died from wounds received while so in service, shall be entitled to receive the bounty and pay to which they would have been entitled had they been regularly mustered into service; *Provided*, That the bounty and pay referred to in this act shall not be payable unless their term of enlistment and service be of such duration as to entitle them to receive the same, according to existing laws.

[Approved, March 25, 1862.]

An act approved, July 14, 1862, entitled "an act to grant pensions," makes the following provision for the invalids of the war of 1861.

AN ACT *to Grant Pensions.*

Be it enacted by the Senate and House of Representatives of the United States of America in Congress assembled, That if any officer, non-commissioned officer, musician or private of the army, including regulars, volunteers and militia, or any officer, warrant or petty officer, musician, seaman, ordinary seaman, flotillaman, marine, clerk, landsman, pilot or other person in the navy or marine corps, has been, since the fourth day of March, eighteen hundred and sixty-one, or shall hereafter be disabled by reason of any wound received or disease contracted while in the service of the United States and in the line of duty, he shall, upon making due proof of the fact according to such forms and regulations as are or may be

[1] By a resolution of July 12, 1862, payments under this act are suspended until the report of the commissioners appointed to investigate claims coming within the purview of this act. The committee are required to report upon the claims of persons who actually served, within sixty days from the time of their appointment.

provided by or in pursuance of law, be placed upon the list of invalid pensisners of the United States, and be entitled to receive, for the highest rate of disability, such pension as is hereinafter provided in such cases, and for an inferior disability an amount proportionate to the highest disability, to commence as hereinafter provided, and continue during the existence of such disability. The pension for a total disability for officers, non-commissioned officers, musicians and privates employed in the military service of the United States, whether regulars, volunteers or militia, and in the marine corps, shall be as follows, viz: Lieutenant-colonel and all officers of a higher rank, thirty dollars per month; major, twenty-five dollars per month; captain, twenty dollars per month; first lieutenant, seventeen dollars per month; second lieutenant, fifteen dollars per month; and non-commissioned officers, musicians and privates, eight dollars per month. The pension for total disability for officers, warrant or petty officers, and others employed in the naval service of the United States, shall be as follows, viz: Captain, commander, surgeon, paymaster and chief engineer, respectively, ranking with commander by law, lieutenant commanding and master commanding, thirty dollars per month; lieutenant, surgeon, paymaster and chief engineer, respectively, ranking with lieutenant by law, and passed assistant surgeon, twenty-five dollars per month; professor of mathematics, master, assistant surgeon, assistant paymaster and chaplain, twenty dollars per month; first assistant engineers and pilots, fifteen dollars per month; passed midshipman, midshipman, captains' and paymasters' clerk, second and third assistant engineer, masters' mate and all warrant officers, ten dollars per month; all petty officers and all other persons before named employed in the naval service, eight dollars per month; and all commissioned officers, of either service, shall receive such and only such pension as is herein provided for the rank in which they hold commissions.

This act will be found entire under the title "INVALID PENSIONS—REGULAR SERVICE," Chapter III, Section I.

The 3d and 4th secs. of what is termed "The New Militia Law," entitled "a bill to amend the act calling forth the militia to execute the laws of the Union, suppress insurrections, and repel invasions, approved, February 28,

1795, and the acts amendatory thereof, and for other purposes," approved July 16, 1862, provides:

SEC. 3. *And be it further enacted*, That the President be, and he is hereby authorized, in addition to the volunteer forces which he is now authorized by law to raise, to accept the services of any number of volunteers, not exceeding one hundred thousand as infantry, for a period of nine months, unless sooner discharged. And every soldier who shall enlist under the provisions of this section shall receive his first month's pay, and also $25 as bounty, upon the mustering of his company or regiment into the service of the United States. And all provisions of law relating to volunteers enlisted in the service of the United States for three years, or during the war, except in relation to bounty, shall be, and the same are extended to, and are hereby declared to embrace the volunteers to be raised under the provisions of this section.

SEC. 4. *And be it further enacted*, That, for the purpose of filling up the regiments of infantry now in the United States service, the President be, and he hereby is, authorized to accept the services of volunteers in such numbers as may be presented for that purpose, for twelve months, if not sooner discharged. And such volunteers, when mustered into the service, shall be in all respects upon a footing with similar troops in the United States service, except as to service bounty, which shall be fifty dollars, one half of which to be paid upon their joining their regiments, and the other half at the expiration of their enlistment.

GENERAL OBSERVATIONS.

In making applications for pensions on behalf of volunteers or militia, in general, the acts which should be consulted are those of April 16, 1816; March 16, 1802; January 11, 1812; January 29, 1813, and March 3, 1815 (some of which will be found noticed under title "INVALID PENSIONS—REGULAR SERVICE," Chapter III, Section I). To these acts all others granting invalid pensions have either direct or indirect relation. The first two acts named have the most general application. It has been held (Commissioner Waldo, February 4, 1854), that the militia of the several States are allowed pensions for injuries received while in the service of the United States only under act of April 24, 1816.

There is at the present time no distinction between regulars, volunteers and militia, so far as relates to the rates of pensions or the manner of obtaining the allowance of the same.

For pensions in cases arising in the war of 1861, reference must be had to the act of July 14, 1862.

SECTION II.

FORMS AND REGULATIONS FOR OBTAINING INVALID PENSIONS—VOLUNTEERS AND MILITIA.

The Forms and Regulations pertaining to applications for pensions in the case of invalids of the regular army, are also applicable to the case of volunteers and militia. These Forms and Regulations will be found at the close of title "INVALID PENSIONS—REGULAR SERVICE," Chapter III, Section II.

A few forms by way of illustration and simplification are here given:

Form of Application for an Invalid Pension.

STATE OF ——, }
—— *County* } *ss.*

On this —— day of ——, 18—, before [*court, judge or clerk*] —— in and for the county and State above named, and by law duly authorized to administer oaths for general purposes, personally appeared ——, a resident of ——, in the State of ——, aged —— years, who being duly sworn according to law, declares that he is the identical ——, who was a private [*or if an officer mention the grade*], in company ——, commanded by Captain ——, in the —— regiment of —— volunteers, commanded by Colonel ——, in the war of 1861 and 1862, for the suppression of rebellion, and the preservation of the Union [*or other war*]. That he volunteered at ——, in the State of——, on or about the —— day of ——, 18—, for the term of ——, and was honorably discharged at ——, on the —— day of ——, 18—, as will appear by his certificate of discharge herewith presented. [*If no certificate was received, that fact should be stated; if received, and afterwards lost or destroyed, state the fact, with the particulars of loss or destruction*].

That while in said service, in the line of his duty, at ——, in the State of ——, on the —— day of ——, 18—. [*Here give details of the manner in which, the time when and the place where the wound was received, or disease contracted; with its nature or character, and its physical effect*].

That since leaving said service this applicant has resided at ——, and his occupation has been ——.

He makes this declaration for the purpose of being placed on the invalid pension roll of the United States, by reason of the disability above stated; and hereby constitutes and appoints ——, his attorney, to prosecute this claim, and procure a pension certificate.[1]

(*Claimant's Signature.*)

Sworn to, subscribed and acknowledged before me, the day and year first above named, and on the same day personally appeared —— and ——, residents of ——, and made oath that they are personally acquainted with ——, who has made and subscribed the foregoing declaration in their presence, and that they have every reason to believe from the appearance of the applicant, and their acquaintance with him, that he is the identical person he represents himself to be; that they reside as above stated, and are disinterested in this claim for a pension; that since leaving the service of the United States, as aforesaid, his habits have been uniformly good, and his occupation ——.

(*Witnesses' Signatures.*)

Sworn to and subscribed before me; and I certify that I am not interested in this claim or concerned in its prosecution; that I know the affiants to be credible witnesses, and that the claimant is the person he represents himself to be.

(*Officer's Signature.*)

This declaration must be made before a Court of Record, or Judge or Clerk of such Court. The certificate of the Clerk, under the seal of the proper Court, must be appended in all cases.

Surgeon's Affidavit to Disability of Invalid.

THE STATE OF ——, }
County of——. } *ss.*

It is hereby certified that ——, late a —— in the company commanded by Captain ——, in the regiment of —— volunteers [*or* volunteer militia, *or* militia, *as the case may be*], commanded by Col. ——, is rendered incapable of performing the duty of a soldier, by reason of wounds received [*or* disease contracted] while he was actually in the service aforesaid, and in the line of his duty, viz.:

1 The better practice is to execute a separate power of attorney.

By satisfactory evidence and accurate examination, it appears that on the —— day of ——, A. D. ——, the said ——, being engaged in ——, at or near a place called ——, in the State of ——, was disabled in the following manner [*Here state fully the manner in which the disability was incurred, its nature, and how it affects the invalid*]; and he is thereby not only incapacitated for military duty, but, in the opinion of the undersigned, is totally [*or* three fourths; *or* one half; *or* one third, *as the degree of disability may be*] disabled from obtaining a subsistence by manual labor.

(*Signature or Signatures.*)

Should this certificate be given by an army surgeon, it is not necessary that it should be sworn to; but if not so given, it must be signed by two reputable surgeons of the vicinity of the claimant's place of residence, who must also make oath to the same. The form for a certificate of the officer administering the oath in the latter case will be found on page 38; where will also be found the forms, regulations and instructions, relating to the execution of other necessary papers in invalid pension cases.

For REGULATIONS and FORMS relating to POWERS OF ATTORNEY, in Pension cases, see Chapter XVI.

OFFICIAL INSTRUCTIONS TO BE OBSERVED IN APPLYING FOR PENSIONS TO INVALID CHEROKEE WARRIORS.

WAR DEPARTMENT, *April* 26, 1842.

In substantiating claims under this law, the following evidence will be required:

The applicant must make a declaration, under oath, before some officer of the United States, or of the Cherokee Nation, duly qualified to administer oaths, stating how, when and where he was wounded, and where he at present resides. He must also produce the testimony of at least two persons of known respectability, stating their knowledge of the claimant, giving his name, residence and age, according to the best of their knowledge and belief; the reputation he has borne in the neighborhood where he resides; and they must be particular in stating the fact whether, during the whole time they have been acquainted with him, he has been considered as one of the Cherokee warriors who was wounded while in the United States service during the late war with Great Britain. The affidavits must be duly authenticated.

The applicant, on obtaining such proof, must present himself to some officer of the medical staff of the army, who will carefully examine him, and give such a certificate respecting his disability as the facts will justify him in giving. The applicant's wound must be particularly described, and the degree of disability arising from the wound must be clearly stated. The examining surgeon is also required to be particular in stating any fact within his knowledge, that may have a tendency to throw light on the claim, whether or not it may relate to the claimant's disability. The annexed form prescribed for granting certificates to persons disabled while in the line of their duty in the United States service, must be followed by the examining surgeons.

No claim will be allowed unless the claimant's name appears on the muster rolls.

The pensions which may be granted will be paid only to the pensioner in person, by or under the direction of some officer of the United States, upon satisfactory evidence of the identity of the applicant. In no case will the powers of attorney be recognized.

J. C. SPENCER, *Secretary of War.*

Surgeon's Certificate in the case of a Cherokee Invalid.

Having been requested by ——, one of the Cherokee tribe, who is now an inhabitant of ——, to examine him with a view of giving him such a certificate as may aid him in procuring a pension from the United States, under the act of 14th April, 1842, I hereby certify that I am fully satisfied, from the affidavits of ——, and ——, two persons in whose statements I repose entire confidence, that the aforesaid ——, an applicant for a pension, did actually serve in the regiment of the Cherokee Indians who were engaged on the side of the United States during the late war with Great Britain; that he was under the command of Captain ——, and that while in said service, and engaged in battle at or near ——, he was wounded by a [*Here particularly describe the wound, and say in what way he is affected by it*], and that in consequence of the injury received by said wound, he is [*Here state the degree of disability—whether one fourth, one third, one half, three fourths or total—as the case may be*], disabled from obtaining his subsistence from manual labor.

Surgeon, U. S. Army.

Dated at ——, this —— day of ——, 18—.

No form for a declaration or other papers necessary to be filed in such cases has been provided by the office having cognizance of such applications; but if any claims under the act remain unadjusted, the regulations established by the Secretary of War, and given in full, with the forms which will be found under title "INVALID PENSIONS—REGULAR SERVICE," page 34, and title "INVALID PENSIONS—VOLUNTEERS AND MILITIA;" page 67, will serve as guides to the draughtsman in his work.

ACT OF JULY 14, 1862.

The Regulations and Forms applicable to this act are given in full under "REGULATIONS and FORMS, INVALID PENSIONS—REGULAR SERVICE," Chapter III, Section II, page 34.

CHAPTER V.

INVALID PENSIONS.

INDIAN WARS—REGULARS, VOLUNTEERS AND MILITIA.

THE first act of the Congress of the United States, after the adoption of the constitution, making provision for repelling the incursions of hostile Indians, was that of September 29, 1789, entitled "an act to recognize and adapt to the Constitution of the United States the establishment of the troops raised under the resolves of the United States in Congress assembled, and for other purposes therein mentioned."[1] This act authorized the President to call out such numbers of the militia of the States as he might, at any time, deem necessary to protect the people of the frontiers; and provides that their pay and subsistence shall be the same as that of the establishment; but makes no provision for pensions in cases of disability.

The next act was that of March 5, 1792, "making further and more effectual provision for the protection of the frontiers of the United States."[2] This adds three regiments to the regular army, to continue in service three years or until peace is secured with the Indian tribes; and prescribes:

SEC. 11. *And be it further enacted*, That all the commissioned and non-commissioned officers, privates and musicians of the said three regiments shall take the same oaths, shall be governed by the

1 U. S. Statutes at Large, vol. i, 95.

2 *Ibid*, vol. i, 241.

same rules and regulations, and, in cases of disabilities, shall receive the same compensations, as are described in the before-mentioned act, entitled "an act for regulating the military establishment of the United States." [1]

The President was empowered, by an act approved January 2, 1812,[2] whenever satisfactorily advised of an actual or threatened incursion of Indian tribes into any State or Territory, to raise, by enlistment or the acceptance of volunteers, for one year,[3] six[4] companies of rangers; who, in cases of disability incurred in the service, were provided for as follows:

SEC. 4. *And be it further enacted,* That the officers, non-commissioned officers and privates, raised pursuant to this act, shall be entitled to like compensation, in case of disability by wounds and otherwise, incurred in the service, as officers, non-commissioned officers and privates in the present military establishment, and with them shall be subject to the rules and articles of war, which have been established or may hereafter by law be established; and the provisions of the act entitled "an act fixing the military peace establishment of the United States," so far as they may be applicable, shall be extended to all persons, matters and things within the intent and meaning of this act, in the same manner as if they were inserted at large in the same. . . .

---

1 This is the act of April 30, 1790. See page 13.

2 U. S. Statutes at Large, vol. ii, 670.

3 This was extended, by act of July 24, 1813, for an additional year, and until the close of the next session of Congress thereafter. (U. S. Statutes at Large, vol. iii, 39.)

4 An act passed July 1, 1812 (U. S. Statutes at Large, vol. ii, 776), authorized the raising of an additional company, under the same "provisions, conditions and restrictions" contained in the act of January, 1812; and an act approved February 25, 1813 (U. S. Statutes at Large, vol. ii, 804), added ten more companies, upon the same terms. The companies last mentioned were intended for use upon the frontiers against the Indian allies of the British, and were originally authorized for one year, but the term of service was extended one year by act of February 24, 1814. (U. S. Statutes at Large, vol. iii, 98.)

An act approved April 10, 1812, entitled "an act for the relief of the officers and soldiers who served in the late campaign on the Wabash,"[1] provides that the officers and men who served under General Harrison against the Indians, on the Wabash, in the year 1811, shall be entitled to the same pay, according to the rank assigned them by General Harrison, as is allowed by law to the militia; and,

SEC. 3. *And be it further enacted*, That every officer, according to the rank which he held as aforesaid, non-commissioned officer and private of the volunteers and militia who served in said campaign, and who have been disabled by known wounds received in said service, shall be placed on the list of invalids of the United States, at such rate of pension as shall be directed by the President of the United States, upon satisfactory proof of such wound and disability being produced to the Secretary of War, agreeably to such rules as he may prescribe: *Provided*, That the rate of compensation for such wounds and disabilities shall never, for the highest disability, exceed half the monthly pay of such officer at the time of being so wounded or disabled, and that the rate of compensation to a non-commissioned officer and private shall never exceed five dollars per month; and all inferior disabilities shall entitle the person so disabled to receive a sum in proportion to the highest disability; but no pension of a commissioned officer shall be calculated at a higher rate than the half-pay of a lieutenant-colonel.

The rate of pensions to certain classes of invalid pensioners was increased by an act approved April 24, 1816. This act will be found at large in Chapter IV, Section I, page 51.

By "an act to authorize the President to raise mounted volunteers for the defense of the frontiers," approved June 15, 1832,[2] provision is made for the acceptance, for

1 U. S. Statutes at Large, vol. ii, 704.

3 *Ibid.*, vol. iv, 533.

one year, of six hundred mounted rangers, for the protection and defense of the north-western frontiers of the United States; and these are promised:

SEC. 4. *And be it further enacted*, That the officers, non-commissioned officers and privates, raised pursuant to this act, shall be entitled to the like compensation, in case of disability by wounds or otherwise incurred in the service, as has heretofore been allowed to officers, non-commissioned officers and privates in the military establishment of the United States; and shall be subject to the rules and articles of war, and such regulations as have been or shall be established, according to law, for the government of the army of the United States, as far as the same may be applicable to the said rangers, within the intent and meaning of this act, for the protection and defense of the north-western frontier of the United States.

In lieu of this battalion of rangers, a regiment of dragoons was added to the regular army, by act of March 2, 1833;[1] and the President was directed to discharge the rangers on their being relieved by the dragoons. This discharge was probably not effected until the term for which the rangers volunteered had expired. The regiment of dragoons was placed upon the same footing in respect to invalid pensions as other regular troops, as will be seen by the following:

SEC. 3. *And be it further enacted*, That the said regiment of dragoons shall be liable to serve on horse or foot, as the President may direct; shall be subject to the rules and articles of war, be recruited in the same manner, and with the same limitations; that the officers, non-commissioned officers, musicians, farriers and privates, shall be entitled to the same provisions for wounds and disabilities, the same provisions for widows and children, and the same allowances and benefits in every respect, as are allowed the other troops constituting the present military peace establishment.

The benefits of existing pension laws were, by act of March 19, 1836, entitled "an act to provide for the pay-

1 U. S. Statutes at Large, vol. iv, 652.

ment of volunteers and militia corps in the service of the United States,"[1] extended to volunteers and militia who had been or might be engaged in subduing the Indians in Florida; as follows:

SEC. 4. *And be it further enacted*, That the volunteers or militia who have been or who may be received into the service of the United States to suppress Indian depredations in Florida, shall be entitled to all the benefits which are conferred on persons wounded or otherwise disabled in the service of the United States.

Hostilities being commenced by the Creek Indians, an act was passed, May 23, 1836,[2] authorizing the President to accept volunteers, either cavalry or infantry, to the number of ten thousand, to serve for six or twelve months after arriving at the place of rendezvous, unless sooner discharged. These were liable to be called out only in case of Indian disturbances, or to repel invasions. Invalid pensions were provided by the act as follows:

SEC. 5. *And be it further enacted*, That the volunteers who may be received into the service of the United States by virtue of the provisions of this act, shall be entitled to all the benefits which may be conferred on persons wounded in the service of the United States.

For a rule forbidding the payment of pensions to persons who are drawing pay in the service, see page 25.

GENERAL OBSERVATIONS.

The acts grouped together under the title "INDIAN WARS," may, with a few exceptions, also be found under the titles "INVALID PENSIONS—REGULAR SERVICE," and "INVALID PENSIONS—VOLUNTEERS AND MILITIA." The forms, regulations, instructions, decisions and opinions

1 U. S. Statutes at Large, vol. v, 7.

2 *Ibid*, vol. v, 32.

applicable to these titles, are of equal application to cases arising under the laws mentioned in this section. These laws, indeed, all relate to certain leading acts referred to in the General Observations at the close of Chapter III, Section I, and Chapter IV, Section I, and are governed by their provisions and the rules adopted for their execution.

CHAPTER VI.

INVALID PENSIONS.

SECTION I.

NAVAL—INCLUDING THE NAVY PROPER, MARINES, SEA-FENCIBLES, PRIVATEERS AND REVENUE CUTTERS, SINCE THE REVOLUTION.[1]

THE first act of Congress, under the constitution, granting naval pensions, was that of July, 1797, entitled "an act providing a naval armament."[2] This provides for manning and employing the frigates United States, Constitution and Constellation, and prescribes the number and rank of the officers, and the number of marines, seamen, midshipmen and ordinary seamen which shall be employed on the several classes of vessels in the navy. Section eleven of this act provides.

SEC. 11. *And be it further enacted*, That if any officer, non-commissioned officer, marine or seaman, belonging to the navy of the United States, shall be wounded or disabled, while in the line of his duty in public service, he shall be placed on the list of the invalids of the United States, at such rate of pay, and under such regulations as shall be directed by the President of the United States: *Provided always*, That the rate of compensation to be allowed for such wounds or disabilities, to a commissioned or warrant officer, shall never exceed, for the highest disability, half the monthly pay of such officer at the time of his being so disabled or wounded; and that the rate of compensation to non-commissioned officers, marines and seamen, shall never exceed five dollars per month: *And provided also*, That all inferior disabilities shall entitle the person so disabled to receive an allowance proportionate to the highest disability.

---

[1] For remarks relating to military and naval invalid pensions during the revolution, see Chap. II, Sec. II.

[2] U. S. Statutes at Large, vol. i, 523.

An act of July 11, 1798, for "establishing and organizing a marine corps,"[1] provides that in addition to the military establishment then existing there shall be raised a corps of marines, to serve on sea or shore, at the discretion of the President. After prescribing the organization, pay and subsistence of the corps, the act proceeds:

SEC. 4. *And be it further enacted*, That the officers, non-commissioned officers, privates and musicians, aforesaid, shall take the same oath, and shall be governed by the same rules and articles of war, as are prescribed for the military establishment of the United States, and by the rules for the regulation of the navy, heretofore, or which shall be established by law, according to the nature of the service in which they shall be employed, and shall be entitled to the same allowance, in case of wounds or disabilities, according to their repective ranks, as are granted by the act "to ascertain and fix the military establishment of the United States."[2]

"An act for the government of the navy of the United States," approved March 2, 1799,[3] prescribes rules for the government of officers and men in the naval service; makes regulations for the distribution of prize money; and provides for disabilities incurred in the service, as follows:

SEC. 8. *And be it further enacted*, That every officer, seaman or mariner disabled in the line of his duty, shall be entitled to receive, for his own life, and the life of his wife, if a married man at the time of receiving the wound, one half his monthly pay.[4]

This act was repealed by an act of April 23, 1800;[5]

---

1 U. S. Statutes at Large, vol. i, 594.

2 Act of May 30, 1796, (p. 15.)

3 U. S. Statutes at Large, vol. i, 709.

4 This is probably the only instance known to the laws of this country in which the right to receive a pension is continued to the beneficiary, personally, after death. The act is evidently based upon the hypothesis that husband and wife are *one*.

5 U. S. Statutes at Large, vol. ii, 45.

but not to the prejudice of any rights acquired under its provisions during the time it remained in force.

The act of April 23, 1800, just referred to, is entitled "an act for the better government of the navy of the United States." It establishes new rules for the regulation of the conduct of officers and men, while on duty; provides pensions for them in case of disability; prescribes the manner in which prizes shall be distributed; and appropriates the moneys accruing to the United States from the sale of prizes to the formation of a fund for the payment of naval pensions. This act, in all its provisions (except as to the management of navy pension fund), is still in force;[1] and the sections which follow will be found to possess interest and importance.

SEC. 5. *And be it further enacted*, That the proceeds of all ships and vessels, and the goods taken on board of them, which shall be adjudged good prize, shall, when of equal or superior force to the vessel or vessels making the capture, be the sole property of the captors; and when of inferior force, shall be divided equally between the United States and the officers and men making the capture.

SEC. 6. *And be it further enacted*, That the prize money, belonging to the officers and men, shall be distributed in the following manner:

1. To the commanding officers of fleets, squadrons or single ships, three twentieths, of which the commanding officers of the fleet and squadron shall have one twentieth, if the prize be taken by a ship or vessel acting under his command, and the commander of single ships, two twentieths; but where the prize is taken by a ship acting independently of such superior officer, the three twentieths shall belong to her commander.

---

1 Since this was written, this act has been repealed (see act of July 17, 1862, p. 91), but the repealing act, so far as relates to invalid pensions, makes provisions for disabilities accruing after March 1, 1861, only. The act of 1800 remains in force as to all claims previous to March 1, 1861.

2. To sea lieutenants, captains of marines, and sailing masters, two twentieths; but where there is a captain, without a lieutenant of marines, these officers shall be entitled to two twentieths and one third of a twentieth; which third, in such case, shall be deducted from the share of the officers mentioned in article No. 3 of this section.

3. To chaplains, lieutenants of marines, surgeons, pursers, boatswains, gunners, carpenters and master's mates, two twentieths.

4. To midshipmen, surgeon's mates, captain's clerks, schoolmasters, boatswain's mates, gunner's mates, carpenter's mates, ship's stewards, sailmakers, masters-at-arms, armorers, cockswains and coopers, three twentieths and a half.

5. To gunner's yeomen, boatswain's yeomen, quartermasters, quartergunners, sailmaker's mates, sergeants and corporals of marines, drummers, fifers and extra petty officers, two twentieths and a half.

6. To seamen, ordinary seamen, marines, and all other persons doing duty on board, seven twentieths.

7. Whenever one or more public ships or vessels are in sight at the time any one or more ships are taking a prize or prizes, they shall all share equally in the prize or prizes, according to the number of men and guns or board each ship in sight.

No commander of a fleet or squadron shall be entitled to receive any share of prizes taken by vessels not under his immediate command; nor of such prizes as may have been taken by ships or vessels intended to be placed under his command, before they have acted under his immediate orders; nor shall the commander of a fleet or squadron, leaving the station where he had the command, have any share in the prizes taken by ships left on such station, after he had gone out of the limits of his said command.

SEC. 7. *And be it further enacted,* That a bounty shall be paid by the United States, of twenty dollars, for each person on board any ship of an enemy at the commencement of an engagement, which shall be sunk or destroyed by any ship or vessel belonging to the United States of inferior force, the same to be divided among the officers and crew in the same manner as prize money.

SEC. 8. *And be it further enacted,* That every officer, seaman or marine, disabled in the line of his duty, shall be entitled to receive for life, or during his disability, a pension from the United States, according to the nature and degree of his disability, not exceeding one half of his monthly pay.[1]

SEC. 9. *And be it further enacted*, That all money accruing, or which has already accrued, to the United States from the sale of prizes, shall be and remain forever a fund for the payment of pension and half-pay, should the same be hereafter granted, to the officers and seamen who may be entitled to receive the same; and if the said fund shall be insufficient for the purpose, the public faith is hereby pledged to make up the deficiency; but if it should be more than sufficient, the surplus shall be applied to the making of further provision for the comfort of the disabled officers, seamen and marines, and for such as, though not disabled, may merit by their bravery, or long and faithful services, the gratitude of their country.

SEC. 10. *And be it further enacted*, That the said fund shall be under the management and direction of the Secretary of the Navy, the Secretary of the Treasury, and the Secretary of War, for the time being,[2] who are hereby authorized to receive any sums to which the United States may be entitled from the sale of prizes, and employ and invest the same, and the interest arising therefrom, in any manner which a majority of them may deem most advantageous. And it shall be the duty of the said commissioners to lay be-

1 The seventh section of an act of April 16, 1816, entitled "an act in addition to an act, entitled 'an act in relation the navy pension fund,'" provides that where, in the opinion of the commissioners of the navy fund, the half-pay allowed by law to an officer, seaman or marine is insufficient for his support, on account of the nature and extent of the disability incurred, they may increase it to an amount not exceeding the monthly pay of the disabled person while in the service.

2 By act of March 26, 1804 (U. S. Statutes at Large, vol. ii, 293), the commissioners of the navy pension fund were authorized and directed to make such regulations as to them might appear expedient, for the admission of persons on the roll of navy pensioners, and for the payment of pensions.

The powers given to the commissioners by the act of March 26, 1804, to make such regulations as might to them appear expedient for the admission of persons on the roll of navy pensioners, authorized the commissioners to fix the period at which the pension should commence, and also the principles by which the amount should be graduated. *Opinion of Attorney-General Taney, December* 21, 1832. (See note following.)

fore Congress, annually, in the first week of their session, a minute statement of their proceedings relative to the management of said fund.[1]

"An act concerning letters of marque, prizes and prize goods," approved June 26, 1812,[2] authorizes the President to grant letters of marque and reprisal, to private armed ships; and provides:

SEC. 17. *And be it further enacted*, That two per centum on the net amount (after deducting all charges and expenditures) of the prize money arising from captured vessels and cargoes, and on the net amount of the salvage of vessels and cargoes, recaptured by the private armed vessels of the United States, shall be secured and paid over to the collector or other chief officer of the customs at the port or place in the United States, at which such captured or recaptured vessels may arrive; or to the consul or other public agent of the United States residing at the port or place, not within the United States, at which such captured or recaptured vessels may arrive. And the moneys arising therefrom, shall be held and hereby is pledged by the government of the United States as a fund for the support of the widows and orphans of such persons as may be slain; and for the support and maintenance of such persons as may be wounded and disabled on board of the private armed vessels of the United States, in any engagement with the enemy, to be assigned and distributed in such manner as shall hereafter by law be pro vided.

---

1 This section was repealed by an act of July 10, 1832, and the entire management of the fund was left to the Secretary of the Navy (U. S. Statutes at Large, vol. iv, 572). It was held by Attorney-General Toucey September 27, 1848), that it rests in the sound discretion of the Secretary of the Navy to decide, according to the regulations in force, when the pension of an applicant shall commence. But (Attorney-General Toucey, February 16, 1849), it does not authorize him to make a statute of limitations. These opinions were concurred in by Attorney-General Johnson, *July* 14, 1849.

Invalids disabled prior to the passage of the act of April 23, 1800, which established the navy pension fund, are not entitled to its benefits. *Attorney-General Grundy, September*, 3, 1838. (See preceding note.)

2 U. S. Statutes at Large, vol. ii, 759.

The per centum coming into the hands of collectors and consuls under the preceding act, was by act of February 13, 1813, "regulating pensions to persons on board private armed ships,"[1] ordered to be paid into the treasury of the United States; and it is also provided by said act as follows:

SEC. 2. *And be it further enacted*, That the Secretary of the Navy be authorized and required to place on the pension list, under the like regulations and restrictions as are used in relation to the navy of the United States, any officer, seaman or marine, who, on board of any private armed ship or vessel bearing a commission of letter of marque, shall have been wounded or otherwise disabled in any engagement with the enemy;[2] allowing to the captain a sum not exceeding twenty dollars per month; to lieutenants and sailing-master a sum not exceeding twelve dollars each per month; to marine officer, boatswain, gunner, carpenter, master's-mate and prize-masters, a sum not exceeding ten dollars each per month; to all other officers a sum not exceeding eight dollars each per month, for the highest rate of disability, and so in proportion; and to a seaman, or acting as a marine, the sum of six dollars per month for the highest rate of disability, and so in proportion; which several pensions shall be paid, by direction of the Secretary of the Navy, out of the fund above provided, and from no other.

Section three requires commanders of vessels bearing letters of marque to keep in their journals lists of the names and rank of persons disabled, describing the nature and extent of the wounds or disabilities.

1 U. S. Stat., vol. ii, 799. The privateer pension fund is exhausted. An act was passed May 21, 1854, appropriating sufficient money from the treasury to pay the arrears of privateer invalid pensions to June 30, 1854.

2 This act grants pensions to those persons only who were wounded in an engagement with the enemy: an amendatory act of August 2, 1813 (U. S. Stats. at Large, vol. iii, 86) authorizes the Secretary of the Navy to "place on the pension list, under the restrictions and regulations of the said act, any officer, seaman or marine, belonging to any private armed ship or vessel of the United States, bearing a commission of letter of marque, who shall have been wounded or otherwise disabled *in the line of their* (*sic*) *duty* as officers, seamen or marines, of such private armed vessel."

Section four requires collectors to transmit, quarterly, to the Secretary of the Navy, transcripts of the entries thus made in the journals reported to him.

By an act of July 26, 1813, entitled "an act to authorize the raising of a corps of sea-fencibles,"[1] the President was authorized to enlist for one year as many companies of sea-fencibles as he might deem necessary, not exceeding ten. These were to be employed on land and water in defense of the ports and harbors of the United States. Invalid pensions were provided in cases of disability, as follows:

SEC. 4. *And be it further enacted*, That the officers, warrant officers, boatswains, and men, raised pursuant to this act, shall be entitled to the like compensation in case of disability incurred by wounds or otherwise in the service of the United States, as officers, warrant officers, and seamen, in the present naval establishment, and shall be subject to the rules and articles which have been or may hereafter be established by law, for the government of the army of the United States.

SEC. 5. *And be it further enacted*, That this act shall be and continue in force during the present war between the United States of America, and their territories, and the united kingdom of Great Britain and Ireland, and the dependencies thereof.

This act was repealed by act of February 27, 1815;[2] but rights acquired under its provisions remain unaffected.

"An act granting pensions to the officers and seamen serving on board the revenue cutters in certain cases," approved April 18, 1814,[3] provides:

Be it enacted by the Senate and House of Representatives of the United States of America in Congress assembled, That the officers and seamen of the revenue cutters of the United States, who have been or

---

[1] U. S. Statutes at Large, vol. iii, 47.

[2] *Ibid*, vol. iii, 219.

[3] *Ibid*, vol. iii, 127.

may be wounded or disabled in the discharge of their duty while co-operating with the navy by order of the President of the United States, shall be entitled to be placed on the navy pension list, at the same rate of pension, and under the same regulations and restrictions as are now provided by law for the officers and seamen of the navy.

The second section of "an act to provide for the payment of navy pensions," approved August 16, 1841,[1] makes the following provision:

SEC. 2. *And be it further enacted*, That no officer, seaman or marine, entitled to a pension from the navy pension fund, who receives pay from the public treasury, shall receive more from the said fund than is sufficient to make the whole amount received from both the above-named sources, equal to the pay fixed by law for the grade to which the officer, seaman or marine may belong as an officer in the services in which he may be engaged, during the year, so that no officer shall receive pay at the same time both as a pensioner and an officer in service.[2]

---

1 U. S. Statutes at Large, vol. v, 440.

2 This section seems confined to persons in the naval service, and does not apply to a person drawing a salary as minister to a foreign government. *Attorney-General Legare, May* 26, 1842. A lieutenant otherwise entitled to a pension, is not entitled to receive it while on duty, and in receipt of his pay as an officer of the navy. Nor can he receive it when not on duty, while in receipt of the pay allowed to his grade. *Attorney-General Clifford, June* 2, 1847. In a subsequent opinion, given on the same day, the Attorney-General modified the preceding opinion in so far as to hold that officers "waiting orders," or "on leave," or "on furlough," can receive only so much on account of their pension as, added to the reduced pay when so "on leave," etc., will amount to their pay when "on duty." This act was modified, by an act of April 30, 1844 (U. S. Stats. at Large, vol. v, 656), which provides that "no person in the army, navy or marine corps, shall be allowed to draw both a pension as an invalid and the pay of his rank or station in the service, unless the alleged disability for which the pension was granted be such as to have occasioned his employment in a lower grade, or in some civil branch of the service." Under this provision it was held that an officer disabled and mustered out of service, and afterwards appointed battalion paymaster, was entitled to both pension and pay—the latter appointment being in a civil branch of the service. *Attorney-General Toucey, November* 1, 1848. Naval pensioners can receive pay and pension too, pro-

A rule for ascertaining and determining the rate of pensions to naval invalids was established by the second section of "an act making an appropriation to supply a deficiency in the navy pension fund," approved August 23, 1842,[1] which enacts :

SEC. 2. *And be it further enacted*, That . . . . . And all pensions to officers and seamen in the naval service shall be regulated according to the pay of the navy as it existed on the first day of January, one thousand eight hundred and thirty-five.[2]

"An act renewing certain naval pensions, and extending the benefits of existing laws, respecting naval pensions, to engineers, firemen, and coal-heavers in the navy, and to their widows," approved August 11, 1848,[3] provides:

SEC. 2. *And be it further enacted*, That engineers, firemen and coal-heavers in the navy shall be entitled to pensions in the same manner as officers, seamen and marines; and the widows of engineers, coal-heavers and firemen in the same manner as the widows of officers, seamen and marines: *Provided*, That the pension of a chief engineer shall be the same as that of a lieutenant in the navy;[4] and a pension of a widow of a chief engineer the same as that of the widow of a lieutenant of the navy: the pension of a first assistant engineer the same as that of a lieutenant of marines; and the pension of the widow of a first assistant engineer the same as that of the widow of a lieutenant of marines;[4] the pension of a second or third assistant engineer the same as that of a forward officer; and the pension of the widow of a second or third assistant engineer the same as that of the widow of a forward officer; the pension of a fireman or coal-heaver the same as that of a seaman; the pension of the widow of a fireman or coal-

vided both do not exceed their lowest duty pay. *Secretary of Interior, April* 30, 1859.

1 U. S. Statutes at Large, vol. v, 521.

2 Monthly pay prior to January 1, 1835, governs navy pension cases, and not the present increased rates of annual pay. *Commissioner Waldo, October* 8, 1853.

3 U. S. Statutes at Large, vol. ix, 282.

4 This was held to mean a *first* lieutenant of marines. *Attorney-General Toucey, Sept.* 26, 1849.

heaver the same as that of the widow of a seaman: *And provided, further,* That an engineer, fireman or coal-heaver shall not be entitled to any pension by reason of a disability incurred prior to the thirty-first of August, eighteen hundred and forty-two, nor shall the widow of an engineer, fireman or coal-heaver be entitled to any pension by reason of the death of her husband, if his death was prior to said date.

SEC. 3. *And be it further enacted,* That the amount of pension in every case arising under this law is not to exceed the half-pay of the deceased officer, seaman or marine as it existed in January, eighteen hundred and thirty-five, or such rate of pension as is allowed by this act

By a joint resolution of August 10, 1848,[1] Congress placed such of the officers and men of the marine corps as served with the army in Mexico, upon the same footing, in respect to bounty land and invalid pensions, as officers and men, according to grade, in the army. That portion of the resolution which relates to this subject is as follows:

Resolved by the Senate and House of Representatives of the United States of America in Congress assembled, That the officers, non-commissioned officers, privates and musicians of the marine corps, who have served with the army in the war with Mexico,[2] and also the artificers and laborers of the ordnance corps serving in said war, be placed, in all respects as to bounty land and other remuneration,[3] in addition to ordinary pay, on a footing with the officers, non-commissioned officers, privates and musicians of the army: *Provided,*

[1] U. S. Statutes at Large, vol. ix, 340.

[2] The entire portion of the marine corps, whether they served on shipboard or land, on the Mexican coast or in the interior, in the Mexican war, are to be considered, within the true meaning of the resolution of the 10th of August, 1848, as having "served with the army in Mexico," and are entitled to the bounty land and other remuneration which that resolution provides. *Attorney-General Johnson, September* 17, 1849.

[3] The phrase "other remuneration," employed in said resolution, must be understood to refer to pensions. *Attorney-General Toucey, November* 21, 1848.

That this remuneration shall be in lieu of prize money and all other extra allowances. . . .

WAR OF 1861.

The second proclamation of the President, calling forth troops to engage in suppressing the rebellion in a portion of the Southern States, is dated May 3, 1861; and directs, among other things, for the enlistment, for not less than one nor more than three years, of eighteen thousand seamen, in addition to the force then constituting the naval establishment of the United States. This proclamation will be found in full on page 57.

An act of July 14, 1862, grants pensions to invalids, who become so by service in the war for the Union, as follows:

AN ACT *to Grant Pensions.*

Be it enacted by the Senate and House of Representatives of the United States of America in Congress assembled, That if any officer, non-commissioned officer, musician or private of the army, including regulars, volunteers and militia, or any officer, warrant or petty officer, musician, seaman, ordinary seaman, flotillaman, marine, clerk, landsman, pilot or other person in the navy or marine corps, has been, since the fourth day of March, eighteen hundred and sixty-one, or shall hereafter be disabled by reason of any wound received or disease contracted while in the service of the United States and in the line of duty, he shall, upon making due proof of the fact according to such forms and regulations as are or may be provided by or in pursuance of law, be placed upon the list of invalid pensioners of the United States, and be entitled to receive, for the highest rate of disability, such pension as is hereinafter provided in such cases, and for an inferior disability an amount proportionate to the highest disability, to commence as hereinafter provided, and continue during the existence of such disability. The pension for a total disability for officers, non-commissioned officers, musicians and privates employed in the military service of the United States, whether regulars, volunteers or militia, and in the marine corps, shall be as follows, viz: Lieutenant-colonel and all officers of a higher rank, thirty dollars per month; major, twenty-five dollars per month; captain, twenty dollars per month; first lieutenant, seventeen dollars per month; second lieutenant, fifteen dollars per month; and non-commissioned officers, musicians and privates, eight dollars per month. The pension for total disability for officers, warrant or petty officers, and others employed in the naval service of the United States, shall be as follows, viz: Captain, commander, surgeon, paymaster and chief engineer, respectively, ranking with commander by law, lieutenant commanding and master commanding, thirty dollars per month; lieutenant, surgeon, paymaster and chief engineer, respectively, ranking with lieutenant by law, and passed assistant surgeon, twenty-five dollars per month; professor of mathematics, master, assistant surgeon, assistant paymaster and chaplain, twenty dollars per month; first assistant engineers and pilots, fifteen dollars per month; passed midshipman, midshipman, captains' and paymasters' clerk, second and third assistant engineer, masters' mate and all warrant officers, ten dollars per month; all petty officers and all other persons before named employed in the naval service, eight dollars per month; and all commissioned officers, of either service, shall receive such and only such pension as is herein provided for the rank in which they hold commissions.

Section six prescribes fees of attorneys for obtaining pensions, pay, etc.

Section seven fixes penalty for making overcharges of fees.

SEC. 10. *And be it further enacted*, That the pilots, engineers, sailors and crews upon the gunboats and war vessels of the United States, who have not been regularly mustered into the service of the United States, shall be entitled to the same bounty allowed to persons of corresponding rank in the naval service, provided they continue in service to the close of the present war; and all persons serving as aforesaid, who have been or may be wounded or incapacitated for service, shall be entitled to receive for such disability the pension allowed by the provisions of this act, to those of like rank, and each and every such person shall receive pay according to corresponding rank in the naval service: *Provided*, That no person receiving pension or bounty under the provisions of this act shall receive either pension or bounty for any other service in the present war.

The entire act may be found on page 28.

A joint resolution of July 16, 1862, extends the benefits of the act of July 14, 1862, to the masters serving on the United States gunboats, as follows:

JOINT RESOLUTION *to Grant Pensions to Masters and other Officers upon the Gunboats in the Service of the United States.*

Resolved by the Senate and House of Representatives of the United States of America in Congress assembled, That the masters serving on board of gunboats employed in the service of the United States, shall be entitled to all the benefits, including bounty and pension, provided for in an act entitled "an act to grant pensions," passed during the present session of Congress, and the widows, mothers and heirs of such officers shall be entitled to all the benefits of said act.

"An act for the better government of the navy of the United States," approved July 17, 1862, contains, among other provisions, the following:

SEC. 2. *And be it further enacted,* That the proceeds of all ships and vessels, and the goods taken on board of them, which shall be adjudged good prize, shall, when of equal or superior force to the vessel or vessels making the capture, be the sole property of the captors; and when of inferior force, shall be divided equally between the United States and the officers and men making the capture.

SEC. 3. *And be it further enacted,* That the prize money belonging to the officers and men shall be distributed in the following manner:

First. To the commanding officer of a fleet or squadron, one twentieth part of all prize money awarded to a vessel or vessels under his immediate command.

Second. To the commander of a single ship, one tenth part of all prize money awarded to the ship under his command, if such ship, at the time of making the capture, was under the immediate command of the commanding officer of a fleet or squadron, and three twentieths if his ship was acting independently of such superior officer.

Third. The share of the commanding officer of the fleet or squadron, if any, and the share of the commander of the ship, being deducted, the residue shall be distributed and apportioned among all others doing duty on board, and borne upon the books, according to their respective rates of pay in the service.

Fourth. When one or more vessels in the navy shall be within signal distance of another making a prize, all shall share in the prize, and money awarded shall be apportioned among the officers and men of the several vessels, according to the rates of pay of all on board who are borne upon the books, after deducting one twentieth to the flag-officer, if there be any such entitled to share.

Fifth. No commander of a fleet or squadron shall be entitled to receive any share of prizes taken by vessels not under his immediate command; nor of such prizes as may have been taken by ships or vessels intended to be placed under his command, before they have acted under his immediate orders; nor shall a commander of a fleet or squadron, leaving the station where he had the command, have any share in the prizes taken by ships left on such station after he has gone out of the limits of his said command, nor after he has transferred his command to a successor.

Sixth. No officer or other person who shall have been temporarily absent on duty from the vessel, on the books of which he continued to be borne while so absent, shall be deprived, in consequence of such absence, of any prize money to which he would otherwise be entitled.

SEC. 6. *And be it further enacted,* That any armed vessel in the service of the United States which shall make a capture, or assist in a capture, under circumstances which would entitle a vessel of the navy to prize money, shall be entitled to an award of prize money in the same manner as if such vessel belonged to the navy; and such prize money shall be distributed and apportioned in the same manner and under the same rules and regulations as provided for persons in the naval service, and paid under the direction of the Secretary of the Navy.

SEC. 11. *And be it further enacted,* That all money accruing or which has already accrued to the United States from sale of prizes, shall be and remain forever a fund for the payment of pensions to the officers, seamen and marines who may be entitled to receive the same; and if the said fund shall be insufficient for the purpose, the public faith is hereby pledged to make up the deficiency; but if it should be more than sufficient, the surplus shall be applied to the making of further provision for the comfort of the disabled officers, seamen and marines.

SEC. 13. *And be it further enacted,* That every officer, seaman or marine, disabled in the line of his duty, shall be entitled to receive for life, or during his disability, a pension from the United States, according to the nature and degree of his disability, not exceeding, in any case, his monthly pay.

SEC. 20. *And be it further enacted,* That all provisions of previous laws, which are inconsistent with those of this act, shall be and are hereby repealed.

GENERAL OBSERVATIONS.

The act to which reference must be had in general, in making applications for pensions for invalids of the navy proper, is that of April 23, 1800. To this act, also, the act of April 18, 1814, granting invalid pensions to officers and seamen on board revenue cutters co-operating with the navy; the act of February 13, 1813, granting like pensions to privateers, and the act of July 26, 1813, granting like pensions to sea-fencibles, relate. The rate of pensions to invalids under these several acts, is regulated according to the pay of the navy as it existed January 1, 1835.

Pensions are granted to invalid engineers, firemen and coal-heavers of the navy who have become disabled since August 31, 1842. The rate of pensions is fixed by the granting act, August 11, 1848.

Invalid pensions to the marine corps are governed by the laws relating to army invalid pensions.

Seamen enlisted under the President's proclamation of May 3, 1861, and others in the naval service, in the war of 1861, are entitled to the benefits of the acts of July 14, 1862, and July 17, 1862, in case of disability incurred in the service. (The acts, proclamations and orders of the President respecting the army and navy, and calling out militia and volunteers, were legalized by act of August 6, 1861. (U. S. Statutes at Large, vol. xii, 326).

SECTION II.

REGULATIONS AND FORMS FOR OBTAINING NAVAL INVALID PENSIONS.

(1)

Form of Application for Navy Invalid Pension.

To the Commissioner of Pensions:

The memorial of the undersigned ——, who was a —— in the United States naval service, respectfully showeth:—

That your memorialist was born at ——, in the State of ——; is —— years of age, —— feet —— inches high; —— complexion, —— eyes, —— hair.

That he entered the United States naval service at ——, in the State of ——, on the —— day of ——, A.D. 18—, and while attached to [*Here give the name and class of vessel*] and holding the rank of —— [*if not an officer, say, after name of vessel,* as a seaman (*or* ordinary seaman, *or* boy, *or otherwise, as the case may be*), he was disabled [*Here state when, where and how the disability was incurred, with a minute description of the injury or sickness, and how the applicant is affected by it*].

That the same was incurred by him in the performance of his duty; and having thereby been disqualified for the naval service, and disabled from obtaining his subsistence by manual labor, he refers to the certificate of Surgeon ——, herewith presented [*If no certificate was obtained, state the fact; if obtained and lost or destroyed, state particulars of loss or destruction*], and claims the benefit of the laws granting navy pensions ——, and that his pension may be made payable at the navy pension agency in ——.

(*Claimant's Signature.*)

Sworn and subscribed to, before ——, this —— day of ——, A.D., 18—. And I certify that I am acquainted with the said ——, and believe him to be the identical person who served as aforesaid, and that I am not interested in his claim for a pension. (*Signature of Officer.*)

This declaration must be made before a Court of Record or before a Judge or Clerk of such Court. Should it be made before a Court, the certificate to the affidavit just given will be omitted, and a certificate of the Clerk according to the form No. 5, following the next form of declaration should be substituted.

(2)

Affidavit of Witnesses.

STATE OF —— }
County of —— } *ss.*

On this —— day of ——, A.D., 18—, before me, the subscriber, a —— in and for said county, duly authorized to administer oaths, personally came ——, aged —— years, and ——, aged —— years, whom I know to be residents of the county and State aforesaid, and persons whom I certify to be respectable and entitled to credit, and who, being duly sworn, say that they were present and saw —— execute the foregoing affidavit by signing the foregoing declaration, and making oath thereto in due form of law, and they further swear that they are acquainted with the said ——, now present, and have every reason to believe from the appearance of the applicant, that he is the identical person he represents himself to be; and further, that they, deponents, do reside in the county aforesaid, and have no interest in the claim of said ——.

(*Signature of Witnesses.*)

Witness:——

Sworn to and subscribed before me, this —— day of ——, A. D. 18—; and I certify that I am acquainted with the said —— and ——, and know them to be credible and disinterested witnesses; and I further certify that I am not interested as agent or otherwise in the prosecution of the foregoing claim.

(*Signatnre of Officer.*)

For FORMS and REGULATIONS relating to POWERS OF ATTORNEY in pension cases, see Chapter XVI.

(3)

Clerk's Certificate

STATE OF —— }
County of —— } *ss.*

I, ——, clerk of the —— court in and for the county and State above named, do hereby certify that ——, Esq., before whom the foregoing affidavits were made, and who has thereunto signed his name, was at the time of so doing a —— in and for the county and State above named, duly commissioned and sworn, that all his official acts as such are entitled to full faith and credit, and that his signature thereto is genuine.

In testimony whereof, I have hereunto signed my name and affixed my official seal this —— day of ——, 18—.

[L. S.] (*Clerk's Signature.*)

(4)

Another Form of Declaration for Naval Invalid Pension.

STATE OF —— } ss.
County of —— }

On this —— day of ——, 18—, before the —— court [*or* before me —— judge *or* clerk of the —— court], a court of record within and for said county, personally appeared ——, a resident of ——, in the county of ——, and State of ——, aged —— years, who being first sworn, according to law, declares that he is the identical —— who was a —— in the naval service of the United States; that he enlisted at ——, in the State of ——, on the —— day of —— A.D., 18—. [*Describe the service in which the claimant was engaged; if on board ship, give the name and class of the vessel, the rank and capacity in which he served, the name of the commanding officer, the engagement or other line of duty or occupation in which the disability was incurred; a full description of the time, place and manner of, in which the wound was received or disease was contracted; and its location, nature and physical effect*].

He further says that he was honorably discharged, as will appear by his certificate of discharge herewith presented [*if no discharge was received, state that fact; if lost or destroyed, detail the circumstances*], on account of said disability, upon the surgeon's certificate for a pension [*if the discharge was upon a certificate of ordinary disability, and the disability continued or increased, these facts should be stated*], and recommending a discharge, as may be found reported by the commanding officer approving the same, on file in the Navy Department at Washington; for the existing degree and continuance of which disability he requests a medical survey may be ordered.

He makes this declaration for the purpose of being placed on the naval invalid pension roll of the United States, and obtaining the pension to which he may be entitled under the act of [*date and title of act*], granting pensions to persons disabled in the naval service of the United States.

(*Claimant's Signature.*)

I certify that the foregoing declaration was sworn to and subscribed before me, this —— day of —— A. D., 18— ; and I further certify that I am acquainted with the said ——, and know [*or* believe] him to be the identical person who served as stated in the foregoing declaration, and that I have no interest in his claim for a pension.

[L. S.] Witness my signature, and the seal of the —— court of —— county, ——. (*Clerk of said Court*).

Should the declaration be made before a Judge, the Clerk's certificate of his official character (under seal) must be attached.

Should the declaration be made before a Court of Record, the Clerk's certificate may be as follows:

(5)

Clerk's Certificate.

STATE OF —— } ss.
County of —— }

I, ——, clerk of the —— court within and for said county, hereby certify that the foregoing declaration was made under oath, and subscribed by ——, before said court, on the —— day of —— A. D. 18—.

[L. S.] In testimony whereof, I hereto set my hand, and affix the seal of our said court, this —— day of —— A. D. 18—.

(*Clerk's Signature.*)

Here must follow the affidavit of two witnesses, according to the form No. 2, given at the close of the first form of declaration for obtaining a naval invalid pension, p. 95. Should the affidavit of the witnesses be made before a Justice of the Peace, the Clerk's certificate to the official character of such justice (under seal of the Court), must also be appended.

For REGULATIONS and FORMS relating to POWERS OF ATTORNEY in pension cases, see Chapter XVI.

(6)

Surgeon's Certificate of Disability.

It is hereby certified that ——, a —— in the United States ship of war ——, commanded by ——, is rendered incapable of performing the duty of a —— by reason of wounds [*or other injuries, or sickness,*] received [*or contracted*] while he was actually in the service aforesaid, and in the line of his duty, viz:

By satisfactory evidence, and accurate examination, it appears that on the —— day of ——, in the year ——, being engaged [*Here state, particularly, the duty in which the applicant was engaged; the harbor, navy-yard, river, bay or ocean, where the ship was, and the time when the injury was received; and give a particular description of the wound, injury or disease, and specify in what manner it has affected the applicant so as to produce disability in the degree stated*], and he is thereby not only incapacitated for duty aforesaid, but in the opinion of the undersigned is totally [*or* three fourths, *or* one half, *or* one third, *or* one fourth, *as the degree of disability may be*] disabled from obtaining his subsistence by manual labor.

(*Date.*) *Surgeon.*
Assistant Surgeon.

(7)

Certificate of Commanding Officer in an Invalid case.

UNITED STATES SHIP ——— —— (*Date.*)

I certify that ——, who was a —— on board of this ship, while under my command, and while engaged in his duty as a ——, was, in consequence of the following circumstances, so injured as to be prevented from any further performance of his duty as a ——, and, I therefore deemed it proper that he should be discharged from the naval service of the United States. He was accordingly discharged on the —— day of ——, 18—.

While he was [*Here state, particularly, all the facts as to the origin of the applicant's disability; the duty in which he was engaged; the particular circumstances which led to the injury, the harbor, navy-yard, river, bay or ocean, where the ship was, and the time when the injury was received.*]

Commander,
U. S. Ship ——.

(8)

Certificate of Ordinary Disability.

I hereby certify that ——, a —— in the United States navy, —— attached to [*if at a navy-yard, ship or hospital, insert name and place*], and holding the rank above-mentioned, as set forth in the record of his case, of which the following is a copy: [*Here insert record made by senior medical officer*], and, therefore, in the opinion of the undersigned, the interests of the service require that he should be discharged. *Surgeon.*

The above-named —— was born at —— in the State of ——, is —— years of age; ——feet and —— inches high; —— complexion; —— eyes; —— hair. He entered the United States naval service at ——, on the —— day of ——, 18—; and —— discharged [*Here insert whether final, or to hospital or ship, for passage home, in which cases the discharges must be furnished by the fourth auditor.*]

—— ———, *Paymaster* [formerly *Purser.*]

Approved: —— ———, *Commanding U. S. Ship* ——.

Discharged from the United States naval service, on the —— day of—— 18—. *Fourth Auditor.*

(9)

Certificate for Pension.

I hereby certify that ——, a —— in the United States navy, —— while attached to [*if at a navy-yard, ship or hospital, mention name and place*], and holding the rank above-mentioned, was disabled by [wound received, *or* casualty occurring, *or* disease contracted], in the United States naval service, and in the line of his duty, as set forth in the record of his case, of which the following is a copy, to-wit: [*copy of record made by senior medical officer*]. He is thereby not only incapacitated for duty, as aforesaid, but, in the opinion of the undersigned, is totally [*or* three fourths, *or* one half, *or other degree of disability, as the case may be*], disabled from obtaining a subsistence by manual labor. *Surgeon.*

The above-named —— was born at ——, in the State of ——, is —— years of age; —— feet, —— inches high; —— complexion; —— eyes; —— hair. He entered the United States naval service at ——, on the —— day of —— A.D. 18—; and —— discharged [*insert whether to hospital, to ship, for passage home, or finally; if for passage home or hospital, the date of final discharge must be furnished by the fourth auditor.*]

—— ——, *Paymaster* [formerly *Purser.*]

Approved: —— ——, *Commanding U. S. Ship* [*or* Navy Yard, etc.]

Finally discharged from the United States naval service, on the —— day of ——, 18—. *Fourth Auditor.*

PRIVATEER PENSIONS.

PENSION OFFICE, June 3, 1854.

Congress having, by the act approved May 31, 1854, made an appropriation for paying the pensions of invalids (who were wounded on board of private armed vessels during the last war with Great Britain), to the thirtieth of the present month, inclusive, parties interested are hereby notified that the following evidence of their being entitled to the benefits of the law will be required, viz:

1. Sworn declaration or memorial, setting forth the vessel to which the pensioner belonged, his rank or station, when and in what manner disabled, monthly rate of pension, and date to which last paid.

2. Evidence of identity, either by affidavit of two credible witnesses, or the certificate of a Justice of the Peace.

The above evidence to be authenticated by the certificate, under seal, of the proper officer, showing the official character of the Justice of the Peace; and to be forwarded, together with the original pension certificate, to this office.

L. P. WALDO, *Commissioner of Pensions.*

(10.)

Declaration for obtaining a Privateer Invalid Pension.

STATE OF —— } ss.
County of —— }

On this —— day of ——, A.D. 18—, personally appeared before the —— court [*or* before me, ——, judge *or* clerk, of the —— court], a court of record within and for said county, ——, a resident of —— in the State of ——, aged —— years, who being first sworn according to law, declares, that he is the identical —— who was a —— on board a private armed vessel of the United States, in the war between the United States and ——; that he enlisted [*or* volunteered] on the —— day of ——, in the year ——, at —— in the State of ——, to serve on board the [*State name and class of private armed vessel, on board which applicant served; the rank or capacity in which he served; the officer in command; the engagement or other occupation in the line of duty in which injury received or disease contracted; the time when and manner how, received or contracted, and nature, continuance and location of the wound or disease; with proper reference to the transcript from the journal of the commanding officer, communicated to the Secretary of the Navy, under the* 3*d and* 4*th sections of the act of February* 13, 1813.]

He makes this declaration for the purpose of being placed on the invalid privateer pension roll of the United States, and of obtaining the pension to which he may be entitled under the act of [*date and title of act*].

(*Claimant's Signature.*)

I certify that the foregoing declaration was sworn to before me, this —— day of ——, A.D. 18—; and that I am acquainted with the said ——, and know [*or* believe] him to be the identical person who served as stated in the foregoing declaration, and that I am not interested in the above claim.

Witness my hand and the seal of the —— court of —— county, [L. S.] ——.

(*Clerk of said Court.*)

[Should the declaration be made before a Court, the certificate of the Clerk should be similar to the one No. 5, page 97. Should it be made before a Judge, his official character must be certified by the Clerk, under seal.]

Here should follow the affidavit of two witnesses, according to the form No. 2, page 95; and if this affidavit should be made before a Justice of the Peace, the certificate of the Clerk, under the seal of the proper Court, should be appended. (See form No. 3, page 95.)

ACT OF JULY 14, 1862.

The regulations established by Commissioner Barrett, for obtaining pensions under this act, will be found in full in Chapter III, Section I, page 39.

The following forms have been provided by the Commissioner, to be used in naval invalid cases:

"A."

Form of Declaration for a Navy Invalid Pension.

STATE OF ——, } ss.
County of —— }

On this —— day of ——, A.D. one thousand eight hundred and ——, personally appeared before —— [*Here state the official character of the person administering the oath*] within and for the county and State aforesaid ——, aged —— years, a resident of ——, in the State of ——, who, being duly sworn according to law, declares that he is the identical —— who enlisted in the naval service of the United States at ——, on the —— day of ——, in the year ——, as a ——, and was honorably discharged on the —— day of ——, in the year ——, at ——; that his personal description is as follows: [*Here state height, complexion, color of hair, occupation, etc.*]; that while in the service aforesaid, and in the line of his duty, he received the following wound (*or other disability, as the case may be*): [*Here give a particular and minute account of the wound or other injury, and state how, when, and where it occurred, where the applicant has resided since leaving the service, and what has been his occupation.*] He makes this application in order to secure the benefits of the act granting pensions, approved July 14, 1862.

(*Signature of Claimant.*)

Also personally appeared —— and ——, residents of (*county, city or town*), persons whom I certify to be respectable and entitled to credit, and who, being by me duly sworn, say that they were present and saw —— sign his name (*or make his mark*) to the foregoing declaration; and they further swear that they have every reason to believe, from the appearance of the applicant and their acquaintance with him, that he is the identical person he represents himself to be; and they further state that they have no interest in the prosecution of this claim.

(*Signatures of Witnesses.*)

Sworn to and subscribed before me, this —— day of ——, A. D., 18—; and I hereby certify that I have no interest, direct or indirect, in the prosecution of this claim.

(*Signature of Judge or other Officer.*)

Applicant's post-office address:

This declaration must be made before a Court of Record, or a Judge or Clerk of such Court. In any case, the Clerk's certificate and seal must be attached.

Affidavits in support of a declaration may be made before a Justice of the Peace, or other officer authorized to administer oaths.

In preparing a declaration under the act of July 14, 1862, it may be well to refer to the forms given in the former part of this section, as the regulations under other laws are, in substance, the same as under this, and useful suggestions may be derived from such reference.

For Regulations and Forms relating to Powers of Attorney, see Chapter XVI.

"F."

Form of Surgeon's Affidavit.

If the claimant for a pension has not been examined, and the degree of his disability certified, before his discharge, by a navy surgeon, and if the certificate of a navy surgeon or a board of survey is not obtainable, on satisfactory explanation of this fact, he may produce the affidavit of two surgeons reputable in their profession, and certified as such by the magistrate before whom their statement is sworn to, in accordance with the following form:

—— (*Date.*)

It is hereby certified that ——, who was a —— in the naval service of the United States [*Here state the vessel or station on which applicant was en-*

gaged, and his particular service], is suffering from[1] ——, and he is thereby not only incapacitated for naval duty, but, in the opinion of the undersigned, is[2] —— disabled from obtaining his subsistence from manual labor. And we further certify that, upon satisfactory evidence and after accurate examination, we believe the said disability was incurred in the naval service of the United States and in the line of duty.

Surgeon.
Surgeon.

Sworn to and subscribed before me, this —— day of ——, A.D. 18—; and I hereby certify that the said —— and ——, are known to me as surgeons in actual practice, reputable in their profession, and that I have no interest, direct or indirect, in the prosecution of this claim.

(*Magistrate's Signature.*)

---

1 Here give a particular description of the wound, injury or disease, and specify in what manner it has affected the applicant so as to produce disability in the degree stated.

2 This blank is to be filled up with the proportional "degree" of disability; for example: "three fourths," "one half," "one third," etc., or 'totally," as the case may be.

CHAPTER VII.

GRATUITOUS PENSIONS.

SECTION I.

WAR OF THE REVOLUTION—MILITARY AND NAVAL.

As AN inducement to the commissioned officers of the revolutionary army to remain in the service until the close of the war, a resolution was passed by the Continental Congress, on the 15th day of May, 1778, promising:

Resolved, unanimously, That all military officers commissioned by Congress, who now are or hereafter may be in the service of the United States, and shall continue therein during the war, and not hold any office of profit under these States or any of them, shall, after the conclusion of the war, be entitled to receive, annually, for the term of seven years, if they live so long, one half of the present pay of such officer: *Provided*, That no general officer of the cavalry, artillery or infantry shall be entitled to receive more than the one half part of the pay of a colonel of such corps, respectively: *And provided*, That this resolution shall not extend to any officer in the service of the United States, unless he shall have taken an oath of allegiance to and shall actually reside within some one of the United States.

The half-pay promised by this resolution is a *bounty* rather than a pension; but as it is *in the nature of a pension*, and, *quasi*, a *gratuity*, it is introduced here as its most appropriate place. The same may be said of several of the resolutions which immediately follow.

The resolution of May, 1778, it will be observed, relates only to officers of the *army*, commissioned by Congress. Naval officers seem to have been overlooked.

Measures having been taken by Congress to reduce and regulate the army, a preamble and resolution were adopted, October 3, 1780, which provide:

And whereas, by the foregoing arrangement, many deserving officers must become supernumerary, and it is proper that regard be had to them:

Resolved, That from the time the reform of the army takes place, they be entitled to half-pay for seven years, in specie or other current money equivalent, and also grants of land at the close of the war, agreeably to the resolution of the 16th of September, 1776.[1]

By a resolution of October 21, 1780, half-pay for life was promised to officers who should remain in the service to the close of the war.

A resolution of January 17, 1781, grants half-pay pension for life to certain officers in the hospital department and medical staff; and introduces a new rule for determining the rate. It is as follows:

Resolved, That all officers in the hospital department and medical staff hereinafter mentioned, who shall continue in service to the end of the war, or be reduced before that time, as supernumeraries, shall be entitled to and receive during life, in lieu of half-pay, the following, viz: The director of the hospital, equal to the half-pay of a lieutenant-colonel; chief physicians and surgeons of the army and hospitals, and hospital physicians and surgeons, purveyor, apothecary and regimental surgeons, each equal to the half-pay of a captain.

The several States were, by a supplementary resolution, recommended to pay these pensions annually, and to draw upon the "Superintendent of Finance" for the repayment of the sums advanced.

Half-pay having been regarded in an unfavorable light, and the officers of the army having memorialized Congress on the subject, resolutions were adopted, on the 22d day of March, 1783, allowing full pay for five years

[1] See title "BOUNTY LAND," page 309.

in lieu of half-pay for life to such officers as might elect to receive such commutation. These resolutions are as follows:

1. *Resolved*, That such officers as are now in service, and shall continue therein to the end of the war, shall be entitled to receive the amount of five years' full pay in money, or securities on interest at six per cent. per annum, as Congress shall find most convenient, instead of the half-pay promised for life by the resolution of the 21st day of October, 1780; the said securities to be such as shall be given to other creditors of the United States: *Provided*, It be at the option of the lines of the respective States, and not of officers individually in those lines, to accept or refuse the same: *And provided, also*, That their election shall be signified to Congress through the commander-in-chief, from the lines under his immediate command, within two months, and through the commanding officer of the southern army, from those under his command, within six months from the date of this resolution.

2. The same commutation shall extend to the corps not belonging to the lines of particular States, and who are entitled to half-pay for life, as aforesaid; the acceptance or refusal to be determined by corps, and to be signified in the same manner and within the same time as above mentioned.

3. That all officers belonging to the hospital department, who are entitled to half-pay by the resolution of the 17th day of January, 1781, may collectively agree to accept or refuse the aforesaid commutation, signifying the same through the commander-in-chief within six months from this time; that such officers as have retired at different periods, entitled to half-pay for life, may collectively, in each state in which they are inhabitants, accept or refuse the same; their acceptance or refusal to be signified, by agents authorized for that purpose, within six months from this period: that with respect to such retiring officers, the commutation, if accepted by them, shall be in lieu of whatever may now be due them since the time of their retiring from service, as well as what might hereafter become due; and that so soon as their acceptance shall be signified, the superintendent of finance be and is hereby directed to take measures for the settlement of their accounts accordingly, and to issue to them certificates bearing interest at six per cent.: that all officers entitled to half-pay

for life, not included in the preceding resolution, may also collectively agree to accept or refuse the aforesaid commutation, signifying the same within six months from this time.[1]

By resolution of January 26, 1784, Congress refused to extend the benefits of the foregoing resolutions to any officer or class of officers not expressly designated therein.

All the preceding resolutions are practically repealed, having become obsolete by subsequent and more favorable legislation; but they belong to the history and exhibit the growth of the system of gratuitous pensions in the United States, and could not, therefore, with propriety, have been omitted from this compilation.

Before March 18, 1818, the payment of money, in the form of gratuities for eminent services rendered in defense of the country, was by law restricted to certain army officers of the revolution. Naval officers, marines, seamen, non-commissioned officers of the army, and private soldiers, who served in the same war, were not admitted to a participation in the benefits thus conferred. But an act of the last-mentioned date, entitled "an act to provide for certain persons engaged in the land and naval service of the United States, in the revolutionary war,"[2] in a measure destroyed the unwarrantable distinctions which, up to that period, had been made in the bestowal of the national bounty. This act is as follows:

Be it enacted by the Senate and House of Representatives of the United States of America in Congress assembled, That every commissioned

---

1 The commutation of five years' full pay, granted to officers under resolution of March 22, 1783, in lieu of half-pay for life, can not be construed to warrant the payment of interest on arrears of the same from the time when such commutation might have been claimed by the party entitled thereto. *Attorney-General Berrien, October* 2, 1830.

2 U. S. Statutes at Large, vol. iii, 410.

officer, non-commissioned officer, musician and private soldier, and all officers in the hospital department and medical staff, who served in the war of the revolution until the end thereof, or for the term of nine months or longer at any period of the war, on the continental establishment, and every commissioned officer, non-commissioned officer, mariner or marine, who served at the same time and for a like term in the naval service of the United States, who is yet a resident citizen of the United States, and who is or hereafter, by reason of his reduced circumstances in life, shall be in need of assistance from his country for support, and shall have substantiated his claim to a pension in the manner hereinafter directed, shall receive a pension from the United States: If an officer, of twenty dollars[1] per month during life; if a non-commissioned officer, musician, mariner, marine or private soldier, of eight dollars per month during life: *Provided*, No person shall be entitled to the provisions of this act until he shall have relinquished his claim to every pension heretofore allowed him by the laws of the United States.[2]

SEC. 2. *And be it further enacted*, That to entitle any person to the provisions of this act, he shall make a declaration, under oath or affirmation, before the district judge of the United States of the district, or before any judge or court of record of the county, State or territory in which the applicant shall reside, setting forth, if he belonged to the army, the company, regiment and line to which he belonged, the time he entered the service, and the time and manner of leaving the service; and in case he belonged to the navy, a like declaration, setting forth the name of the vessel and particular service in which he was employed, and the time and manner of leaving the service, and shall offer such other evidence as may be in his power; and on its appearing, to the satisfaction of the said judge, that the applicant served in the revolutionary war, as aforesaid, against the common enemy, he shall certify and transmit the testimony in the case and the proceedings had thereon to the Secretary of the Department of War, whose duty it shall be, if satisfied the applicant comes under the provisions of this act, to place such officer,

1 This was no advantage to invalid officers above the grade of first lieutenant, as their pensions already exceeded the amount here fixed. (*Act of April* 24, 1816.)

2 A pensioner under this act can not receive an invalid pension also. *Attorney-General Butler, February* 27, 1834.

musician, mariner, marine or soldier on the pension list of the United States, to be paid in the same manner as pensions to invalids who have been placed on the pension list are now paid, and under such restrictions and regulations, in all respects, as are prescribed by law.

SEC. 3. *And be it further enacted*, That every pension by virtue of this act shall commence on the day that the declaration under oath or affirmation, prescribed in the foregoing section, shall be made.[1]

SEC. 4. *And be it further enacted*, That from and after the passage of this act, no sale, transfer or mortgage, of the whole, or any part, of the pension payable in pursuance of this act, shall be valid; and any person who shall swear or affirm falsely in the premises, and be thereof convicted, shall suffer as for willful and corrupt perjury.

The benefits of the provisions of this act are limited, as will be seen, to officers and soldiers of the continental line, and officers, seamen and marines belonging to the naval service of the United States. State and independent troops are not embraced in these terms.

An act was subsequently (May 1, 1820),[2] passed requiring every person applying for or receiving a pension under the act of March 18, 1818, to exhibit a sworn schedule of his whole estate and income, and an affidavit to the effect that he had not, in any manner disposed of his property, or any part of it, with the intention of bringing himself within the provisions of the last-named act, and that he had no property, securities contracts or debts, or income, except what was contained in his schedule. A copy of this schedule was to be certified by the Clerk of the Court before which the schedule should be exhibited,

1 This was afterwards (act of March 1, 1823, U. S. Statutes at Large, vol iii, 782), so amended as to make the commencement of the pension date from the time of completing the proof.

2 U. S. Statutes at Large, vol. iii, 569.

with the opinion of the Court as to the value of the property also certified thereon.

Upon receipt of the certified schedule the Secretary of War was required to strike from the pension list the name of any person who, in his opinion, did not require the assistance of the government in supporting himself.[1] "*Provided*, That every person, who shall have been placed on the pension list in consequence of disability, from known wounds received in the revolutionary war, and who shall have relinquished such pension in order to avail themselves (*sic*) of the benefit of the provisions of the act, to which this is an amendment, who by virtue of this section, may be stricken from the pension list, shall be forthwith restored to the pension so relinquished."

The Attorney-General (Wirt) having decided that no authority existed for restoring to the pension rolls the names of such indigent persons as were stricken off by the Secretary, and who, upon subsequent proof being made were found to be entitled to relief, Congress, by act of March 1, 1823,[2] made provision for such cases, and authorized their restoration to all the benefits of the act of March, 1818.

The act of March 1, 1823, also provided that in case a claimant, by reason of great bodily infirmity, was unable to exhibit his schedule in open Court, a Judge or Justice

1 If indigents acquire property after being placed on the pension roll, they may be dropped. *Attorney-General Taney, March* 23, 1832. The rule is understood to be not to withhold a pension on account of property, unless the yearly value of the property possessed by the claimant shall exceed the amount of the pension. *Secretary Porter, October* 15, 1828. Also *Decisions of same, December* 26, 1828; and *February* 2, 1829.

2 U. S. Statutes at Large, vol. iii, 782.

of a Court of Record, might attend at his place of residence, and receive his schedule.

It also provided that all pensions under the act of March 18, 1818, and the acts amendatory and supplemental thereto, should commence from the time of completing the proof.

Thus the law remained until May 15, 1828, when another act was passed, enlarging still further the bounty of the government to the heroes of the revolution. This act is entitled "an act for the relief of certain officers and soldiers of the army of the revolution." [1]

This act is as follows:

Be it enacted by the Senate and House of Representatives of the United States of America in Congress assembled, That each of the surviving officers of the army of the revolution,[2] in the continental line, who was entitled to half-pay by the resolve of October twenty-first, seventeen hundred and eighty, be authorized to receive out of any money in the Treasury, not otherwise appropriated,[3] the amount of his full pay in said line, according to his rank in the line, to begin on the third of March, one thousand eight hundred and twenty-six, and to continue during his natural life: *Provided,* That under this act no officer shall be entitled to receive a larger sum than the full pay of a captain in said line.[4]

SEC. 2. *And be it further enacted,* That whenever any of said officers has received money of the United States, as a pensioner, since the third day of March, one thousand eight hundred and twenty-six, aforesaid, the sum so received shall be deducted from what said officer would otherwise be entitled to under the first sec-

[1] U. S. Statutes at Large, vol. iv, 269.

[2] Hospital surgeons and surgeons' mates, are not entitled to the benefits of this act. *Commissioner Waldo, October* 4, 1853.

[3] This restriction repealed, by act of April 5, 1856. U. S. Statutes at Large, vol. xi, 3.

[4] Surgeons are entitled to the pay of a captain of infantry, under this act. *Secretary Woodbury, October* 22, 1834; *Secretary Porter, February* 17, 1844; and *Commissioner Edwards, February* 13, 1844.

tion of this act; and every pension to which said officer is now entitled shall cease after the passage of this act.[1]

SEC. 3. *And be it further enacted*, That every surviving non-commissioned officer, musician or private in said army, who enlisted therein for and during the war, and continued in service until its termination, and thereby became entitled to receive a reward of eighty dollars, under a resolve of Congress, passed May fifteenth, seventeen hundred and seventy-eight, shall be entitled to receive his full monthly pay in said service, out of any money in the Treasury not otherwise appropriated;[2] to begin on the third day of March, one thousand eight hundred and twenty-six, and to continue during his natural life: *Provided*, that no non-commissioned officer, musician or private in said army, who is now on the pension list of the United States, shall be entitled to the benefits of this act.[3]

SEC. 4. *And be it further enacted*, That the pay allowed by this act shall, under the direction of the Secretary of the Treasury, be paid to the officer or soldier entitled thereto, or to their authorized attorney, at such places and days as said Secretary may direct; and that no foreign officer shall be entitled to said pay, nor shall any officer or soldier receive the same, until he furnish to said Secretary satisfactory evidence that he is entitled to the same in conformity to the provisions of this act; and pay allowed by this act shall not, in any way, be transferable or liable to attachment, levy or seizure, by any

---

1 An act to amend this act, passed May 31, 1830 (U. S. Statutes at Large, vol. iv, 426), provides that the second section of this act shall not be construed to embrace invalid pensioners; and that the pension of invalid soldiers shall not be deducted from the amount receivable by them under this act. Under this amended act it has been held: That invalid pensions restored under the amended act, do not commence from the time when first withheld. *Attorney-General Berrien, June* 19, 1830; *Attorney-General Butler, December* 19, 1834.

2 This restriction in the first section of this act was repealed by an act of April 5, 1856; but for some reason it is retained in this section.

3 An act of July 14, 1832 (U. S. Statutes at Large, vol. iv, 600), prescribes that this section shall not be construed to embrace invalid pensioners; and that the pension of invalid soldiers shall not be deducted from the amount receivable by them under this act.

legal process whatever, but shall inure wholly to the personal benefit of the officer or soldier entitled to the same by this act.[1]

SEC. 5. *And be it further enacted*, That so much of said pay as accrued by the provisions of this act before the third day of March, eighteen hundred and twenty-eight, shall be paid to the officers and soldiers entitled to the same, as soon as may be, in the manner and under the provisions before mentioned; and the pay which shall accrue after said day shall be paid semi-annually, in like manner, and under the same provisions.

This act is also restricted in its operation—the benefits of its provisions being limited to officers and soldiers in the continental line, who served during the war. Naval officers, marines, seamen, State troops, etc., are not embraced within its terms.

But justice, though tardy, came at last. An act approved June 7, 1832, entitled "an act supplementary to the 'act for the relief of certain surviving officers and soldiers of the revolution,'"[2] swept away all invidious distinctions in dispensing the benefactions of government, and placed all who served their country, for at least six months in the war of the revolution, in the land or naval forces, without regard to the line of service, upon an equal footing.

This act is as follows:

Be it enacted by the Senate and House of Representatives of the United States of America in Congress assembled, That each of the surviving officers,[3] non-commissioned officers, musicians, sol-

1 Where a pensioner pledged his certificate of pension for debt, it was held that payment might be made to him, upon proof of identity, without a renewal of the certificate. *Attorney-General Taney, October* 27, 1832.

2 U. S. Statutes at Large, vol. iv, 529.

3 Service in a military office, even though the commission may not be issued, or may not date back to the commencement of the service, entitles the person to a pension for such service. *Secretary Cass, January*, 15, 1833. But in such cases strict proof of service, and that the claimant was pre-

diers,[1] and Indian spies, who shall have served in the continental line or State troops, volunteers or militia, at one or more terms, a period of two years,[2] during the war of the revolution, and who are not entitled to any benefit under the act for the relief of certain surviving officers and soldiers of the revolution, passed the fifteenth day of May, eighteen hundred and twenty-eight,[3] be authorized to receive, out of any money in the Treasury, not otherwise appropriated,[4] the amount of his full pay in the said line, according to his rank, but not exceeding in any case the pay of a captain in the said line;[5] such pay to commence from the fourth day of March, one thousand eight hundred and thirty-one, and shall continue during his natural

vented from receiving a commission by circumstances not under his control, will be required. *Secretary Cass, February* 21, 1833.

1 Those only are entitled to pensions, under this act, who formed a component part of the army, and were not only *mechanics*, but *enlisted* as *soldiers*. *Secretary Ewing, July* 18, 1849.

2 The war of the revolution did not terminate until April, 1783, upon ratification of the treaty of peace. *Attorney-General Wirt, February* 12, 1825. The deficiency of two years' service as captain can not be made up by service in an inferior rank. *Attorney-General Butler, May*, 2, 1834. Desertion forfeits all right to a pension. *Secretary Porter and Commissoner Edwards, June* 27, 1843. It is morally certain, from historical facts, that the Virginia militia served at least two years, at intervals, in the revolution. *Assistant Secretary Goddard, September* 9, 1850.

A resolution of July 14, 1832 (U. S. Statutes at Large, vol. iv, 608), provides that the time of imprisonment as a prisoner of war shall be computed as a part of the term of service.

A resolution of March 2, 1833 (U. S. Statutes at Large, vol. iv, 668), directs that the period of an applicant's service shall be computed from the time when he entered the service until the 11th day of April, 1783 (the date of the definitive treaty of peace), provided he served until that period.

3 These exclusive words should apply to cases in which the party applies in the same character in which he was entitled under act of 1827, and for the same description of service. *Attorney-General Taney, May* 18, 1833.

4 This restriction was repealed by act of April 5, 1856 (U. S. Statutes at Large, vol. xi, 3).

5 A surgeon in the revolution is not entitled to a pension higher than that of a captain of infantry. *Attorney-General Butler, December* 19, 1834. Surgeons, under the act of June 7, 1832, are entitled to the highest rate of pensions, according to length of service, including staff service. *Secretary Porter, November* 14, 1843.

life; and that any such officer, non-commissioned officer, musician or private, as aforesaid, who shall have served in the continental line, State troops, volunteers or militia, a term or terms in the whole less than the above period, but not less than six months, shall be authorized to receive out of any unappropriated money in the Treasury, during his natural life, each according to his term of service, an amount bearing such proportion to the annuity granted to the same rank for the service of two years, as his term of service did to the term aforesaid; to commence from the fourth day of March, one thousand eight hundred and thirty-one.

SEC. 2. *And be it further enacted*, That no person receiving any annuity or pension under any law of the United States providing for revolutionary officers and soldiers, shall be entitled to the benefits of this act, unless he shall first relinquish his further claim to such pension;[1] and in all payments under this act, the amount which may have been received under any other act, as aforesaid, since the date at which the payments under this act shall commence, shall first be deducted from such payment.

SEC. 3. *And be it further enacted*, That the pay allowed by this act shall, under the direction of the Secretary of the Treasury, be paid to the officer, non-commissioned officer, musician or private entitled thereto, or his or their authorized attorney, at such places and times as the Secretary of the Treasury may direct, and that no foreign officer[2] shall be entitled to said pay, nor shall any officer, non-commissioned officer, musician or private receive the same until he furnish the said Secretary satisfactory evidence that he is entitled to the same, in conformity to the provisions of this act; and the pay hereby allowed shall not be in any way transferable or lia-

1 An act approved February 19, 1833, prescribes that this shall not be construed to embrace invalid pensioners; and that the pensions of invalid soldiers shall not be deducted from the amount receivable by them under this act (U. S. Statutes at Large, vol. iv, 612). A pensioner can not at the same time receive half-pay under the act of July 5, 1832, providing for the claims of the State of Virginia, and a pension under the act of June 7, 1832. *Attorney-General Legare, September 30*, 1841.

2 All persons, whether residents or non-residents of the United States, who are embraced by the description contained in the first section, except "foreign officers," are entitled to avail themselves of its provisions. *Attorney-General Taney, October 27*, 1832.

ble to attachment, levy or seizure, by any legal process whatever, but shall inure wholly to the personal benefit of the officer, non-commissioned officer, musician or soldier entitled to the same. [1]

SEC. 4. *And be it further enacted*, That so much of the said pay as accrued before the approval of this act, shall be paid to the person entitled to the same, as soon as may be, in the manner, and under the provisions above-mentioned; and the pay which shall accrue thereafter, shall be paid semi-annually, in the manner above directed; and in case of death of any person embraced by the provisions of this act, or of the act to which it is supplementary, during the period intervening between the semi-annual payments directed to be made by said acts, the proportionate amount of pay which shall accrue between the last preceding semi-annual payment and the death of such person, shall be paid to his widow, [2] or, if he leave no widow, to his children. [3]

1 Where a pensioner has pledged his certificate of pension for debt, a renewal of the certificate is not necessary, but payment may be made without it, on proof of identity. *Attorney-General Taney, October* 27, 1832.

2 Under this act an administrator could never have been recognized by this office as a claimant, until the act of June 19, 1840, permitted it to be paid to him "for the sole use and benefit of the children, to be distributed among them in equal shares, and never to be regarded as assets." *Commissioner Heath, October* 17, 1851, and *Secretary Stuart, March* 17, 1852.

3 See title "ARREARS OF PENSIONS," page 274. In case of the death of the pensioner, leaving neither widow nor child, the arrears of pensions go to his legal representative. *Attorney-General Butler, February* 28, 1834. If a soldier dies after March 4, 1831, and before June 7, 1832, leaving a widow, who also dies before June 7, 1832, the children of the widow who are not children of the soldier, can not claim the arrears of pension due under this act; but the children of the soldier *may* claim the same. *Attorney-General Butler, April* 13, 1837. The children of soldiers or of their widows may draw what was due the parents when they died, although not claimed, or proof not perfected, at their death. *Secretaries Woodbury and Poinsett and Commissioner Edwards, April*, 1839. Under the act of Congress, passed on 7th of June, 1832, providing for the relief of certain surviving officers of the revolution, and its several supplements, the word children in the act embraces the grand-children of a deceased pensioner, whether their parents died before or after his decease, and they are entitled, *per stirpes*, to a distributive share of the deceased parent's pension. *Walton et al.* v. *Cotton et al.*, 19 Howard, 355.

An act of April 2, 1862, prohibits the allowance of a claim for a pension,

SEC. 5. *And be it further enacted,* That the officers, non-commissioned officers, mariners or marines, who served for a like term in the naval service,[1] during the revolutionary war, shall be entitled to the benefits of this act, in the same manner as is provided for the officers and soldiers of the army of the revolution.

GENERAL OBSERVATIONS.

The acts to which reference should be had, in preparing applications for pensions for revolutionary soldiers, are those of March 18, 1818, May 15, 1828, and June 7, 1832. The first named act is applicable, only, to persons in indigent circumstances, who served in the continental line, or in the naval service. Applications should not be made under this act, unless unavoidable, as the act of June 7, 1832, is much more favorable to the applicant.[2] The act of May 15, 1828, applies to persons—officers and soldiers of the army, but not of the naval forces—who served in the continental line during the entire war. It extends to field and line officers, major and brigadier-generals, directors of the hospital, chief physicians and surgeons of the army or hospital, hospital physicians, surgeons, purveyors and apothecaries, and regimental surgeons. No other staff officers are entitled to its benefits. The act of June 7, 1832, has the widest application. This embraces every description of persons belonging either

or an increase of pension, to the children or other descendants of a person who served in the revolution, or of his widow, when the soldier or his widow died without having established a claim to a pension.

1 This language can not be construed to apply to privateers. *Attorney-General Taney, July* 21, 1832.

2 It is more favorable in this: at least nine months' service must be proved, to obtain the benefits of the act of March 18, 1818; and under this law a pension commences at the time when the proof is completed. Under the act of June 7, 1832, pensions commence from March 4, 1831. In the latter case the pension, though smaller *for each year,* would be much greater *in the aggregate,* on account of the accumulation.

to the land or naval forces, whether serving as regulars, state troops, Indian spies, volunteers or militia; and who served for at least six months, in one or more tours. Those who served two years in all, are entitled to full pay, during life; but in no case can this exceed the pay of a captain in the line. A service of less than two years, and *not less* than six months, entitles the claimant to pay for life, proportioned in equal ratio, to the term served. Persons entitled to the benefits of the act of May 15, 1828, are not entitled to pensions under the act of June 7, 1832.

Invalid pensioners of the revolution are entitled to the benefits of the acts of May 15, 1828, and June 7, 1832, without relinquishing their pensions as invalids.

Foreign officers are not entitled to the benefits of the acts of May 15, 1828, and June 7, 1832.

Applications for gratuitous pensions must be made to the Commissioner of Pensions, to whom all letters and papers should be addressed. Postage on letters to him, upon official business, need not be paid.

SECTION II.

REGULATIONS AND FORMS FOR OBTAINING GRATUITOUS PENSIONS FOR SURVIVORS OF THE REVOLUTION.

As the act of June 7, 1832, is more favorable to claimants, *at the present time*, than that of March 18, 1818, it is not deemed necessary to provide forms to be used in making applications under the latter act.

Nor is it deemed necessary to insert a series of forms applicable to the act of May 15, 1828; as it is not probable that any claims under this act remain unadjusted.

The following regulations govern applications for pensions under the act of June 7, 1832.

DEPARTMENT OF WAR, *June* 27, 1832.

The following regulations have been adopted by the Secretary of War for carrying into effect the act of Congress passed June 7, 1832, entitled "an act supplementary to 'an act for the relief of the surviving officers and soldiers of the revolution.'"

This law has been construed to extend as well to the line as to every branch of the staff of the army, and to include, under the terms "continental line," "State troops," "militia" and "volunteers," all persons enlisted, drafted, or who volunteered, and who were bound to military service; but not to those who were occasionally employed with the army upon civil contracts, such as clerks to commissaries and to storekeepers, etc., teamsters, boatmen, etc.

Four general classes of cases are embraced in this law:

I. The regular troops.

II. The State troops, militia and volunteers.

III. Persons employed in the naval service.

IV. Indian spies.

I. As rolls of the regular troops in the revolutionary war exist in this department, all persons claiming the benefit of this law, as officers, non-commissioned officers, musicians or privates, will, in the first instance, make application by transmitting the following declaration [see No. 1, page 123], which will be made before a Court of Record of the county where such applicant resides. And every Court having, by law, a seal and clerk, is considered a Court of Record.

If, on examination of the proper record, the names of applicants making this declaration [No. 1, page 123] can not be found, they will receive detailed instructions respecting the nature and form of the testimony they must produce, to be placed on the pension roll. As the presumption will, in such case, be against the applicants, in consequence of the omission of their names in the muster rolls, they will be required to furnish as near as may be, the same evidence as has heretofore been required by the regulations and practice adopted for carrying into effect the act of Congress of March 18, 1818, and the acts supplementary thereto, with such relaxations as have been from time to time sanctioned by the Department, on account of the rapid decrease of the survivors of the revolutionary army, and the consequent difficulty of procuring direct positive testimony in every case.

Whenever an officer or non-commissioned officer is now in the receipt of a pension, he should make application, if he should be entitled to the benefits of this act, by letter merely, setting forth his rank, and the regiment, corps or vessel in which he served, and his present place of residence. His pension certificate must accompany his letter.

In those cases where the applicants have once been on the pension roll, under the act of March 18, 1818, and have been dropped therefrom on account of property, or from any other reason; or, when the application has been made under the act of May 15, 1828, and the evidence of service is in the Department; or, having made application and proof of service, and having been rejected, instead of the declaration before mentioned, they will make a statement, setting forth, under oath, their having been previously on the pension roll, and their having been struck from the same, showing their rank, regiment, corps or vessel, in which they served, their present place of residence, when the first application was made, or of their application under the act of 15th May, 1828.

In a case where a claimant may make personal application at this Department, and can produce satisfactory proof of service, and of his identity, also, at the seat of Government, he may make his declaration before a Justice of the Peace.

II. The case of the State troops, volunteers and militia, is different. There are, in the Department, no rolls of the State troops, except those of Virginia; and no rolls of militia except those of New Hampshire.

Applicants who served in the State troops of Virginia, and applicants who served in the militia of New Hampshire, will be required to produce the same proof as is prescribed for those who served upon the continental establishment. But with respect to the other State troops and militia, there is no record to advert to, and no presumption to be rebutted. The nature of the case, therefore, demands a different rule of proceeding.

Every applicant who claims a pension by virtue of service in the State troops, volunteers or militia, except as is above provided, will make and subscribe the following declaration. [See No. 2, page 126.]

The form of the proceedings, and of the certificates, will be so varied as to meet the case, when the declaration is made out of Court, before a Judge, as heretofore provided for.

Every applicant will produce the best proof in his power. This is the original discharge or commission; but if neither of these can be obtained, the party will so state under oath; and will then procure, if possible, the testimony of at least one credible witness, stating, in detail, his personal knowledge of the services of the applicant, and such circumstances connected therewith as may have a tendency to throw light upon the transaction.

If such surviving witness can not be found, the applicant will so state in his declaration; and he will also, whether he produce such evidence or not, proceed to relate all the material facts which may be useful in the investigation of his claim, and in the comparison of his narrative with the events of the period of his alleged service, as they are known at the Department. A very full account of the services of each person will be indispensable to a favorable action on his case. The facts stated will afford one of the principal means of corroborating the declaration of the applicant, if true, or of detecting the imposition, if one be attempted; and unless, therefore, these are amply and clearly set forth, no favorable decision can be expected. All applicants will appear before some Court of Record in the county in which they reside, and there subscribe and be sworn to one of the declarations provided, according to the nature of his case.

The Court will propound the following interrogatories, to all applicants for a pension, on account of service in the militia, State troops or volunteers, except the militia of New Hampshire, and the State troops of Virginia:

1. Where, and in what year were you born?
2. Have you any record of your age; and if so, where is it?
3. Where were you living when called into service; where have you lived since the revolutionary war; and where do you now live?
4. How were you called into service; were you drafted; did you volunteer, or were you a substitute; and if a substitute, for whom?
5. State the names of some of the regular officers who were with the troops where you served; such continental and militia regiments as you can recollect; and the general circumstances of your service?
6. *To an Officer.*—Did you ever receive a commission; and if so, by whom was it signed; and what has become of it? *To a Soldier.*—Did you ever receive a discharge from the service; and if so, by whom was it given; and what has become of it?

7. State the names of persons to whom you are known in your present neighborhood, and who can testify as to your character for veracity, and their belief of your service as a soldier of the revolution.

The Court will see that the answers to these questions are embodied in the declaration, and they are requested to annex their opinions of the truth of the statement of the applicant.

The applicant will further produce in Court, if the same can be done, in the opinion of the Court, without too much expense and inconvenience to him, two respectable persons (one of whom should be the nearest clergyman, if one lives in the immediate vicinity of such applicant), who can testify from their acquaintance with him, that they believe he is of the age he represents, and that he is reputed and believed in the neighborhood to have been a revolutionary soldier, and that they concur in that opinion. If one of these persons is a clergyman, the Court will so certify; and they will also certify to the character and standing of other persons giving such certificates.

The traditionary evidence of service is deemed very important, in the absence of any direct proof, except the declaration of the party; and the Courts are requested to be very particular in the inquiry whether the belief is general, and whether any doubts have ever existed on the subject. To require from the applicants positive proof of service from a contemporary survivor, would, after the lapse of so many years, be to deprive many of them of the benefit of the law; and as no presumption is raised against the militia by the existence of rolls in the Department, there is no good reason why this requisition should be extended to them. On the other hand, to receive the declaration of the parties as a sufficient ground for placing them upon the pension roll, without corroborating circumstances, would be to open the Treasury to great frauds. A just medium seems to present the best rule for carrying into effect the objects of Congress.

If the two persons whose certificates are required can not be produced in Court without too much inconvenience and expense to the applicant, then the statement of the facts and opinions above mentioned will be made under oath, before some Judge or Justice of the Peace, and the certificate of the Court to the situation and credibility of the persons making the statement will be given. Applicants unable to appear in Court by reason of bodily infirmity, may make the declaration before required, and submit to the examination before a Judge or Justice of a Court of Record of the proper county, and the Judge or Justice will execute the duties which the Court is herein requested to perform, and will also certify that the applicant can not, from bodily infirmity, attend the Court.

Whenever any official act is required to be done by a Judge or Justice of a Court of Record, or by a Justice of the Peace, the certificate of the Secretary of State or Territory, or of the proper Clerk of the Court or county, under his seal of office will be annexed, stating that such person is a Judge or Justice of a Court of Record, or a Justice of the Peace, and the signature annexed is his genuine signature.

III. Persons serving in the marine forces.

IV. Indian spies.

Each of these two latter classes of cases will produce proof as nearly as may be, conformably to the preceding regulations, and authenticated in a similar manner, with such variations as the different nature of the service may require. No payments can be made on account of the services of any person who may have died before the taking effect of the act of June 7, 1832;[1] and in case of death subsequent thereto, and before the declaration herein required is made, the parties interested will transmit such evidence as they can procure, taken and authenticated before a Court of Record, showing the services of the deceased, the period of his death, the opinion of the neighborhood respecting such services, the title of the claimant and the opinion of the Court upon the whole matter.

By the resolution of Congress of the 14th July, 1832, the time of imprisonment as a prisoner of war shall be taken and computed as a part of the period of service, in the execution of the act of June 7, 1852. JAMES L. EDWARDS, *Commissioner of Pensions.*

Declaration No. 1. (*For Regular Troops.*)

STATE OF —— }
County of —— } *ss.*

On this —— day of ——, A.D. ——, personally appeared before 2 the —— court within and for the State and county aforesaid ——, a resident

1 Since this was written by the Commissioner the benefits of the act of June 7, 1832, have been extended to the widows of persons who served as mentioned in the act, and died.

2 The declarant must appear in open court, unless prevented from doing so by reason of bodily infirmity, in which case he will follow the rule laid down for his guidance.

of —— county,[1] in the State of ——, aged [2] —— years, who being first duly sworn according to law, doth, on his oath, make the following declaration, in order to obtain the benefit of the provision made by the act of Congress passed June 7, 1832: that he enlisted in the army of the United States in the year ——, with [3] —— and served in the —— regiment of the —— line, under the following named officers. [*Here set forth the names*

[1] The declarant must make his declaration in the county where he resides. If he should fail to do so, he must assign a sufficient reason for not conforming to the rule.

[2] The age of the claimant must invariably be mentioned. The declarant must mention the period or periods of the war when he served.

[3] Every continental officer or soldier must give the name of the colonel under whom he served; otherwise a satisfactory examination of the claim can not be had. Every claimant, must state, with precision, the length of his service, and the different grades in which he served, in language so definite as to enable the Department to determine to what amount of pension he is entitled. In a case where the applicant can not, by reason of the loss of memory, state precisely how long he served, he should amend his declaration by making an affidavit in the following words:

"Personally appeared before me, the undersigned, a justice of the peace, etc. ——, who being duly sworn, deposeth and sayeth that, by reason of old age, and the consequent loss of memory, he can not swear positively as to the precise length of his term of service, but according to the best of his recollection, he served not less than the period mentioned below, and in the following grades: For —— years, —— months and —— days, I served as a ——. For —— months and —— days, I served as a ——; and for such service I claim a pension."

It is important, in all cases, to determine with precision the period for which each applicant served, and the particular rank he held, as the law directs the pension to be paid according to the grade of the pensioner, and the length of his service. The use of the phrase *about three or four months*, is too indefinite, and all such qualifying expressions are objectionable. Some persons who apply for pensions merely state that they served two years in the militia, etc., without specifying the tours, the names of the officers and other particulars respecting their service. This form of a declaration is highly objectionable. It must, in every case, be clearly shown under what officers the applicant served; the duration of each term of engagement; the particular place or places where the service was performed; that the applicant served with an embodied corps called into service by competent authority; that he was either in the field or in the garrison; and for the time during which the service was performed, he was not employed in any civil pursuit.

and rank of the field and company officers; the time he left the service (and if he served under more than one term of enlistment, he must specify the particular period, and the rank and names of his officers); the town, or county, or State in which he resided when he entered the service; the battles, if any, in which he was engaged; and the country through which he marched].

He hereby relinquishes every claim[1] whatever to a pension or an annuity except the present, and he declares that his name is not on the pension roll of any agency, in any State [*or, if any,* only on that of the agency in the State of ——]. (*Claimant's Signature.*)

And then will follow the certificate of the court:

And the said court do hereby declare their opinion,[2] that the above-named applicant was a revolutionary soldier, and served as he states.

(*Signature of Presiding Judge.*)

I, ——, clerk of the —— court, within and for the county of —— and State of ——, do hereby certify[3] that the foregoing contains the original proceedings of the said court, in the matter of the application of —— for a pension.

[L. S.] In testimony whereof, I have hereunto set my hand and affixed the seal of said court,[4] this —— day of ——, 18—.

(*Clerk of —— Court, —— County, ——.*)

---

[1] The law makes the relinquishment indispensable, except by invalids.

[2] The opinion of the court is always required.

[3] The clerk must give his certificate in every case.

[4] The clerk must affix his seal, and if it has no device or inscription by which it can be distinguished from any other seal, or if he has no public seal of office, the certificate of a member of Congress, proving the official character and signature of the certifying officer, should accompany the papers.

Mode of Authenticating Papers.—In every instance where the certificate of the certifying officer who authenticates the papers is not written on the same sheet of paper which contains the affidavit or other papers authenticated, the certificate must be attached thereto by a piece of tape or narrow ribbon, the ends of which must pass under the seal of office of the certifying officer, so as to prevent any paper from being improperly attached to the certificate.

Proof of Service.—In a case where the name of the applicant is not found on the records of the Department, he must prove his service by two credible witnesses, who are required to set forth in their affidavits the time of the claimant's entering the service, and the time and manner of his leaving the same, as well as the regiment, company and line to which he belonged. The magistrates who administer the oaths must certify to the

Declaration No. 2. (For State Troops and Militia.)

STATE OF —— }
County of —— } *ss.*

On this —— day of ——, 18—, personally appeared ——, in open court, before the —— court, within and for the county and State aforesaid, now sitting, ——, a resident of ——, in the county of —— and State of ——, aged —— years, who being first duly sworn according to law, doth on his oath make the following declaration, in order to obtain the benefit of the act of Congress passed June 7, 1832: That he entered the service of the United States under the following named officers, and served as herein stated. [*Here set forth the names and rank of the field and company officers; the day (if possible) and the month and the year when the claimant entered the service, and the time when he left the same; and, if under more than one engagement, he must specify the particular periods, and the rank and names of his officers; the town, county and State in which he resided when he entered the service; whether he was drafted, was a volunteer or a substitute; the battles, if any, in which he was engaged; the country through which he marched; the continental regiments or companies with which he served* (i. e., *which were in same division*), *and the names of some of the regular officers whom he knew; together with such other particulars as may be useful in the investigation of his claim; and also, if the facts be so, that he has no documentary evidence, and that he knows of no person, whose testimony he can procure, who can testify to his service.*[1]]

He hereby relinquishes every claim whatever to a pension or annuity except the present, and declares that his name is not on the pension roll of the agency of any State [*or, if any*, only on that of the agency of the State of ——]. (*Claimant's Signature.*)

And then will be annexed the following certificate:

We, ——, a clergyman, residing in ——, in the county of —— and State of ——, and ——, residing ——, hereby certify that we are well acquainted with ——, who has subscribed and sworn to the above declaration; that we believe him to be —— years of age; that he is reputed and believed, in the

---

credibility of the witnesses, and the official character and signature of the magistrate must be certified by the proper officer, under his seal of office.

1 The notes to No. 1 are also applicable to No. 2, except as to "*proof of service.*" This (*proof of service*) must also be observed in militia cases, where muster rolls are on file in the Department.

The answers to the interrogatories propounded by the court, in accordance with the regulations of the Commissioner, must all be written, and sent to the office with the declaration.

neighborhood where he resides, to have been a soldier of the revolution;[1] and that we concur in that opinion.

(*Signatures of Witnesses.*)

Sworn to and subscribed before me the day and year aforesaid.

(*Officer's Signature.*)

And then will follow the certificate of the court:

And the said court do hereby declare their opinion, after the investigation of the matter, and after putting the interrogatories prescribed by the Commissioner of Pensions, that the above-named applicant was a revolutionary soldier, and served as he states. And the court further certifies, that it appears to them that ——, who has signed the preceding certificate, is a clergyman, resident in ——, and that —— [*the other witness*] is a credible person; and that their statement is entitled to credit.

(*Presiding Judge.*)

I, ——, clerk of the —— court, within and for the county of —— and State of ——, do hereby certify that the foregoing contains the original proceedings of the said court, in the matter of the application of —— for a pension.

[L. S.] In testimony whereof, I hereunto set my hand and the seal of said court, this —— day of ——, A.D. 18—.

(*Clerk's Signature.*)

For REGULATIONS and FORMS relating to POWERS OF ATTORNEY, see Chapter XVI.

The forms immediately preceding are intended as guides only to the draughtsman. He should not rely upon them solely, but should study carefully the regulations prescribed by the Commissioner, which point out more fully what will be required of the applicant in support of his claim.

Should interlineations or erasures be made in drawing up pension papers, they should be referred to at the bottom of the declaration or the officer's certificate before signing.

---

1 This traditionary evidence is indispensable in militia cases.

CHAPTER VIII.

GRATUITOUS PENSIONS.

SECTION I.

WIDOWS AND ORPHANS—REVOLUTIONARY WAR.

ALL pensions to widows and orphans, whether in the form of full or half-pay for a term of years or for life, are mere gratuities, and will be so considered in this compilation.

The provisions of the resolution of the Continental Congress, passed May 15, 1778,[1] granting half-pay for seven years to the commissioned officers of the army, were, by a resolution of August 24, 1780, extended to the widows and orphans of those officers who had died, or might die, in the service, as follows:

Resolved, That the resolution of the 15th day of May, 1778, granting half-pay for seven years to the officers of the army who should continue in service to the end of the war, be extended to the widows of those officers who have died, or shall hereafter die, in the service; to commence from the time of such officers' death, and continue for the term of seven years; or, if there be no widow, or in case of her death or intermarriage, the said half-pay be given to the children of the officer dying as aforesaid, if he shall have left any; and that it be recommended to the Legislatures of the respective States to which such officers belong, to make provision for paying the same, on account of the United States.

This resolution makes provision for half-pay for seven years to the widows and orphans of commissioned officers of the continental line only.

No further general legislation was had upon the sub-

[1] See Chapter VII, Section I.

ject until nearly fifty-six years after the date of this resolution, when the act of July 4, 1836,[1] was passed. This act is of so much importance that it is here given entire.

AN ACT *granting Half-pay to Widows or Orphans, where their Husbands and Fathers have died of wounds received in the Military Service of the United States, in certain cases, and for other purposes.*

Be it enacted by the Senate and House of Representatives of the United States of America in Congress assembled, That when any officer, non-commissioned officer, musician, or private of the militia, including rangers, sea-fencibles and volunteers, shall have died while in the service of the United States, since the twentieth of April, eighteen hundred and eighteen, or who shall have died in consequence of a wound received while in the service, since the day aforesaid, and shall have left a widow, or, if no widow, a child, or children under sixteen years of age, such widow, or, if no widow, such child or children, shall be entitled to receive half the monthly pay to which the deceased was entitled at the time of his death, or receiving such wound, for and during the term of five years; and in case of the death or marriage of the said widow before the expiration of said five years, the half-pay for the remainder of time shall go to the children of the said decedent; *Provided*, That the half-pay aforesaid shall be half the monthly pay of the officers, non-commissioned officers, muscians, and privates of the infantry of the regular army, and no more; *Provided, also*, That no greater sum shall be allowed to the widow, or the child, or children, of any officer than the half-pay of a lieutenant-colonel.

SEC. 2. *And be it further enacted*, That if any officer, non-commissioned officer, musician, soldier, Indian spy, mariner or marine, whose service during the revolutionary war was such as is specified in the act passed the seventh of June, eighteen hundred and thirty-two, entitled "an act supplementary to the act for the relief of certain surviving officers and soldiers of the revolution," have died since the fourth of March, eighteen hundred and thirty-one, and before the date of said act, the amount of pension that would have accrued from the fourth of March, eighteen hundred and thirty-one, to the time of his death and become payable to him by virtue of that act, if he had survived the passage thereof, shall be paid to his widow; and if he left no

[1] U. S. Statutes at Large, vol. v, 127.

widow, to his children, in the manner prescribed in the act hereby amended.

SEC. 3. *And be it further enacted*, That if any person who served in the war of the revolution in the manner specified in the act passed the seventh day of June, eighteen hundred and thirty-two, entitled "an act supplementary to the act for the relief of certain surviving officers and soldiers of the revolution," have died, leaving a widow, whose marriage took place before the expiration of the last period of his service, such widow shall be entitled to receive during the time she may remain unmarried, the annuity or pension which might have been allowed to her husband, by virtue of the act aforesaid, if living at the time it was passed.[1]

1 The subsequent marriage of the widow does not preclude her from claiming the benefits of the third section of this act, provided she was a widow at the time the act passed. (See act of March 3, 1837, page 131.)

A resolution of July 7, 1838, directs that pensions under the third section of the act of July 4, 1836, shall be granted to widows whose husbands had died, or should die, after the passage of the act of 1836. (See the resolution, page 132.)

The children of a widow who was living on the 4th of July, 1836, and was entitled to the benefit of the third section of the act of that date, can draw the amount due up to the date of her death, although she failed to apply. *Attorney-General Butler, April* 13, 1837.

In all cases where the husband was in receipt of a pension under any of the revolutionary pension acts, until the time of his death, the pension of the widow, under the act of July 4, 1836, can only commence from the date of her husband's death. *Ibid.*

The word children, under the act of June 7, 1832, and its supplements, embraces the grandchildren of the deceased pensioner, whether their parents died before or after his decease, and they are entitled, *per stirpes*, to a distributive share of the deceased parent's pension.— *Walton et al.* v. *Colton et al.*, 19 Howard's Reports, 355.

As the act of 1837 removed the objection to a second marriage, and allowed the pension to the widow although she married again, provided she was a widow on the 4th of July, 1836, and as the resolution of July 7, 1838, removes the impediment to the time of the death of the husband, I think, a just construction of the resolution, when taken in connection with former acts, will embrace the widows of revolutionary officers and soldiers who married a second time, whenever they shall again become widows.— *Attorney-General Grundy, October* 2, 1839.

Where a widow applies for a pension under the act of 1836, and dies before a certificate issues (having bequeathed the pension by will made pre-

SEC. 4. *And be it further enacted*, That any pledge, mortgage, sale, assignment or transfer of any right, claim, or interest in any money or half-pay granted by this act, shall be utterly void and of no effect: each person acting for, and in behalf of, any one entitled to money under this act, shall take and subscribe an oath, to be administered by the proper accounting officer, and retained by him, and put on file, before a warrant shall be delivered to him, that he has no interest in said money by any pledge, mortgage, sale, assignment, or transfer, and that he does not know or believe that the same has been so disposed of to any person whatever.

SEC. 5. *And be it further enacted*, That the Secretary of War shall adopt such forms of evidence, in applications under this act, as the President of the United States may prescribe.

An act "explanatory" of the last named act, approved March 3, 1837,[1] is as follows:

Be it enacted by the Senate and House of Representatives of the United States of America in Congress assembled, That the benefits of the third section of the act entitled "an act granting half-pay to widows and orphans, where their husbands and fathers have died of wounds received in the military service of the United States, and for other purposes," approved the fourth day of July, eighteen hundred thirty-six, shall not be withheld from any widow in consequence of her having married after the decease of the husband, for whose services she may claim to be allowed a pension or annuity under said act; *Provided*, That she was a widow at the time it was passed.

SEC. 2. *And be it further enacted*, That the widow of any person who continued in the service of the United States, until the third day of November, seventeen hundred and eighty-three, and was married before that day, and while her husband was in such service, shall be entitled to the benefits of the third section of the aforesaid act.

Subsequently, by a resolution of July 7, 1838, entitled "a resolution for the benefit of the widows of certain revolutionary officers and soldiers, the third section

vious to her death), her executor is not entitled to receive the pension for distribution according to the will—it goes to her children. *Attorney-General Poinsett, January* 25, 1830.

1 U. S. Statutes at Large, vol. v, 187.

of the act of July 4, 1836, was still further modified. This resolution is as follows:

Resolved by the Senate and House of Representatives of the United States of America in Congress assembled, That the benefits of the third section of an act entitled, "an act granting half-pay to widows or orphans where their husbands and fathers have died of wounds received in the military service of the United States, in certain cases, and for other purposes," approved the fourth day of July, eighteen hundred and thirty-six, shall not be withheld from any widow whose husband has died since the passage of the said act, or who shall hereafter die, if said widow shall otherwise be entitled to the same.[1]

On the same day an act was approved, which still further extends the benefits of previous acts of Congress towards the widows of deceased revolutionary officers, soldiers, mariners and seamen. This act is as follows:

AN ACT *Granting Half-Pay and Pensions to certain Widows.*[2]

Be it enacted by the Senate and House of Representatives of the United States of America in Congress assembled, That if any person who served in the war of the revolution in the manner specified in the act passed the seventh day of June, eighteen hundred and thirty-two, entitled "an act supplementary to the act for the relief of certain surviving officers and soldiers of the revolution," have died, leaving a widow, whose marriage took place after the expiration of the last period of his service, and before the first day of January, seventeen hundred and ninety four,[3] such widow shall be entitled to receive,

---

1 As the act of 1837 removed the objection to a second marriage, and allowed the pension to the widow although she married again, provided she was a widow on the 4th of July, 1836, and as the resolution of July 7, 1838, removes the impediment as to the time of the death of the husband, I think, a just construction of the resolution, when taken in connection with the former acts, will embrace the widows of revolutionary officers and soldiers who married a second time, whenever they shall again become widows. *Attorney-General Grundy, October 2, 1839.*

2 U. S. Statutes at Large, vol. v, 305.

3 Widows of officers who died before the passage of the act of June 7

for and during the term of five years from the fourth day of March, eighteen hundred and thirty-six,[1] the annuity or pension which might have been allowed to her husband, in virtue of said act, if living at the time it was passed.[2] *Provided*, That in the event of the marriage of such widow said annuity or pension shall be discontinued.

SEC. 2. *And be it further enacted*, That no pledge, mortgage, sale, assignment, or transfer of any right, claim, or interest in any an-

---

1832, are not entitled to pensions under act of July 7, 1838. *Attorney-General Legare and Secretary Spencer, May* 31, 1842.

The act of July 7, 1838, was intended to provide pensions for widows who were not embraced in the third section of the act of July 4, 1836, or other prior laws. *Attorney-General Butler, August* 24, 1838.

1 This was renewed for one year from March 4, 1843, by an act of March 3, 1843 (U. S. Statutes at Large, vol. v, 647), and for four additional years from March 4, 1844, by act of June 17, 1844 (U. S. Statutes at Large, vol. v, 680). Under the last-named act, Secretary Wilkins decided (June 20, 1844), that where a widow died between March 4, 1844, and June 17, 1844, her children were entitled to the benefits of the last-named act. A joint resolution of March 3, 1851, explaining the acts of 1838, 1843 and 1844 (U. S. Statutes at Large, vol. ix, 647), provides that the benefits of those acts "shall not be withheld from any widow whose husband died since the passage of either of said acts, if said widows shall be otherwise entitled to the same: *Provided*, That no pension shall be granted to said widow for the same time her husband received one."

2 Under the act of 1838, the pension to a widow begins at the time of the death of her husband. *Commissioner Edwards, and Secretary Poinsett, April* 1, 1839. Widows of deceased pensioners, whose husbands were living at the passage of the act of July 7, 1838, can not receive a pension for the same time their husbands drew a pension. *Commissioner Waldo, June* 30, 1854. Widows take for five years, beginning in 1836, and are to be paid, according to the letter of the law, from that time. *Attorney-General Legare, Sept.* 2, 1842. The children of soldiers, or of their widows, may draw what was due their parents when they died, although not claimed, or the proof might not have been perfected at their death. This applies to act of July 7, 1838. *Commissioner Edwards, confirmed by Secretary Poinsett, April* 5, 1839. But this decision is set aside by an act of Congress of April 2, 1862. (See that act, page 139.) Widows who became such after July 7, 1838, and died before July 1, 1848, were not entitled to the benefits of either the act of Congress, or the joint resolution of the above dates; nor are their representatives entitled. *Commissioner Waldo, June* 10, 1853.

nuity, half-pay, or pension, granted by this act, shall be valid; nor shall the half-pay, annuity, or pension granted by this act, or any former act of Congress, be liable to attachment, levy, or seizure, by any process in law or equity, but shall inure wholly to the personal benefit of the pensioner or annuitant entitled to the same; and that, before a warrant shall be delivered to any person acting for or in behalf of any one entitled to money under this act, such person shall take and subscribe an oath or affirmation, to be administered by the proper accounting officer, and put on file, that he has no interest in said money by any pledge, mortgage, transfer, agreement, understanding, or arrangement, and that he does not know or believe that the same has been so disposed of to any other person.

SEC. 3. *And be it further enacted*, That the Secretary of War shall adopt such regulations and forms of evidence in relation to applications and payments under this act, as the President of the United States may prescribe.

This act was amended by "an act to amend the acts of July, eighteen hundred and thirty-six, and eighteen hundred and thirty-eight, allowing pensions to certain widows," approved August 23, 1842,[1] which declares:

. . . That the marriage of the widow, after the death of her husband, and for whose services she claims a pension, under the act of the seventh of July, eighteen hundred and thirty-eight, shall be no bar to the claim of such widow to the benefit of that act, she being a widow at the time she makes application for a pension.

A resolution, also modifying the act of July 7, 1838, was passed on the 16th day of August, 1842.[2] This resolution is as follows:

Resolved by the Senate and House of Representatives of the United States of America in Congress assembled, That the benefits of the act, entitled "an act granting half-pay and pensions to certain widows," approved the seventh day of July, eighteen hundred and thirty-eight, shall not be withheld from any widow whose husband died after the passage of the act of the seventh of June, eighteen hun-

1 U. S. Statutes at Large, vol. v, 521.

2 *Ibid*, vol. v, 584.

dred and thirty-two, and before the act of seventh July, eighteen hundred and thirty-eight, if otherwise entitled to the same.[1]

"An act making appropriations for the payment of revolutionary and other pensioners of the United States, for the fiscal year ending on the thirtieth of June, one thousand eight hundred and forty-five," approved, April 30, 1844,[2] provides, among other things, that "no pension shall hereafter be granted to a widow for the same time that her husband received one."

A rule of evidence was established by the second section of an appropriation act of May 7, 1846,[3] as follows:

SEC. 2. *And be it further enacted*, That no widow entitled to a pension under existing laws, and claiming a pension, whose husband was drawing a pension at the time of his decease, shall be required, in any such case, to furnish any further evidence that said husband was entitled to a pension; nor shall any evidence, in any case, be required to entitle the widow to a pension, when the evidence is in the archives of the government, other than such proof as would be sufficient to establish the marriage between the applicant and the deceased pensioner in civil personal actions in a court of justice.[4 5]

---

1 I am of opinion that no pension accrued to the said Polly Knight, in her life-time, from the 4th March, 1836, to the death of her husband, she having died before the passage of the joint resolution of the 16th August, 1842, and, therefore, her representatives have no right to the arrearages of pension which they claim. *Secretary Stuart, Nov.* 15, 1850. The benefits of the resolution of August 16, 1842, are intended for those widows only who were living at the time of its passage. *Commissioner Edwards, confirmed by Secretary Spencer, Feb.* 4, 1843.

2 U. S. Statutes at Large, vol. v, 656. This act operates on claims filed in the office prior to the passage of the act, as well as to all subsequent cases. *Secretary Wilkins, May* 1, 1844.

3 U. S. Statutes at Large, vol. ix, 6.

4 5 The fact that the husbands were upon the roll, and drew pensions, is presumptive evidence that they were entitled to them; yet, if they were not, that fact may be proved. The *onus*, however, is upon the government, to show that they were not entitled. *Attorney-General Mason, January* 23, 1846. To establish their claims, it is sufficient for the widows to prove that their husbands were pensioners, and that they are their widows. *Ibid.* General reputation and cohabitation are, in general, sufficient evidence

The bounty of Congress to the widows of soldiers of the revolution was still further enlarged by the act of February 2, 1848,[1] by which all the benefits of the act of June 7, 1832, granting pensions to surviving soldiers of the revolution, for life, were extended to the widows of such soldiers as had died, or might subsequently die. This act is as follows:

AN ACT *making further provisions for Surviving Widows of the Soldiers of the Revolution.*

Be it enacted by the Senate and House of Representatives of the United States of America in Congress assembled, That if any person who served in the war of the revolution in the manner specified in the act passed the seventh day of June, eighteen hundred and thirty-two, entitled "an act supplementary to an act for the relief of certain surviving officers and soldiers of the revolution," have died, or shall hereafter die, leaving a widow, whose marriage took place before the first day of January, one thousand seven hundred and ninety-four, such widow shall be entitled to receive, for and during her natural life, from and after the fourth day of March, eighteen hundred and forty-eight, the annuity or pension which might have been allowed to her husband, in virtue of said act, if living at the time it was passed, under the

of marriage; but this is only presumptive—it may be rebutted. *Ibid.* The continuous cohabitation of the parties as man and wife, for so many years, and the birth of so many children, consecutively acknowledged and treated as legitimate, *being proven*, the marriage might well be presumed.—*Acting Secretary of Interior Goddard, September* 23, 1840.

The rule of evidence in this section is in effect repeated by a joint resolution of July 1, 1848 (U. S. Statutes at Large, vol. ix, 336), which is as follows:

Resolved, by the Senate and House of Representatives of the United States of America in Congress assembled, That in all cases where a pension may have been granted to any officer or soldier of the revolution, in his life-time, the evidence upon which such pension was granted shall be conclusive of the service of such officer or soldier in the application of any widow, or woman who may have been the widow, of such officer or soldier, for a pension; and upon proof by her that she was married to any such officer or soldier prior to January first, seventeen hundred and ninety-four, and that she is a widow, she shall thereupon be placed upon the pension rolls, at the same rate as such officer or soldier received during his life-time.

[1] U. S. Statutes at Large, vol. ix, 210.

same rules, regulations, and restrictions as are prescribed in the act approved July seventh, eighteen hundred and thirty-eight, entitled "an act granting half-pay and pensions to certain widows." *Provided,* That in the event of the marriage of such widow, said annuity or pension shall be discontinued.

SEC. 2. *And be it further enacted,* That such widows as have been admitted by special acts of Congress to the benefit of the pension act approved the seventh day of July, one thousand eight hundred and thirty-eight, or to the benefit of the act approved the seventeenth day of June, one thousand eight hundred and forty-four, shall be entitled, and shall be admitted to the benefit of this act; subject, however, to the rules, limitations, and restrictions in and by said acts prescribed.

An act containing still more liberal provisions was passed July 29, 1848.[1] This act is entitled "an act for the relief of certain surviving widows of officers and soldiers of the revolutionary army," and provides:

Be it enacted by the Senate and House of Representatives of the United States of America in Congress assembled, That the widows[2] of all officers, non-commissioned officers, musicians, soldiers, mariners or marines, or Indian spies who shall have served in the continental line, State troops, volunteers, militia, or in the naval service, in the revolutionary war with Great Britian, shall be entitled to a pension during such widowhood, of equal amount per annum that their husbands would have been entitled to, if living, under existing pension laws; to commence on the fourth day of March, eighteen hundred and forty-eight, and to be paid in the same manner that other pensions are paid to widows; but no widow now receiving a pension shall be entitled to receive a further pension under the provisions of this act; and no widow married after the first day of January, one thousand eight hundred, shall be entitled to receive a pension under this act.

Section two makes void any assignment or transfer of a pension granted under the provisions of the act, and

[1] U. S. Statutes at Large, vol. ix, 265.

[2] No widow receiving a pension at the time of the passage of the act of July 29, 1848, can receive a further pension under said act. *Commissioner Waldo, January* 11, 1854.

exempts it from seizure for debt. It also provides that the existing regulations governing applications for, and the payment of, pensions shall apply to cases under the act.

Section three provides that the act shall take effect immediately.

With the second section of an act of February 3, 1853, "to continue half-pay to certain widows and orphans,"[1] the bounty of Congress to this class of beneficiaries culminated, and the last distinction between the widows of officers and soldiers of the revolution was removed. This second section is found in strange company (the first section of the act continuing for five years, half-pay to the widows and orphans of certain soldiers who served after the revolution), but is not the less operative. It is as follows:

SEC. 2. *And be it further enacted*, That the widows of all officers, non-commissioned officers, musicians, and privates of the revolutionary army, who were married subsequent to January, A. D. eighteen hundred, shall be entitled to a pension in the same manner as those who were married before that date.[2]

Section three of the act making appropriations for the support of the army for the year ending June 30, 1855, approved August 5, 1854,[3] provides:

SEC. 3. *And be it further enacted*, That the act approved September twenty-eight, one thousand eight hundred and fifty, entitled "an act granting bounty land to certain officers and soldiers who have been engaged in the military service of the United States," the act approved March twenty-second, one thousand eight hundred and fifty-two, entitled "an act to make land warrants assignable, and for other purposes;" and the act approved February third, one thou-

1 U. S. Statutes at Large, vol. x, 154.

2 The commencement of a pension under this section of the act is from the passage of the act. *Commissioner Waldo, May* 4, 1853.

3 U. S. Statutes at Large, vol. x, 581.

sand eight hundred and fifty-three, entitled "an act to continue half-pay to certain widows and orphans," shall not be so construed as to deprive any widow from (*sic*) the benefits therein granted for the services of her husband, though she may have married again: *Provided, however*, That the applicant is a widow at the time of making the claim: *Provided*, such party shall not receive a pension during coverture.

This provision was subsequently (act of February 28, 1855[1]), extended to the widows of naval officers, marines, and seamen, as follows:

SEC. 3. *And be it further enacted*, That the widows of the officers, non-commissioned officers, marines or mariners who served in the navy of the United States during the revolutionary war, and who were married since the first day of January, eighteen hundred, shall be entitled to pensions in the same manner, and to the same extent, as the widows of the officers and soldiers of the army of the revolution, under the second section of the act of February third, eighteen hundred and fifty-three.

By an act of April 2, 1862, the children and other descendants of persons who served in the revolution are precluded from claiming a pension or increase of pension by reason of such services, where the soldier or his widow died without establishing a claim to a pension. This act is as follows:

AN ACT *to prohibit the allowance or payment of Pensions to the Children of Officers and Soldiers of the Revolution.*

Be it enacted by the Senate and House of Representatives of the United States of America in Congress assembled, That from and after the passage of this act no claim for a pension or for an increase of pension, shall be allowed in favor of the children or other descendants of any person who served in the war of the revolution, or of the widow of such person, when such person or his widow died without having established a claim to a pension.

---

1 U. S. Statutes at Large, vol. x, 615.

GENERAL OBSERVATIONS.

The act of July 3, 1836, may be said to lie at the foundation of all acts of Congress granting *pensions* to the widows and orphans of revolutionary officers, soldiers, marines and seamen, as it is to this act that all subsequent legislation upon the subject relates.

This act, in its turn, has retrospective relation to the act of June 7, 1832, granting pensions to survivors of the revolution.

A widow can claim a pension under the act of July 4, 1836, only when her husband, were he still living, would be entitled to such pension; and it is the amount to which he would be entitled, if living, which governs the rate of pension to her. This act limits its benefits to such widows as were married before the expiration of the husband's last term of service; but by act of March 3, 1837, this was extended to widows married before November 3, 1783, and to such as had married the second time, and were again widows, at the passage of the act. This was still further extended by the joint resolution of July 7, 1838, which allowed those widows whose husbands had died since the passage of the act of July 4, 1836, or who might afterwards die, to claim the benefits of that act.

An act, passed on the same day on which the resolution was adopted, gave to those widows who were married after the expiration of the husband's last term of service, and before January 1, 1794, the same pension, for five years, from March 4, 1836, which the husbands, if living, might claim under the act of June 7, 1832.

This allowance of half-pay was extended five years from March 4, 1843, by acts of March 3, 1843, and June 17, 1844. A joint resolution of March 3, 1851, extended the benefits of the last-named acts, and of the act of June

7, 1838, to widows whose husbands died after the passage of said acts, but not to include any portion of time for which the husband received a pension. The acts of 1843 and 1844, just referred to grant no original pension. They merely continue the payment of pensions already granted.

An act of August 23, 1842, provides that the second marriage of a widow shall not bar her right to a pension under the act of July 7, 1838, if she be a widow at the time she makes application for a pension.

By joint resolution of August 16, 1842, it was ordered that the benefits of the act of July 7, 1838, should not be withheld from a widow whose husband died after June 7, 1832, and before July 7, 1838. This was, however, restricted by act of April 30, 1844, which provided that no pension should be granted to a widow for the same time her husband received one.

The act of February 2, 1848, gave for life, to such widows as were married before January 1, 1794, the pensions which their husbands, if living at the time of the application, might claim under the act of June 7, 1832, to commence on the 4th day of March, 1848.

The act of July 29, 1848, granted pensions during widowhood to the widows of all persons who served in the army or navy during the revolution, whether as officers, musicians, soldiers, mariners, marines, or Indian spies, in the continental line, State troops, volunteers or militia, at the same rates which their husbands, if living, might claim under existing laws; but no widow, then receiving a pension, nor any widow married after January 1, 1800, could claim such pension.

The restriction as to time of marriage was removed by act of February 3, 1852; as to a second marriage by act of August 5, 1854, and by act of February 28, 1855, the benefits of the act of February 3, 1853, were extended to the widows of those who served in the navy of the United States during the war of the revolution.

To sum up these laws, the result will be found to be, that the widows of all commissioned and non-commissioned officers, musicians, soldiers, and Indian spies of the army, whether belonging to the continental line, State troops, volunteers or militia; and the officers, seamen and marines of the navy, during the revolution, who served at least six months, are entitled to the same pensions, during widowhood, which their husbands might claim under any existing laws, if living. And this claim may be made by a widow, although married a second time, provided she be a widow at the time of making the application.

The act of July 29, 1848, may be considered as most favorable to widows, as this may, in some cases, yield them a greater pension than any other law. It can in no case yield a *less* pension, as the applicant has the entire range of laws granting pensions to those who served in the revolution, from which to select one under which her husband, if living, might claim his pension.

Under the act of April 2, 1862, no further claim for a pension or increase of a pension can be presented by the children or other descendants of revolutionary worthies, when the claim to such pension was not established by the soldier or his widow, before their death. This virtually cuts off all claims on the part of children of such persons; as there remains but the bare possibility that amounts may be due heirs upon pension claims established by their ancestors before death, which have remained unsettled. For the manner of applying for the payment of such sums claimants are referred to the title "ARREARS OF PENSIONS."

SECTION II.

REGULATIONS AND FORMS FOR OBTAINING PENSIONS FOR WIDOWS OF PERSONS WHO SERVED IN THE WAR OF THE REVOLUTION.

ACT OF JULY 4, 1836.

PENSION OFFICE, *July* 9, 1836.

In order to carry into effect the act of Congress of the 4th of July, 1836, entitled "an act granting half-pay to the widows or orphans, where their husbands and fathers have died of wounds received in the military service of the United States, in certain cases and for other purposes," the following rules have been prescribed by the President of the United States, and adopted by the Secretary of War; and they are now published for the information of applicants under that law:

1. Applicants under the first section of the act must produce the best proof the nature of the case will allow as to the service of the deceased officer or soldier, the time when he died, and the complaint of which he died, and the supposed cause of his disease. It must be clearly shown in what company and regiment, or corps, he served, and the grade he held.[1] Such proof must be had, either from the records of the War Department, the muster rolls, the testimony of commissioned officers, or the affidavits of persons of known respectability. From similar sources evidence must be derived as to the period and cause of the death of the officer or soldier.

2. The legality of the marriage, name of the widow, with those of her children who may have been under sixteen years of age at the time of the father's decease,[2] with the State or Territory and county in which she and they reside, should be established. The legality of the marriage may be ascertained by the certificate of the clergyman who joined them in wedlock,[3] or the testimony of respectable persons having knowledge of the fact. The age and number of children may be ascertained by the deposition of the mother, accompanied by the testimony of respectable persons having knowledge of them, or by transcripts from the parish registers duly authen-

[1] The act of May 7, 1846, (page 135), dispenses with this proof where the husband was a pensioner at the time of his death.

[2] This is no longer necessary.

[3] This certificate must be proved by the testimony of witnesses who knew the handwriting of the clergyman, or saw him sign the certificate. It must also appear by proof that the clergyman *was such*, and was authorized to solemnize marriages.

ticated. The widow, at the time of allowing the half-pay, or placing her on the list for it, must show that she has not again married; and must, moreover, repeat this at the time of receiving each and every payment thereof; because, in case of her marrying again, the half-pay to her ceases, and the half-pay for the remainder of the time shall go to the child or children of the decedent. This may be done by the affidavits of respectable persons having knowledge of the case.

3. In cases where there are children, and no widow, their guardian will, of course, act for them and establish their claims as prescribed in the foregoing regulations, and receive their stipends for them.

4. Applicants under the second section of the law will make a declaration before a court of record, setting forth, according to the best of her (or their) knowledge or belief, the names and rank of the field and company officers, the day (if possible) and the month and year when the claimant's husband or father (as the case may be) entered the service, and the time when he left the same; and, if under more than one engagement, the claimant must specify the particular periods, and the rank and names of the officers under whom the service was performed; the town or county and State in which the claimant's husband or father resided when he entered the service; whether he was drafted, was a volunteer, or substitute; the battles, if any, in which he was engaged; the country through which he marched;[1] with such further particulars as may be useful in the investigation of the claim; and, also, if the fact be so, that the claimant has no documentary evidence in support of the claim.

5. The same description of proof as to the relationship of the claimant to the deceased officer or soldier will be required, as the rule under the first section points out.

6. Claimants under the third section of the law must not only produce such proof as the foregoing regulations direct in relation to widows' claims, but they must, in all cases, as an indispensable requisite, show when they were legally married to the deceased officer or soldier on account of whose services the claim is presented, and that the marriage took place before the last term of service of the husband expired.[2] They must also prove that they were never afterwards married.

1 The act of May 7, 1846, (p. 170), dispenses with this proof where the husband was a pensioner at the time of his death.

2 This has been dispensed with by late acts.

7. In a case where the service of the deceased officer or soldier is clearly proved by record or documentary evidence, or the affidavit of a commissioned officer, showing the grade and length of service of the deceased, the particulars in relation to the service are not required to be set forth in the claimant's declaration, except so far as to show that the claimant or claimants is or are the widow or children of the deceased.

8. The claimant must, in every case where there is no record or documentary proof of the revolutionary service of the deceased officer or soldier, produce the testimony of at least one credible witness. Traditionary evidence will be deemed useful in every such case.

9. Applicants unable to appear in court by reason of bodily infirmity, may make their declarations, before required, before a judge or justice of a court of record of the county in which they reside, and the judge or justice will certify that the applicant can not, from bodily infirmity, attend the court.

10. Whenever any official act is required to be done by a judge or justice of a court of record, or by a justice of the peace, the certificate of the Secretary of State or of the Territory, or of the proper clerk of the court of the county, under his seal of office, will be annexed, stating that such a person is a judge or justice of a court of record, or a justice of the peace, and that the signature annexed is his genuine signature.

11. The widows of those who served in the navy, or as Indian spies, will produce proof, as nearly as may be, conformably to the preceding regulations, and authenticated in a similar manner, with such variations as the different nature of the service may require.

12. The form prescribed for claimants under the third section of the act will be observed by every other description of claimants, so far as the same may be applicable to their cases.

The judge or justice who may administer an oath, must, in every instance, certify to the credibility of the affiant.

13. In every case in which the deceased officer or soldier was a pensioner, the fact should be so stated, and the deceased pensioner so described as to enable the Department to refer immediately to the evidence upon which he was pensioned, and thus facilitate the investigation of the claim of his widow or children.

JAMES L. EDWARDS, *Commissioner of Pensions.*

Declaration.

STATE OF —— } ss.
County of —— }

On this —— day of ——, in the year 18—, personally appeared before the —— court, a court of record within and for said county, Mrs. ——, aged —— years; a resident of ——, in the county of ——, and State of ——, who being first duly sworn, according to law, doth, on her oath, in open court,[1] make the following declaration, in order to obtain the benefit of the provision made by the act of Congress, passed July 4, 1836: That she is the widow of —— who was a [*Here set forth the rank the husband held, the regiment, company or vessel, the colonel's and captain's names, the time when the husband entered the service* (*if possible*), *and the time when discharged, and the other particulars required by regulation No.* 4. *But should the husband have been a pensioner at the time of his death, it will be sufficient to say*], who was a ——, in the company commanded by ——, in the regiment of [*Here state whether State troops, volunteers, militia, or regulars*], commanded by Colonel ——, in the war of the revolution, and was, at the time of his death, a pensioner of the United States, under the act of [*date of act*]. She further declares that she was married to the said ——, on the —— day of ——, in the year ——; that her husband, the said ——, died on the —— day of ——, 18—; and that she has remained a widow ever since that period, as will more fully appear by reference to the proofs hereto annexed. [*If there should be no public or private record of the marriage, state the fact here. Should there be no public record, so state. So, also, in case there should be no living witnesses of the marriage.*]

(*Claimant's Signature.*)

Sworn to and subscribed by the said ——, in open court.

[L. S.] In testimony whereof, I hereto set my hand and affix the seal of said —— court, this —— day of ——, 18—.

Clerk of said Court.

Should the declaration be made before a Judge or Clerk, the declaration and the certificate of the Clerk will be altered to correspond to the facts.

Proof of the marriage of the claimant and the person for whose services she claims, must accompany the declaration. The best proof is that furnished by a public re-

---

[1] This may be made before a judge or clerk of a court of record, but not before any other officer. Any proof necessary to be filed with a declaration, may be made before any officer authorized to administer oaths in general.

cord. If there be such record, a copy of the same, certified by the officer having such record in custody, must be procured. The officer, in making the copy, will use no figures, but will write the dates in words. Having made the copy he will attach the following certificate.

I certify that the above is a true copy of the record, with the exception of the date and figures, which are expressed in the record in fair and legible date and figures, as follows :—[*Insert them here as in the record.*]

(*Officer's Signature.*)

Then add the following affidavit:

STATE OF ——, } ss.
County of—— }

—— ——, being sworn, says that he is [*Name his office*] within and for said county ; that by virtue of his office he is custodian of the marriage records of said county ; and that the above is a correct extract taken from said records, with the exception above named, as certified by me.

(*Signature.*)

Sworn to and subscribed before me, this —— day of ——, A.D. 18—.

(*J. P.*
Or other officer authorized to administer oaths generally.)

Then will follow the certificate of the proper officer, under his seal of office, that the person administering the oath is a Justice of the Peace, or other officer authorized to administer such oath.

In case there should be no public record of the marriage, but a private record, the book containing such private record, or the leaves upon which the same appears, must be sent to the Pension Office. Proof that it is a private, family record, must also be forwarded. This should consist of the affidavit of the person in whose custody the record is, or of at least two persons who have no interest in the claim, who can state from their own knowledge, that it is a family record, and that they know the entries to have been made at the time of or soon after the occurrence of the transaction noted; or that, from long acquaintance with the family, and knowledge of the record, they believe the entries to have been made at the time of or soon after the events recorded took place. They should also state in whose handwriting the entries appear to have been made.

This affidavit may be made before any officer authorized to administer oaths; whose official character must be certified, as in other cases.

The family record may be sent by mail, directed to the Commissioner of Pensions. It will be returned after it has been examined by the Commissioner.

Should there be no private record of the marriage, the next best proof will be the testimony of at least two witnesses who were present at the marriage, and can so state under oath, detailing particulars of time, place, by whom ceremony performed, etc.

But if there be neither public nor private record of the marriage, and no witnesses living (or if living, should their place of residence be unknown) who were present at the marriage, an affidavit stating the facts must be made by the claimant (or she may include them in her declaration), and then proof of cohabitation and reputation of marriage will be admitted. The witnesses to the reputation of marriage must state that they were acquainted with the claimant and her husband, in the lifetime of the latter; that they knew them for many years to live and cohabit together as man and wife; that they were recognized as married persons by all their friends and acquaintances; and that they never heard the fact of their marriage called in question.

The widowhood of the claimant must also be proved.

Proof of cohabitation, death of husband, and widowhood, may be embodied in an affidavit as follows:

STATE OF ——, } *ss.*
County of——. }

On this —— day of ——, A.D. 18—, before me, a justice of the peace within and for the county and State aforesaid, personally came —— and ——, residents of said county, who being by me duly sworn, depose and say that they are, and for at least —— years have been, well acquainted with Mrs. ——, who has made application to be placed on the pension rolls of the United States. That they were also acquainted with ——, her late husband, and knew him for at least —— years previous to his death. That the said —— and ——, to the personal knowledge of deponents, lived and cohabited together as husband and wife, and were so recognized and acknowledged for many years before the death of the husband; and their marriage was never questioned, to the knowledge of deponents. That the said —— died on the —— day of ——, A.D. 18—, as these deponents well know, having been present at his funeral [*or* having seen his corpse, after death]. That the said —— has remained a widow ever since the death of her said husband, within the personal knowledge of deponents. [*In case of the second marriage of the widow, and death of her second husband, these facts must also be shown.*]

Deponents say that they are disinterested witnesses.

(*Signatures of Witnesses.*)

Sworn to and subscribed before me, the day and year aforesaid. And I certify that I know the said —— and —— to be credible and disinterested witnesses; and that I have no interest in the claim of —— for a pension.

Justice of the Peace,
[*or other officer authorized to administer oaths.*]

Here must follow the certificate of the proper officer, under his seal of office, to the official character of the Justice or other officer administering the oath.

For FORMS and REGULATIONS relating to POWERS OF ATTORNEY in pension cases, *see* Chapter XVI.

ACT OF MARCH 3, 1837.

PENSION OFFICE, *March* 15, 1837.

In a case where the claimant has married after the decease of the husband for whose services she may claim the pension, it can not, under the explanatory act of March 3, 1837, be withheld on account of her last marriage, provided she was a widow on the 4th July, 1836. The latter part of the 6th rule of the regulations of the 9th July, 1836, is not, of course, applicable to such a case. The facts in relation to the marriage of the last husband, and his death, should be fully set forth in the claimant's declaration. The following is the form of the declaration in such a case:

Declaration in order to obtain the Benefits of the third Section of the Act of 4th July, 1836, and of the first Section of the Act of 3d March, 1837.

STATE OF ——}
County of ——} *ss.*

On this —— day of ——, personally appeared before [*court, judge or clerk*, ——, a resident of ——, in the county of —— and State of ——, aged —— years, who, being first duly sworn according to law, doth, on her oath, make the following declaration in order to obtain the benefit of the provision made by the act of Congress passed July 4, 1836, and the act explanatory of said act passed March 3, 1837: That she was married to ——, who was [*Here insert the particulars respecting the service of the deceased husband for whose services she may claim a pension, as directed in rule No. 4, of the foregoing regulations of July 9, 1836, page* 143].

She further declares, that she was married to the said —— on the —— day of ——, in the year seventeen hundred and ——; that her husband, the aforesaid ——, died on the —— day of ——; that she was afterwards married to ——, who died on the —— day of ——; and that she was a widow on the 4th of July, 1836, and still remains a widow, as will more fully appear by reference to the proof hereto annexed.

Sworn and subscribed, on the day and year above written, before ——

The declaration, page 146, for applications under the act of July, 1836, may be used in cases under the act of March, 1837, by making a few slight changes which will be apparent at a glance.

The same regulations as are prescribed to be observed in making applications under the act of July 4, 1836, are applicable to the act of March 3, 1837, and the same proof of marriage, death and widowhood, must be made under the latter as under the former act.

ACT OF JULY 7, 1838.

PENSION OFFICE, July 17, 1838.

The following rules, prescribed by the President of the United States, and adopted by the Secretary of War, in order to carry into effect the act of Congress of the 7th July, 1838, entitled "an act granting half-pay and pensions to certain widows," are published for the information of applicants under that law:

1. Applicants must produce the best proof the nature of the case will allow, as to the service of the deceased officer or soldier, and the time when he died. It must be clearly shown in what troop or company, and regiment or corps, he served, and the grade he held. Proof as to service must be had, either from the records of the War Department, the muster rolls, the testimony of commissioned officers, or the affidavits of persons of known respectability. Every applicant will make a declaration, according to the subjoined form, before a Court of Record,[1] setting forth, according to the best of her knowledge or belief, the name and rank of the person on account of whose service the claim is presented; the day, month and year (if possible), when he entered the service, and the time when he left the same; and, if under more than one engagment, the claimant must specify the particular periods, and the rank and name of the officers under whom the service was performed; the town or county and State, in which he resided when he entered the service; whether he was drafted, was a volunteer, or a substitute; the battles, if any, in which he was engaged; the country through which he marched, with such further particulars as may be useful in the investigation of the claim; and also, if the fact be so, that the claimant has no documentary evidence in support of the claim. From the best sources of information evidence must be derived as to the period of the death of the officer or soldier.[2]

2. The legality of the marriage, and the time when it took place, must be clearly established; and it must also be shown that the widow was never afterwards married. Record proof, as to the marriage, is always required whenever it can be obtained. In a case where the town, county, parish or family records afford no proof as to the period when the marriage took place, the fact must be estab-

1 The declaration of the widow who claims, must be made, in all cases, in open court, unless she is prevented by bodily infirmity from appearing before court. [This regulation, which was established after the passage of the act, has since then been so far relaxed as to allow the declaration to be made before the judge or clerk of a court of record.]

2 It must, in all cases, be shown in what year the husband died. The testimony on this point must be positive, and the language must be free from all ambiguity.

lished by the testimony of one or more respectable persons, whose credibility must be certified by the officer who may administer the oath. And, in order to prevent any mistake or improper use that may be made of the affidavit of an officer who may have the custody of records, from which he may make transcripts of the record in relation to a marriage, the officer who may give his affidavit will, instead of copying the figures contained in the record, certify "that it is a true copy of the record, with the exception of the date, which is expressed on the record in fair legible figures, as follows:" [Here copy the day, month, and year, in letters and figures, in exact conformity with the original.] Then let him add the following words:

"I, ——, above named, depose and say, that I hold the office of —— in the county, town, and State aforesaid, and that the above is a true extract from the records of said —— with the exception above-named, as certified by me. *Clerk of the* ——

(*or* Rector, *or* Pastor, *as the case may be.*)

Sworn before me,

——, *Justice of the Peace.*"

And then will follow the certificate of the proper officer, under his seal of office, as to the official character and signature of the magistrate who may administer the oath. Where no record proof exists, other than the family record, the original record must be produced and sworn to by the person in whose possession it has been kept. [1]

3. In a case where the service of the deceased officer or soldier is clearly proved by record or documentary evidence, or the affidavit of a commissioned officer, showing the grade and length of service of the deceased, the particulars in relation to the service are not required to be set forth in the claimant's declaration; but she must swear, in positive terms, that she is the widow of the person whose service is proved. And no claim whatever can be sustained without positive proof of service.

4. In every case in which the deceased officer or soldier was a pensioner, the fact should be so stated, and the deceased pensioner

1 The family record must be sent to the Pension Office, if there be no other record, accompanied by the oath of the person in whose possession it has remained. The person who may swear to the genuineness of the record should give the name of the person in whose handwriting the record was made.

so described as to enable the Department to refer immediately to the evidence upon which he was pensioned, and thus facilitate the investigation of the claim of the widow.

5. Applicants unable to appear in Court, by reason of bodily infirmity, may make the declaration before required before a Judge or Justice[1] [or Clerk or Prothonotary] of a Court of Record in the county in which the applicant resides, and the Judge or Justice will certify that the applicant can not, from bodily infirmity, attend the Court.

6. Whenever any official act is required to be done by a Judge or Justice of a Court of Record, or by a Justice of the Peace, the certificate of the Secretary of the State or Territory, or of the proper officer or Clerk of the Court or county, under his seal of office, will be annexed, stating that such a person is a Judge, or a Justice of the Peace, and that the signature annexed is his genuine signature.

7. The widows of those who served in the navy, or as Indian spies, will produce proof, as nearly as may be, conformably to the preceding regulations, and authenticated in a similar manner, with such variations as the different nature of the service may require.

J. L. EDWARDS, *Commissioner of Pensions.*

Declaration.

STATE OF —— }
County of —— } *ss.*

On this —— day of ——, A. D. 18—, before the —— court [*or* judge, *or* clerk of the —— court] a court of record within and for said county, personally appeared ——, a resident of said county, aged —— years, who being first duly sworn according to law, doth on her oath make the following declaration, in order to obtain the benefit of the provision made by the act of Congress, passed July 7, 1838, entitled "an act granting half-pay and pensions to certain widows:" That she is the widow of —— who was a [*Here state the rank of the husband, the captain of the company and colonel of the regiment or name of the vessel and her commander, in which he served, the time when he entered the service, time when he was discharged, etc., as directed by rule No.* 1 *of the regulations. In case her husband was a pensioner at the time of his death it will be sufficient to say*]: That she is the widow of —— who was a —— in the company of [regulars, State troops, volunteers *or* militia], commanded by Captain —— in the regiment commanded by Colonel ——, in the war of the revolution, who was, at the time of his death a pensioner of the United States, under the act of ——.

[1] But not a justice of the peace. Evidence accompanying the declaration may be taken before a justice of the peace.

She further declares that she was married to the said—— on the —— day of ——, in the year 18—; that her husband, the aforesaid ——, died on the —— day of ——, A. D. 18—. [*If married the second time the claimant should so state, giving the date of such second marriage, and death of second husband*], and that since his death she has remained unmarried, and is now a widow. (*Claimant's Signature.*)

For further forms and regulations applicable to claims under this act, see Regulations and Forms, act of July 4, 1836, page 143.

ACTS OF MARCH 3, 1843, AND JUNE 7, 1844.

As these acts grant no original pensions, but merely extend the operation of the act of July 7, 1838, and are, practically, obsolete, it is not deemed necessary to insert here forms and instructions applicable to them.

ACT OF JULY 29, 1848.

The rules of evidence and forms prescribed in cases arising under the act of July 29, 1848, are identical with those provided for in cases under the act of July 7, 1838, to which applicants are referred, page 150.

ACTS OF FEBRUARY 3, 1853, AND FEBRUARY 28, 1855.

PENSION OFFICE, *March* 25, 1853.

The following regulations, approved by the Secretary of the Interior, have been adopted for carrying into effect the provisions of the act of February 3, 1853, entitled "an act to continue half-pay to certain widows and orphans."

[The first and second parts of these regulations relate to the first section of the act, which has no reference to revolutionary pensions.]

3. Under the provisions of the second section, the widows of all officers non-commissioned officers, musicians and privates of the revolutionary army, who were married subsequent to January, A.D. 1800, are entitled to a pension in the same manner as those who were married before that date.

In applications for the benefits of these provisions, the party must prove the service of the officer or soldier in whose right she claims; her marriage with such officer and soldier, and his death.

In case such officer or soldier has received a pension in his lifetime, a reference to the evidence filed in his application will be sufficient to prove the service.

Every applicant will make a declaration according to the form hereto appended, before a Court of Record [or Judge or Clerk of such Court], setting forth, according to the best of her knowledge and belief, the name and rank of the person on account of whose service the claim is asserted; the time when he entered and left the service; the names and rank of the officers under whom the service was performed; the place in which he resided when he entered the service; the time and place of his death; that she was lawfully joined in marriage with said officer or soldier, and that she is now a widow.

In case such officer or soldier was a pensioner, that fact should also be stated, as well as the act under which he was pensioned, and the agency at which he was paid.

If the applicant is unable to appear in Court, by reason of bodily infirmity, she may make the declaration before a Judge or Justice [or Clerk] of a Court of Record of the county in which she resides, and the Judge or Justice [or Clerk] will certify that the applicant, from bodily infirmity, is unable to attend Court.

The official character of the magistrate or other person before whom any papers are verified, should be authenticated in the usual form.

L. P. Waldo, *Commissioner of Pensions.*

Declaration: Act of February 3, 1853. (*Army.*)

State of —— } ss.
County of —— }

On this —— day of ——, A.D., 18—, before the —— court [*or* before —— judge, *or* —— clerk, of the —— court], a court of record, within and for the county and State aforesaid, personally appeared ——, a resident of said county, aged —— years, who being first sworn, according to law, doth, on her oath, make the following declaration in order to obtain the benefits of the provision made by the act of Congress passed on the third day of February 1853, granting pensions to the widows of persons who served during the revolutionary war; that she is the widow of —— who was a [*Here insert the rank the husband held in the army, and give the details of his service according to the requirements of the above regulations. If the husband was a pensioner at the time of his death, that fact must be noted, and the particulars of his service need not, in that case, be so specifically given*].

She further declares that she was married to the said ——, on the —— day of ——, A.D., 18—; that her said husband died on the —— day of ——, A.D., 18— [*if she was married a second time, state the fact, with the date of her second marriage, and of the death of her second husband*]: and that she is now a widow.

She hereby appoints ——, her attorney, with power of substitution, to prosecute this her claim for a pension, to receive the certificate when issued, and to do all other acts necessary in order to effect the object of his appointment.[1]

(*Declarant's Signature.*)

Sworn to and subscribed by said ——, in open court (*or* before me —— judge, *or* —— clerk of the —— court within and for the county of —— and State of ——) the day and year aforesaid.

[L. S.] Witness my hand, and the seal of said court.

(*Clerk of said Court*).

Should the oath be administered by a Judge, the certificate of the Clerk of the Court, under its seal, to his official character, must be attached.

For further forms pertaining to applications for pensions under the act of February 3, 1853, see Forms and Regulations, Act of July 4, 1836, page 146, and July 7, 1838, page 150. It may be well also, to consult the forms of declarations under these acts, before using the one above given, as useful hints may thus be obtained.

Declaration under Act of February 28, 1855. (*Naval.*)

STATE OF ——
County of —— } *ss.*

On this —— day of ——18—, before the —— court, [*or* before me ——, judge, *or* clerk of the —— court], a court of record, within and for the county aforesaid, personally appeared ——, a resident of said county, aged —— years, who being first duly sworn according to law, doth, on her oath, make the following declaration in order to obtain the benefits of the provision made by the act of Congress passed on the 25th February, 1855, granting pensions to widows of persons who served in the navy of the United States during the revolutionary war; that she is the widow of —— who was a [*Here state the rank of the husband; the vessel he served in, and*

[1] Better omit this, and execute a separate power.

the name of her commander; the time of entering the service, and time of discharge. If the husband was a pensioner at the time of his death, state the fact, and mention the act under which, and the place where he was paid. The particulars of service need not be so minutely detailed in case the husband was a pensioner].

She further declares that she was married to the said ——, on the —— day of ——, A. D., 18—, that her said husband died on the —— day of ——, A. D., 18— [*if she was married a second time, state the fact, with the date of her second marriage, and of the death of her second husband*]; and that she is now a widow.

She hereby appoints ——, her attorney, with power of substitution, to prosecute this her claim for a pension, to receive the certificate when issued, and to do all other acts necessary in order to effect the object of his appointment.

(*Declarant's Signature.*)

Applicants will refer to the forms pertaining to the acts of July 4, 1836, page 146, and July 7, 1838, page 150, for additional forms applicable to the act of February, 1855, and also to obtain hints and suggestions which may be serviceable in preparing papers under the act last mentioned.

CHAPTER IX.

GRATUITOUS PENSIONS.

SECTION I.

WIDOWS AND ORPHANS—REGULARS, SINCE REVOLUTION.

THE first section of "an act in addition to the 'act making further and more effectual provision for the protection of the frontiers of the United States,'" approved June 7, 1794,[1] provides:

Be it enacted by the Senate and House of Representatives of the United States of America in Congress assembled, That if any commissioned officer in the troops of the United States shall, while in the service of the United States, die, by reason of wounds received in actual service of the United States, and shall leave a widow, or, if no widow, shall leave a child or children under age, such widow, or, if no widow, such child or children shall be entitled to and receive the half of the monthly pay to which the deceased was entitled at the time of his death, for and during the term of five years. And in case of the death or intermarriage of such widow, before the expiration of the said term of five years, the half-pay for the remainder of the term shall go to the child or children of such deceased officer, while under the age of sixteen years; and, in like manner, the allowance to the child or children of such deceased, where there is no widow, shall be paid no longer than while there is a child or children under the age aforesaid: *Provided*, That no greater sum shall be allowed, in any case, to the widow or to the child or children of any officer, than the full pay of a lieutenant-colonel.

These provisions are still in force, if any widows of commissioned officers who died or were killed in the line of duty, while serving under the act to which the above

1 U. S. Statutes at Large, vol. i, 390.

act is an addition, remain, whose claims are unadjusted. In case any widows died, without having married again, and without claiming the half-pay to which they were entitled under the act, their children, whether over or under sixteen years of age, may claim the amounts to which their mothers were entitled when living.[1] These remarks are also applicable to some of the acts which follow.

An act, approved March 16, 1802, "fixing the military peace establishment of the United States,"[2] provides, among other things:

SEC. 15. *And be it further enacted*, That if any commissioned officer in the military peace establishment of the United States[3] shall, while in the service of the United States, die, by reason of any wound received in actual service of the United States, and leave a widow, or, if no widow, a child or children under sixteen years of age, such widow, or, if no widow, such child or children shall be entitled to and receive half the monthly pay to which the deceased was entitled at the time of his death, for and during the term of five years. But in the case of the death or intermarriage of such widow before the expiration of the said five years, the half-pay for the remainder of the time shall go to the child or children of such deceased officer: *Provided, always*, That such half-pay shall cease on the decease of such child or children.

These benefits are restricted to the widows and orphans of deceased commissioned officers.

By an act of April 12, 1808, "to raise, for a limited time, an additional military force,"[4] five regiments of

---

[1] For method of obtaining such unclaimed pensions, see title "ARREARS OF PENSIONS."

[2] U. S. Statutes at Large, vol. ii, 132.

[3] A paymaster is a commissioned officer within the meaning of this act, and his widow is entitled to a pension under the fifteenth section. *Attorney-General Grundy, March* 22, 1839.

[4] U. S. Statutes at Large, vol. ii, 481.

infantry, one regiment of riflemen, one regiment of light artillery, and one regiment of light dragoons were added to the military establishment; and the widows and children of those who enlisted under the act were provided for as follows:

SEC. 5. *Be it further enacted*, That . . . and that the provisions of the act entitled "an act fixing the military peace establishment of the United States," relative to the widow, child or children of any commissioned officer who shall die, while in the service of the United States, by reason of any wound received in actual service of the United States, . . . shall be in force, and be applied to all matters, persons and things within the intent and meaning of this act, in the same manner as if they were inserted at large in the same.

These provisions are also limited to the widows and orphans of commissioned officers who died in the service.

As preparatory to the struggle with Great Britain, which had become inevitable, Congress passed an act, on the 11th day of January, 1812, "to raise an additional military force,"[1] by which ten regiments of infantry, two regiments of artillery, and one regiment of light dragoons (to be enlisted for five years, unless sooner discharged) were added to the army. Provision was made by this act for the widows of such commissioned officers of the regular army as might, *while in the service*, die of wounds received, as follows:

SEC. 15. *And be it further enacted*, That if any commissioned officer[2] in the military establishment of the United States shall, while in the service of the United States, die, by reason of any wound received in the actual service of the United States, and leave a widow, or, if no widow, a child or children under sixteen years of age, such widow, or, if no widow, such child or children shall be

1 U. S. Statutes at Large, vol. ii, 671.

2 A paymaster is a commissioned officer. *Attorney-General Grundy, March* 22, 1839.

entitled to and receive half the monthly pay to which the deceased was entitled at the time of his death, for and during the term of five years. But in the case of the death or intermarriage of such widow before the expiration of the said term of five yerrs,[1] the half-pay for the remainder of the time shall go to the child or children of such deceased officer: *Provided, always,* That such half-pay shall cease on the decease of such child or children.

An act "in addition" to the last-named act, approved January 29, 1813,[2] authorizes the raising of twenty additional regiments of infantry, and provides:

SEC. 11. *And be it further enacted,* That if any commissioned officer shall, while in the service of the United States, die, by reason of any wound received in actual service of the United States, and leave a widow, or, if no widow, a child or children under sixteen years of age, such widow, or, if no widow, such child or children shall be entitled to and receive half the monthly pay to which the deceased was entitled at the time of his death, for and during the term of five years. But in case of the death or intermarriage of such widow before the expiration of the said term of five years, the half-pay for the remainder of the time shall go to the child or children of such deceased officer: *Provided,* That such half-pay shall cease on the decease of such child or children.

At the conclusion of the war of 1812, by an act entitled "an act fixing the military peace establishment of the United States," approved March 3, 1815,[3] the army was reduced to a peace footing. After prescribing the details of the new organization, the act proceeds:

SEC. 7. *And be it further enacted,* That the several corps authorized by this act shall be subject to the rules and articles of war, be recruited in the same manner and with the same limitations, and that officers, non-commissioned officers, musicians and privates shall

1 The right of a widow to a pension is a vested right. *Attorney-General Butler, January* 17, 1837.

2 U. S. Statutes at Large, vol. ii, 794.

3 *Ibid,* vol. iii, 224.

be entitled to the same provision for wounds and disabilities, the same provision for widows and children, and the same benefits and allowances, in every respect, not inconsistent with the provisions of this act, as are authorized by the act of sixteenth March, one thousand eight hundred and two, entitled "an act fixing the military peace establishment of the United States," and the act of the twelfth April, one thousand eight hundred and eight, entitled "an act to raise, for a limited time, an additional military force;" and that the bounty to the recruit and compensation to the recruiting officer shall be the same as are allowed and paid by the aforesaid act of the twelfth of April, one thousand eight hundred and eight.

Thus far the legislation of Congress, in favor of the widows of persons who served in the regular army, was confined to the widows of commissioned officers; but an act of April 16, 1816, entitled "an act making further provision for military services during the late war, and for other purposes,"[1] dispensed with this distinction, and extended the bounty of the nation to the widows of *others* who had faithfully served the country in "the tented field." This act made the following provision:

Be it enacted by the Senate and House of Representatives of the United States of America in Congress assembled, That when any officer or private soldier of the militia, including rangers, sea-fencibles and volunteers, or any non-commissioned officer, musician or private, enlisted for either of the terms of one year or eighteen months, or any commissioned officer of the regular army, shall have died while in the service of the United States, during the late war, or in returning to his place of residence, after being mustered out of service, or who shall have died at any time thereafter, in consequence of wounds received while in the service, and shall have left a widow, or if no widow, a child or children under sixteen years of age, such widow, or if no widow, such child or children shall be entitled to receive half the monthly pay to which the deceased was entitled at the time of his death, for and during the term of five years; and in case of death or intermarriage of such widow before

[1] U. S. Statutes at Large, vol. iii, 285.

the expiration of said five years, the half pay for the remainder of the time shall go to the child or children of said decedent;[1] *Provided always*, That the Secretary of War shall adopt such forms of evidence under this act as the President may prescribe; . . .

SEC. 2. *And be it further enacted*, That when any non-commissioned officer, musician or private soldier, of the regular army of the United States, shall have been killed in battle, or have died of wounds or disease, while in the service of the United States, during the late war, and have left a child or children under sixteen years of age,[2] it shall be lawful for the guardian of such child or children, within one year from the passage of this act,[3] to relinquish the bounty land to which such non-commissioned officer, musician or private soldier, had he survived the war, would have been entitled; and, in lieu thereof, to receive half the monthly pay to which such deceased person was entitled at the time of his death, for and during the term of five years, to be computed from and after the seventeenth day of February, one thousand eight hundred and fifteen; the payment thereof to be made when and where other military pensions are or shall be paid; and when a warrant for the military bounty land aforesaid shall have been issued to or for the use of the child or children of any such deceased non-commissioned officer, musician or private soldier, such child or children, or either of them, being under sixteen years of age, it shall be lawful for the guardian of such minor or minors, to surrender and deliver such warrant into the office for the Department of War, within one year from the passing of this act; of which surrender and delivery the Secretary of that Department shall give notice to the Secretary of the Treasury, who shall thereupon give the requisite orders for the payment of the half-pay hereby provided for.[4]

1 Under the act of March 3, 1817, which relates back to the act of April 16, 1816, it was decided by Secretary Stuart (December 1, 1851), that the arrears of pension due the widow at her death, are payable to the children of the widow, legitimate or illegitimate.

2 Under the second section of the act of April 16, 1816, minor children must have been under sixteen years of age at the time when the father died. *Attorney-General Rush, December* 24, 1816.

3 Extended two years by act of March 3, 1817, page 164, and three additional years by act of March 3, 1819. See the act, page 165.

4 This section was amended in several respects by act of March 3, 1817, which see, page 164.

An act to amend the foregoing act, approved March 3, 1817,[1] contains the following provisions:

Be it enacted by the Senate and House of Representatives of the United States of America in Congress assembled, That the widows and children of soldiers, of the militia, the volunteers, the rangers, and the sea-fencibles, who served during the late war, and for whom half-pay for five years was provided, by an act passed on the sixteenth day of April, one thousand eight hundred and sixteen, entitled "an act making further provision for military service during the late war, and for other purposes," shall be placed on an equality as to their annual allowance; that is to say: such widows, and in case of no widow such children, as may be embraced in the before-recited act, shall be entitled to receive (as the half-pay to which they are entitled), at the rate of forty-eight dollars per annum, and no more; and the widows and children aforesaid, of the officers of the different corps aforesaid, shall be entitled to the half-pay of the officers of the infantry.

SEC. 3. *And be it further enacted*, That the further time of two years shall be allowed to the guardians of the minor children of deceased soldiers to relinquish their claims to bounty lands for five years' half-pay, according to the second section of the above-recited act, to which this is a supplement, passed the sixteenth day of April, one thousand eight hundred and sixteen.

SEC. 4. *And be it further enacted*, That the widows and children of the non-commissioned officers of the rangers shall be placed on the same footing as to half-pay for five years, with the widows and children of the infantry.

SEC. 5. *And be it further enacted*, That the provisions of the second section of the act to which this is a supplement shall be, and the same are hereby, extended to all cases where either of the children therein mentioned shall have been under sixteen years of age at the time of the father's decease: *Provided*, The guardian of such minor children shall, in addition to the relinquishment by said act required, file, in the office of the Department of War, evidence of the assent of all the other heirs, if any there be, of said deceased soldier, or of their guardians, to such relinquishment.

SEC. 6. *And be it further enacted*, That in all cases where the child

[1] U. S. Statutes at Large, vol. iii, 394.

or children of a regular soldier, deceased, have the right, under the laws of the United States, to relinquish their bounty in land for five years' half-pay, the said child or children shall be entitled to the same amount as is given by the act to the widows of the militia soldiers who died in the service during the late war, viz.: four dollars per month.

The second section of the act of April 16, 1816, was further amended by an act approved March 3, 1819, entitled "an act concerning the allowance of pensions upon a relinquishment of bounty lands.[1] This act is as follows:

Be it enacted by the Senate and House of Representatives of the United States of America in Congress assembled, That the second section of the act making further provision for military services during the late war, and for other purposes, approved April sixteenth, one thousand eight hundred and sixteen, and so much of the act to amend the same, approved March third, one thousand eight hundred and seventeen, as relates to the subject of that section, shall be continued in force for the term of three years from and after the passing of this act: *Provided, nevertheless*, That no pension shall be granted under said acts, after the sixteenth day of April, next, unless at the time of relinquishing the bounty land, in manner therein described, the children, for whose benefit the same may be granted, or one of them, shall be under sixteen years of age: *And provided, also*, That the pensions shall commence at the date of the relinquishments respectively.

"An act for the more perfect defense of the frontiers," approved March 2, 1833,[2] authorizes the enlistment of a regiment of dragoons, and provides:

SEC. 3. *And be it further enacted*, That the said regiment of dragoons shall be liable to serve on horse or foot, as the President may direct; shall be subject to the rules and articles of war, be recruited in the same manner, and with the same limitations; that the officers, non-commissioned officers, musicians, farriers and privates

1 U. S. Statutes at Large, vol. iii, 521.

2 *Ibid*, vol. iv, 652.

shall be entitled to the same provisions for wounds and disabilities, the same provisions for widows and children, and the same allowances and benefits, in every respect, as are allowed the other troops constituting the present military peace establishment.

An act approved July 4, 1836, granting pensions to the widows and children of rangers and others, will be found more fully noticed under "WIDOWS AND ORPHANS—VOLUNTEERS AND MILITIA," Chapter X, Section I, page 202.

A proviso to a pension appropriation act of April 30, 1844,[1] directs that "no pension shall hereafter be granted to a widow for the same time that her husband received one."[2]

A rule of evidence in applications by widows for pensions, is established by the second section of "an act making appropriations for the payment of revolutionary and other pensions of the United States for the year ending the thirtieth of June, one thousand eight hundred and forty-seven, and for other purposes," approved May 7, 1846,[3] as follows:

SEC. 2. *And be it further enacted*, That no widow entitled to a pension under existing laws, and claiming a pension, whose husband was drawing a pension at the time of his decease, shall be required, in any such case, to furnish any further evidence that said husband was entitled to a pension, nor shall any evidence, in any case, be required to entitle the widow to a pension, when the evidence is in the archives of the government, other than such proof as would be sufficient to establish the marriage between the applicant and the deceased pensioner in civil personal actions in a court of justice.

By an act of May 19, 1846,[4] a regiment of mounted

---

1 U. S. Statutes at Large, vol. v, 656.

2 This applies to applications before and after the passage of the act. *Secretary Wilkins, May* 1, 1844.

3 U. S. Statutes at Large, vol. ix, 6.

4 *Ibid*, vol. ix, 13.

riflemen was added to the regular army, for service at military stations on the route to Oregon. Section three of this act provides:

SEC. 3. *And be it further enacted*, That the said regiment of riflemen shall be subject to the rules and articles of war, and shall be recruited in the same manner as other troops in the service of the United States, and with the same conditions and limitations; and the officers, non-commissioned officers, musicians, privates, blacksmiths and farriers, shall be entitled to the same provisions for wounds and disabilities, and the same provisions for widows and children, and the same allowances and benefits in every respect, as are allowed to other troops composing the army of the United States.

An act approved July 21, 1848, entitled "an act amending an act, entitled 'an act granting half-pay to widows or orphans, when their husbands and fathers have died of wounds received in the military service of the United States,' in case of deceased officers and soldiers of the militia and volunteers, passed July fourth, eighteen hundred and thirty-six,"[1] extends the benefits of the first section of the act of July 4, 1836, to the widows and orphans of officers and soldiers who died or were killed, in the war with Mexico. This act is as follows:

Be it enacted by the Senate and House of Representatives of the United States of America in Congress assembled, That the provisions of the first section of the act entitled "an act granting half-pay to the widows or orphans, where their husbands and fathers have died of wounds received in the military service of the United States, in certain cases, and for other purposes," approved July fourth, eighteen hundred and thirty-six,[2] shall be applicable to all widows and orphans of officers, musicians and soldiers of the army of the United States, who were in the army of the United States on the

[1] U. S. Statutes at Large, vol. ix, 249.

[2] This act will be found at large, page 129. The first section with notes, will also be found on page 100.

first day of March, eighteen hundred and forty-six; or at any subsequent period during the present war between the United States and Mexico.

SEC. 2. *And be it further enacted*, That all widows and orphans of officers, non-commissioned officers, musicians and privates, whether of the regular army or of volunteers, who have died since the first day of April, one thousand eight hundred and forty-six, or who may die during the war with Mexico, from wounds received, or from disease contracted, while in the line of duty,[1] shall be entitled to the same rate of pension as is provided for in the first section of the before-mentioned act, under like limitations and restrictions:[2] *Provided*, Said death has occurred or may hereafter occur, while said officers, non-commissioned officers, musicians or privates, were in the service of the United States, and in the line of duty; or while returning to their usual places of residence in the United States, after having received a discharge upon a surgeon's certificate of disability incurred from wounds received, or disease contracted, while in the line of duty, or while on their march to join the army in Mexico: *And provided further*, That this act shall not be applicable to the widows and orphans of such officers, non-commissioned officers, musicians or privates, who have not served in Mexico, or at posts or stations on the borders of Mexico, except where such officers, non-commissioned officers, musicians or privates, have died while on their march to join the army in Mexico.

SEC. 3. *And be it further enacted*, That all pensions under this act shall be granted under such rules, regulations, restrictions and limitations as the Secretary of War, with the approbation of the President of the United States may prescribe..

---

[1] Death occasioned by intemperance will not entitle widow to pension. *Decision of Secretary Stuart, October* 10, 1850.

[2] A widow pensioner under the act of July 21, 1848, is entitled to her pension up to the date of her death or intermarriage, if either occur within the five years for which the pension runs; and for the remainder of the time, if any, the pension inures to the child or children under sixteen years of age. *Regulations of Second Comptroller*. The acts of February 3, 1853, and June 3, 1858, confirm this ruling.

The five years' half-pay provided by this act was continued for an additional five years by act of February 3, 1853, (p. 170), and for life, by act of 1858, (page 172.)

By an act of February 22, 1849,[1] the second section of the foregoing act was construed to "embrace all widows and orphans of officers, non-commissioned officers, musicians and privates, whether of the regular army or of volunteers, who have received an honorable discharge, or who remained to the date of their death in the military service of the United States, and who have died since their return to their usual places of residence, of wounds received or from disease contracted while in the line of duty, subject to such rules, regulations and restrictions as the Secretary of War, by the third section of said act, is authorized to impose."[2]

And a "joint resolution relative to evidence in applications for pensions by widows of deceased soldiers under the act of July twenty-first, eighteen hundred and forty-eight," passed March 3, 1849,[3] prescribes:

Resolved by the Senate and House of Representatives of the United States of America in Congress assembled, That in all applications for pensions by the widows of deceased soldiers under the act of July twenty-first, eighteen hundred and forty-eight, the returns on the rolls of the disease of which the soldier died, and the opinion of the surgeon-general founded thereon, that from the nature of the disease it was contracted while the soldier was in the line of his duty, shall be considered satisfactory evidence thereof, without the proof now required at the Pension Office; and that it shall be the duty of the Commissioner of Pensions in all cases of application for pensions under said act, to apply to the proper officers for said evidence, without requiring the applicant to furnish the same.

---

1 U. S. Statutes at Large, vol. ix, 347.

2 By act of February 3, 1853, (page 170), the provisions of this second section were construed to embrace the widows of officers and soldiers of the war of 1812, and the Indian wars since 1790.

3 U. S. Statutes at Large, vol. ix, 418.

An additional resolution, giving construction to the act of July 21, 1848, was passed September 28, 1850,[1] is as follows:

Resolved by the Senate and House of Representatives of the United States of America in Congress assembled, That the provisions of the second section of the act entitled "an act granting half-pay to widows or orphans when their husbands and fathers have died of wounds received in the military service of the United States," approved July twenty-one, eighteen hundred and forty-eight, extended by the act of February twenty-two, eighteen hundred and forty-nine, shall be construed to embrace the widows and orphans of all persons designated therein, who died while in actual service in the late war with Mexico, or in going to or returning from the same; and also to the widows and orphans of all such pensioners, as having been honorably discharged, or having resigned, shall have died after the passage of said last-mentioned act, or who may hereafter die, from wounds received, or from disease contracted while in said service: ***Provided,*** That the army rolls showing the death of any of said persons in the army shall be sufficient evidence to establish that fact.

The half-pay allowed widows and orphans under the acts of July 21, 1848, and February 22, 1849, was continued five years by an act of February 3, 1853,[2] which is as follows:

AN ACT *to continue Haf-pay to certain Widows and Orphans.*

Be it enacted by the Senate and House of Representatives of the United States of America in Congress assembled, That all widows and orphans who were granted and allowed five years' half-pay by the provisions of the act approved the twenty-first day of July, one thousand eight hundred and forty-eight, entitled "an act amending the act granting half-pay to widows or orphans, where their husbands or fathers have died of wounds received in the military service of the United States, in case of deceased officers and soldiers of the militia and volunteers,

[1] U. S. Statutes at Large, vol. ix, 564.

[2] *Ibid,* vol. x, 154.

passed July fourth, one thousand eight hundred and thirty-six," or an act approved the twenty-second day of February, one thousand eight hundred and forty-nine, entitled "an act granting five years' half-pay, to certain widows and orphans of officers, non-commissioned officers, musicians and privates, both regulars and volunteers," be, and they are hereby granted a continuance of said half-pay,[1] under like limitations and restrictions, for a further period of five years, to commence at the expiration of the half-pay provided for by the aforesaid acts: *Provided, however*, That in case of the death or marriage[2] of said widow before the expiration of said term of five years, the half-pay for the remainder of the term, shall go to the child or children of the deceased officer or soldier, while under the age of sixteen years; and in like manner the child or children of such deceased, when there is no widow, shall be paid no longer than while there is a child or children under the age aforesaid: *And provided further*, That no greater sum shall be allowed in any case to the widow, or to the child or children of any officer, than the half-pay of a lieutenant-colonel: *Provided further*, That the act approved the twenty-second of February, one thousand eight hundred and forty-nine, "granting five years' half-pay to certain widows and orphans of officers, non-commissioned officers, musicians and privates, both regular and volunteer," be so extended and construed as to embrace the widows and minor heirs of the officers, non-commissioned officers, musicians and privates, of the regulars, militia and volunteers of the war of eighteen hundred and twelve, and of the various Indian wars since 1790.[3]

---

1 Pensions under special acts are not renewed by the act of February 3, 1853. *Commissioner Waldo, November* 16, 1853.

2 An act of August 5, 1854 (U. S. Statutes at Large, vol. x, 576), provides that the act of February 3, 1853, "shall not be so construed as to deprive any widow from the benefits therein granted for the services of her husband, though she may have married again: *Provided, however,* That the applicant is a widow at the time of making the claim: *Provided,* Such party shall not receive pension during coverture."

3 The widow of a soldier killed by the Indians, in time of peace, is not entitled to the benefits of the act of February 3, 1853. *Commissioner Waldo, December* 2[illegible], 1853.

The second section relates to the widows of officers and and soldiers of the revolution.

Half-pay was granted for life to all widows, and until sixteen years of age to all children, who were entitled to five years' half-pay, under existing laws, by an act of June 3, 1858,[1] which is as follows:

AN ACT *to extend an act entitled "an act to continue Half-pay to certain Widows and Orphans," approved February three, eighteen hundred and fifty-three.*

Be it enacted by the Senate and House of Representatives of the United States of America in Congress assembled, That all those surviving widows and minor children who have been, or may be, granted and allowed five years' half-pay under the provisions of any law or laws of the United States, be, and they are hereby, granted a continuance of such half-pay, under the following terms and limitations, viz: to such widows during life, and to such child or children, where there is no widow, while under the age of sixteen years, to commence from the expiration of the half-pay provided for by the first section of the act entitled "an act to continue half-pay to certain widows and orphans," approved February three, eighteen hundred and fifty-three: *Provided, however*, That in case of the marriage or death of any such widow, the half-pay shall go to the child or children of the deceased officer or soldier while under the age of sixteen years; and, in like manner, the child or children of such deceased officer or soldier, when there is no widow, shall be paid no longer than while there are children or a child under the age aforesaid; *And provided further*, That the half-pay of such widows and orphans shall be half the monthly pay of the officers, non-commissioned officers, musicians and privates of the infantry of the regular army of the United States, and no more, and that no greater sum shall be allowed to any such widow or minor children than the half-pay of a lieutenant-colonel; *And provided, also*, That this act shall not be construed to apply to or embrace the case of any person or persons now receiving a penson for life: and, further, that wherever half-pay shall have been granted by any special act of Congress, and is renewed or continued under the provisions of this act, the same shall commence from the date hereof.

[1] U. S. Statutes at Large, vol. xi, 309.

SEC. 2. *And be it further enacted,* That the provisions renewed and continued by this act shall be payable out of any money in the Treasury not otherwise appropriated.

By a special act, approved March 27, 1854,[1] pensions were granted to the widows and children of the regular troops who perished in the steamship San Francisco, as follows:

SEC. 2. *And be it further enacted,* That . . .; and that the widows and minor children of those officers, non-commissioned officers and privates, who perished by this disaster, or who have died from disease in consequence thereof, shall be allowed pensions in the same manner, in all respects, as if the said officers, non-commissioned officers and privates, had been killed in battle.

WAR OF 1861.

A general act, granting pensions to the sufferers by the war of 1861, for the maintenance of the Government, approved July 14, 1862, provides as follows:

AN ACT *to Grant Pensions.*

Be it enacted by the Senate and House of Representatives of the United States of America in Congress assembled, That if any officer, non-commissioned officer, musician or private of the army, including regulars, volunteers and militia, or any officer, warrant or petty officer, musician, seaman, ordinary seaman, flotillaman, marine, clerk, landsman, pilot or other person in the navy or marine corps, has been, since the fourth day of March, eighteen hundred and sixty-one, or shall hereafter be disabled by reason of any wound received or disease contracted while in the service of the United States and in the line of duty, he shall, upon making due proof of the fact according to such forms and regulations as are or may be provided by or in pursuance of law, be placed upon the list of invalid pensions [pensioners] of the United States, and be entitled to receive, for the highest rate of disability, such pension as is hereinafter provided in such cases, and for an inferior disability an amount

1 U. S. Statutes at Large, vol. x, 269.

proportionate to the highest disability, to commence as hereinafter provided, and continue during the existence of such disability. The pension for a total disability for officers, non-commissioned officers, musicians and privates employed in the military service of the United States, whether regulars, volunteers or militia, and in the marine corps, shall be as follows, viz: Lieutenant-colonel and all officers of a higher rank, thirty dollars per month; major, twenty-five dollars per month; captain, twenty dollars per month; first lieutenant, seventeen dollars per month; second lieutenant, fifteen dollars per month; and non-commissioned officers, musicians and privates, eight dollars per month. The pension for total disability for officers, warrant or petty officers, and others employed in the naval service of the United States, shall be as follows, viz: Captain, commander, surgeon, paymaster and chief engineer, respectively, ranking with commander by law, lieutenant commanding and master commanding, thirty dollars per month; lieutenant, surgeon, paymaster and chief engineer, respectively, ranking with lieutenant by law, and passed assistant surgeon, twenty-five dollars per month; professor of mathematics, master, assistant surgeon, assistant paymaster and chaplain, twenty dollars per month; first assistant engineers and pilots, fifteen dollars per month; passed midshipman, midshipman, captains' and paymasters' clerk, second and third assistant engineer, masters' mate and all warrant officers, ten dollars per month; all petty officers and all other persons before named employed in the naval service, eight dollars per month; and all commissioned officers, of either service, shall receive such and only such pension as is herein provided for the rank in which they hold commissions.

SEC. 2. *And be it further enacted,* That if any officer or other person named in the first section of this act has died since the fourth day of March, eighteen hundred and sixty-one, or shall hereafter die, by reason of any wound received or disease contracted while in the service of the United States, and in the line of duty, his widow, or, if there be no widow, his child or children under sixteen years of age, shall be entitled to receive the same pension as the husband or father would have been entitled to had he been totally disabled, to commence from the death of the husband or father, and to continue to the widow during her widowhood, or to the child or children until they severally attain to the age of sixteen years, and no longer.

SEC. 4. *And be it further enacted*, That . . . *And provided, further*, That no moneys shall be paid to the widow or children, or any heirs of any deceased officer, on account of bounty, back pay or pension, who have in any way been engaged in, or who have aided or abetted, the existing rebellion in the United States; but the right of such disloyal widow or children, heir or heirs of such soldier, shall be vested in the loyal heir or heirs of the deceased, if any there be.

SEC. 6. *And be it further enacted*, That the fees of agents and attorneys, for making out and causing to be executed the papers necessary to establish a claim for a pension, bounty and other allowance before the Pension Office under this act, shall not exceed the following rates: For making out and causing to be duly executed a declaration by the applicant, with the necessary affidavits, and forwarding the same to the Pension Office, with the requisite correspondence, five dollars. In cases wherein additional testimony is required by the Commissioner of Pensions, for each affidavit so required and executed and forwarded (except the affidavits of surgeons, for which such agents and attorneys shall not be entitled to any fees), one dollar and fifty cents.

SEC. 7. *And be it further enacted*, That any agent or attorney who shall, directly or indirectly, demand or receive any greater compensation for his services under this act than is prescribed in the preceding section of this act, or who shall contract or agree to prosecute any claim for a pension, bounty or other allowance under this act, on the condition that he shall receive a per centum upon or any portion of the amount of such claim, or who shall wrongfully withhold from a pensioner or other claimant the whole or any part of the pension or claim allowed and due to such pensioner or claimant, shall be deemed guilty of a high misdemeanor, and upon conviction thereof shall, for every such offense, be fined not exceeding three hundred dollars, or imprisoned at hard labor not exceeding two years, or both, according to the circumstances and aggravations of the offense.

The remaining sections of this act may be found on page 28.

GENERAL OBSERVATIONS.

The acts of June 7, 1794; March 16, 1802; April 12, 1808; January 11, 1812; January 29, 1813; and March

3, 1815, made provision for the widows and children of commissioned officers alone, who died in the service. The act of April 16, 1816, granted half-pay for five years to the widows and children of non-commissioned officers, musicians and privates of the regular army, who enlisted for either eighteen months or one year, and the widows and children of commissioned officers of the regular army, who died before or after being mustered out of service, of wounds received in the war of 1812. It also authorized the guardians of children of deceased non-commissioned officers, musicians and privates, who died of wounds or disease while in service in the war of 1812, to relinquish the bounty land to which the dead soldier, had he survived the war, would have been entitled, and to accept in lieu thereof half the monthly pay to which such deceased person was entitled at the time of his death, for five years. The time for making these relinquishments was by the act limited to one year, and subsequently extended five additional years; but this portion of the act, having expired by limitation, is no longer in force.

The act of March 3, 1817, fixes the pension of widows and children of soldiers at forty-eight dollars per annum, and of officers at half the pay of officers of the infantry. The act also places the widows and children of rangers on an equality, as to half-pay, with the widows and children of the infantry.

The act of March 2, 1833, relating to certain dragoons; the act of July 4, 1836, relating, in part, to rangers; and the act of May 19, 1846, relating to mounted riflemen, allow the widows and children of such persons as served in these corps, and died in the service, the same benefits as were by law granted to other portions of the army. These acts relate back to the acts of April 16, 1816, and March 3, 1817.

A rule of evidence was established by the act of May 7, 1846, relieving widows of the trouble and expense of proving the service of their husbands, when the latter were pensioners at the time of their death.

By the act of July 21, 1848, the benefits of the first section of the act of July 4, 1836 (given in full in the preceding section), were extended to the widows and children of officers and soldiers who had died in the service since March 1, 1846, including the Mexican war. It also provided like pensions to the widows and children of officers and soldiers who had died since April 1, 1846, or might die during the war with Mexico, from wounds received or disease contracted in the line of duty, or while returning to their homes upon a discharge for disability, or while on the march to join the army in Mexico.

This act was enlarged by the act of February 22, 1849, so as to embrace the widows and children of persons who were wounded or contracted disease in the service, of which they died after their discharge and return home. By the joint resolution of September 28, 1850, the acts of July 21, 1848, and February 22, 1849, were construed to embrace the widows and children of those who had died, after the passage of those acts, from disability accruing in the service, as well as of those who might thereafter die. It also makes army rolls showing the death of such persons sufficient evidence to establish that fact.

The joint resolution of March 3, 1849, directed that the returns on the rolls of the disease of which a soldier died, and the opinion of the surgeon-general thereon, that the disease was contracted in the service, should be taken as conclusive evidence of that fact.

The act of February 3, 1853, extended for five additional years the half-pay granted the 21st of July, 1848, and the 22d day of February, 1849; and directed that the last-mentioned act should be construed to apply to the widows and children of officers and soldiers who served in the war of 1812, and the Indian wars since 1790.

The act of June 3, 1858, granted half-pay for life, or during widowhood, to such widows as were entitled to half-pay for five years, and to children under sixteen years of age, in certain cases, to commence at the expiration of the five years' half-pay allowed by the act of February 3, 1853. The act of August 5, 1854, provides that this act shall not deprive widows of deceased officers and soldiers who had married again from claiming a pension, provided they were widows when making their claim.

The act of July 14, 1862, makes provisions for the widows of persons who have died since March 1, 1861, or who may hereafter die of disability incurred in the war of 1861.

The acts to which reference should be had in making applications for widows and orphans of regulars, in general, are those of April 16, 1816 (this relates to the war of 1812 only); February 22, 1849; and June 3, 1858. For widows and orphans made so by the war with Mexico, the acts of July 21, 1848; February 22, 1849; and June 3, 1858; and the joint resolution of September 28, 1850, should be consulted. For widows of the war of 1861, the act of July 14, 1862, is the most favorable.

The special act in the case of those who perished in the steamship San Francisco, relates to the general acts granting pensions to the widows and orphans of regulars.

SECTION II.

REGULATIONS AND FORMS FOR OBTAINING PENSIONS FOR WIDOWS AND ORPHANS OF REGULARS.

PENSION OFFICE, *February*, 1862.

To procure the half-pay provided under the various acts of Congress, for the widows or minor children of officers and soldiers who have died in the military service of the United States, or of wounds or disease incurred in such service, in the line of duty, applicants must make their declarations and establish their proof substantially in accordance with the subjoined instructions and forms:

1. The declaration of the widow, or of the guardian duly appointed and qualified in the case of a minor child or children, must be made, under oath or affirmation before a Court of Record [or before a Judge or Clerk of such Court] (unless satisfactory reason is shown for making such affidavit before some other magistrate having authority to administer oaths), according to the forms accompanying these instructions. In all cases the official character of the magistrate must be duly certified by the proper officer, under his seal of office.

2. If the applicant be a widow, she must prove the legality of her marriage, the death of her husband, and that she is still a widow. She must also furnish the names and ages of her children under sixteen years of age at her husband's decease, and the place of their residence. On a subsequent marriage her pension will cease, and the minor child or children of the deceased officer or soldier, if any be living, under the age of sixteen years, will be entitled to the same, in her stead, from the date of such marriage.

3. If application be made in behalf of a minor child of the deceased officer or soldier, the marriage of his parents must be proved, the death of his father, the death or re-marriage of his mother, and that he is still a minor, under sixteen years of age.

4. In case the deceased officer or soldier was a pensioner, that fact should also be stated, as well as the act under which he was pensioned, and the agency at which he was paid. In such case, a reference to the evidence filed in his application will be sufficient to prove the service.

5. Proof of the service of the deceased officer or soldier must be had from the muster rolls or other documentary evidence in custody of the executive Departments (which the claimant is not required to

produce), or else from the testimony of commissioned officers or the affidavits of persons of known respectability. It must also be clearly shown in what company and regiment, or corps, the deceased served, and in what grade.

6. Applicants, other than the widows of revolutionary soldiers, must furnish the best proof the nature of the case will allow, not only as to the place and time of the death of the deceased officer or soldier, but also as to the complaint of which he died, and the supposed cause of his disease.

7. The legality of the marriage may be ascertained by the certificate of the clergyman who joined them in wedlock, or by the testimony of respectable persons having knowledge of the fact, in default of record evidence. The ages and number of children may be ascertained by the deposition of the mother, accompanied by the testimony of respectable persons having knowledge of them, or by transcript from the parish registers, duly authenticated. The widow must show, at the time of receiving each and every payment of her pension, that she has not again married. This may be done by the affidavits of respectable persons having knowledge of the case.

8. The claimant must, in every case where there is no record or documentary proof of the revolutionary service of the deceased officer or soldier, produce the testimony of at least one credible witness. Traditionary evidence will be deemed useful in every such case.

9. Under the provisions of the first section of the act of February 3, 1853, all widows and orphans who were granted and allowed five years' half-pay by the provisions of the act of July 4, 1836, extended by the act of July 21, 1848, and further extended by the act of February 22, 1849, are entitled to a continuance of said half-pay for a further period of five years, to commence at the expiration of the half-pay provided for by the aforesaid acts, under the restrictions and limitations specified in the said acts.

10. Under the last proviso of the first section of the act of February 3, 1853, the widows of officers, non-commissioned officers, musicians and privates of the regulars, militia and volunteers of the war of 1812, and also in the various Indian wars since 1790, who remained to the date of their death in the service of the United States, or who, having received an honorable discharge, and having died since their return to their usual place of residence of wounds received, or from disease contracted while in the line of their duty,

are entitled to receive half the monthly pay to which the deceased was entitled at the time of his death, or at the time of receiving such wounds, or contracting such disease, for and during the term of five years, to commence at the time of completing the evidence in said case.

11. Under the provisions of the second section of the act of February 3, 1853, the widows of all officers, non-commissioned officers, musicians and privates of the revolutionary army, who served six months, and who were married subsequently to January, 1800, are entitled to a pension in the same manner as those who were married before that date.

12. Applications based upon service in the war of 1861, for the suppression of rebellion, should be made in accordance with the foregoing regulations and the subjoined forms.

13. Agents must, in all cases, have proper authority from the claimants in whose behalf they appear. No power of attorney will be recognized as sufficient unless signed in the presence of two witnesses, and acknowledged before a duly qualified officer, whose authority is certified under seal.

JOSEPH H. BARRETT, *Commissioner.*

(1) *Declaration of Widow: applying in general.*

STATE OF ——
County of —— } *ss.*

On this —— day of ——, A. D. 18—, personally appeared before the —— of the ——, ——, a resident of the county of ——, and State of ——, aged —— years, who, being first duly sworn according to law, doth, on her oath, make the following declaration, in order to obtain the benefits of the provision made by the act of Congress approved ——; that she is the widow of ——, who was a [*Here insert the rank the husband held, and specify the service performed.*]

She further declares that she was married to the said —— on the —— day of ——, in the year ——; that her husband, the aforesaid ——, died on the —— day of ——, [1] and that she has remained a widow ever since

---

[1] Should there be children, here should be inserted:

That there were born to them, during their said marriage, the following children, who were under sixteen years of age at the time of the death of said decedent, viz: —— born —— 18—; —— born —— 18—, etc.; and that these are still living, and at the following places: [*Here give the places of residence of the children.*]

The names and ages of the children must also be proved by the affidavits of at least two credible witnesses who have knowledge of the facts.

that period,[1] as will more fully appear by reference to the proof hereto annexed. (*Declarant's Signature.*)

Sworn to and subscribed on the day and year first above written, before ——. (*Officer's Signature.*)

The foregoing form, furnished by the Commissioner of Pensions, is substantially the same as the forms appertaining to applications by widows of the revolution. The regulations, and rules of evidence, are also, in substance the same, in the last-named cases, as in applications by the widows of regulars *since* the revolution. Applicants are referred to the Regulations and Forms to be found under "WIDOWS AND ORPHANS—REVOLUTIONARY WAR," page 143, for many hints and suggestions that will be found serviceable in applying for pensions for widows of regulars.

ACT OF JULY 21, 1848—MEXICAN WAR.

PENSION OFFICE, August 21, 1848.

The following regulations have been adopted by the Secretary of War, with the approbation of the President of the United States, for carrying into effect the provisions of the act of the 21st July, 1848, entitled "an act amending the act entitled 'an act granting half-pay to the widows or orphans, where their husbands and fathers have died of wounds received in the military service of the United States,' in cases of deceased officers and soldiers of the militia and volunteers, passed July fourth, eighteen hundred and thirty-six."

1. All applicants are required to show, either by the official certificate or testimony of a commissioned officer, or the muster or pay rolls, or some record evidence from the Adjutant-General's Office, that the deceased officer or soldier, on account of whose service the pension is claimed, died of wounds received, or from disease contracted while in the line of his duty, and that he served either in Mexico, or at some post or station on the borders of Mexico. If he did not die in the service, it must be shown that he died while on

[1] If the widow was subsequently married, the name of her second husband, the date of the marriage, and death of second husband must be stated in the declaration and proved.

his return to his usual place of residence in the United States, after having received a discharge upon a surgeon's certificate of disability incurred from wounds received, or disease contracted while in the line of duty, or while on his march to join the army in Mexico, or at some post or station on the borders of Mexico.

2. The legality of the marriage, the name of the widow, with those of her children who may have been under sixteen years of age at the time of the father's decease, with the State or Territory and county in which she and they reside, should be established. The legality of the marriage may be ascertained by the certificate of the clergyman who joined them in wedlock, or the testimony of respectable persons having knowledge of the fact. The age and number of the children may be ascertained by the deposition of the mother, accompanied by the testimony of respectable persons having knowledge of them, or by transcripts from the parish registers, duly authenticated. The widow, at the time of allowing the half-pay, or placing her on the list for it, must show that she has not again married; and must, moreover, repeat this at the time of receiving each and every payment thereof; because, in case of her marrying again, the half-pay to her ceases, and the half-pay for the remainder of the time shall go to the child or children of the deceased soldier. This may be done by the affidavits of respectable persons having knowledge of the case.

3. In cases where there are children, and no widow, their guardian will, of course, act for them, and establish their claims as prescribed in the foregoing regulations, and receive their stipends for them.

4. The credibility of the witness must in every case be certified by the magistrate who may administer the oath; and the official character and signature of the magistrate must be certified by the proper officer, under his seal of office.

5. In every case the applicant, if a widow, must make a declaration according to the form annexed. If there be no widow, and the claim is made on behalf of orphan children, there must be a guardian appointed tc act for them, and he must make a declaration, varying the form to suit the case.

JAMES L. EDWARDS, *Commissioner of Pensions.*

Declaration in order to obtain the Benefits of the act of the 21st July, 1848.

STATE OF —— }
County of —— } *ss.*

On this —— day of ——, personally appeared before the —— of the ——, ——, resident of ——, in the county of ——, and State of ——, aged —— years, who, being first duly sworn according to law, doth, on her oath, make the following declaration, in order to obtain the benefit of the provision made by the law of the United States, passed on the 21st of July, 1848: That she is the widow of ——, who was a —— in the —— regiment of United States ——; that she was married to the said ——, on the —— day of —— in the year eighteen hundred and ——; that her husband, the aforesaid ——, died on the —— day of ——, at ——, in ——, in consequence of ——; and that she has remained a widow ever since that period, as will more fully appear by reference to the proofs hereto annexed.

(*Declarant's Signature.*)

Sworn to and subscribed on the day and year above-written, before ——.

(*Officer's Signature.*)

The official character and signature of the magistrate must be certified by the proper officer, under his seal of office.

The foregoing regulations, and the accompanying form, are also substantially like the regulations and forms provided for widows of the revolution. It is not deemed necessary, therefore, to repeat these forms here; but applicants are referred to them under "WIDOWS AND ORPHANS—REVOLUTIONARY WAR," page 143. The act of July 21, 1848, specially refers to the act of July 4, 1836. This act, with the regulations provided by the Commissioner, and the forms necessary in executing the same, will also be found under the above-mentioned title.

ACT OF FEBRUARY 3, 1853.

PENSION OFFICE, March, 25, 1853.

The following regulations, approved by the Secretary of the Interior, have been adopted for carrying into effect the provisions of the act of 3d February, 1853, entitled "an act to continue half-pay to certain widows and orphans."

1. Under the provisions of the first section of this act, all widows

and orphans who were granted and allowed five years' half-pay by the provisions of the act of 4th July, 1836, extended by the act of 21st of July, 1848, and further extended by the act of 22d February, 1849, are entitled to a continuance of said half-pay for a further period of five years, to commence at the expiration of the half-pay provided for by the aforesaid acts, under the restrictions and limitations in the said acts specified.

To obtain these benefits the applicant must make a declaration, under oath, before some magistrate in the county where the declarant resides, or before some other person qualified to administer an oath (which declaration must be duly authenticated), according to the form appended hereto, marked "A," page 186.

The official character of the magistrate must be duly certified by the proper officer, under his seal of office, and the person administering the oath must certify that the declarant is personally known to him.

It will be observed, that in the event of the death or marriage of the widow, and the application is made on behalf of a child or children under sixteen years of age, the half-pay is not continued after such child or children shall have passed the age of sixteen.

2. Under the last proviso of the first section, the widows of officers, non-commissioned officers, musicians and privates of the regulars, militia and volunteers of the war of 1812, who were not entitled by the provisions of the act of 16th April, 1816, and also in the various Indian wars since 1790, who remained to the date of their death in the service of the United States, or who having received an honorable discharge, and who have died since their return to their usual place of residence, of wounds received, or of disease contracted, while in the line of their duty, are entitled to receive half the monthly pay to which the deceased was entitled at the time of his death, or at the time of receiving such wound, or contracting such disease, for and during the term of five years, to commence at the time of completing the evidence in said case.

In case there be no such widow, or in case of her marriage or death, before the expiration of five years, the half-pay or such part thereof as remains at the time of her marriage or decease, will go to the minor heirs of the deceased.

In applications for these benefits, the party must make a declaration in writing, before a Court of Record, according to the form appended hereto, marked "B," page 187, and must produce proof of the service of the deceased officer or soldier; the time of his death; and that it was occasioned by wounds received, or from disease contracted, while in service, in the line of his duty.[1]

If the applicant be a widow, she must prove the legality of her marriage, and that she has remained a widow since the death of her husband [or, if subsequently married, she must show that she is a widow at the time of making the application].

If the applicant be a minor child of the deceased officer or soldier, he must prove the marriage of his parents, their death and his minority.

3. [This portion of the regulations relates to applications by widows of officers and soldiers of the revolution, and will be found with form accompanying the same, on page 154].

L. P. WALDO, *Commissioner of Pensions.*

"A."

Declaration in order to obtain the Renewal of the Half-Pay provided for in the first section of the act of February 3, 1853.

STATE OF —— }
County of —— } *ss.*

On this —— day of ——, A. D. ——, personally appeared before me, a —— within and for the county and State aforesaid, ——, a resident of said county, aged —— years, who being first duly sworn according to law, doth, on her oath, make the following declaration in order to obtain the benefits of the provision made by the act of Congress, passed the 3d February, 1853, granting the renewal of half-pay to certain widows and orphans: That she is the widow of ——, who was a [*Here insert the rank the husband held, the company and regiment in which he served, and the monthly amount of the half-pay which she received under the first section of the act of July* 4, 1836, *or July* 21, 1848]. She further declares that she is still a widow.

(*Declarant's Signature.*)

Sworn to and subscribed before me, the day and year above written.

(*Officer's Signature.*)

1 This is subject to these qualifications: Where the deceased husband was a pensioner at the time of his death, proof of service need not be made. Again: the act of February 22, 1849, specially provides, that when the army rolls show the death of the husband, this shall be deemed sufficient evidence of the fact. And the joint resolution of March 3, 1849, directs that the returns on the rolls of the disease of which a soldier died, and the opinion of the surgeon-general thereon that the disease was contracted in the service, shall be taken a sufficient proof of the fact.

This declaration may be made before any officer authorized to administer oaths, generally; whose official character must be shown by the certificate and seal of the Clerk of the proper court.

The affidavit of two disinterested persons, that they are acquainted with the widow; that she is the identical person to whom half-pay for five years was granted as stated in her declaration; and that she is a widow, must accompany the foregoing declaration.

"B."

Declaration in order to obtain the Benefits of the last proviso of the first section of the Act of February 3, 1853.

STATE OF —— } ss.
County of —— }

On this —— day of ——, 18—, before the —— court [*or* before ——, judge, *or* ——, clerk of the —— court], a court of record, within and for the county and State aforesaid, personally appeared ——, a resident of said county, aged —— years, who being first duly sworn according to law, doth, on her oath, make the following declaration in order to obtain the benefit of the provision made by the law of the United States, passed the 3d day of February, 1853: That she is the widow of ——, who was a —— in company ——, in the —— regiment of regulars [*or* militia, *or* volunteers—*if militia or volunteers, mention the war in which service was performed.*] That she was married to the said ——, on the —— day of ——, in the year ——; that her husband, the aforesaid ——, died on the —— day of ——, 18—, at ——, in consequence of ——, and that she has remained a widow ever since that period, as will more fully appear by reference to the proofs hereto annexed.

(*Declarant's Signature.*)

Sworn to and subscribed before me, the day and year above written.

(*Officer's Signature.*)

As there is a close similarity in the regulations prescribed for executing the various acts of Congress granting half-pay pensions to widows, it is not deemed necessary to repeat the forms given in "WIDOWS AND ORPHANS—REVOLUTIONARY WAR," nor those which have preceded under this title. At best, the forms which are furnished for preparing the necessary papers in pension cases are but skeletons; and much is left to the tact and skill of the draughtsman, aided by the regulations prescribed at the Pension Office. There is no danger of *proving too much, in any case*, and it is well, therefore, always to consult the regulations and forms applicable to acts of a similar character to the one under which it is desired to make an application, to obtain such assistance as may be found; and should superfluous proof be furnished, by mistake, it can do no harm.

It may be remarked, in passing, that the form "B," and the first form given under this title, are applicable to the same class of cases, viz: regulars in the war of 1812, in the peace establishment, and in Indian wars since 1790.

ACT OF JUNE 3, 1858: (HALF-PAY CONTINUED FOR LIFE.)

PENSION OFFICE, *August* 12, 1858.

1. The foregoing act is published in the form of a circular, for the convenience and information of those entitled to its benefits.

2. It will be observed that it creates no new class of pensions, but simply renews and continues to widows, or children while under sixteen years of age, certain pensions provided for by previous laws. Persons claiming its benefits have therefore only to prove their identity and their continued widowhood, or prescribed minority.

3. This must be done in the form of a declaration, in writing, under oath, by the widow or the guardian of such of the children of the deceased officer, or soldier, as may be still under the age of sixteen years. The declaration must state the age and residence of the claimant, the name and rank of the deceased husband or father, and the company or regiment to which he belonged; the date of the act under which the former pension was allowed—its rate per month, the agency where paid, and the dates of its commencement and termination; and that it is made for the purpose of obtaining the benefits of the said act of June 3, 1858.

4. The declaration must be sworn to, and subscribed before a justice of the peace, or other officer duly authorized to administer oaths for general purposes, in the presence of at least two persons who know the claimant to be a widow, and otherwise the person she represents herself to be, who shall make oath thereto, and particularly as to their means of knowledge concerning the facts about which they testify.

5. Applications in behalf of minors must be accompanied by the best evidence attainable of their respective ages, if it have not already been furnished in a former application.

6. It is required that the State, county, and post-office address of the claimant, shall in every case be set forth in the declaration, and the length of time the same has been her place of residence, and the official position and genuineness of signature of the magistrate, or other officer before whom papers are executed or acknowledged, shall be duly attested by a certificate under seal from the proper officer; which certificate, if not written on the sheet of paper containing the signature to be authenticated, must be attached thereto by a piece of tape or ribbon, the ends of which must pass under the official seal, so as to prevent any paper being improperly attached to said certificate.

7. No officer before whom any paper may be executed, or testimony taken, will be recognized as the agent of the claimant; but in every case such officer must certify that he is in no wise interested in the result of the application; and if the certificate is to be sent to any person other than the claimant, she must, in her declaration, give the name and address of the person to whom she may desire it to be sent.

8. The above requirements will be rigidly enforced, and a careful observance of the same, in the preparation of their cases in the first instance, will save claimants much trouble and delay in the adjudication of their claims.

GEO. C. WHITING, *Commissioner.*

No forms have been furnished by the Commissioner for carrying the act of June 3, 1858, into effect; but reference to other forms under this title, particularly form "A," page 186, act of February 3, 1853, will give applicants, or their agents, all the assistance that will be required in preparing papers for presentation under the former act.

Form of Declaration for Guardian of Minor Children in order to obtain Half-Pay.

STATE OF ——, } ss.
County of—— }

On this —— day of ——, A. D. ——, personally appeared before the —— court of the ——, ——, a resident of ——, in the county of ——, and State of——, aged —— years, who, being first duly sworn according to law, doth, on oath, make the following declaration, as guardian of the minor child —— of ——, deceased, in order to obtain the benefits of the provision made by the act of Congress approved ——, granting half-pay to minor children (under 16 years of age), of deceased officers and soldiers: that he is the guardian of——, [*Naming the minor child or children, his ward or wards*], whose father was a —— [*Naming the rank of such deceased officer or soldier, and reciting his service*]; that the parents of his said wards were married at ——, on the —— day of ——, 18—, by ——; that the said —— [*the father*], died at ——, on the —— day of ——, in the year ——; that the mother of the child aforesaid died (or again married, being now the wife of ——), on the —— day of ——, in the year ——; and that the date- of the birth of his said ward —— as follows: ——.

(*Guardian's Signature.*)

Sworn to and subscribed, on the day and year first above written, before,

(*Officer's Signature.*)

This declaration must be made before a Court of Record, or before a Judge or Clerk of such Court. The Clerk's certificate and seal must be attached, in any event.

An authenticated copy of the letters of guardianship must accompany the declaration, together with proof of marriage, of death, of the children being those of the deceased officer or soldier, etc., as in applications by widows. Forms for preparing this proof will be found under this title, and under title "WIDOWS AND ORPHANS—REVOLUTIONARY WAR," Chapter VIII, Sec. II, page 143.

ACT OF MARCH 27, 1854: TROOPS LOST ON THE SAN FRANCISCO.[1]

The regulations for executing this act are the same as in other cases where pensions are claimed for the service of an officer or soldier in the regular army. The officers and soldiers referred to in the act belonged to the establishment, and were lost off the coast of South America, on their way to California.

The following alterations may be made in the ordinary forms, to apply them to this act:

. . . In order to obtain the benefit of the second section of the act entitled "an act for the relief of the United States troops, who were sufferers by the recent disaster to the steamship San Francisco," approved, March 27, 1854: that she is the widow of ——, deceased, who was a —— in company ——, commanded by Captain ——, in the third regiment of United States Artillery, commanded by Colonel William Gates; and was on board the steamship San Francisco, on the 21st day of December, 1853, and remained on board said ship until the disaster by which said ship was lost; that her said husband perished on or about the —— day of ——, 1854 (or died of disease contracted in consequence of said disaster, on the —— day of —— 18--).

PENSION ACT OF JULY 14, 1862.

GENERAL PROVISIONS.

Under the act of Congress approved July 14, 1862, pensions are granted to the following classes of persons:

[1] The troops on board the San Francisco were the following:

Companies A, B, D, G, H, I, K, L, of the Third Regiment U. S. Artillery. Colonel, William Gates; Maj. and Brev. Lieut. Col., J. M. Washington; Maj., Charles S. Merchant; Surgeon, R. S. Satterlee; Asst. Surg., H. R. Wirtz; First Lieut., S. L. Fremont, Reg. Quartermaster and Acting Adjutant; First Lieut. L. Loeser, Acting Assistant Commissary. Company A was commanded by Capt. and Brev. Maj. George Taylor; Company D, by Capt. Brev. Maj. F. O. Wyse; Company G, by First Lieut. W. A. Winder; Company H, by First Lieut. C. S. Winder; Company I, by Capt. Brev. Lieut. Col. M. Burke; Company K, by First Lieut. Brev. Capt. H. B. Field; Capt. H. P. Judd commanding detachment of recruits to constitute companies B and L. In addition to these were Capt. J. W. T. Gardiner, First Dragoons, on his way to join his regiment in California; Lieut. F. K. Murray, U. S. Navy, on way to join squadron at Rio Janeiro; First Lieut. R. H. Smith; Second Lieut. J. Van Vosst; Brev. Second Lieut. J. G. Chandler.

1. Invalids, disabled since March 4, 1861, in the military or naval service of the United States, in the line of duty.

2. Widows of officers, soldiers or seamen dying of wounds received or of disease contracted in the military or naval service, as above.

3. Children, under sixteen years of age, of such deceased persons, if there is no widow surviving, or from the time of the widow's re-marriage.

4. Mothers (who have no husband living) of officers, soldiers or seamen, deceased as aforesaid, provided the latter have left neither widow nor children under sixteen years of age, and provided, also, that the mother was dependent, wholly or in part, upon the deceased for support.

5. Sisters, under sixteen years of age, of such deceased persons, dependent on the latter, wholly or in part, for support, provided there are no rightful claimants of either of the three last preceding classes.

The rates of pension to the several classes and grades are distinctly set forth in the first section of the act, a copy of which is herewith published. Only one full pension in any case will be allowed to the relatives of a deceased officer, soldier or seaman, and in order of precedence as set forth above. When more than one minor child or orphan sister thus becomes entitled to pension, the same must be divided equally between them.

Invalid pensions, under this law, will commence from the date of the pensioner's discharge from service, provided application is made within one year thereafter. If the claim is not made until a later date, the pension will commence from the time of the application. Pensions of widows and minors will commence from the death of the officer, soldier or seaman, on whose service the claim is based.

ARMY PENSIONS.

Declarations are required to be made before a court of record, or before some officer of such court duly authorized to administer oaths, and having custody of its seal. *Testimony* may be taken before a justice of the peace, or other officer having like authority to administer oaths, but in no case will any evidence be received that is verified before an officer who is concerned in prosecuting the claim, or has a manifest interest therein.

The subjoined forms, marked, respectively, A, B, C, D, E, and, F, will guide applicants for pensions, of the army branch, in the several classes. The forms should be exactly followed in every instance. No attorney will be regarded as having filed the necessary declaration and affidavits, as contemplated by the seventh section of the act, unless the *forms*, as well as the instructions given in this pamphlet, are strictly complied with.

In support of the allegations made in the claimant's declaration, testimony will be required in accordance with the following rules:

1. The claimant's identity must be proved by two witnesses, certified by a judicial officer to be respectable and credible, who are present and witness the signature of the declarant, and who state, upon oath or affirmation, their belief, either from personal acquaintance or for other reasons given, that he or she is the identical person he or she represents himself or herself to be.

2. Every applicant for an invalid pension must, if in his power, produce the certificate of the captain, or of some other commissioned officer under whom he served, distinctly stating the time and place of the said applicant's having been wounded or otherwise disabled, and the nature of the disability; and that the said disability arose while he was in the service of the United States and in the line of his duty.

3. If it be impracticable to obtain such certificate, by reason of the death or removal of said officers, it must be so stated under oath by the applicant, and his averment of the fact proved by persons of known respectability, who must state particularly all the knowledge they may possess in relation to such death or removal; then secondary evidence can be received. In such case the applicant must produce the testimony of at least two credible witnesses (who were in a condition to know the facts about which they testify), whose good character must be vouched for by a judicial officer, or by some one known to the Department. The witnesses must give a minute narrative of the facts in relation to the matter, and must show how they obtained a knowledge of the facts to which they testify.

4. The surgeon's certificate for discharge should show the character and degree of the claimant's disability; but when that is wanting, and when the certificate of an army surgeon is not obtainable, the certificate of two respectable civil surgeons will be received, in accordance with form F. These surgeons must give in their certificate a particular description of the wound, injury, or disease, and specify how and in what manner his present condition and disability

are connected therewith. The degree of disability for obtaining subsistence by manual labor must also be stated.

5. The habits of the applicant, and his occupation since he left the service, must be shown by at least two credible witnesses.

If the applicant claims a pension as the widow of a deceased officer or soldier, she must prove the legality of her marriage, the death of her husband, and that she is still a widow. She must also furnish the names and ages of her children under sixteen years of age at her husband's decease, and the place of their residence. On a subsequent marriage her pension will cease, and the minor child or children of the deceased officer or soldier, if any be living, under the age of sixteen years, will be entitled to the same in her stead, from the date of such marriage.

Proof of the marriage of the parents and of the age of claimants will, in like manner, be required in all applications in behalf of minor children.

The legality of the marriage may be ascertained by the certificate of the clergyman who joined them in wedlock, or by the testimony of respectable persons having knowledge of the fact, in default of record evidence. The ages and number of children may be ascertained by the deposition of the mother, accompanied by the testimony of respectable persons having knowledge of them, or by transcripts from the parish or town registers duly authenticated.

Similar proof will be required of the marriage of the claimant, if the mother of a deceased officer or soldier, and that she remains a widow.

If the claimant be a dependent sister, like proof will be required of the marriage of her parents, and of her relationship to the deceased.

Guardians of minor claimants must, in all cases, produce evidence of their authority as such, under the seal of the court from which their appointment is obtained.

Applicants of the last four classes above given, who have in any manner aided or abetted the rebellion against the United States government, are not entitled to the benefits of this act.

Attorneys for claimants must have proper authority from those in whose behalf they appear. Powers of attorney must be signed in the presence of two witnesses, and acknowledged before a duly qualified officer, whose official character must be certified under seal.

In all cases the post-office address of the claimant must be distinctly stated.

Applications under this act will be numbered and acknowledged, to be acted on in their turn. In filing additional evidence, correspondents should always give the number of the claim as well as the name of the claimant.

JOSEPH H. BARRETT, *Commissioner.*

PENSION OFFICE, *July* 21, 1862.

"B."

Form of Declaration for obtaining a Widow's Army Pension.

STATE OF ——
County of —— } *ss.*

On this —— day of ——, A.D. ——, personally appeared before me——, of the ——, ——, a resident of ——, in the county of ——, and State of ——, aged —— years, who, being first duly sworn according to law, doth, on her oath, make the following declaration, in order to obtain the benefit of the provision made by the act of Congress approved July 14, 1862: That she is the widow of ——, who was a —— in company ——, commanded by ——, in the —— regiment of ——, in the war of 1861, who [*Here specify the time, place and cause of death*]. She further declares, that she was married to the said —— on the —— day of ——, in the year ——; that her husband, the aforesaid ——, died on the day above mentioned, and that she has remained a widow ever since that period (*or if she has re-married and again become a widow, the fact must be stated*), as will more fully appear by reference to the proof hereto annexed. She also declares that she has not in any manner been engaged in, or aided or abetted, the rebellion in the United States.

(*Declarant's Signature.*)

Also personally appeared —— and ——, residents of (*county, city or town*), persons whom I certify to be respectable and entitled to credit, and who, being by me duly sworn, say that they were present and saw —— sign her name (*or make her mark*) to the foregoing declaration; and they further swear that they have every reason to believe, from the appearance of the applicant and their acquaintance with her, that she is the identical person she represents herself to be; and that they have no interest in the prosecution of this claim.

(*Signatures of Witnesses.*)

Sworn to and subscribed before me, this —— day of ——, A. D., 18—; and I hereby certify that I have no interest, direct or indirect, in the prosecution of this claim.

(*Signature of Judge or other Officer.*)

Applicant's post-office address:

This must be accompanied by the same proof as in other applications by widows. The Regulations and Forms prescribed in cases arising under the act of July 14, 1862, are, in every essential particular, similar to those provided under other acts granting pensions to widows. By reference, therefore, to preceding forms under this title, claimants will find suggestions which will aid them in preparing their papers.

For FORMS and REGULATIONS relating to POWERS OF ATTORNEY, in pension cases, see Chapter XVI.

"C."

Form of Declaration for Guardian of Minor Children in order to obtain Army Pension.[1]

STATE OF —— } ss.
County of —— }

On this —— day of ——, A.D. one thousand eight hundred and ——, personally appeared before the —— of the ——, ——, a resident of ——, in the county of ——, and State of ——, aged —— years, who, being first duly sworn according to law, doth on oath make the following declaration, as guardian of the minor child of ——, deceased, in order to obtain the benefits of the provision made by the act of Congress, approved July 14, 1862, granting pensions to minor children, under sixteen years of age, of deceased officers and soldiers ; that he is the guardian of ——, [*naming the minor child or children, his ward or wards*], whose father was a —— in company ——, commanded by ——, in the —— regiment of ——, in the war of 1861, and that the said —— died at ——, on the —— day of ——, in the year —— [*here state the cause of death*] ; that the mother of the child, ——, aforesaid died (*or* again married, being now the wife of ——), on the —— day of ——, in the year —— ; and that the date of birth of his said ward— as follows :

He further declares, that the parents of his said ward— were married at ——, on the —— day of ——, in the year ——, by ——.

(*Guardian's Signature.*)

Sworn to and subscribed on the day and year first above written, before ——; and I hereby certify that I have no interest, direct or indirect, in the prosecution of this claim.

(*Signature of Judge or other Officer.*)

[1] For forms in cases of minor sisters of deceased officers and soldiers, see pages 261-2.

This must be accompanied by a certified copy of the letters of guardianship, and by the same proof as in the case of declarations by widows. The forms for preparing this proof will be found under this title, and title "WIDOWS AND ORPHANS—REVOLUTION," pages 143–157. By reference to other forms of declarations in the case of guardians of minors, under this title and "WIDOWS AND CHILDREN—NAVAL," hints may be obtained which may aid claimants in drawing up their papers.

For FORMS and REGULATIONS relating to POWERS OF ATTORNEY, in pension cases, see Chapter XVI.

CHAPTER X.

GRATUITOUS PENSIONS.

SECTION I.

WIDOWS AND ORPHANS—VOLUNTEERS AND MILITIA, SINCE REVOLUTION.

By an act of March 14, 1798,[1] entitled "an act to provide for the widows and orphans of certain deceased officers," the provisions of the act of June 7, 1794,[2] are extended to the widows and orphan children of the commissioned officers of the militia, who died by reason of wounds received since the fourth day of March, one thousand seven hundred and eighty-nine, in the actual service of the United States. Two years' time was allowed in which to make applications for the benefits of the act.

"An act for the relief of the officers and soldiers who served in the late campaign on the Wabash," approved April 10, 1812,[3] provides:

Sec. 2. *And be it further enacted*, That the officers, according to the rank which they held as aforesaid, the non-commissioned officers and soldiers of the volunteers and militia, who served in the said campaign, and who were killed or died of wounds received in said service, leaving a widow, or, if no widow, shall have left a child or

---

1 U. S. Statutes at Large, vol. i, 540.

2 See "Widows and Orphans—Regulars," page 158.

3 U. S. Statutes at Large, vol. ii, 704. This act was passed for the benefit of officers and soldiers, and their widows and children, in the campaign on the Wabash, conducted by General Harrison against the Indians. The rank referred to in the second section is the rank assigned officers by General Harrison.

children under the age of sixteen, such widow, or, if no widow, such child or children shall be entitled to and receive the half of the monthly pay to which the deceased was entitled at the time of his death, or receiving the wound of which he died, for and during the term of five years; and in case of the death or intermarriage of such widow before the expiration of the term of five years, the half-pay for the remainder of the term shall go to the child or children of such deceased officer or soldier, while under the age of sixteen years; and, in like manner, the allowance to the child or children of such deceased, where there is no widow, shall be paid no longer than while there is a child or children under the age aforesaid: *Provided*, That no greater sum shall be allowed, in any case, to the widow or to the child or children of any officer, than the half-pay of a lieutenant-colonel.

Provision was made for the widows and children of commissioned officers of the militia and volunteers, who might die by reason of wounds received in the service, by an act approved August 2, 1813, entitled "an act to provide for the widows and orphans of militia slain, and for militia disabled, in the service of the United States;"[1] as follows:

Be it enacted by the Senate and House of Representatives of the United States of America in Congress assembled, That if any commissioned officer of the militia or of any volunteer corps shall, while in the service of the United States, die, by reason of wounds received in actual service of the United States, and leave a widow, or, if no widow, a child or children under sixteen years of age, such widow, or, if no widow, such child or children shall be entitled to and receive half the monthly pay to which the deceased was entitled at the time of his death, for and during the term of five years. But in the case of the death or intermarriage of such widow, before the expiration of the said term of five years, the half-pay for the remainder of the term shall go to the child or children of such deceased officer: *Provided, always*, That such half-pay shall cease on the death of such child or children.

1 U. S. Statutes at Large, vol. iii, 73.

SEC. 3. *And be it further enacted*, That the provisions of this act shall be construed to have effect from and after the eighteenth day of June, one thousand eight hundred and twelve.

By an act approved April 16, 1816, entitled "an act making further provision for military services during the late war, and for other purposes,"[1] it is prescribed:

Be it enacted by the Senate and House of Representatives of the United States of America in Congress assembled, That when any officer or private soldier of the militia, including rangers, sea-fencibles and volunteers, or any non-commissioned officer, musician or private, enlisted for either of the terms of one year or eighteen months, or any commissioned officer of the regular army, shall have died while in the service of the United States, during the late war, or in returning to his place of residence, after being mustered out of service, or who shall have died at any time thereafter, in consequence of wounds received while in the service, and shall have left a widow, or if no widow, a child or children under sixteen years of age, such widow, or if no widow, such child or children shall be entitled to receive half the monthly pay to which the deceased was entitled at the time of his death, for and during the term of five years; and in case of the death or intermarriage of such widow before the expiration of said five years, the half pay for the remainder of the time shall go to the child or children of said decedent; *Provided, always*, That the Secretary of War shall adopt such forms of evidence, in applications under this act, as the President of the United States may prescribe;[2] . . .

These provisions, as will have been observed, are confined to the widows and orphans of certain persons who died from disability incurred in the war of 1812.

An act amendatory of the last-named act, approved March 3, 1817,[3] prescribes the rate of pensions to be allowed to those who are entitled to the benefits of the act, as follows:

1 U. S. Statutes at Large, vol. iii, 285.

2 For the remainder of this act, see page 163.

3 U. S. Statutes at Large, vol. iii, 394.

Be it enacted by the Senate and House of Representatives of the United States of America in Congress assembled, That the widows and children of soldiers of the militia, the volunteers, the rangers, and the sea-fencibles, who served during the late war, and for whom half-pay for five years was provided, by an act passed on the sixteenth day of April, one thousand eight hundred and sixteen, entitled "an act making further provision for military services during the late war, and for other purposes," shall be placed on an equality as to their annual allowance; that is to say: such widows, and in case of no widow such children, as may be embraced in the before-recited act, shall be entitled to receive (as the half-pay to which they are entitled), at the rate of forty-eight dollars per annum, and no more; and the widows and children aforesaid, of the officers of the different corps aforesaid, shall be entitled to the half-pay of the officers of the infantry.

By an act of April 20, 1818, entitled "an act to increase the pay of militia while in actual service, and for other purposes,"[1] provision was made for the widows and children of the militia who had served or might serve in the war against the Seminole Indians, and who had died or been killed, or who might die or be killed, in the service, as follows:

SEC. 2. *And be it further enacted*, That the widows and orphans of the militia who have been called into the service of the United States since the first day of September, eighteen hundred and seventeen, or who hereafter may be called into the said service, in prosecuting said war, or who may have died or been killed, or hereafter may die or be killed, in such service, shall be entitled to the same half-pay, for five years, and pensions allowed, by the laws now in force, to the widows and orphans of the militia who died or were killed in the service of the United States during the late war with Great Britain.

"An act to provide for the payment of volunteers and militia corps in the service of the United States," approved March 19, 1836,[2] makes provision for the widows

[1] U. S. Statutes at Large, vol. iii, 459. [2] *Ibid*, vol. v, 7.

and children of deceased volunteers and militia who died of disabilities incurred in the Florida war, as follows:

SEC. 5. *And be it further enacted,* That when any officer, non-commissioned officer, artificer or private of said militia or volunteer corps,[1] who shall die in the service of the United States or returning to his place of residence after being mustered out of service, or at any time in consequence of wounds received in service, and shall leave a widow, or if no widow, a child or children under sixteen years of age, such widow, or if no widow, such child or children, shall be entitled to receive half the monthly pay to which the deceased was entitled at the time of his death, for and during the term of five years; and in case of the death or intermarriage of such widow before the expiration of five years, the half-pay for the remainder of the time shall go to the child or children of said decedent: *Provided, always,* That the Secretary of War shall adopt such forms of evidence, in applications under this act, as the President of the United States may prescribe.

By the first section of an act approved July, 4, 1836, entitled "an act granting half-pay to widows or orphans, when their husbands and fathers have died of wounds received in the military service of the United States in certain cases, and for other purposes,"[2] it is provided:

Be it enacted by the Senate and House of Representatives of the United States of America in Congress assembled, That when any officer, non-commissioned officer, musician or private, of the militia, including rangers, sea-fencibles, and volunteers, shall have died while in the service of the United States, since the twentieth day of April, eighteen hundred and eighteen, or who shall have died in consquence of a wound received while in the service, since the day aforesaid,[3] and shall have left a widow, or, if no widow, a child or

1 The preceding section grants invalid pensions to persons disabled in the service, in suppressing Indian depredations in Florida; and the clause in this section, "said militia or volunteer corps," evidently refers to the troops thus engaged.

2 U. S. Statutes at Large, vol. v, 127.

3 Pensions under the first section of the act of July 4, 1836, commence

children under sixteen years of age, such widow, or if no widow, such child or children shall be entitled to receive half the monthly pay to which the deceased was entitled at the time of his death, or receiving such wound, for and during the term of five years;[1] and in case of the death or marriage of such widow before the expiration of said five years, the half-pay for the remainder of the time shall go to the said decedent:[2] *Provided*, That the half-pay aforesaid shall be half the monthly pay of the officers, non-commissioned officers, musicians and privates of the infantry of the regular army, and no more: *Provided, also*, That no greater sum shall be allowed to the widow or to the child or children of an officer, than the half-pay of a lieutenant-colonel.

A proviso to a pension appropriation act of April 30, 1844,[3] directs that "no pension shall hereafter be granted to a widow for the same time that her husband received one."

---

from the death of the husband, when the death occurred prior to the passage of the act; and when it occurred subsequently, from the time of the death of the husband. The first section embraces the cases of widows and orphans whose husbands and fathers may hereafter die in the service, as well as those who had died before the passage of the law. *Attorney-General Butler, Oct.* 24, 1836.

This act was amended by acts of July 21, 1848, page 204, and February 22, 1849, (page 206), and construed by the joint resolution of September 28, 1850, (page 207).

1 Pensions under the act of July 4, 1836, are renewed by the act of February 3, 1853. *Commissioner Waldo, Nov.* 16, 1853. By the act of June 3, 1858, all half-pay pensions were continued during life or widowhood, to widows; and until sixteen years of age to children.

When a soldier embraced in the first section of the act of the 4th of July, 1836, has died, leaving a widow and children, and the widow has married before the passage of the act, the children, within the equity of the law, and by a liberal construction of its provisions, are entitled to its benefits. *Attorney-General Butler, August* 3, 1836.

2 A widow pensioner under the law of July 4, 1836, is entitled to her pension up to the date of her death, or intermarriage, if either occur within the five years for which the pension runs; and for the remainder of the time, if any, the pension inures to the child or children under sixteen years of age. *Second Comptroller.*

3 U. S. Statutes at Large, vol. v, 656.

A rule of evidence, applicable to all widows whose husbands were pensioners at the time of their death, was established by an act of May 7, 1846,[1] as follows:

SEC. 2. *And be it further enacted*, That no widow entitled to a pension under existing laws, and claiming a pension, whose husband was drawing a pension at the time of his decease, shall be required, in any such case, to furnish any further evidence that said husband was entitled to a pension; nor shall any evidence, in any case, be required to entitle the widow to a pension, when the evidence is in the archives of the government, other than such proof as would be sufficient to establish the marriage between the applicant and the deceased pensioner in civil personal actions in a court of justice.[2]

An act of July 21, 1848, entitled "an act amending the act entitled 'an act granting half-pay to widows or orphans, where their husbands and fathers have died of wounds received in the military service of the United States,' in case of deceased officers and soldiers of the militia and volunteers, passed July fourth, eighteen hundred and thirty-six,"[3] extends the benefits of the first section of the act of July 4, 1836, to the widows and orphans of officers and soldiers of the regular army and volunteers, who died of disabilities which accrued in the service, as follows:

SEC. 2. *And be it further enacted*, That all widows[4] and orphans

1 U. S. Statutes at Large, vol. ix, 6.

2 The fact that the husband was upon the rolls is presumptive evidence that he was entitled to it. It is for the government to show that he was not so entitled. General reputation, and cohabitation, are, in general, sufficient evidence of marriage; but the presumption arising in such cases may be rebutted. *Attorney-General Mason, June* 23, 1846.

3 U. S. Statutes at Large, vol. ix, 249.

4 Where a widow, pensioned under the act of July 21, 1848, contracts another marriage, the agent must require her pension certificate to be surrendered, on paying her pension to the date of such intermarriage. If she has a child entitled to the reversion of the pension, application must be made, with proper proof, to the Commissioner of Pensions, for a new certi-

of officers, non-commissioned officers, musicians and privates, whether of the regular army or of volunteers, who have died since the first day of April, one thousand eight hundred and forty-six, or who died during the war with Mexico, from wounds received, or from disease contracted, while in the line of duty, shall be entitled to the same rate of pension as is provided for in the first section of the before-mentioned act,[1] under like restrictions: *Provided*, Said death has occurred or may hereafter occur, while said officers, non-commissioned officers, musicians or privates, were in the service of the United States, and in the line of duty;[2] or while returning to their usual place of residence in the United States, after having received a discharge upon a surgeon's certificate for disability while in the line of duty, or while on their march to join the army in Mexico: *And provided further*, That this act shall not be applicable to the widows and orphans of such officers, non-commissioned officers, musicians or privates, who have not served in Mexico, or at posts or stations on the borders of Mexico; except where such officers, non-commissioned officers, musicians or privates, have died while on their march to join the army of the United States in Mexico.

SEC. 3. All pensions under this act shall be granted under such rules, regulations, restrictions and limitations as the Secretary of War, with the approbation of the President of the United States, may prescribe.

The provisions of this second section were, by act of February 22, 1849, extended to the widows and orphans of all regulars and volunteers who died, by any means,

---

ficate in the name of the child. *Regulations of Second Comptroller.* See also notes to act of July 4, 1836, just preceding. See also joint resolution of March 3, 1849, on page 206.

1 That is, the act of July 4, 1836. The act of July 21, 1848, was amended by act of February 22, 1849; the pension granted therein was extended five years by act of February 3, 1853; and extended for life, etc., by act of June 3, 1858. A construction was given by resolution of September 28, 1850; and a rule of evidence established by resolution of March 3, 1849.

2 Under this act it was decided by Secretary Stuart (Oct. 10, 1850), that death caused by intemperance, is not a case of death occurring in the line of duty.

while in the service, or while returning to their homes, after being honorably discharged. The act is as follows:

AN ACT *granting five years' Half-pay to certain Widows and Orphans of Officers, Non-commissioned Officers, Musicians and Privates, both Regulars and Volunteers.*[1]

Be it enacted by the Senate and House of Representatives of the United States of America in Congress assembled, That the provisions of the second section of the act entitled "an act amending the act, entitled 'an act granting half-pay to widows or orphans where their husbands or fathers have died of wounds received in the military service of the United States, in cases of deceased officers and soldiers of the militia and volunteers,' " approved July 21, 1848, shall be so construed as to embrace all widows and orphans of officers, non-commissioned officers, musicians and privates, whether of the regular army or of volunteers, who have received an honorable discharge, or who remained to the day of their death in the military service of the United States, and who have died since their return to their usual places of residence, of wounds received, or from disease contracted while in line of duty, subject to such rules, regulations and restrictions as the Secretary of War, by the third section of said act is authorized to impose.[2]

A "joint resolution relative to evidence in applications for pensions by widows of deceased soldiers, under the act of July twenty-first, eighteen hundred and forty-eight," passed March 3, 1849,[3] prescribes:

Resolved by the Senate and House of Representatives of the United States of America in Congress assembled, That in all applications for pensions by the widows of deceased soldiers under the act of July twenty-first, eighteen hundred and forty-eight, the

---

[1] U. S. Statutes at Large, vol. ix, 347.

[2] A construction of this act was given by joint resolution of September 28, 1850; and by act of February 3, 1853, the pensions granted thereby were extended five years, and by act of June 3, 1858, were extended during life, etc. The act of February 3, 1853, also provides that officers and soldiers of the war of 1812, and of Indian wars since 1790, shall be embraced in the provisions of the act of February 22, 1849.

[3] U. S. Statutes at Large, vol. ix, 418.

returns on the rolls of the disease of which the soldier died, and the official opinion of the surgeon-general founded thereon, that from the nature of the disease it was contracted while the soldier was in the line of his duty, shall be considered satisfactory evidence thereof, without the proof now required at the Pension Office; and that it shall be the duty of the Commissioner of Pensions in all cases of application for pensions under said act, to apply to the proper officers for said evidence, without requiring the applicant to furnish the same.

By a joint resolution of the 28th September, 1850,[1] it was directed that the second section of the act of July 21, 1848, extended by the act of February 22, 1849, be construed to embrace the widows and orphans of all persons designated therein, who died while in actual service in the war with Mexico, or in going to and returning from the same; and also to the widows and orphans of all such persons as, having been honorably discharged, or having resigned, shall have died after the passage of said last-mentioned act, or who may hereafter die, of wounds received or from disease contracted while in said service: *Provided*, That the army rolls showing the death of any of said persons in the army shall be sufficient evidence to establish that fact.

The half-pay allowed by certain acts to certain widows and children was renewed five years, by an act of February 3, 1853, entitled "an act to continue half-pay to certain widows and orphans."[2] This act is as follows:

Be it enacted by the Senate and House of Representatives of the United States of America in Congress assembled, That all widows[3] and orphans

1 U. S. Statutes at Large, vol. ix, 564.

3 *Ibid*, vol. x, 154.

3 An act of August 5, 1854, provides that the second marriage of a widow shall not bar her of her right to a pension under the act of February 3, 1853, provided she is a widow at the time of making the claim.

who were granted and allowed five years' half-pay by the provisions of the act approved the twenty-first day of July, one thousand eight hundred and forty-eight, entitled "an act amending the act granting half-pay to widows or orphans, where their husbands or fathers have died of wounds received in the military service of the United States, in case of deceased officers and soldiers of the militia and volunteers, passed July fourth, one thousand eight hundred and thirty-six," or an act approved the twenty-second day of February, one thousand eight hundred and forty-nine, entitled "an act granting five years' half-pay, to certain widows and orphans of officers, non-commissioned officers, musicians and privates, both regulars and volunteers," [1] be, and they are hereby granted a continuance of said half-pay, under like limitations and restrictions, for a further period of five years, to commence at the expiration of the half-pay provided for by the aforesaid acts: *Provided, however*, That in case of the death or marriage of such widow before the expiration of said term of five years, the half-pay for the remainder of the term, shall go to the child or children of the deceased officer or soldier, while under the age of sixteen years; and in like manner the child or children of such deceased, when there is no widow, shall be paid no longer than while there is a child or children under the age aforesaid: *And provided further*, That no greater sum shall be allowed in any case to the widow, or to the child or children of any officer, than the half-pay of a lieutenant-colonel: *Provided further*, That the act approved the twenty-second of February, one thousand eight hundred and forty-nine, "granting five years' half-pay to certain widows and orphans of officers, non-commissioned officers, musicians and privates, both regular and volunteer," be so extended and construed as to embrace the widows and minor heirs of the officers, non-commissioned officers, musicians and privates, of the regulars, militia and volunteers of the war of eighteen hundred and twelve, and of the various Indian wars since 1790. [2]

1 Pensions under the act of February 22, 1849, July 21, 1848, and July 4, 1836, are renewed by the act of February 3, 1853; but pensions under special acts are not renewed by said acts. *Commissioner Waldo, November* 16, 1853.

2 The widow of a soldier killed by the Indians in a time of peace, is not entitled to the benefits of the act of February 3, 1853. *Commissioner Waldo, December* 21, 1853.

The third section of an army appropriation act of August 5, 1854,[1] provides a rule of construction applicable to cases under the act of February 3, 1853, as follows:

SEC. 3. *And be it further enacted*, That . . . the act approved February third, one thousand eight hundred and fifty-three, entitled "an act to continue half-pay to certain widows and orphans," shall not be so construed as to deprive any widow from the benefits therein granted for the services of her husband, though she may have married again: *Provided, however*, That the applicant is a widow at the time of making the claim: *Provided*, Such party shall not receive pension during coverture.

By an act of June 3, 1858, entitled "an act to extend 'an act to continue half-pay to certain widows and orphans,' approved February three, eighteen hundred and fifty-three."[2] Congress continued the half-pay of widows in all cases, for life, and of orphans until the age of sixteen years. This important act is as follows:

Be it enacted by the Senate and House of Representatives of the United States of America in Congress assembled, That all those surviving widows and minor children who have been, or may be, granted and allowed five years' half-pay under the provisions of any law or laws of the United States, be and they are hereby, granted a continuance of such half-pay, under the following terms and limitations, viz: to such widows during life, and to such child or children, where there is no widow, while under the age of sixteen years, to commence from the expiration of the half-pay provided for by the first section of the act entitled "an act to continue half-pay to certain widows and orphans," approved February three, eighteen hundred and fifty-three: *Provided, however*, That in case of the marriage or death of any such widow, the half-pay shall go to the child or children of the deceased officer or soldier while under the age of sixteen years; and, in like manner, the child or children of such deceased officer

1 U. S. Statutes at Large, vol. x, 581.

2 *Ibid*, vol. xi, 309.

or soldier, when there is no widow, shall be paid no longer than while there are children or a child under the age aforesaid: *And provided further*, That the half-pay of such widow and orphans shall be half the monthly pay of the officers, non-commissioned officers, musicians and privates of the infantry of the regular army of the United States, and no more, and that no greater sum shall be allowed to such widow or minor children than the half-pay of a lieutenant-colonel; *And provided, also*, That this act shall not be construed to apply to or embrace the case of any person or persons now receiving a pension for life; and, further, that wherever half-pay shall have been granted by any special act of Congress, and is renewed or continued under the provisions of this act, the same shall commence from the date hereof.

WAR OF 1861.

An act of July 14, 1862, granting pensions in general for wounds, disease or death, incurred in the war of 1861, for the suppression of rebellion, contains the following provisions:

AN ACT *to Grant Pensions.*

Be it enacted by the Senate and House of Representatives of the United States of America in Congress assembled, That if any officer, non-commissioned officer, musician or private of the army, including regulars, volunteers and militia, or any officer, warrant or petty officer, musician, seaman, ordinary seaman, flotillaman, marine, clerk, landsman, pilot or other person in the navy or marine corps has been, since the fourth day of March, eighteen hundred and sixty-one, or shall hereafter be disabled by reason of any wound received or disease contracted while in the service of the United States and in the line of duty, he shall, upon making due proof of the fact according to such forms and regulations as are or may be provided by or in pursuance of law, be placed upon the list of invalid pensions [pensioners] of the United States, and be entitled to receive for the highest rate of disability, such pension as is hereinafter provided in such cases, and for an inferior disability an amount proportionate to the highest disability, to commence as hereinafter provided, and continue during the existence of such disability. The pension for a total disability for officers, non-commissioned officers, musicians and privates employed in the military service of the United States, whether regulars, volunteers or militia, and in the marine corps, shall be as follows, viz: Lieutenant-colonel and all officers of a higher rank, thirty dollars per month; major, twenty-five dollars per month; captain, twenty dollars per month; first lieutenant, seventeen dollars per month; second lieutenant, fifteen dollars per month; and non-commissioned officers, musicians and privates, eight dollars per month. The pension for total disability for officers, warrant or petty officers, and others employed in the naval service of the United States, shall be as follows, viz: Captain, commander, surgeon, paymaster and chief engineer, respectively, ranking with commander by law, lieutenant commanding and master commanding, thirty dollars per month; lieutenant, surgeon, paymaster and chief engineer, respectively, ranking with lieutenant by law, and passed assistant surgeon, twenty-five dollars per month; professor of mathematics, master, assistant surgeon, assistant paymaster and chaplain, twenty dollars per month; first assistant engineers and pilots, fifteen dollars per month; passed midshipman, midshipman, captains' and paymasters' clerk, second and third assistant engineer, masters' mate and all warrant officers, ten dollars per month; all petty officers and all other persons before named employed in the naval service, eight dollars per month; and all commissioned officers, of either service, shall receive such and only such pension as is herein provided for the rank in which they hold commissions.

SEC. 2. *And be it further enacted*, That if any officer or other person named in the first section of this act has died since the fourth day of March, eighteen hundred and sixty-one, or shall hereafter die, by reason of any wound received or disease contracted while in the service of the United States, and in the line of duty, his widow, or, if there be no widow, his child or children under sixteen years of age, shall be entitled to receive the same pension as the husband or father would have been entitled to had he been totally disabled, to commence from the death of the husband or father, and to continue to the widow during her widowhood, or to the child or children until they severally attain to the age of sixteen years, and no longer.

SEC. 4. *And be it further enacted*, That . . . *And provided, further*, That no moneys shall be paid to the widow or children, or any heirs of any deceased officer, on account of bounty, back pay or pension, who have in any way been engaged in, or who have aided or abetted, the existing rebellion in the United States; but the right of such disloyal widow or children, heir or heirs of such soldier, shall be vested in the loyal heir or heirs of the deceased, if any there be.

SEC. 6. *And be it further enacted*, That the fees of agents and attorneys, for making out and causing to be executed the papers necessary to establish a claim for a pension, bounty and other allowance before the Pension Office under this act, shall not exceed the following rates: For making out and causing to be duly executed a declaration by the applicant, with the necessary affidavits, and forwarding the same to the Pension Office, with the requisite correspondence, five dollars. In cases wherein additional testimony is required by the Commissioner of Pensions, for each affidavit so required and executed and forwarded (except the affidavits of surgeons, for which such agents and attorneys shall not be entitled to any fees), one dollar and fifty cents.

SEC. 7. *And be it further enacted*, That any agent or attorney who shall, directly or indirectly, demand or receive any greater compensation for his services under this act than is prescribed in the preceding section of this act, or who shall contract or agree to prosecute any claim for a pension, bounty or other allowance under this act, on the condition that he shall receive a per centum upon or any portion of the amount of such claim, or who shall wrongfully withhold from a pensioner or other claimant the whole or any part of the pension or claim allowed and due to such pensioner or claimant, shall be deemed guilty of a high misdemeanor, and upon conviction thereof shall, for every such offense, be fined not exceeding three hundred dollars, or imprisoned at hard labor not exceeding two years, or both, according to the circumstances and aggravations of the offense.

The other sections of the act may be found on pages 28 to 33.

GENERAL OBSERVATIONS.

The act of April 16, 1816, makes provision for the widows and orphans of officers and soldiers who served in the war of 1812.

The amount of the half-pay to widows and orphans of

the militia and volunteers, and certain others troops, is fixed by the act of March 3, 1817.

The benefits of all laws granting half-pay to widows and orphans of regulars, were extended to the widows and children of militia who died in the Seminole war, by act of April 20, 1818.

Half-pay was granted to the widows and orphans of volunteers and militia who served on the Wabash, under General Harrison, by act of April 10, 1812; and like provision was made by act of March 19, 1836, for the widows and orphans of volunteers and militia who served in the Florida war.

The act of July 4, 1836, makes provision for the widows of volunteers, militia, and others who served after April 20, 1818.

The act of July 21, 1848, extends the benefits of the first section of the act of July 4, 1836, to the widows and orphans of those who served in the Mexican war. These benefits were by act of February 22, 1849, also extended to the widows and orphans of all regulars and volunteers who died in the service, or after discharge, from wounds or disease, received or contracted in the service.

The joint resolution of September 28, 1850, construed the acts of July 21, 1848, and February 22, 1849.

The act of February 3, 1853, continued for five additional years the half-pay granted by acts of July 21, 1848, and February 22, 1849, and by relation (according to the decision of the Commissioner of Pensions), the half-pay provided in the first section of the act of July 4, 1836. This act also extended the benefits of the act of February 22, 1849, to the widows and orphans of officers and soldiers of the war of 1812, and Indian wars since 1790.

The act of August 5, 1854, prescribes that the marriage of a widow, after the death of her soldier-husband, shall not bar her of a pension, if she be again a widow at the time of making her application.

The act of June 3, 1858, renews for life or widowhood, to widows, and until the age of sixteen years, to orphans, the half-pay granted under any act of Congress.

The act of July 14, 1862, makes provisions for the widows and orphans of the war of 1861.

SECTION II.

REGULATIONS AND FORMS FOR OBTAINING PENSIONS FOR WIDOWS AND ORPHANS OF VOLUNTEERS AND MILITIA.

The same regulations and forms (with slight variations) which appertain to the claims of widows and orphans of regulars, apply to those of the widows and orphans of volunteers and militia. To the former, therefore, claimants under this title are referred. They may also consult "Regulations and Forms for obtaining pensions for widows of persons who served in the war of the revolution," with profit.

A few forms, applicable to claims under the various acts granting pensions to the widows of volunteers and militia, in general, here follow, by way of illustration:

Widow's Declaration.

STATE OF ——, }
County of——. } *ss.*

On this —— day of 18—, before —— in and for the county and State above-named, personally appeared ——, a resident of ——, in the State of ——, aged —— years, who being duly sworn according to law, declares that she is the widow of ——, who was a —— in company ——, commanded by Captain —— of the —— regiment of volunteers, commanded by Colonel ——, and who —— at —— on or about the —— day of —— 18—, while in the service of the United States —— [*Here give the particulars of death, stating particularly whether it was caused in battle or by wounds received, of which the husband subsequently died, or by disease (describing it) contracted in the line of duty; also the time of his death.*]

That she was married to the said —— on the —— day of —— 18—, at —— by one —— a ——, that her name before her said marriage was ——; that there were born to her and her said husband, during the existence of said marriage the following children, who are now under sixteen years of age, viz: [*Here give names, date of birth, and residence of all the children under sixteen years of age.*] That she has remained a widow since the death of her said husband; all which will appear by the proof hereto annexed. [*Should there be no public record of the marriage, that fact should be stated; should there be neither public nor private record, this should be stated; and so, if there should be no living witnesses of the marriage, or if their places of residence should be unknown.*]

She makes this declaration for the purpose of obtaining the half-pay pension to which she is entitled by reason of the services and death of her said husband, and hereby constitutes and appoints —— her attorney to prosecute the claim and procure a certificate.[1]

(*Claimant's Signature.*)

Sworn to and subscribed before —— the day and year first above-written, and on the same day, personally came —— and ——, residents of ——, who being duly sworn according to law, declare that they are personally acquainted with Mrs. —— widow of —— who has made and subscribed the foregoing declaration, and were acquainted with her and her said husband before he entered the service, and know that they lived together as man and wife, and were so reputed. That she is the widow of the identical —— who performed the military service mentioned in said declaration, and has remained a widow since his death. That their knowledge of the identity of her husband with the soldier is derived from personal knowledge [*or otherwise*].

And they further testify that they reside as above-stated, and are disinterested in this claim. (*Witnesses' Signatures.*)

Sworn to and subscribed before ——, and I certify that I am not interested in this claim, or concerned in its prosecution; that I believe the affiants to be credible persons, and the declarant is the person she represents herself to be. (*Officer's Signature.*)

This declaration must be made before a Court of Record, or before a Judge or Clerk of such Court.

For Forms of Affidavits and other proof which must accompany the foregoing declaration, and also for general instructions relative to such claims, applicants are re-

[1] A separate power of attorney is preferable.

ferred to "WIDOWS AND ORPHANS—REVOLUTIONARY WAR," and "WIDOWS AND ORPHANS—REGULARS." Such accompanying proof may be made before any officer authorized to administer oaths in general. The official character of such officer must be attested as follows:

STATE OF —— }
County of —— } *ss.*

I, ——, clerk of the —— court, in and for the county and State above-named, do hereby certify that ——, before whom the foregoing affidavits were made, and who has thereunto signed his name, was at the time of so doing a —— in and for the county and State aforesaid, duly commissioned and sworn, that all his official acts, as such, are entitled to full faith and credit, and that his signature thereto is genuine.

[L. S.] In testimony whereof, I have hereunto signed my name and affixed my official seal this —— day of ——, 18—.

Clerk of the —— Court —— County.

For REGULATIONS and FORMS relating to POWERS OF ATTORNEY in pension cases, see Chapter XVI.

ACT OF JULY 14, 1862.

The regulations and forms prescribed by the Commissioner, to be observed in making applications under this act, in behalf of widows and orphans, will be found under title "WIDOWS AND ORPHANS—REGULARS."

CHAPTER XI.

GRATUITOUS PENSIONS.

SECTION. I.

WIDOWS AND ORPHANS—INDIAN WARS.

THE President was empowered by an act approved January 2, 1812,[1] entitled "an act authorizing the President of the United States to raise certain companies of rangers, for the protection of the frontier of the United States," whenever satisfactorily advised of an actual or threatened incursion of Indian tribes into any State or Territory, to raise, by enlistment or the acceptance of volunteers, for one year,[2] six[3] companies of rangers, for whom the following provision was made:

SEC. 4. *And be it further enacted*, That the officers, non-commissioned officers, and privates, raised pursuant to this act, shall be entitled to like compensation in case of disability by wounds, and otherwise incurred in the service, as officers, non-commissioned officers, and privates, in the present military establishment, and with them shall be subject to the rules and articles of war, which have

1 U. S. Statutes at Large, vol. ii, 670.

2 This was extended one year, and until the close of the next session of Congress thereafter, by act of July 24, 1813. (U. S. Statutes at Large, vol. iii, 39.)

3 An act passed July 1, 1812 (U. S. Stats. at Large, vol. ii, 776), authorized the raising of an additional company, under the same provisions, conditions and restrictions contained in the act of January, 1812; and an act approved February 25, 1813 (U. S. Stats. at Large, vol. ii, 804), added ten more companies, upon the same terms. These ten companies were intended for service upon the frontiers, against the Indian allies of the British, and were originally authorized for one year; but by act of February 24, 1814 (U. S. Stats. at Large, vol. iii, 98), the term of service was extended one year.

been established, or may hereafter be by law established; and the provisions of the act entitled "an act fixing the military peace establishment of the United States," so far as they may be applicable, shall be extended to all persons, matters, and things, within the intent and meaning of this act, in the same manner as if they were inserted at large in the same.[1] . . .

An act approved April 10, 1812, entitled "an act for the relief of the officers and soldiers who served in the late campaign on the Wabash," provides that the officers and men who served under General Harrison, against the Indians on the Wabash, shall receive the same pay, according to the rank assigned them by General Harrison, as is allowed the militia; and that the widows or orphans of such as were slain, or died of wounds received in the service, should receive half the monthly pay to which the deceased husband or father was entitled at the time of his death, for five years. Section two of this act, which contains the latter provision, may be found in full on page 198.

Half-pay is granted to the widows and orphans of rangers and others, in certain cases, by an act of April 16, 1816, entitled "an act making further provision for military services during the late war, and for other purposes.[3] (See page 200).

By an act of April 20, 1818, entitled "an act to increase the pay of the militia while in actual service, and

[1] The act of 1802, here referred to, makes provision for the widows and orphans of commissioned officers only. See section 15 of this act, on page 159.

[2] U. S. Statutes at Large, vol. ii, 704.

[3] U. S. Statutes at Large, vol. iii, 285. An act of March 3, 1817, fixes the amount of half-pay to which widows and orphans of soldiers shall be entitled under this act at forty-eight dollars per annum; and of widows and orphans of officers at half the pay of officers of the infantry.—(U. S. Satutes at Large, vol. iii, 394).

for other purposes,"[1] the same provision was made for the widows and children of the militia who had served, or might serve, in the war against the Seminole Indians, and who had died or been killed, or might die or be killed, in such service, as for the widows and orphans of the militia who died or were killed in the service of the United States during the war of 1812. Section two of this act, which contains this provision, is given at large on page 201.

"An act for the more perfect defense of the frontiers," approved March 2, 1833,[2] authorizes the enlistment of a regiment of dragoons, for service upon the border, and provides:

SEC. 3. *And be it further enacted*, That the said regiment of dragoons shall be liable to serve on horse or foot, as the President may direct; shall be subject to the rules and articles of war, be recruited in the same manner, and with the same limitations; that the officers, non-commissioned officers, musicians, farriers and privates, shall be entitled to the same provisions for wounds and disabilities, the same provisions for widows and children, and the same allowances and benefits, in every respect, as are allowed the other troops constituting the present military peace establishment.

Provision was made by act of March 19, 1836, entitled "an act to provide for the payment of volunteers and militia corps in the service of the United States,"[3] for the widows and orphans of the volunteers and militia who had been or might be engaged in the service of the United States, in suppressing Indian hostilities in Florida, and had died, or might die, in the service. The section of the act in which this provision is made will be found on page 202.

1 U. S. Statutes at Large, vol. iii, 459.

2 *Ibid*, vol. iv, 652.

3 *Ibid*, vol. v, 7.

The first section of the act of July 4, 1836, entitled "an act granting half-pay to widows or orphans, where their husbands and fathers have died of wounds received in the military service of the United States in certain cases, and for other purposes," grants half-pay to the widows or orphans of militia, volunteers, rangers, and sea-fencibles, who died since April 20, 1818; a rule of evidence is established by act of May 7, 1846; another rule of evidence is prescribed by a joint resolution of September 28, 1850; an act of February 3, 1853, extends the benefits of the act of February 22, 1849, to the widows and orphans of officers and soldiers who served in the various Indian wars since 1790, and also extends the half-pay granted by said act of February 22, 1849, for five years. An act of August 5, 1854, provides that the widow of a deceased officer or soldier who has married again, may claim the benefits of the act of February 3, 1853, if she be a widow at the time of making her application; and an act of June 3, 1858, continues for life or widowhood, to widows, and until sixteen years of age, to orphans, the half-pay that may have been granted them for five years, by any former laws: all which acts and resolutions, with accompanying notes, will be found under "WIDOWS AND ORPHANS—VOLUNTEERS AND MILITIA," page 198.

Reference is also here made to an act of May 19, 1846, adding a regiment of mounted riflemen to the regular army for service on the route to Oregon, and making provision for the widows and children of such of these troops as might die, or be slain; which act will be found on page 167.

SECTION II.

REGULATIONS AND FORMS FOR OBTAINING PENSIONS FOR WIDOWS AND ORPHANS: INDIAN WARS.

As all the acts grouped in the preceding section may be found under either "WIDOWS AND ORPHANS—REGULARS," or "WIDOWS AND ORPHANS—VOLUNTEERS AND MILITIA," claimants are referred to those titles for the necessary form and regulations in making applications for widows or orphans whose husbands or fathers served in Indian wars.

CHAPTER XII.

GRATUITOUS PENSIONS.

SECTION I.

WIDOWS AND ORPHANS—NAVAL, SINCE REVOLUTION—INCLUDING NAVY PROPER, PRIVATEERS, SEA-FENCIBLES AND MARINES.

An act approved March 2, 1799, entitled "an act for the government of the navy of the United States,"[1] contains the following:

SEC. 8. *And be it further enacted,* That every officer, seaman or marine, disabled in the line of his duty, shall be entitled to receive, for his own life and the life of his wife, if a married man at the time of receiving the wound, one half his monthly pay.

This act was repealed by an act of April 23, 1800; but not to the prejudice of any rights acquired while it was in existence.

By an act of January 20, 1813, entitled "an act providing navy pensions in certain cases,"[2] half-pay for five years is granted to the widows or children of officers of the navy and marines, who may be killed or die in the service. This act is as follows:

Be it enacted by the Senate and House of Representatives of the United States of America in Congress assembled, That if any officer of the navy or marines shall be killed or die, by reason of a wound received in the line of his duty,[3] leaving a widow, or, if no widow, a child or

1 U. S. Statutes at Large, vol. i, 716.

2 *Ibid,* vol. ii, 790.

3 This embraces all the operations of the ship, whether civil or military, and takes in the whole of her navigation during the entire cruise. The officer who is killed or dies by reason of a wound received by the falling of a spar in a tempest, is as entirely within the description of being killed or

children under sixteen years of age, such widow, or, if no widow, such child or children shall be entitled to receive half the monthly pay to which the deceased was entitled at the time of his death, which allowance shall continue for and during the term of five years; but in case of the death or intermarriage of such widow, before the expiration of the said term of five years, the half-pay for the remainder (*sic*) shall go to the child or children of the said deceased officer: *Provided*, That such half-pay shall cease on the death of such child or children; and the money required for this purpose shall be paid out of the navy pension fund, under the direction of the commissioners of that fund.

A general act, granting pensions to the widows and orphans of officers, seamen and marines belonging to the public and private armed vessels of the United States, who died or might die in such service, was passed on the 4th day of March, 1814;[1] and is as follows:

AN ACT *giving Pensions to the Orphans and Widows of Persons Slain in the Public and Private Armed Vessels of the United States.*

Be it enacted by the Senate and House of Representatives of the United States of America in Congress assembled, That if any officer,[2] seaman or marine, serving on board any private armed ship or vessel, bearing a commission of letter-of-marque, shall die, or shall have died since the eighteenth day of June, in the year of our Lord one thousand eight hundred and twelve, by reason of a wound[3] received in

dying by reason of a wound received in the line of his duty, as the officer who is killed or dies by a wound in battle. *Attorney-General Wirt, March* 31, 1825.

Under the navy pension act of January 20, 1813, and the second section of a like act of March 4, 1814, it does not occur to me that the death need occur in the naval service, provided it be proved to have been occasioned by a wound received while in the service, and in the line of his duty. *Attorney-General Butler, April* 6, 1838.

1 U. S. Statutes at Large, vol. iii, 103.

2 A navy agent is not "an officer, seaman or marine," and his widow is not entitled to a pension. *Attorney-General Butler, April* 7, 1837.

3 This was amended and explained by act of April 16, 1818.

the line of his duty, leaving a widow,[1] or, if no widow, a child or children under sixteen years of age, such widow, or, if no widow, such child or children shall be placed on the pension list by the Secretary of the Navy, who shall allow to such widow, child or children half the monthly pension to which the rank of the deceased would have entitled him, for the highest rate of disability, under "an act regulating pensions to persons on board private armed ships,"[2] which allowance shall continue for the term of five years;[3] but in case of the death or intermarriage of such widow, before the expiration of the term of five years, the half-pay for the remainder of the term shall go to the child or children of the deceased: *Provided*, That the half-pay shall cease on the death of such child or children. And the several pensions hereby granted shall he paid, by direction of the Secretary of the Navy, out of the fund provided by the seventeenth section of an act entitled "an act concerning letters-of-marque, prizes and prize goods," and from no other.[4]

SEC. 2. *And be it further enacted*, That if any seaman or marine belonging to the navy of the United States shall die, or if any officer,[5] seaman or marine belonging to the navy of the United States shall have died[6] since the eighteenth day of June, in the year of our Lord

---

1 A widow entitled to a pension, who marries again, may make application for the amount due up to the time of her marriage; and, in case of her death, her legal representatives may claim. *Attorney-General Wirt, June* 9, 1825; *Attorney-General Butler, April* 5, 1836. Two decisions. See also notes to preceding act.

2 See, for this act, "INVALID PENSIONS—NAVAL," page 84.

3 This was continued for an additional five years, by acts of April 16, 1818 (U. S. Statutes at Large, vol. iii, 427); April 9, 1824 (U. S. Statutes at Large, vol. iv, 18); May 23, 1828 (U. S. Statutes at Large, vol. iv, 288); and June 19, 1834 (U. S. Statutes at Large, vol. iv, 679).

4 This fund is exhausted.

5 The act of March 14, 1814, deals only with the past case of officers, and makes no provision for future cases, but leaves the future to stand solely upon the provisions of the act of January 20, 1813. *Attorney-General Wirt, March* 31, 1825.

6 Under the second section of the navy pension act of March 4, 1814, it does not appear to me that the death need occur in the naval service, provided it be proved to have been occasioned by a wound received while in the service, and in the line of duty. *Attorney-General Butler, April* 6, 1838.

one thousand eight hundred and twelve, by reason of a wound received in the line of his duty, leaving a widow,[1] or, if no widow, a child or children under sixteen years of age, such widow, or, if no widow, such child or children shall be entitled to and receive half the monthly pay to which the deceased was entitled at the time of his death, which allowance shall continue for the term of five years.[2] But in the case of the death or intermarriage of said widow, before the expiration of the said term of five years, the half-pay for the remainder of the term shall go to the child or children of the deceased: *Provided*, That such half-pay shall cease on the decease of such child or children. And the money required for this purpose shall be paid out of the navy pension fund, under the direction of the commissioners of that fund.

Provision was made, by an act of April 16, 1816, for the widows and children of sea-fencibles, who served in the war of 1812. This act, with notes, forms and regulations, will be found at large under title "WIDOWS AND ORPHANS—VOLUNTEERS AND MILITIA," page 200. Under this title will also be found an act passed on the 3d day of March, 1817, fixing the half-pay under the act of April 16, 1816.

"An act to amend and explain 'an act giving pensions to the widows and orphans of persons slain in the public and private armed vessels of the United States,'" approved March 3, 1817,[3] provides:

Be it enacted by the Senate and House of Representatives of the United States of America in Congress assembled, That if any officer, seaman or marine belonging to the navy of the United States[4] shall die or shall

1 See notes to preceding act.

2 This was extended, in periods of five years, by acts of March 3, 1819; January 22, 1824; May 23, 1828; June 23, 1832; June 30, 1834; March 3, 1845; and August 11, 1848; and by act of June 3, 1858, was continued for life to widows, and until sixteen years of age to orphans.

3 U. S. Statutes at Large, vol. iii, 373.

4 The provisions of this act are confined to officers, seamen and marines of the navy, and do not apply to private armed vessels. *Attorney-General*

have died since the 18th day of June, in the year of our Lord one thousand eight hundred and twelve, in consequence of disease contracted, or of casualties or injuries received, while in the line of his duty, and which shall be satisfactorily proved to the commissioners of the navy pension fund, leaving a widow,[1] or, if no widow, a child or children[2] under sixteen years of age, such widow, or, if no widow, such child or children shall be entitled to receive half the monthly pay to which the deceased was entitled at the time of his death, which allowance shall continue for the term of five years. But in case of the death or intermarriage of such widow, before the expiration of the said term of five years, the half-pay for the remainder of the term shall go to the child or children of the deceased: *Provided*, That such half-pay shall cease on the death of such child or children. And the money required for this purpose shall be paid out of the navy pension fund, under the direction of the commissioners of that fund.

This act was repealed by an act of January 22, 1824; but it is expressly provided in the repealing act that pensions already granted should be paid in full, and the repeal should not impair or affect the rights of persons acquired during the existence of the act.

The half-pay granted the widows of privateers, by act of March 4, 1814, was continued five years by act of April 16, 1818, entitled "an act in addition to 'an act giving pensions to the orphans and widows of persons slain in the public or private armed vessels of the United States,'"[3] as follows:

Be it enacted by the Senate and House of Representatives of the

---

Wirt, March 31, 1825. A navy agent is not an "officer, seaman or marine," and his widow is not entitled to a pension. *Attorney-General Butler, April* 7, 1837.

1 See notes to preceding acts.

2 If the widow have married before the passage of this act, the children of the deceased are entitled to the pension. *Attorney-General Butler, April* 7, 1837. *Same, April* 11, 1837.

3 U. S. Statutes at Large, vol. iii, 427.

United States of America in Congress assembled, That in every case where a person has been put on the pension list, or granted a certificate of pension by virtue of the first section of an act passed the fourth day of March, in the year eighteen hundred and fourteen, entitled "an act giving pensions to the orphans and widows of persons slain in the public or private armed vessels of the United States," the Secretary of the Navy be, and he is hereby authorized, at the expiration of the term of five years, for which any pension certificate shall have been granted as aforesaid, to allow the full monthly pension to which the rank of the deceased would have entitled him for the highest rate of disability, and that such pension shall continue to such person for the further term of five years: *Provided*, That such pension shall cease on the death of such widow, child or children.

SEC. 2. *And be it further enacted*, That if any officer, seaman, or marine, shall have died since the eighteenth day of June, in the year eighteen hundred and twelve, in consequence of an accident or casualty, which occurred in the line of his duty [1] on board [2] a private armed vessel, leaving a widow,[1] or if no widow, a child or children under sixteen years of age, the Secretary of the Navy be, and he is hereby authorized to place such widow, child or children, on the pension list, and allow to such widow, child or children, the same monthly pension as if the deceased had died by reason of wounds received in the line of his duty: *Provided*, That all moneys paid by virtue of this act shall be paid out of the privateer pension fund, and no other.

By an act approved March 3, 1819, entitled "an act extending the term of half-pay pensions to the widows and children of certain officers, seamen and marines, who died in the public service," [3] it is provided:

Be it enacted by the Senate and House of Representatives of the United States of America in Congress assembled, That in all

[1] See notes to preceding acts.

[2] This includes casualties which occur in the line of duty, whether "on board" the vessel, or other place where the rules of the service require the officer or seaman to be. *Attorney-General Wirt, March* 31, 1825.

[3] U. S. Statutes at Large, vol. iii, 502.

cases where provision has been made by law for five years half-pay to the widows [1] and children of officers, seamen and marines, who were killed in battle, or died of wounds received in battle, or who died in the naval service [1] of the United States, during the late war, the said provision shall be continued for the additional term of five years, to commence at the end of the first term of five years, in each case, respectively, making the provision equal to ten years half-pay; which shall be paid in the manner, and out of the fund, heretofore designated by law; and the said pensions shall also cease for the reasons mentioned in said law.

"An act further extending the term of half-pay pensions to the widows and children of officers, seamen and marines, who died in the public service," approved January 22, 1824,[2] provides:

Be it enacted by the Senate and House of Representatives of the United States of America in Congress assembled, That in all cases where provision has been made by law for five years' half-pay to the widows and children of officers, seamen and marines who were killed in battle, or who died in the naval service of the United States, during the late war; and, also, in all cases where provision has been made for extending the term for five years, in addition to the first term of five years, the said provision shall be further extended for an additional term of five years, to commence at the end of the second term of five years, in each case, respectively, making the provision equal to fifteen years' half-pay; which shall be paid out of the fund heretofore provided by law; and the said provisions shall cease for the causes mentioned in the laws providing the same, respectively.

The half-pay granted by former acts to the widows and orphans of privateers was extended for a third term of five years, by act of April 9, 1824, entitled "an act extending the term of pensions, granted to persons disabled, and to the widows and orphans of those who have been

[1] See notes to preceding acts.

[2] U. S. Statutes at Large, vol. iv, 4.

slain, or who have died, in consequence of wounds or casualties received while in the line of their duty, on board the private armed ships of the United States during the late war,"[1] as follows:

Be it enacted by the Senate and House of Representatives of the United States of America in Congress assembled, That the pensions of all persons, who are now in the receipt thereof, under the provisions of the following laws of the United States, or either of them, to-wit: An act passed March fourth, one thousand eight hundred and fourteen, entitled "an act giving pensions to the orphans and widows of persons slain in the public or private armed vessels of the United States," and an act passed April sixteenth, one thousand eight hundred and eighteen, entitled "an act in addition to an act giving pensions to the orphans and widows of persons slain in the public or private armed vessels of the United States," so far as regards persons receiving pensions from the funds arising from captures and salvage made by the private armed vessels of the United States be, and the same are hereby continued, under the restrictions and regulations in the said acts contained, for and during the additional term of five years, from and after the period of the expiration of the said pension, respectively: *Provided, however*, That the said pensions shall alone be paid from the proceeds of the privateer pension fund, so called, and without recourse to the United States for any deficiency (should such occur), which may hereafter arise thereon: *And provided, further*, That no pension shall be paid to such widow after her intermarriage, nor to any orphan children of such officer, seaman and marines, after they shall have attained the age of sixteen years.[2]

The pensions to the widows and children of privateers, renewed by the foregoing act, were continued for five additional years, by act of May 23, 1828;[3] and to widows only were continued five years beyond that, by act of

1 U. S. Statutes at Large, vol. iv, 18.

2 See notes to the acts referred to in this section.

3 U. S. Statutes at Large, vol. iv, 288.

June 19, 1834.[1] These continuing acts are nearly *verbatim*, like the act of April 9, 1824. The privateer pension fund having been exhausted, all laws granting pensions to the widows of privateers were permitted to expire by limitation.

The pensions granted by former acts to the widows and children of officers, seamen and marines, who died in the naval service of the United States, were by the first section of an act of May 23, 1828, entitled "an act to provide for extending the term of certain pensions, chargeable on the navy and privateer pension fund,"[2] continued for five additional years; as follows:

Be it enacted by the Senate and House of Representatives of the United States of America in Congress assembled, That in all cases where provision has been made by law for the five years' half-pay to the widows and children of officers, seamen and marines, who were killed in battle, or who died in the naval service of the United States during the last war; and also in all cases where provision has been made for extending the term for five years in addition to any term of five years, the said provision shall be extended for an additional term of five years, to commence at the current or last expired term of five years, in each case, respectively; making the provision equal to twenty years' half-pay; which shall be paid out of the fund heretofore provided for by law, and the said pensions shall cease for the causes mentioned in the laws providing the same respectively.[3]

The pensions renewed by the foregoing act, were continued to widows only, by an act of June 28, 1832, entitled "an act further to extend the pension heretofore granted to the widows of persons killed or who died in the naval service,"[4] for five additional years; by act of

1 U. S. Statutes at Large, vol. iv, 679.

2 *Ibid*, vol. iv, 288.

3 See notes to preceding laws.

4 U. S. Statutes at Large, vol. iv, 550.

June 30, 1834, entitled "an act concerning naval pensions, and the navy pension fund,[1] were continued to widows only for five additional years; by act of March 3, 1845, entitled "an act renewing certain naval pensions for the term of five years,"[2] were continued to widows only for five additional years; by act of August 11, 1848, were continued for five years, to widows and orphans; and by act of June 3, 1858, were continued for life, to widows, and until the age of sixteen years, to orphans. The acts of June 30, 1834, August 11, 1848 and June 3, 1858, will be further referred to in their proper places in the sequel of this section.

An act of June 30, 1834, entitled "an act concerning naval pensions, and the navy pension fund,"[3] provides:

Be it enacted by the Senate and House of Representatives of the United States of America, in Congress assembled, That all the provisions and benefits of the act of the twenty-eighth of June, one thousand eight hundred and thirty-two, entitled "an act further to extend the pensions heretofore granted to the widows of persons killed, and who have died in the naval service," be continued for another term of five years to all those widows who have heretofore had the benefit of the same; and the same are hereby also extended to the widows of officers,[4] seamen and marines, who have died in the naval service since the first day of January, one thousand eight hundred and twenty-four; or who may die in said service by reason of disease contracted, or of casualties by drowning or otherwise, or of injuries received while in the line of their duty;[5] and the pensions

1 U. S. Statutes at Large, vol. iv, 714.

2 *Ibid*, vol. v, 731.

3 *Ibid*, vol. iv, 714.

4 Engineers appointed under the act of August 24, 1842, are not entitled to pensions under this act, and, consequently, their widows are not entitled. *Attorney-General Clifford, October* 14, 1847.

A navy agent is not an "officer" within the meaning of this act, and his widow is not entitled to pension. *Attorney-General Butler, April* 7, 1837.

5 The act of June 30, 1834, provides pensions for widows whose husbands

of such widows shall commence from the passage of this act:[1] *Provided*, That every pension hereby granted shall cease on the death or marriage of such widow.

Half-pay for five years is granted the widows and orphans of sea-fencibles who died in the service since April 20, 1818, by act of July 4, 1836. This act, with the forms and regulations applicable thereto, and accompanying notes, will be found under "WIDOWS AND ORPHANS—VOLUNTEERS AND MILITIA," page 198.

By "an act for the more equitable administration of the navy pension fund," approved March 3, 1837,[2] it is provided:

Be it enacted by the Senate and House of Representatives of the United States of America, in Congress assembled, That if any officer, seaman or marine, have died,[3] or may hereafter die, in the naval service;[4] leaving a widow,[5] and, if no widow, a child or children,[6]

---

died in the naval service since January 1, 1824; and therefore the widow of a person who died from the causes specified in the act, prior to that date, is not entitled to a pension. *Attorney-General Butler, October* 17, 1834.

1 Pensions under this act, where the husband died before its passage, should commence from the date of the act; but if the death took place subsequently, the pension should commence from the time of such death. *Attorney-General Clifford, October* 14, 1847.

2 U. S. Stat. at Large, vol. v, 180. Navy pensions can not be granted under the act of March 3, 1837, the same having been repealed by act of August 3, 1842. *Commissioner Waldo, August* 23, 1853, *and Attorney-General Nelson, April* 15, 1844.

3 A child pensioned under the act of 3d March, 1817, until sixteen years of age, may subsequently claim a pension for five additional years under the act of March 3, 1837. *Attorney-General Butler, April* 10, 1837.

4 The first section of the act of March 3, 1837, is confined to cases where the death occurred while the person was in the naval service. *Attorney-General Butler, April* 6, 1838.

5 Where a widow, who, if living, would have been entitled to a pension under this act, died before its passage, her legal representative can not claim the benefits of the act. *Attorney-General Butler, April* 11, 1837.

6 If she be married, the children may claim a pension under this act. *Attorney-General Butler, April* 7, 1837, *and April* 11, 1837.

Where a navy officer died in 1820, and his widow in 1835, and there

such widow, and if no widow, such child or children, shall be entitled to receive half the monthly pay to which the deceased would have been entitled, under the acts regulating the pay of the navy, in force on the first day of January, one thousand eight hundred and thirty-five, to commence from the time of the death of such officer, seaman or marine; but in case of the death or intermarriage of such widow, the half-pay shall go to the child or children of such deceased officer, seaman or marine: *Provided*, That the half-pay granted to the child or children, shall cease on their death, or on their attaining the age of twenty-one years.

By a proviso to the first section of "an act to provide for the payment of navy pensions," approved August 16, 1841,[1] the foregoing act was modified; and by an act of August 23, 1842, repealed. The proviso to the act of August 16, 1841, is as follows:

"All widows or children of all naval officers, seaman or marines, now deceased, and entitled to receive or make proof of their pensions under the act of the third of March, eighteen hundred and thirty-seven, shall receive the same until the close of the next session of Congress; but no widow or children of any naval officer, seaman or marine, who may hereafter die, shall be entitled to any pension by virtue only of any provision in the said act."

The section of the act of August 23, 1842,[2] by which the act of March 3, 1837, was repealed, is as follows:

An Act making Appropriation to supply a Deficiency in the Navy Fund.

SEC. 2. *And be it further enacted*, That the act, entitled "an act to provide for the more equitable administration of the navy pension fund," approved March third, eighteen hundred and thirty-seven

were children who were under twenty-one years of age, at the time of the father's death, but over twenty-one at the time of making the claim, it was held that they were entitled to a pension from the time of the death of the father, until they reached the age of twenty-one. *Attorney-General Butler, April* 11, 1837, in two cases, and one April 12, 1837.

[1] U. S. Stat. at Large, vol. v, 440.

[2] *Ibid*, vol. v, 519.

be, and the same is hereby, repealed, from and after the first day of July, eighteen hundred and forty-two. And all pensions to officers and seamen in the naval service shall be regulated according to the pay of the navy as it existed on the first day of January, one thousand eight hundred and thirty-five.[1]

"An act making appropriations for the payment of revolutionary and other pensions," for the year ending June 30, 1845, approved April 30, 1844,[2] provides among other things, that "no pension shall hereafter be granted to a widow for the same time her husband received one."[3]

"An act for the relief of the widows and orphans of the officers, seamen and marines, of the United States schooner Grampus, and for other purposes," approved June 15, 1844,[4] directs:

Be it enacted by the Senate and House of Representatives of the United States of America in Congress assembled, That for the purpose of fixing the time at which shall commence the pensions, under the existing laws, of the widows of the officers, seamen and marines, who were lost in the United States schooner Grampus, as well as the time to which the pay of said officers, seamen and marines, shall be allowed, the twentieth day of March, one thousand eight hundred and forty-three, shall be deemed and taken to be the day on which the said schooner Grampus foundered at sea. . . . .

SEC. 2. *And be it further enacted*, That if any of the said officers, seamen or marines, shall have left no widow, or having left a widow, she shall have died before the passage of this act, and there shall be living at the date of the passage of this act a child or children of said officers, seamen or marines, un-

1 Monthly pay, prior to January 1, 1835, governs the navy pension cases, and not the present increased rates of pay. *Commissioner Waldo, October* 8, 1853.

2 U. S. Statutes at Large, vol. v, 656.

3 This applies to claims filed before as well as after the passage of the act. *Secretary Wilkins, May* 1, 1844.

4 U. S. Statutes at Large, vol. v, 665.

der sixteen years of age, such child or children shall be entitled to the same pension to which the widow, had there been one as aforesaid, would have been entitled, for the like period of five years; but in case of the death or intermarriage of the widow before the expiration of the said term of five years, the said pension for the remainder of the said term shall go to the child or children of the said deceased officer, seamen or marine:[1] *Provided*, That such pension shall cease upon the death of such child or children.

A rule of evidence was established by the second section of "an act making appropriations for the payment of revolutionary and other pensions of the United States for the year ending the thirtieth June, one thousand eight hundred and forty-seven, and for other purposes," approved May 7, 1846,[2] as follows:

Be it enacted by the Senate and House of Representatives of the United States of America in Congress assembled, That no widow, entitled to a pension under existing laws, and claiming a pension, whose husband was drawing a pension at the time of his decease, shall be required, in any case, to furnish any further evidence that said husband was entitled to a pension; nor shall any evidence in any case be required, to entitle the widow to a pension, where the evidence is in the archives of the government, other than such proof as would be sufficient to establish, the marriage between the applicant and the deceased pensioner in civil personal actions in a court of justice.[3]

---

1 Where a widow drew a pension under this act, but died before the expiration of the five years, it was held that a child of the deceased was not entitled to a full pension for five years, but only for the remainder of the term for which the mother was pensioned.—*Att'y Gen'l Nelson, January* 4, 1845.

2 U. S. Statutes at Large, vol. ix, 5.

3 To establish their claims it is sufficient for the widows to prove that their husbands were entitled to pensions, and that they are their widows. If the husbands were upon the pension rolls, it is presumptive evidence that they were entitled to pensions; and it is for the government to show that they were not entitled.

General reputation and co-habitation are, in general, sufficient evidence of marriage: the presumption raised by such proof may, however, be rebutted —*Att'y Gen'l Mason, June* 23, 1846.

"An act renewing certain naval pensions, and extending the benefits of existing laws, respecting naval pensions, to engineers, firemen and coal-heavers in the navy, and to their widows," approved August 11, 1848,[1] is as follows:

Be it enacted by the Senate and House of Representatives of the United States of America in Congress assembled, That all those widows, and such child or children, as are now receiving a pension under any of the laws of Congress, passed prior to the first day of August, eighteen hundred and forty-one (excepting the law passed the third of March, eighteen hundred and thirty-seven), and those widows and children, who have received pensions at any time within five years prior to the passage of this act, may and shall continue to receive the same amount as they received under any special act, from the time such special act expired; *Provided*, Such act ceased on or after the first day of September, eighteen hundred and forty-five, or may hereafter terminate.[2] And all such pensions as are now in force, and such as are renewed by this act, shall be paid out of any money in the treasury not otherwise appropriated,[3] so long as the said widows shall live as widows, and in case of the death, before or after the passage of this act, of the widows, to the orphan child or children of the deceased parties, until they respectively arrive at the age of sixteen years; and to the child or children of said widows in case of marriage by said widows, until said child or children shall respectively arrive at the age of sixteen years; and that the act approved 30th April, 1844, shall not be so construed as to exclude officers, seamen or marines, from their pensions when disabled for sea service; *Provided*, That the whole amount received by the pensioner, including pay for his service and pension, shall not exceed his lowest duty pay. That the orphan child or children of

1 U. S. Statutes at Large, vol. ix, 282.

2 The first section of the act of August 11, 1848, embraces all such widows and children as were receiving pensions under any act of Congress passed prior to August 1, 1841. Also all such widows and children as received pensions within five years prior to the passage of the act. The word "special" is not used in the sense of "private."—*Att'y Gen'l Toucey, Sept.* 26, 1849.

3 This restriction was repealed by act of April 5, 1856. (U. S. Statutes at Large, vol. xi, 3.)

the deceased parties shall have a pension in case the widow has died after drawing a five years' pension, to commence at the time when the widow dies, and to continue until the child or children shall respectively reach the age of sixteen years; and that any casualty by which an officer, seaman or marine, has lost or may lose his life while in the line of his duty, shall be considered sufficient to entitled the widow, child or children to all the benefits of this act.

SEC. 2. *And be it further enacted*, That engineers, firemen and coal-heavers, in the navy, shall be entitled to pensions in the same manner as officers, seamen and marines; and the widows of engineers, coal-heavers and firemen, in the same manner as the widows of officers, seamen and marines: *Provided*, That the pension of a chief engineer shall be the same as that of a lieutenant[1] in the navy; and a pension of a widow of a chief engineer the same as that of the widow of a lieutenant in the navy; the pension of a first assistant engineer the same as that of a lieutenant[1] of marines; and the pension of the widow of a first assistant engineer, the same of that of the widow of a lieutenant of marines; the pension of a second or third assistant engineer, the same as that of a forward officer; and the pension of the widow of a second or third assistant engineer, the same as that of the widow of a forward officer; the pension of a fireman or coal-heaver, the same as that of a seaman; the pension of the widow of a fireman or coal-heaver, the same as that of the widow of a seaman: *And provided further*, That an engineer, fireman or coal-heaver shall not be entitled to any pension by reason of a disability incurred prior to the thirty-first of August, eighteen hundred and forty-two, nor shall the widow of any engineer, fireman or coal-heaver, be entitled to any pension by reason of the death of her husband, if his death was prior to that date.

SEC. 3. *And be it further enacted*, That the amount of pension in every case arising under this law is not to exceed the half-pay of the deceased officer, seaman or marine, as it existed in January, eighteen hundred and thirty-five, or such rate of pension as is allowed by this act.

By an act approved June 3, 1858, entitled "an act to extend 'an act to continue half-pay to certain widows and

[1] This means a first lieutenant.—*Att'y Gen'l Toucey, Sept.* 26, 1849.

orphans,' approved February three, eighteen hundred and fifty-three,"[1] continues under certain limitations, to surviving widows, during life or widowhood, and to minor children, until sixteen years of age, the half-pay granted them for five years, under any law or laws of the United States. This act will be found at large under "WIDOWS AND ORPHANS—VOLUNTEERS AND MILITIA," page 209.

The first section of an act of August 1, 1856, entitled "an act for the relief of the widows and orphans of the officers, seamen and marines of the United States sloop-of-war Albany, and for other purposes,"[2] prescribes:

Be it enacted by the Senate and House of Representatives of the United States of America in Congress assembled, That for the purpose of fixing the time at which shall commence the pensions, under the existing laws, of the widows and orphan children of the officers, seamen, marines and others in service, who were lost in the United States sloop-of-war Albany, as well as the time at which the pay of said officers, seamen, marines and others in service, shall be allowed, the eighteenth day of April, one thousand eight hundred and fifty-five, shall be deemed and taken to be the day on which the said sloop-of-war Albany, foundered at sea; and that, for the like purposes, the twenty-ninth day of June, one thousand eight hundred and fifty-five, shall be deemed and taken to be the day on which the United States brig Porpoise was lost in like manner.

A like act was passed, July 24, 1861,[3] fixing the date of the loss of the United States sloop-of-war Levant on the 30th day of June, 1861.

WAR OF 1861.

An act of July 14, 1862, granting pensions to persons disabled, and to the widows, children, mothers and orphan sisters of persons killed, or who die, in war of 1861, against rebellion, makes the following provisions:

1 U. S. Statutes at Large, vol. xi, 309.

2 Ibid, vol. xi, 29.

3 Ibid, vol. xii, 273.

AN ACT *to Grant Pensions.*

Be it enacted by the Senate and House of Representatives of the United States of America in Congress assembled, That if any officer, non-commissioned officer, musician or private of the army, including regulars, volunteers and militia, or any officer, warrant or petty officer, musician, seaman, ordinary seaman, flotillaman, marine, clerk, landsman, pilot or other person in the navy or marine corps, has been, since the fourth day of March, eighteen hundred and sixty-one, or shall hereafter be disabled by reason of any wound received or disease contracted while in the service of the United States and in the line of duty, he shall, upon making due proof of the fact according to such forms and regulations as are or may be provided by or in pursuance of law, be placed upon the list of invalid pensions [pensioners] of the United States, and be entitled to receive, for the highest rate of disability, such pension as is hereinafter provided in such cases, and for an inferior disability an amount proportionate to the highest disability, to commence as hereinafter provided, and continue during the existence of such disability. The pension for a total disability for officers, non-commissioned officers, musicians and privates employed in the military service of the United States, whether regulars, volunteers or militia, and in the marine corps, shall be as follows, viz: Lieutenant-colonel and all officers of a higher rank, thirty dollars per month; major, twenty-five dollars per month; captain, twenty dollars per month; first lieutenant, seventeen dollars per month; second lieutenant, fifteen dollars per month; and non-commissioned officers, musicians and privates, eight dollars per month. The pension for total disability for officers, warrant or petty officers, and others employed in the naval service of the United States, shall be as follows, viz: Captain, commander, surgeon, paymaster and chief engineer, respectively, ranking with commander by law, lieutenant commanding and master commanding, thirty dollars per month; lieutenant, surgeon, paymaster and chief engineer, respectively, ranking with lieutenant by law, and passed assistant surgeon, twenty-five dollars per month; professor of mathematics, master, assistant surgeon, assistant paymaster and chaplain, twenty dollars per month; first assistant engineers and pilots, fifteen dollars per month; passed midshipman, midshipman, captains' and paymasters' clerk, second and third assistant engineer, masters' mate and all warrant officers, ten dollars per month; all petty officers and all other persons before named employed in the naval service, eight dollars per month; and all commissioned officers, of either service, shall receive such and only such pension as is herein provided for the rank in which they hold commissions.

SEC. 2. *And be it further enacted,* That if any officer or other person named in the first section of this act has died since the fourth day of March, eighteen hundred and sixty-one, or shall hereafter die, by reason of any wound received or disease contracted while in the service of the United States, and in the line of duty, his widow, or, if there be no widow, his child or children under sixteen years of age, shall be entitled to receive the same pension as the husband or father would have been entitled to had he been totally disabled, to commence from the death of the husband or father, and to continue to the widow during her widowhood, or to the child or children until they severally attain to the age of sixteen years, and no longer.

SEC. 4. *And be it further enacted,* That . . . *And provided, further,* That no moneys shall be paid to the widow or children, or any heirs of any deceased soldier, on account of bounty, back pay or pension, who have in any way been engaged in, or who have aided or abetted, the existing rebellion in the United States; but the right of such disloyal widow or children, heir or heirs of such soldier, shall be vested in the loyal heir or heirs of the deceased, if any there be.

Sections six and seven, regulate fees for procuring pensions, etc., and prescribe penalties for over-charge.

SEC. 10. *And be it further enacted,* That the pilots, engineers, sailors and crews upon the gunboats and war vessels of the United States, who have not been regularly mustered into the service of the United States, shall be entitled to the same bounty allowed to persons of corresponding rank in the naval service, provided they continue in service to the close of the present war; and all persons serving as aforesaid, who have been or may be wounded or incapacitated for service, shall be entitled to receive for such disability the pension allowed by the provisions of this act, to those of like rank, and each and every such person shall receive pay according to corresponding rank in the naval service: *Provided,* That no person receiving pension or bounty under the provisions of this act shall receive either pension or bounty for any other service in the present war.

SEC. 11. *And be it further enacted*, That the widows and heirs of all persons described in the last preceding section who have been or may be employed as aforesaid, or who have been or may be killed in battle, or of those who have died or shall die of wounds received while so employed, shall be paid the bounty and pension allowed by the provisions of this act, according to rank, as provided in the last preceding section.

The entire act will be found on pages 28 to 32.

A joint resolution of Congress, approved July 16, 1862, extends the benefits of the foregoing act to the masters serving on the gunboats of the United States, as follows:

JOINT RESOLUTION *to grant Pensions to Masters and other Officers upon the Gunboats in the service of the United States.*

Resolved by the Senate and House of Representatives of the United States of America in Congress assembled, That the masters serving on board of gunboats employed in the service of the United States shall be entitled to all the benefits, including bounty and pension, provided for in an act entitled "an act to grant pensions," passed during the present session of Congress, and the widows, mothers and heirs of such officers shall be entitled to all the benefits of said act.

GENERAL OBSERVATIONS.

The act of January 13, 1813, grants half-pay to the widows and orphans of officers, only.

The first act making general provision for the widows and orphans of officers, seamen and marines, who served in the navy proper, and on board privateers, was that of March 4, 1814, which was amended by act of March 3, 1817, and the second section of the act of April 16, 1818. These acts all related to the war of 1812, except that of March 3, 1817, which acts retrospectively and prospectively.

The pensions to widows of persons who served in the navy proper, were continued by sundry acts, in periods of five years, until by act of June 3, 1858, when they were renewed to widows during life or widowhood, and to orphans until sixteen years of age.

The pensions to widows of privateers were continued by various acts until 1839, when they were permitted to expire by limitation—the privateer pension fund being exhausted.

Pensions were granted to the widows and orphans of sea-fencibles who served in the war of 1812, by act of April 16, 1816, and of those who died since April 20, 1818, by act of July 4, 1836. These pensions are also renewed by act of June 3, 1858.

The act of March 3, 1817, explains what kinds of disability will entitle to a pension. It relates to past and future cases.

The act of June 30, 1834, grants pensions to the widows of officers, seamen and marines who died in the naval service since January 1, 1824, or may die after the passage of the act.

The act of March 3, 1837, made general provision for the widows and orphans of persons who died in the naval service; but this act is no longer in force.

The act of August 23, 1842, repeals the act of March 3, 1837, and provides that pensions shall be regulated by the pay in the navy as it existed on the first day of January, 1835.

By the special act of June 15, 1844, pensions are allowed to widows and orphans of persons lost in the United States schooner Grampus, and the date of the loss of the vessel fixed, for pension purposes.

A rule of evidence is established by the act of May 7, 1846.

Pensions were renewed for five years to such widows and children as were then receiving them, by act of August 11, 1848; and the same act grants half-pay for five years to the widows and children of engineers, firemen and coal-heavers.

The act of June 3, 1858, extends for life, to widows, and until the age of sixteen years, to orphans, the half-pay, granted by any acts of Congress.

By act of August 1, 1856, the time of the loss of the sloop Albany and brig Porpoise, was determined, for pension purposes; and by act of July 24, 1861, the time of the loss of the sloop Levant was also fixed, for like purposes.

No law exists granting pensions to the widows or orphans of persons dying in the revenue cutter service, even though such revenue cutter be co-operating with the navy proper.

The act of July 14, 1862, makes provision for pensions to the widows and orphans of persons dying in the naval service, in the war of 1861.

SECTION II.

REGULATIONS AND FORMS FOR OBTAINING PENSIONS FOR WIDOWS AND ORPHANS IN NAVY CASES.

PENSION OFFICE, *May* 23, 1853.

Sir: For your information I inclose a form of application for widow's navy pension, together with a printed sheet exhibiting the description of evidence furnished to this office under the general order of the 17th February, 1851, in every case of disability or death in the naval service.

In all claims for widow's pension, or a renewal thereof, it must be shown by evidence, accompanying the application, or already on file, that the husband lost his life while in the naval service, by reason of wounds or injuries received, casualty incurred, or disease contracted in the line of duty. In cases of a date subsequent to that of the general order, such evidence may generally be found here; but if of prior date must, if practicable, be furnished by the certificates of medical or other commissioned officers of the navy, cognizant of the facts. If, after using due diligence, such certificates can not be obtained, the applicant can then present such other testimony as would be taken in a court of justice.

The usual legal proof of marriage must be produced, accompanied by a statement of the names and ages of all children of the parties, whether the fruit of their own or of former marriage. This last is to be desired, not only as a security to the Government, but as facilitating any future claim on the part of the children.

The widowhood and identity of the applicant should be stated in the memorial, and certified by the officiating magistrate or established by the affidavit of credible witnesses; and all evidence (excepting the certificates of naval officers), must be given by affidavit before a magistrate, whose official character must be certified by the clerk of the county in which he acts, under his seal of office.

Applications for orphans' navy pension may be made in the following cases:

1. Death of mother before the father.
2. Death of mother since the father, but without having received the benefit of the pension laws.
3. Death or intermarriage of their mother, since having received such benefit.

In the first and second cases, the same testimony would be required as in widow's applications, together with legal proof of the names and ages of the children.

In the third case, the latter only.

Orphans' applications can be made by the legally appointed guardian, in any form embracing a statement of facts. Claims of arrearages of pension may be paid to the orphans themselves, if adults, or to an administrator, for the sole and exclusive use and benefit of the children of the deceased parties.

Very respectfully, your obedient servant,

LOREN P. WALDO, *Commissioner.*

Form of Application for Widow's Navy Pension.

TO THE COMMISSIONER OF PENSIONS:

The memorial of the undersigned [*widow's name*], the widow of [*husband's name*], who was a [*Here give the rank of the husband*], in the naval service of the United States, respectfully showeth:

That the said [*husband's name*], entered the service in the year ——, and died therein, while holding the rank above-mentioned, on the —— day of ——, 18—; by reason of [*Here give minute description of the injury, accident, or disease by which the death was caused; mention when, where and how it happened, and whether the deceased was at the time serving on board ship (and if so, naming her, with the name of her commander), or in the hospital, and at what place or station*], in the line of duty.

That the undersigned was married to the said ——, on the —— day of ——, in the year ——; and that the following is a correct statement of the names and ages of the children of the parties, now living. [*Here give names of children, with the dates of their birth, including the children of either of the parties by a former marriage.*]

That your memorialist has, since the death of her said husband, remained unmarried, and the widow of the said —— [*If the widow married a second time, but is unmarried at the time of the application, the date of such subsequent marriage and the time of the death of her last husband must be stated and proved*]; for the truth of which statements she refers to the testimony herewith filed [*or* already on file in the Pension Office]. She claims the benefits of the laws granting navy pensions to the widows of officers, seamen and marines who have died in the naval service, and requests that her name may be inscribed on the roll of pensioners, payable at the Navy Pension Agency, at ——. (*Declarant's Signature.*)

Sworn to and subscribed before the —— court [*or*, before me, ——, judge; *or*, before me, ——, clerk of the —— court], a court of record, within and for the county of —— and State of ——, this —— day of ——, A. D. 18—.

[L. S.] Witness my signature and the seal of said court, the day and year aforesaid. (*Clerk's Signature.*)

This declaration must be made before a Court of Record, or before a Judge or Clerk of such Court. If made before a Judge, the certificate of the Clerk, under the seal of the Court, as to his official character, must be appended.

Accompanying this declaration must be the following proof:

1. Proof of service and the cause of the death of the husband. Where the husband was a pensioner while living, proof of service need not be made. If record

evidence of the service and cause of death of the husband is in the archives of the Government, the facts of the service and death may be stated in brief in the declaration, and reference be made to the place where such record evidence may be found. The character of the proof necessary (whenever required) may be learned by consulting the regulations which precede the foregoing declaration.

2. Proof of the marriage. This must be made by one of the methods mentioned under "WIDOWS AND ORPHANS — REVOLUTIONARY WAR;" or, "WIDOWS AND ORPHANS — VOLUNTEERS AND MILITIA;" or, "WIDOWS AND ORPHANS—REGULARS."

3. Proof of the death of the husband.

4. Proof of the names and ages of the children.

5. Proof of present widowhood.

6. Proof of the date of subsequent marriage, and death of last husband, when required by facts.

All which may be made according to the forms prescribed under the titles referred to above, in item two.

Affidavits of witnesses to any of the facts to be proved may be made before any person authorized to administer oaths generally. The certificate of the Clerk, under the seal of the proper Court, must attest the official character of the persons administering the oaths.

The form of declaration applicable in obtaining a pension may also be used in applying for the renewal of a pension. The only alterations necessary are these: 1. It should appear that the claimant formerly obtained a pension for the service of her husband mentioned in her declaration. 2. That the declaration is made to obtain a renewal of the pension, mentioning the act under which such renewal is claimed.

The accompanying proof in the case of renewal is the same as in original applications.

Claimants may consult, with possible profit, the regulations and forms prescribed in the cases of navy invalids, widows and orphans of the revolution, and widows and orphans of regulars, volunteers and militia.

For FORMS and REGULATIONS for executing POWERS OF ATTORNEY, in pension cases, see Chapter XVI.

The following form of certificate of the death of a person in the naval service accompanies the general order issued by the Secretary of the Navy, on the 17th day of February, 1851.

I hereby certify that ——, who was a —— in the United States navy, while attached to [*Here insert the name of the vessel, hospital or navy-yard*], and holding the rank above-mentioned, departed this life at ——, on the —— day of ——, 18—; and that he died of [*wound, casualty or disease, as the case may be*], as set forth in the record of his case, of which the following is a copy: [*Here give copy of record.*] (*Surgeon's Signature.*)

The above-named ——, deceased, was born at ——, in the county of ——, and State of ——; about —— years of age; —— feet —— inches high; —— complexion; —— eyes; —— hair; and entered the United States naval service at ——, on the —— day of ——, in the year ——.

(*Purser's Name.*)

Approved: (*Commander's Name.*)

Declaration of Guardian of Minor Children.

TO THE COMMISSIONER OF PENSIONS:

The memorial of the undersigned [*insert guardian's name*], guardian of [*here insert names of the children*], minor children of [*here insert the name of the father*], who was a —— in the naval service of the United States, respectfully showeth:

That the said [*the father*] entered the service in the year ——, and died therein, while holding the rank above-mentioned, on the —— day of ——, by reason of [*a wound, casualty or disease*], in the line of duty.

That the parents of his wards were married at ——, on the —— day of ——, A. D. 18—, by one ——, a ——; that the mother of his said wards died [*or*, was again married, being now the wife of ——] on the —— day of ——, A. D. 18—; and that the dates of the birth of his said wards are as follows: [*Here give the date of the birth of each child.*] He makes this declaration for the purpose of obtaining for his said wards the benefit of the laws granting navy pensions to the minor children of officers, seamen and marines who have died in the naval service; and requests that the names of his said wards may be inscribed on the roll of pensioners, payable at the Navy Pension Agency at ——, in the State of ——.

(*Declarant's Signature.*)

This must be sworn to before a Court of Record, or Judge or Clerk of such Court. For form of certificate of oath, see the form attached to the widow's declaration last preceding.

The declaration of the guardian must be accompanied by a copy of his letters of guardianship, and the same proof (except in the cases mentioned in the regulations given under this title) as in applications by widows.

ACT OF JULY 14, 1862.

The regulations established by Commissioner Barrett, to be observed in executing this act, will be found at large on page 179.

The following forms have also been provided:

"B."

Form of Declaration for obtaining a Widow's Navy Pension.

STATE OF —— } ss.
County of —— }

On this —— day of ——, A.D. ——, personally appeared before me——, of the ——, ——, a resident of ——, in the county of ——, and State of ——, aged —— years, who, being first duly sworn according to law, doth, on her oath, make the following declaration, in order to obtain the benefits of the provision made by the act of Congress approved July 14, 1862, granting pensions: That she is the widow of ——, who was a —— [*here state decedent's service*], who [*here specify the time, place and cause of death*]. She further declares, that she was married to the said —— on the —— day of ——, in the year ——; that her husband, the aforesaid ——, died on the day above mentioned, and that she has remained a widow ever since that period (*or if she has re-married and again become a widow, the fact must be stated*), as will more fully appear by reference to the proof hereto annexed. The personal description of the said ——, her deceased husband, is as follows: [*Here state his age, height, complexion, occupation, etc.*] She also declares that she has not in any manner been engaged in, or aided or abetted, the rebellion in the United States.

(*Declarant's Signature.*)

Also personally appeared —— and ——, residents of (*county, city or town*), persons whom I certify to be respectable and entitled to credit, and who, being by me duly sworn, say that they were present and saw —— sign her name (*or make her mark*) to the foregoing declaration; and they further swear that they have every reason to believe, from the appearance of the applicant and their acquaintance with her, that she is the identical person she represents herself to be; and that they have no interest in the prosecution of this claim.

(*Signatures of Witnesses.*)

Sworn to and subscribed before me, this —— day of ——, A. D., 18—; and I hereby certify that I have no interest, direct or indirect, in the prosecution of this claim.

(*Signature of Judge or other Officer.*)

Applicant's post-office address:

This must be accompanied by like proof as in other applications by widows. The forms for preparing this proof may be found under "WIDOWS AND ORPHANS—REVOLUTIONARY WAR," and "WIDOWS AND ORPHANS—REGULARS." As the forms and regulations under the act of July 14, 1862, are essentially the same as those applicable to other acts granting pensions to widows, claimants should refer to the forms and instructions given in the former part of this section.

For FORMS and REGULATIONS for the execution of POWERS OF ATTORNEY, in pension cases, see Chapter XVI.

"C."

Form of Declaration for Guardian of Minor Children in order to obtain Navy Pension.

STATE OF ——
County of —— } *ss.*

On this —— day of ——, A.D. one thousand eight hundred and ——, personally appeared before the —— of the ——, ——, a resident of ——, in the county of ——, and State of ——, aged —— years, who, being first duly sworn according to law, doth on oath make the following declaration, as guardian of the minor child of ——, deceased, in order to obtain the benefits of the provision made by the act of Congress, approved July 14, 1862, granting pensions to minor children, under sixteen years of age, of deceased officers and seamen; that he is the guardian of ——, [*naming the minor child or children, his ward or wards*], whose father was a —— [*here state decedent's service*]; and that the said —— died at ——, on the —— day of ——, in the year —— [*here state the cause of death*]; that the mother of the child, ——, aforesaid, died (*or* again married, being now the wife of ——), on the —— day of ——, in the year ——; and that the date of birth of his said ward— as follows:

He further declares, that the parents of his said ward— were married at ——, on the —— day of ——, in the year ——, by ——.

(*Guardian's Signature.*)

Sworn to and subscribed on the day and year first above written, before ——; and I hereby certify that I have no interest, direct or indirect, in the prosecution of this claim.

(*Signature of Judge or other Officer.*)

This must be accompanied by a certified copy of the letters of guardianship, and the same proof as in the case of widows.

CHAPTER XIII.

GRATUITOUS PENSIONS.

SECTION I.

PENSIONS TO MOTHERS—MILITARY AND NAVAL.

AN act "to grant pensions," approved July 14, 1862, makes an innovation upon existing pension laws, by granting pensions to the mothers of persons who die, or are killed in the service of the United States, in certain cases. This law is in part as follows :

AN ACT *to Grant Pensions.*

Be it enacted by the Senate and House of Representatives of the United States of America in Congress assembled, That if any officer, non-commissioned officer, musician or private of the army, including regulars, volunteers and militia, or any officer, warrant or petty officer, musician, seaman, ordinary seaman, flotillaman, marine, clerk, landsman, pilot or other person in the navy or marine corps, has been, since the fourth day of March, eighteen hundred and sixty-one, or shall hereafter be disabled by reason of any wound received or disease contracted while in the service of the United States and in the line of duty, he shall, upon making due proof of the fact according to such forms and regulations as are or may be provided by or in pursuance of law, be placed upon the list of invalid pensions [pensioners] of the United States, and be entitled to receive, for the highest rate of disability, such pension as is hereinafter provided in such cases, and for an inferior disability an amount proportionate to the highest disability, to commence as hereinafter provided, and continue during the existence of such disability. The pension for a total disability for officers, non-commissioned officers, musicians and privates employed in the military service of the United States, whether regulars, volunteers or militia, and in the marine corps, shall be as follows, viz: Lieutenant-colonel and all officers of a higher rank, thirty dollars per month; major, twenty-five dollars per month; captain, twenty dollars per month; first lieutenant, seventeen dollars per month; second lieutenant, fifteen dollars per month; and non-commissioned officers, musicians and privates, eight dollars per month. The pension for total disability for officers, warrant or petty officers, and others employed in the naval service of the United States, shall be as follows, viz: Captain, commander, surgeon, paymaster and chief engineer, respectively, ranking with commander by law, lieutenant commanding and master commanding, thirty dollars per month; lieutenant, surgeon, paymaster and chief engineer, respectively, ranking with lieutenant by law, and passed assistant surgeon, twenty-five dollars per month; professor of mathematics, master, assistant surgeon, assistant paymaster and chaplain, twenty dollars per month; first assistant engineers and pilots, fifteen dollars per month; passed midshipman, midshipman, captains' and paymasters' clerk, second and third assistant engineer, masters' mate and all warrant officers, ten dollars per month; all petty officers and all other persons before named employed in the naval service, eight dollars per month; and all commissioned officers, of either service, shall receive such and only such pension as is herein provided for the rank in which they hold commissions.

SEC. 3. *And be it further enacted*, That where any officer or other person named in the first section of this act, shall have died subsequently to the fourth day of March, eighteen hundred and sixty-one, or shall hereafter die, by reason of any wound received or disease contracted while in the service of the United States, and in the line of duty, and has not left or shall not leave a widow nor legitimate child, but has left or shall leave a mother who was dependent upon him for support, in whole or part, the mother shall be entitled to receive the same pension as such officer or other person would have been entitled to had he been totally disabled; which pension shall commence from the death of the officer or other person dying as aforesaid: *Provided, however*, That if such mother shall herself be in receipt of a pension as a widow, in virtue of the provisions of the second section of this act, in that case no pension or allowance shall be granted her on account of her son, unless she gives up the other pension or allowance. *And provided, further*, That the pension given to a mother on account of her son, shall terminate on her re-marriage: *And provided, further*, That nothing herein shall be so construed as to entitle the mother of an officer or other person dying, as aforesaid, to more than one pension at a time under the provisions of this act.

SEC. 4. *And be it further enacted*, That . . . *And provided, further*, That no moneys shall be paid to the widow or children, or any heirs of any deceased soldier, on account of bounty, back pay or pension, who have in any way been engaged in, or who have aided or abetted, the existing rebellion in the United States; but the right of such disloyal widow or children, heir or heirs of such soldier, shall be vested in the loyal heir or heirs of the deceased, if any there be.

SEC. 6. *And be it further enacted*, That the fees of agents and attorneys, for making out and causing to be executed the papers necessary to establish a claim for a pension, bounty and other allowance before the Pension Office under this act, shall not exceed the following rates: For making out and causing to be duly executed a declaration by the applicant, with the necessary affidavits, and forwarding the same to the Pension Office, with the requisite correspondence, five dollars. In cases wherein additional testimony is required by the Commissioner of Pensions, for each affidavit so required and executed and forwarded (except the affidavits of surgeons, for which such agents and attorneys shall not be entitled to any fees), one dollar and fifty cents.

SEC. 7. *And be it further enacted*, That any agent or attorney who shall, directly or indirectly, demand or receive any greater compensation for his services under this act than is prescribed in the preceding section of this act, or who shall contract or agree to prosecute any claim for a pension, bounty or other allowance under this act, on the condition that he shall receive a per centum upon or any portion of the amount of such claim, or who shall wrongfully withhold from a pensioner or other claimant the whole or any part of the pension or claim allowed and due to such pensioner or claimant, shall be deemed guilty of a high misdemeanor, and upon conviction thereof shall, for every such offense, be fined not exceeding three hundred dollars, or imprisoned at hard labor not exceeding two years, or both, according to the circumstances and aggravations of the offense.

SEC. 10. *And be it further enacted*, That the pilots, engineers, sailors and crews upon the gunboats and war vessels of the United States, who have not been regularly mustered into the service of the

United States, shall be entitled to the same bounty allowed to per sons of corresponding rank in the naval service, provided they continue in service to the close of the present war; and all persons serving as aforesaid, who have been or may be wounded or incapacitated for service, shall be entitled to receive for such disability the pension allowed by the provisions of this act, to those of like rank, and each and every such person shall receive pay according to corresponding rank in the naval service: *Provided*, That no person receiving pension or bounty under the provisions of this act shall receive either pension or bounty for any other service in the present war.

SEC. 11. *And be it further enacted*, That the widows and heirs[1] of all persons described in the last preceding section who have been or may be employed as aforesaid, or who have been or may be killed in battle, or of those who have died or shall die of wounds received while so employed, shall be paid the bounty and pension allowed by the provisions of this act, according to rank, as provided in the last preceding section.

This act will be found at large on pages 28 to 33. The provisions of the foregoing act were extended to masters of gunboats, and to their widows, mothers and heirs, by a joint resolution of July 16, 1862, as follows:

JOINT RESOLUTION *to grant Pensions to Masters and Officers upon the Gunboats in the service of the United States.*

Resolved by the Senate and House of Representatives of the United States of America in Congress assembled, That the masters serving on board of gunboats employed in the service of the United States shall be entitled to all the benefits, including bounty and pension, provided for in an act entitled "an act to grant pensions," passed

---

1 No official construction of this section has yet been made known, but it is believed that by the word "heirs" in this place, it was the intention of Congress to embrace all those persons designated in the former part of the act as entitled to pensions, according to the order of priority there established. The opinion that this was intended to include mothers, is strengthened by the joint resolution of July 16, 1862, which is in the nature of an amendment or addition to this and the preceding section, and specially designates mothers. Unless this construction is given to the joint resolution, mothers are preferred to children of the deceased person.

during the present session of Congress, and the widows, mothers and heirs of such officers shall be entitled to all the benefits of said act.

SECTION II.

REGULATIONS AND FORMS TO BE OBSERVED IN APPLYING FOR PENSIONS FOR MOTHERS.

For Regulations, see "INVALID PENSIONS—REGULARS," Chapter III, Section II, page 39.

"D."

Form of Declaration for Mother's Application for Army Pension.

STATE OF —— }
County of —— } *ss.*

On this —— day of ——, A. D. ——, personally appeared before the ——, of the ——, ——, a resident of ——, in the county of ——, and State of ——, aged —— years, who, being first duly sworn according to law, doth on her oath make the following declaration, in order to obtain the benefits of the provisions made by the act of Congress approved July 14, 1862: That she is the widow of ——, and mother of ——, who was a —— in company ——, commanded by ——, in the —— regiment of ——, in the war of 1861, who —— [*here state the time, place, and cause of death.*]

She further declares that her said son, upon whom she was wholly or in part dependent for support, having left no widow or minor child under sixteen years of age surviving, declarant makes this application for a pension under the above-mentioned act, and refers to the evidence filed herewith, and that in the proper department, to establish her claim.

She also declares that she has not, in any way, been engaged in, or aided or abetted, the rebellion in the United States; that she is not in the receipt of a pension under the second section of the act above mentioned, or under any other act, nor has she again married since the death of her son, the said ——.

(*Declarant's Signature.*)

Also personally appeared —— and ——, residents of (*county, city or town*) persons whom I certify to be respectable and entitled to credit, and who, being by me duly sworn, say that they were present and saw —— sign her name (*or,* make her mark) to the foregoing declaration; and they further swear that they have every reason to believe, from the appearance of the applicant and their acquaintance with her, that she is the identical person she represents herself to be.

(*Signature of Witnesses.*)

Sworn to and subscribed before me this —— day of——, A. D. 18—;

and I hereby certify that I have no interest, direct or indirect, in the prosecution of this claim.

(*Signature of Judge or other Officer.*)

Applicant's post-office address:

"D."

Form of Declaration for Mother's Application for Navy Pension.

STATE OF —— }
County of —— } *ss.*

On this —— day of ——, A. D. ——, personally appeared before the ——, of the ——, ——, a resident of ——, in the county of ——, and State of ——, aged —— years, who, being first duly sworn according to law, doth on her oath make the following declaration, in order to obtain the benefits of the provisions made by the act of Congress approved July 14, 1862, granting pensions: That she is the widow of ——, and mother of ——, who was a ——[*here state decedent's service and personal description*], who —— [*here state the time, place and cause of death.*]

She further declares that her said son, upon whom she was wholly or in part dependent for support, having left no widow or minor child under sixteen years of age surviving, declarant makes this application for a pension under the above-mentioned act, and refers to the evidence filed herewith, and that in the proper department, to establish her claim.

She also declares that she has not, in any way, been engaged in, or aided or abetted, the rebellion in the United States; that she is not in the receipt of a pension under the second section of the act above mentioned, or under any other act, nor has she again married since the death of her son, the said ——.

(*Declarant's Signature.*)

Also personally appeared —— and ——, residents of (*county, city or town*), persons whom I certify to be respectable and entitled to credit, and who, being by me duly sworn, say that they were present and saw —— sign her name (*or*, make her mark) to the foregoing declaration; and they further swear that they have every reason to believe, from the appearance of the applicant and their acquaintance with her, that she is the identical person she represents herself to be.

(*Signatures of Witnesses.*)

Sworn to and subscribed before me this —— day of ——, A. D. 18—; and I hereby certify that I have no interest, direct or indirect, in the prosecution of this claim.

(*Signature of Judge or other Officer.*)

Applicant's post-office address:

These declarations must be made before a Court of Record, or before a Judge or Clerk of such Court. The certificate and seal of the Clerk must be attached in all cases.

The declarations must be accompanied by proof of marriage of the claimant; of the relationship between the claimant and the deceased; of the widowhood of the claimant, and her total or partial dependence upon the deceased for support; that the deceased left neither widow nor children, and of the loyalty of the claimant. And where the death of the son has occurred since his return from service, from wounds or disease received or contracted in the service; or where such death does not appear upon the rolls, or other government records, proof of the death and cause of the death must also be sent in with the declarations. Affidavits in the nature of proof may be made before a Justice of the Peace, or other officer authorized to administer oaths generally; but his official character must appear by the certificate of the Clerk of the proper Court, under seal.

The proper forms for preparing this proof may be found under "WIDOWS AND ORPHANS—REVOLUTIONARY WAR," and "WIDOWS AND ORPHANS—REGULARS;" and it is not deemed necessary to repeat them here.

For REGULATIONS and FORMS for preparing POWERS OF ATTORNEY in pension cases, see Chapter XVI.

CHAPTER XIV.

GRATUITOUS PENSIONS.

SECTION I.

PENSIONS TO SISTERS—MILITARY AND NAVAL.

"AN act to grant pensions," approved July 14, 1862, was the first to provide pensions for the orphan sisters of persons who die or are killed in the military or naval service of the United States. This act is in part as follows:

Be it enacted by the Senate and House of Representatives of the United States of America in Congress assembled, That if any officer, non-commissioned officer, musician or private of the army, including regulars, volunteers and militia, or any officer, warrant or petty officer, musician, seaman, ordinary seaman, flotilla-man, marine, clerk, landsman, pilot or other person in the navy or marine corps, has been, since the fourth day of March, eighteen hundred and sixty-one, or shall hereafter be, disabled by reason of any wound received or disease contracted while in the service of the United States, and in the line of duty, he shall upon making due proof of the fact, according to such forms and regulations as are or may be provided by or in pursuance of law, be placed upon the list of invalid pensions [pensioners] of the United States, and be entitled to receive, for the highest rate of disability, such pension as is hereinafter provided in such cases, and for an inferior disability an amount proportionate to the highest disability, to commence as hereinafter provided, and continue during the existence of such disability. The pension for a total disability for officers, non-commissioned officers, musicians and privates, employed in the military service of the United States, whether regulars, volunteers or militia, and in the marine corps, shall be as follows, viz.: Lieutenant-colonel, and all officers of a higher rank, thirty dollars per month; major, twenty-five dollars per month; captain, twenty dollars per month; first lieutenant, seventeen dollars per month; second lieutenant fifteen dollars per month; and non-commissioned officers, musicians and privates, eight dollars per month. The pension for total disability for officers, warrant or petty officers, and others employed in the naval service of the United States, shall be as follows, viz.: Captain, commander, surgeon, paymaster and chief engineer, respectively, ranking with commander by law, lieutenant commanding, and master commanding, thirty dollars per month; lieutenant, surgeon, paymaster and chief engineer, respectively, ranking with lieutenant by law, and passed assistant surgeon, twenty-five dollars per month; professor of mathematics, master, assistant surgeon, assistant paymaster, and chaplain, twenty dollars per month; first assistant engineers and pilots, fifteen dollars per month; passed midshipman, midshipman, captain's and paymaster's clerk, second and third assistant engineer, master's mate and all warrant officers, ten dollars per month; all petty officers, and all other persons before named, employed in the naval service, eight dollars per month; and all commissioned officers of either service shall receive such and only such pension as is herein provided for the rank in which they hold commissions.

SEC. 4. *And be it further enacted*, That when any officer or other person named in the first section of this act shall have died subsequently to the fourth day of March, eighteen hundred and sixty-one, or shall hereafter die, by reason of any wound received or disease contracted while in the service of the United States, and in the line of duty, and has not left or shall not leave a widow, nor legitimate child, nor mother, but has left or may leave an orphan sister or sisters, under sixteen years of age, who were dependent upon him for support, in whole or in part, such sister or sisters shall be entitled to receive the same pension as such officer or other person would have been entitled to had he been totally disabled; which pension to said orphan shall commence from the death of the officer or other person dying as aforesaid, and shall continue to the said orphans until they severally arrive at the age of sixteen years, and no longer: *Provided, however*, That nothing herein shall be so construed as to entitle said orphans to more than one pension at the same time, under the provisions of this act: *And provided, further*, That no moneys shall be paid to the widow or children, or any heirs of any deceased soldier, on account of bounty, back pay or pension, who have in any way been engaged in or who have aided or abetted the existing rebellion in the United States; but the right of such disloyal widow or children, heir or heirs of such soldier, shall be vested in the loyal heir or heirs of the deceased, if any there be.

Section six prescribes the fees of agents for obtaining pensions, etc.

Section seven fixes the penalty for charging excessive fees.

SEC. 10. *And be it further enacted*, That the pilots, engineers sailors and crews upon the gunboats and war vessels of the United States, who have not been regularly mustered into the service of the United States, shall be entitled to the same bounty allowed to persons of corresponding rank in the naval service, provided they continue in service to the close of the present war; and all persons serving as aforesaid, who have been or may be wounded or incapacitated for service, shall be entitled to receive for such disability the pension allowed by the provisions of this act to those of like rank, and each and every such person shall receive pay according to corresponding rank in the naval service: *Provided*, That no person receiving pension or bounty under the provisions of this act shall receive either pension or bounty for any other service in the present war.

SEC. 11. *And be it further enacted*, That the widows and heirs[1] of all persons described in the last preceding section who have been or may be employed as aforesaid, or who have been or may be killed in battle, or of those who have died or shall die of wounds received while so employed, shall be paid the bounty and pension allowed by the provisions of this act, according to rank, as provided in the last preceding section.

1 This has not yet received an official construction, but it is believed that the word "heirs," as here employed, was intended to embrace those persons who are designated in the former part of the act as entitled to pensions for the service of the deceased person, according to the order of priority there established. That it was meant to include *mothers* is evident from the joint resolution of July 16, 1862, which supplies an omission in the tenth and eleventh sections of the act of July 14, 1862, and may be considered as an addition to that act. Unless this construction is adopted, the joint resolution will prefer the mother to the children of the deceased person.

For this act entire, see pages 28 to 33.

A joint resolution of July 16, 1862, supplies an omission in the foregoing act, and extends its provisions to mates on board gunboats in the service, and to those dependent upon them. This resolution is as follows:

JOINT RESOLUTION *to grant Pensions to Masters and Officers upon the Gunboats in the service of the United States.*

Resolved by the Senate and House of Representatives of the United States of America in Congress assembled, That the masters serving on board of gunboats employed in the service of the United States shall be entitled to all the benefits, including bounty and pension, provided for in an act entitled "an act to grant pensions," passed during the present session of Congress, and the widows, mothers and heirs of such officers shall be entitled to all the benefits of said act.

SECTION II.

REGULATIONS AND FORMS TO BE OBSERVED IN APPLYING FOR PENSIONS FOR SISTERS.

For Regulations, see "INVALID PENSIONS—REGULARS," page 39.

Form of Declaration of Guardian of Orphan Sisters for Army Pension.

STATE OF ——, } *ss.*
County of—— }

On this —— day of ——, A. D., ——, personally appeared before the ——, of the ——, —— a resident of ——, in the county of ——, and State of ——, aged —— years, who, being first duly sworn according to law, doth on oath make the following declaration, in order to obtain a pension under the act of July 14, 1862: That he is the legally appointed guardian of [*here give the names and ages of his ward or wards*], who —— the only surviving child ——, under sixteen years of age, of ——, and ——, his wife, and sister — of ——, who was a —— in company ——, commanded by ——, in the —— regiment of ——, in the war of 1861, who [*here state the time, place and cause of his death*]. That the brother of his said ward —, upon whom they were wholly or in part dependent for support, having left no widow, minor child or children, or mother, declarant as guardian and on behalf of his ward —, refers to the accompanying evidence, and such as may be found in the department, to establish her (or their) claim under the law above named.

He further declares that his said ward —— not in the receipt of any pension under said act.

He also declares that his ward —— not, in any way, been engaged in, or aided or abetted, the rebellion in the United States.

(*Guardian's Signature.*)

Applicant's post-office address.

Sworn to and subscribed before me this —— day of ——, A. D., 18—; and I hereby certify that I have no interest, direct or indirect, in the prosecution of this claim.

(*Signature of Judge or other Officer.*

Form of Declaration of Guardian of Orphan Sisters for Navy Pension.

STATE OF —— } ss.
County of —— }

On this —— day of ——, A. D., ——, personally appeared before the ——, of the ——, ——, a resident of ——, in the county of ——, and State of ——, aged —— years, who, being first duly sworn according to law, doth on oath make the following declaration, in order to obtain a pension under the act of July 14, 1862: That he is the legally appointed guardian of [*here give the names and ages of his ward or wards*] who —— the only surviving child ——, under sixteen years of age, of ——, and ——, his wife, and sister — of ——, who was a [*here state decedent's service and personal description*] who [*here state the time, place and cause of his death*]. That the brother of his said ward —, upon whom they were wholly or in part dependent for support, having left no widow, minor child or children, or mother, declarant as guardian, and on behalf of his ward —, refers to the accompanying evidence, and such as may be found in the department, to establish her (or their) claim under the law above named.

He further declares that his said ward —— not in the receipt of any pension under said act.

He also declares that his ward —— not, in any way, been engaged in, or aided, or abetted the rebellion in the United States.

(*Guardian's Signature.*)

Sworn to and subscribed before me, this —— day of ——, A.D. 18—; and I hereby certify that I have no interest, direct or indirect, in the prosecution of this claim. (*Signature of Judge or other Officer.*)

Applicant's post-office address.

These declarations must be made before a Court of Record, or the Judge or Clerk of a Court of Record. In any case the seal of the Court must be appended.

The declaration must be supported by the following proof:

1. The marriage of the parents of the claimant or claimants.

2. The death or marriage of the mother of the deceased.

3. The relationship between the claimant or claimants and the deceased.

4. The names and ages of the sisters under sixteen years of age who were dependent upon the deceased, in whole or part, for support.

5. That the deceased left neither widow nor children.

6. In case the death of the brother took place after his return from service, of disability incurred while in the line of duty; or where such death does not appear upon the rolls, or other government records, the death, and cause of the death of the brother must also be proved.

7. Proof of loyalty.

Affidavits in proof of these several facts may be made before a Justice or other officer authorized to administer oaths generally; but his official character must be certified by the Clerk of the proper Court, under its seal.

The requisite forms for preparing the foregoing proof will be found under "WIDOWS AND ORPHANS, REVOLUTIONARY WAR," and "WIDOWS AND ORPHANS—REGULARS."

For REGULATIONS and FORMS pertaining to POWERS OF ATTORNEY, in pension cases, see Chapter XVI.

CHAPTER XV.

OFFICIAL OPINIONS AND DECISIONS RELATING TO INVALID PENSIONS.

ARMY--INCLUDING REGULARS, VOLUNTEERS, AND MILITIA.

WHO ENTITLED:

Cadets at West Point and corps of engineers are entitled to pensions under act of March 16, 1802. *Attorney-General Wirt, April* 8, 1820.

An aid-de-camp is not entitled to pay or pension as such aid, but according to the commission actually held. *Attorney-General Wirt, December* 5, 1820.

Where a soldier dies after March 4, 1831, and before June 7, 1832, and leaves a widow, who also dies before June 7, 1832, the children of the *soldier* are entitled to a pension; but not the children of the widow by another husband. *Attorney-General Butler, April* 13, 1837.

A paymaster is a commissioned officer, and his wife is entitled to a pension under the act of March 16, 1802. *Attorney-General Grundy, March* 22, 1839.

Commodore Porter, who was minister to Turkey, was held to be entitled to his pay as minister, and as a pensioner, at the same time. *Attorney-General Legare, May* 26, 1842.

An officer who lost a limb in the war of 1812, was mustered out of the service upon a captain's pension. He was subsequently appointed battalion paymaster, and it was held that this appointment was to a civil branch of the service, and that he was entitled to both pay and pension. *Attorney-General Toucey, Nov.* 1, 1848.

The word children embraces grandchildren of a deceased pensioner, under the act of June 7, 1832, and its supplements. *Walton et al.* v. *Cotton et al.*, 19 *Howard*, 355.

A person not mustered into the service is not entitled to a pension. *Secretary Calhoun, Oct.* 24, 1821.

A minor wounded in the service, and subsequently discharged for minority, does not lose his right to a pension. *Secretary Cass, Feb.* 10, 1836.

A person who fails to return to duty after release from captivity is not entitled to a pension; being viewed as a deserter. *Secretary Poinsett and Commissioner Edwards, Aug.* 31, 1840.

Desertion forfeits all right to a pension. *Secretary Porter and Commissioner Edwards, June* 27, 1843.

It is not sufficient that a man should be employed in a mechanical occupation by the Government to make him an artificer of the army. A person to be entitled to a pension must be regularly enlisted. *Secretary Ewing, July* 18, 1849.

Divorce is a bar to a wife's claim to a pension; and the Pension Office can not decide upon the legality of a divorce. *Commissioner Waldo, May* 23, 1853.

The armed police of a State are not entitled to invalid pensions. *Commissioner Waldo, February* 4, 1854.

PENSIONS A VESTED RIGHT:

A widow entitled to a pension and not claiming the same before marrying a second time, may claim it afterwards. *Attorney-General Wirt, June* 9, 1825; *Attorney-General Butler, April* 5, 1836 (two opinions); *Same, January* 17, 1837; *Attorney-General Grundy, March* 23, 1839; *Attorney-General Legare, June* 24, 1842; *Secretary Woodbury, Commissioner Edwards, and Secretary Poinsett, April*, 1839; *Commissioner Waldo, August* 13, 1853.

INCREASE OF PENSION:

Increase of pension, on account of increased disability, to commence from the date of increased disability. *Secretary Marcy, August* 28, 1845.

LINE OF DUTY:

It would not, I think, be going too far to say that, in every case where an officer or private loses his health while in the service, to such a degree as to be disabled from performing duty any more, he is contemplated *prima facie*, as an object of this charitable relief from the legislature. *Attorney-General Rush, April* 6, 1838, *Secretarg Dallas, July* 29, 1815.

Disability incurred in attempt to escape from captivity is "in the line of duty." *Attorney-General Wirt, April* 17, 1821.

It extends to all the operations of the ship, whether civil or military, and takes in the whole of her navigation during the entire cruise. The officer who is killed, or dies by reason of a wound received by the falling of a spar in a tempest, is as entirely within the description of being killed, or dying by reason of a wound received in the line of his duty, as the officer who is killed or dies by a wound in battle. Death by drowning, on board a prize ship which founders, is death in the line of duty. *Attorney-General Wirt, March* 21, 1825.

The law is understood to embrace only those who have been injured in the service of the United States, while actually employed in duties peculiar to them as soldiers; or from exposure to the inclemencies of the weather at the posts or stations at which they may have been put on duty; or while on the march to such stations. Such complaints or injuries, therefore, as are merely the effect of time, or of peculiarity of constitution, or are produced by accidents to which they would have been equally liable in their ordinary occupations in civil life, or which have occurred by their own fault, can not of course be entitled to a pension from the United States. *Surgeon-General Lovell, July* 15, 1824.

A soldier is always in the line of duty, except when under arrest, in confinement, on furlough, or absent without leave. *Secretary Ewing, April* 10, 1849.

Disability of a soldier incurred in the line of his duty in removing Indians, entitles him to a pension. *Secretary Ewing, July* 2, 1850.

Death from intemperance is not a case of death in the line of duty. *Secretary Stuart, October* 10, 1850.

A soldier on parole is considered to be still in captivity. *Secretary Graham, October* 15, 1850.

A soldier who has a furlough, or leave of absence, is still regarded as in the service. *Secretary Stuart, January* 27, 1852.

Insanity, when the effect of injury received, or exposure incurred in the line of duty, and resulting in suicide, entitles the widow to the benefits of the pension laws. *Commissioner Waldo June* 4, 1853.

COURTS OF RECORD:

All are courts of record, within the contemplation of the act of Congress: 1. Which are expressly made courts of record by the law of the State which creates them. 2. Which have been solemnly adjudged by the tribunals of the several States to be courts of record. 3. Which proceed according to the course of common law, with a jurisdiction unlimited in point of amount, keeping a record of their proceedings. 4. Which have the power of fine and imprisonment. *Attorney-General Wirt, May* 9, 1820.

Probate courts in Vermont are courts of record. *Secretary Cass, November* 2, 1832.

A justice of the peace in Tennessee is a court of record. *Secretary Ewing, June* 11, 1849.

A justice of the peace in Virginia is a court of record. *Secretary Ewing, July* 13, 1849. But only when the court is in session. *Commissioner Waldo, February* 10, 1854.

COMMENCEMENT OF PENSIONS:

Act of May 15, 1820, prescribing that pensions shall commence at the time of completing the testimony, applies to all laws then in force. *Attorney-General Wirt, July* 2, 1822. Never is it complete until every objection to its reception is removed. *Attorney-General Wirt, July* 19, 1822.

Under the act of May 15, 1820, a pension commences from the time when the testimony is closed before the officer taking it. *Attorney-General Butler, March*, 31, 1836.

Pensions under the first section of the act of July 4, 1836, commence from the time of the passage of the act, where the death of the party serving occurred before that time; but if the death occurred after the passage of the act, a pension will commence from the date of the death. *Attorney-General Butler, October* 24, 1836. This rule should be applied to all laws granting pensions to widows. *Attorney-General Black, November*, 15, 1858.

Pensions granted to widows and orphans, by act of March 3, 1845, commence from the time when they cease under former acts. *March* 19, 1845.

Under the act of June, 1834, pensions commence from the date of the passage of the act, where the death of the husband occurred before that time, but where it took place afterwards, the pension will commence at the time of such death. *Attorney-General Clifford, October*, 14, 1847.

It rests in the sound discretion of the Secretary of the Navy (as the successor to the commissioners of the navy fund) to decide, according to the regulations in force, when a pension shall commence.

Under the second section of act of February 3, 1853, it is from the passage of the act. *Commissioner Waldo, May* 4, 1853.

Commencement of an invalid pension is from the completion of the testimony, and not from the soldier's discharge from the army. *Commissioner Waldo, January* 11, 1854.

MISCELLANEOUS POINTS:

Error in allowing a pension does not make the recipient a debtor of the government. *Attorney-General Taney, October* 24, 1832.

False swearing in making an affidavit in support of a claim for pension subjects the party to a prosecution for perjury. *Attorney-General Butler, January* 21, 1835.

A contract of marriage entered into by parties capable of contracting, in the presence of a competent witness, is a valid marriage in New York. *Attorney-General Butler, August* 18, 1837.

Where a pension is overpaid, the excess may be deducted from the next payment. *Attorney-General Legare, July* 2, 1842.

General reputation and cohabitation are, in general, sufficient evidence of marriage; but this being merely presumptive, it may be rebutted. *Attorney-General Mason, June* 23, 1846.

No appeal lies to the President in pension cases. *Attorney-General Mason, August* 4, 1846.

The opinions of attorneys-general are advisory only. *Attorney-General Butler*, 1836; *Attorney-General Johnson, May* 8, 1849; *Attorney-General Cushing, February*, 11, 1854; *Secretary Ewing, June* 28, 1849.

Actual and not brevet rank governs in pension cases. *Attorney-General Cushing, August* 30, 1853; *Commissioner Waldo, September* 1, 1853.

A resolution of Congress is not mandatory. *Attorney-General Cushing, August* 23, 1854.

An officer wounded while serving in a higher grade than his commission, is entitled to a pension according to the pay of the higher grade, though not commissioned. *Secretary Cass, January* 15, 1833.

The nearest relatives of an insane person entitled to a pension may make a declaration for him. *Secretary Cass* (no date).

A right to be promoted to a higher grade does not entitle an officer to the pay or pension attaching to such higher grade. *Secretary Wilkins, June* 15, 1844.

No claim for a pension shall be taken up out of its order. *Secretary Ewing, August* 10, 1849.

A claim rejected upon appeal is considered finally disposed of. *Secretary Ewing, August* 25, 1849. Except upon new and important evidence, which could not have been obtained prior to the decision. *Secretary Ewing, April* 17, 1850.

Papers on file in one public office, necessary to establish claims before another office, should be examined and copied by the latter, to do justice to the claimant. *Secretary Ewing, October* 12, 1849.

Interest upon interest is not allowed in the settlement of claims before the Pension Office. *Secretary Ewing, January* 7, 1850.

The arrear of pension due to a pensioner at his death, is different from arrear of pension that had never been claimed before the death of him or her entitled to it; in the latter case, the arrear must go to his or her personal representatives. *Secretary Ewing, March* 5, 1850.

A discharge is honorable unless forfeited by some crime or misconduct. *Adjutant-General Jones, March* 4, 1850.

A person gone to parts unknown, and not heard from for seven years, is by common law presumed to be dead. *Secretary Ewing, May* 7, 1850.

The mother of illegitimate children may inherit from them; but their putative father can not. *Secretary Ewing, July* 5, 1850.

If the certificate of a commissioned officer can not be obtained to prove that a widow's husband died of disease contracted in the line of his duty, the testimony of other witnesses may be admitted. *Acting Secretary Goddard, September* 9, 1850.

Parties living together for many years as man and wife, and their children being acknowledged and treated as legitimate, with the affidavit of the surviving party, their marriage may well be presumed. *Acting Secretary Goddard, September* 13, 1850.

A debtor for money erroneously paid him or her (as a pension or otherwise) is chargeable, with interest on the same, to be calculated and deducted out of subsequent payments to the creditor. *Secretary Stuart, October* 29, 1851.

Papers filed with applications for pensions can not be withdrawn; but certified copies of the same may be obtained. *Secretary Stuart, November* 1, 1851.

Persons entitled to pensions under both a general and special act, may elect which to accept; but, having made a choice, they can not afterwards alter it. *Commissioner Waldo, October* 15, 1852.

Calendar months govern the computation of time in military service. *Commissioner Waldo, October 26*, 1853.

NAVAL—INCLUDING NAVY PROPER, PRIVATEERS AND MARINES.

For LINE OF DUTY, see preceding opinions and decisions in army cases.

WHO ENTITLED:

A navy agent is not an "officer, seaman or marine," and his widow is not entitled to a pension for his services. *Attorney-General Butler, April* 7, 1837.

A widow having married before the passage of an act, the children under sixteen years of age of the deceased husband are entitled to a pension. *Attorney-General Butler, April* 7, 1837, and *April* 11, 1837. (Two opinions.)

Mrs. Decatur was held by Attorney-General Butler (April 11, 1837) not to be entitled to a pension under a special act in her favor and also under a general law; and this opinion was confirmed by the Supreme Court of the United States, in the case of *Decatur* v. *Paulding*, 14 Peters, 497.

The widow of any person borne on the ship's books as one of the crew, is entitled to a pension, in case of his death from wounds or sickness. *Attorney-General Butler, November* 18, 1837.

Invalids disabled before the passage of the act of April 23, 1800, establishing the navy pension fund, are not entitled to its benefits. *Attorney-General Grundy, September* 3, 1838.

A lieutenant, otherwise entitled to a pension, is not entitled to receive it while on duty and in receipt of pay as an officer of the navy; nor can he receive it while not on duty, but in receipt of the pay allowed to his grade. *Attorney-General Clifford, May* 24, 1847. This opinion the attorney-general reviewed on the 2d June, 1847, and held that officers on leave, waiting orders, etc., may draw such sum as a pension as will make, by adding the same to his "leave" pay, the amount of pay to which he would be entitled if on duty. This was concurred in by Attorney-General Cushing, September 14, 1854.

An invalid may receive a pension while in the public service, for a disability which only renders him less able to support himself. *Attorney-General Taney, December* 17, 1832.

MISCELLANEOUS POINTS:

Monthly pay, prior to January 1, 1835, governs navy pension cases, and not the present increased rates of annual pay. *Commissioner Waldo, October* 8, 1853.

Where a wound is received in the service, and an officer is not in a situation to certify the fact, or may be dead, the evidence of a private individual will be taken. *Secretary Ewing, February* 27, 1850.

The power conferred upon the Secretary of the Navy to make regulations for the admission of persons upon the pension roll, does not authorize him to make a statute of limitations. *Attorney-General Toucey, February* 16, 1849.

See also OPINIONS and DECISIONS in army cases, page 264, for holdings applicable to navy cases.

CHAPTER XVI.

POWERS OF ATTORNEY IN PENSION CASES.

REGULATIONS AND FORMS.

DEPARTMENT OF THE INTERIOR,
PENSION OFFICE, *April* 18, 1851.

THE following rules and regulations, approved by the Secretary of the Interior, will be observed in the settlement of pension claims against the Government:

1. An agent or attorney asking to examine papers filed in any pension claim, or for the re-consideration of a claim heretofore adjudicated, must produce a power of attorney giving him the necessary authority to act as agent of the claimant, which power of attorney must be acknowledged before a justice of the peace or other person qualified to take acknowledgments or administer oaths, and must be certified under a recognized official seal. The party moreover executing such power must have taken an oath that he or she is directly interested as one of the claimants, and a certificate to that effect must accompany the power.

2. On the presentation of such authority, the commissioner will, in his discretion, furnish an abstract of the proofs appearing in the papers filed, or permit a personal inspection of such papers.

3. Upon the presentation of the power, as required in the first rule, if it appear that the original party performing the alleged service, or his widow, is the applicant for the re-consideration of a claim heretofore adjudicated, such claim may be re-examined as a matter of right, but there shall not be more than two re-examinations without the production of further material evidence.

4. In other cases than those of the person performing service, or his widow, as prescribed in the third rule next preceding, no pension case which has been finally adjudicated shall be re-opened, unless on the production of satisfactory proof that the adjudication was erroneous, accompanied by an affidavit of the party applying therefor, showing that such proof has been discovered since the adjudication was made.

5. Appeals may be taken from the decision of the Commissioner of Pensions within six months from the time the decision is made and communicated to the party or his agent.

6. No application for a re-hearing will be entertained after the expiration of two years from the final adjudication of a claim and notice thereof to the applicant or his agent. After that time the party will be left to seek redress by an appeal to Congress.

J. E. HEATH, *Commissioner of Pensions.*

PENSION OFFICE,——186 .

SIR: In relation to the application of——under act of——you are informed that when an inquiry is made concerning claims pending in this bureau, the party inquiring must file authority from the claimant, or an agent appointed by him, with full power of substitution. Powers of attorney must in all cases, be signed in the presence of two witnesses, and acknowledged before a duly qualified officer, who is certified under seal. When such authority is received at this office, you will be promptly notified of the condition of the claim. Very respectfully,

JOSEPH H. BARRETT, *Commissioner.*

Forms.

Know all men by these presents, that I ——, of the county of —— and State of ——, do hereby constitute and appoint ——, my true and lawful agent and attorney, for me and in my name to prosecute the claim presented by me for an invalid pension [*or*, for a half-pay pension as widow of —— deceased ; *or*, the claim presented by me, as guardian for ——, minor heirs of —— deceased, for a pension for said wards; *or*, for an increase of pension; *or*, for a renewal of pension; *or*, for arrears of pension, *or otherwise, as the case may be*]; and I do hereby authorize my said attorney to examine the papers, documents and records on file in any department of the government or the several offices thereof, relating to my said claim, to appoint one or more substitutes to assist him in the business aforesaid; to file additional evidence or arguments, whenever required; to receive the certificate which may issue in my name upon said claim; and to do any and all acts necessary in attaining the object of his said appointment.

In testimony whereof I hereto set my hand and seal, this —— day of —— A. D. 18—.

Executed in presence of:
(*Two witnesses.*) [L. S.]

STATE OF —— } ss.
County of —— }

On this —— day of ——, A. D. 18—, before me, a justice of the peace in and for the county aforesaid, personally appeared ——, and acknowledged the foregoing power of attorney to be —— act and deed, for the purposes therein mentioned.

In testimony whereof, I hereunto set my hand, the day and year aforesaid. (*J. P.*)

STATE OF —— } ss.
County of —— }

[L. S.] I, ——, clerk of the —— court, within and for said county, certify that —— Esq., whose genuine signature appears to the foregoing certificate of acknowledgment, was, at the time of subscribing the same, and still is, an acting justice of the peace, in and for said county, duly commissioned and sworn, and that his official acts are entitled to full faith and credit.

In testimony whereof, I hereto set my hand and affix the seal of said court, at ——, this —— day of ——, A. D. 18 —.

(*Clerk.*)

When a power of attorney is executed by one of several claimants, the regulations require that the party executing shall make oath that he or she has a direct interest in the claim.

Where the power is intended merely to authorize an attorney to present the claim, and receive the certificate that may be issued thereon, it will be sufficient if this power be included within the claimant's declaration, provided the officer administering the oath also certifies that the execution of the power was acknowledged before him, and the witnesses certify that it was subscribed in their presence.

CHAPTER XVII.

ARREARS OF PENSIONS.

LAWS, REGULATIONS AND FORMS.

UNDER this title will be considered only arrears of pensions proper.[1]

An act of March 2, 1829, entitled "an act making provision for the payment of pensions to the widows or children of pensioners, in certain cases, and for other purposes,"[2] contains the following provisions:

SEC. 2. *And be it further enacted*, That whenever any revolutionary pensioner shall die, the Secretary of War shall cause to be paid the arrears of the pension due to the said pensioner at the time of his death; and all payments under this act, shall be made to the widow of the deceased pensioner or to her attorney; or if he left no widow, or she be dead, to the children of the pensioner, or to their guardian, or his attorney; and if no child or children, then to the legal representatives of the deceased.[3]

---

1 Arrears of pensions, properly speaking, are moneys due pensioners, their widows, children or legal representatives, upon a claim presented and allowed. Unclaimed pensions are such as have never been claimed, although provision has been made by law for their payment, when proved.

2 U. S. Statutes at Large, vol. iv, 350.

3 Where by special act the widow of a deceased pensioner is placed upon the pension roll at the same rate that the deceased received in his lifetime, and she dies before the passage of the act, her children are entitled to the arrear; and if there be no children, then the arrear goes to the legal representatives of the widow. *Attorney-General Gilpin, May* 25, 1840.

Attorney-General Mason (July 14, 1846) held, that the law of 1829 is superseded by the law of 1840. This opinion certainly admits of doubt. The act of 1829 provides (among other things), for cases where the pensioner leaves a *widow*, and directs that she shall first be entitled to the arrears of pension due her deceased husband. The act of 1840 provides for cases

In case a pensioner under this act should leave neither widow nor child, the arrears of pension due him at the time of his death will be paid to his executor or administrator, to defray the expenses of his last illness and funeral, and if there be no such expenses, the money due will revert to the government.

An act of June 19, 1840, entitled "an act making provision for the payment of pensions to executors or administrators of deceased persons in certain cases,"[1] provides:

Be it enacted by the Senate and House of Representatives of the United States of America in Congress assembled, That in case any male pensioner[2] shall die, leaving children,[3] but no widow, the amount of

---

where there is *no widow* of the deceased pensioner. The former act is not in express terms repealed, and, therefore, so far as relates to arrears of pensions, where there is a surviving widow, the act of March 2, 1829, it would seem, is still in full force.

The term "legal representatives" of a deceased pensioner, as used in the act of March 2, 1829, means the executor of the last will and testament of the deceased pensioner or the administrator on his estate. *Second Comptroller.*

The Department of the Interior will not issue a certificate to an administrator of a revolutionary officer, or otherwise recognize such a claim, where neither widow nor children survive; nor in the case of the administrator of a widow, where no children survive. But if a certificate has been issued to a male pensioner, who afterwards dies, the amount of pension accruing after the last semi-annual payment to the time of his death, will be paid by the Treasury Department *to his administrator*, if neither widow nor children *survive*, and in case of a female pensioner, to her *administrator*, if no children *survive*. *Commissioner Waldo, Letter to Dr. Mayo, May* 29, 1855.

1 U. S. Statutes at Large, vol. v, 385.

2 The act of June 19, 1840, applies to "pensioners," which means persons receiving a pension, not to those who are entitled to pensions but have not made their claim. *Secretary Ewing, March* 5, 1850.

3 The law of 1840 authorizes the payment to administrators and executors only in cases where there are children or a child; where there is no child, the executor or administrator can not claim. *Secretary Marcy, April*

pension due to such pensioner at the time of his death, shall be paid to the executor or administrator [1] on the estate of such pensioner, for the sole and exclusive benefit of the children, [2] to be by him distributed among them in equal shares, and the same shall not be considered as a part of the assets of said estate, nor liable to be applied to the payment of the debts of said estate, in any case whatever.[3]

SEC. 2. *And be it further enacted*, That in case any pensioner who is a widow, shall die, leaving children,[4] the amount of pension due at the time of her death shall be paid to the executor or administrator for the benefit of her children, as directed in the foregoing section.

SEC. 3. *And be it further enacted*, That in case of the death of any pensioner, whether male or female, leaving children, the amount of pension may be paid to any one or each of them, as they may prefer, without the intervention of an administrator.[1]

These are the only acts making general provision for the payment of arrears. Special provision is made in some cases by the acts granting particular pensions.

REGULATIONS.

Under the act of March 2, 1829, the widow or children of a deceased pensioner, as the case may be, must prove that they are such, before a court of record, and get a certificate of the fact from a

---

21, 1845; also *Second Comptroller;* also *Commissioner Heath, October* 17, 1851; also *Secretary Stuart, March* 17, 1852.

1 Arrears due a deceased pensioner may be paid to the administrator, unless some one or more of the heirs entitled make known to the pension agent a preference that their shares should be paid without the intervention of an administrator. *Second Comptroller.*

2 This includes grandchildren. *Walton et al.* v. *Colton et al.*, 19 Howard 355.

3 Except to pay the expenses of the last illness and funeral of the pensioner.

4 This includes illegitimate children. *Secretary Stuart, December* 1, 1851. Where there are no children of a deceased widow, the arrears of pension due her can not be claimed by her executor or administrator. *Attorney-General Mason, July* 14, 1846. See note page 275.

clerk of the court, under his seal of office, before the arrears can be paid, according to said act.

Approved, Dec. 22, 1829. J. H. EATON.

WAR DEPARTMENT, *Nov.* 9, 1833.

In a case where the residence of all the children of a deceased pensioner can not be ascertained, those who are known to be living must prove their relationship to the deceased before a court of record. They must show that the pensioner left no widow; that the children who are in parts unknown, have not been heard of for at least one full year, and that exertions have been made, without success, to ascertain their residence. Their names must be given. The court must give a certificate containing the facts, and the clerk of the court must sign the same, and annex thereto his seal of office. In such case, the amount due will be paid to those who are known to be living; and all that is due must be paid at one time.

In a case where there is no widow, and the children who survive reside at a considerable distance from each other, and it is difficult or impracticable to obtain information or powers of attorney from those who live remote from the pension agency, the amount due to each child may be paid, upon proper voucher when demanded, without requiring all the children to make application at the time.

LEWIS CASS.

The following instructions and forms prescribed by the Second Comptroller to be observed by Pension Agents for keeping and stating their accounts for settlement at the Treasury, were approved September 1, 1846:

[Only so much is taken from these instructions as is applicable to the payment of arrears of pensions.]

6. Under the provisions of the acts of 2d March, 1829, and 29th June, 1840, in case of the death of any pensioner, the arrears of pension due to him at the time of his death must be paid—

I. "To the widow of the deceased pensioner or to her attorney;" proving herself to be such before a court of record.

II. If there be no widow, then to the executor or administrator on the estate of such pensioner, for the sole and exclusive benefit of the children, to be by him distributed among them in equal shares; and the law of 1840 declares that the arrears of pension "shall not be considered a part of the assets of said estate, nor liable to be applied to the payments of the debts of said estate in any case whatever."

III. In case of the death of any pensioner who is a widow leaving children, the amount of pension due at the time of her death must be paid to the executor or administrator for the benefit of her children, as directed in the foregoing paragraph.

IV. In case of the death of any pensioner, whether male or female, leaving children, the amount of pension may be paid to any one or each of them, as they may prefer, without the intervention of an administrator. If one of the children is selected to receive the amount due, he or she must produce a power of attorney from the others for that purpose, duly authenticated.

V. If there be no widow, child or children, then the amount due such pensioner at the time of his death must be paid to the legal representative of the decedent.

VI. When an executor or administrator shall apply for the pension due to a deceased person, he must deposit with you a certificate of the clerk of the court, judge of probate, register of wills, ordinary or surrogate (as the case may be), stating that he is duly authorized to act in that capacity on the estate of the deceased pensioner, and, if a male, that it has been proved to his satisfaction that there is no widow of the said pensioner living.

7. In all cases of payments being made of moneys due a deceased pensioner, the original pension certificate must be surrendered, as evidence of the identity of the person to whom the pension claimed was due, or other substantial evidence of such identity must be produced in case such certificate can not be obtained for surrendry, and that due search and inquiry have been made for said certificate, and that it can not be found. The date of said pensioner's death must be proved before a court of record.

8. A certificate of the facts proved must be obtained from the clerk of the court. It is not necessary for the clerk to give the evidence in detail, but only to state the facts that have been proved, and certify under his seal of office that the testimony adduced was satisfactory to the court; and in case a pension certificate is illegally withheld from a pensioner, he (or she, as the case may) must produce evidence of identity and the facts.

Oath of Identity where Arrears are due, and Certificate to be surrendered.

STATE OF —— } ss.
County of—— }

On this —— day of —— A.D. 18—, before me, a justice of the peace within and for said county, duly authorized by law to administer oaths, personally appeared ——, and made oath in due form of law, that he is the identical person named in an original certificate, dated at the Department of the Interior on the —— day of —— A.D. 18—, and to be herewith surrendered, and of which the following is a copy, viz.: [*Here copy certificate at length* : that he now resides at ——, in ——, and has resided there for the space of —— years past; and that previous thereto he resided in ——; of the truth of which statement I am satisfied. (*Signature.*)

Sworn to and subscribed, before me this —— day of —— A.D. 18—.

(*J. P.*)

For form of acknowledgment and power of attorney, to accompany this affidavit, see below:

Oath of Identity of Widow or Child, or Executor or Administrator of a deceased person.

STATE OF —— } ss.
County of —— }

Be it known, that before me, ——, a ——, in and for the county aforesaid, duly authorized by law to administer oaths, personally appeared ——, and made oath in due form of law, that she (*or* he, *as the case may be*) is the widow [*or* son, *or* daughter, *or* executor of the last will and testament, *or* administrator of the estate, *as the case may be*], of —— , the identical person who was a pensioner, and is now dead, and to whom a certificate of pension was issued, which is herewith surrendered.[1]

That the deceased pensioner resided in ——, in the State of ——, for the space of —— years before his death; and that previous thereto he resided in ——. (*Signature.*)

Sworn to and subscribed this —— day of ——, 18—, before me.

(*J. P.*)

[Certificate and seal of clerk of court.]

This must be supported by proof, as required in the

[1] In case the pension certificate has been lost, insert, immediately after the name or names of the widow, child or children, as the case may be, the following: "And that the pension certificate of said pensioner has been lost, and, after due search and inquiry therefor, it can not be found."

foregoing regulations, which claimants will particularly examine.

In case the pension has been due and unclaimed for *fourteen* months, the application should be presented to the Third Auditor of the Treasury; if less than fourteen months, at the agency where the certificate is made payable.

Power of Attorney.

Know all men by these presents, that I, ——, of ——, in the county of ——, State of ——, widow (or child, *or otherwise, as the case may be*), of ——, who was an invalid pensioner of the United States, do hereby constitute and appoint ——, my true and lawful attorney, for me, and in my name, to receive from the agent of the United States for paying pensions in ——, State of ——, the balance of said pension from the —— day of ——, 18—, to the —— day of ——, being the day of his death.

Witness my hand and seal, this —— day of ——, 18—.

Sealed and delivered in presence of

(*Witness.*) [SEAL.]

STATE OF ——}
County of ——} *ss.*

On this —— day of ——, A.D. 18—, before the undersigned authority within and for said county, personally came —— [widow, *or* child, *or* executor, *or* administrator] of —— deceased, and acknowledged the signing and sealing of the foregoing power of attorney, for the purposes therein expressed.

Given under my hand, the day and year aforesaid.

(*J. P.*)

The official character of the magistrate or other officer taking the acknowledgment, must be certified by the Clerk of the proper Court, under its seal, as in other cases.

Certificate of the Court as to the Death of a Pensioner.

STATE OF ——}
County of ——} *ss.*

I, ——, clerk of the court of ——, holden at ——, in and for ——, do hereby certify, that satisfactory evidence has been exhibited to said court that —— was a pensioner of the United States at the rate of —— dollars per ——; was a resident of the county of ——, in the State of —— and died at ——, in the State of ——, in the year ——, on the —— day of ——;

that he left a widow [*or* no widow] (*or* child *or* children, *as the case may be*), whose name is (*or* are, *as the case may be*) ——.

In testimony whereof, I have hereunto set my hand and affixed [L. S.] my seal [seal of the court] —— of office at ——, this —— day of ——, in the year of our Lord 18—.

(*Clerk of the* ——.)

No arrears are due, where the person in whose right they are claimed was not living at the date of the act granting the pension. And by a recent act the children of revolutionary soldiers are precluded from claiming pensions or back pensions where their fathers or mothers died without having established their claim.

For further rulings and orders relative to the payment of arrears of pensions, see page 292.

CHAPTER XVIII.

RENEWAL OF PENSIONS.

THE regulations and forms for the renewal of pensions may, in some cases, be found in the chapters which contain the renewing acts. A few forms are here given by way of illustration merely.

Declaration for renewal [Military Case].

STATE OF ——
County of —— } *ss.*

On this —— day of —— A.D. 18—, before the —— court [*or* before me ——, judge, *or* clerk of the —— court], a court of record within and for said county, personally appeared ——, a resident of said county, aged —— years, who being first duly sworn, according to law, doth, on her oath, make the following declaration in order to obtain the benefits of the act of ——, renewing half-pay to certain widows and orphans.

That she is the widow of ——, who was a ——, in company ——, commanded by Captain ——, in the —— regiment of ——, commanded by Colonel ——, in the war with ——; for proof of which she refers to the papers on file in her original application, upon which she formerly obtained a pension at the rate of —— dollars per month, payable at the agency for paying pensions in ——, in the State of ——; the certificate of which pension has been surrendered.

She now claims the benefits of the act of ——, and asks that her name may be placed upon the list of pensioners payable at the agency in ——, in the State of ——.

She further declares that she is still a widow. (*Signature of Claimant.*)

Sworn to and subscribed in open court [*or*, before me ——, judge, *or* clerk of said court of ——] the day and year aforesaid. And I certify that I believe [*or* know] the declarant to be the person she represents herself to be, and that I am not interested in her said claim.

[L. S.] In testimony whereof I hereto set my hand, and affix the seal of said court, this —— day of —— A.D. 18—.

(*Clerk's Signature.*)

If sworn to before a Judge, his official character must be certified by the Clerk, under the seal of the Court.

STATE OF —— }
County of —— } *ss.*

On this —— day of, —— A.D. 18—, personally appeared before the —— court [*or*, before me —— judge, *or* —— clerk, of the —— court] a court of record within and for said county, ——, and ——, who are [to me well known to be] residents of the county of ——, and credible witnesses, and who being first duly sworn, depose and say, that they are well acquainted with Mrs. ——, who subscribed and made oath to the above declaration in their presence, and have known her for at least —— years last past; that she is the widow of ——, who served in the manner specified in said declaration; that she is the identical person to whom a pension was granted for such service, at the rate of —— dollars per month; and that she is still a widow. (*Signature.*)

[Certificate of oath.]

In case the widow married again after her original pension was granted, such marriage, with the death of the second husband, must be mentioned and proved.

To these must be added a power of attorney [see Chapter XVI], and the certificate of the Clerk thereto.

Declaration for renewal [Naval Case].

TO THE COMMISSIONER OF PENSIONS:

The memorial of the undersigned, the widow of the late ——, who was a —— in the navy of the United States, respectfully shows:

That her husband, the aforesaid ——, entered the service of the United States in the year ——; that while in the said service, and holding the rank above-mentioned, he departed this life, at ——, on the —— day of ——, in the year ——; that the undersigned was married to the said —— on the —— day of ——, in the year ——, and in proof thereof, she refers to papers on file in the pension office, upon which she obtained a pension for five years. She therefore claims the benefits of the act of Congress of the ——, granting pensions to the widows of officers, seamen and marines, who have died in the service aforesaid; and she requests that her name may be inscribed on the roll of pensioners under that law, who are paid at ——, in the State of ——. (*Claimant's Signature.*)

Here must follow a certificate of the Judge or Clerk, as in the case of a widow whose husband was in the military service.

The same proof as in the last-mentioned case must accompany the declaration, and a power of attorney must also be executed in such cases.

CHAPTER XIX.

INCREASE OF PENSIONS.[1]

REGULATIONS.

NO APPLICATION for an increase of an invalid pension will be examined, unless the proof be first presented to the Pension Agent, where the payment is made. He will forward the "surgeon's affidavit," the "pension certificate," etc., to the Department of the Interior.

If the applicant was pensioned on account of a wound received previous to the war of 1812, he should be examined by two surgeons, under a commission issued by a judge of one of the United States Courts, in order to obtain an increase of his pension.

The magistrate who may administer the oath to the surgeons must certify that they are respectable in their professions, or believes, on the information of others, that they are so. And the official character of the magistrate must be certified by a proper officer under his seal of office.

If the claimant be within thirty miles of an army surgeon, he must obtain his testimony.

The oath may be made before any officer duly authorized to administer oaths. J. L. EDWARDS, *Commissioner of Pensions.*

Application for Increase: [Army Case.]

STATE OF —— } ss.
County of —— }

On this —— day of —— A. D. 18—, before me, a —— within and for said county, personally appeared ——, a resident of said county, aged —— years, who being by me first duly sworn, declares that he is the same person in whose favor a certificate of pension was issued on the —— day of ——, 18—, by the Secretary of the Interior, at the rate of ——, per month,

[1] The increase can in no case exceed a full pension.

Where the increase of a pension is claimed on account of the amputation of a limb, injured in the service, it will commence from the time when such increased disability occurred. *Secretary Marcy, August* 28, 1845

from the —— day of —— 18—; and which pension has been paid to him to the —— day of ——, 18—, at the agency at ——, in the State of ——.

That the disability for which the said pension was allowed was caused by ——, in the line of his duty as a —— in company ——, in the —— regiment of ——, in the war with ——, and was graduated for [*State the degree of disability for which the said pension was allowed, as:* one fourth, one half, *or otherwise*], disability from manual labor. That said disability has since increased [*Here give the nature and effect of the increase*], and renders him less able than formerly to perform manual labor, as will appear by the surgeon's affidavit herewith filed.

He makes this declaration for the purpose of obtaining an increase of his pension, corresponding with the increase of his disability as aforesaid.

(*Claimant's Signature.*)

Sworn to and subscribed before me, the day and year aforesaid; and I certify that I have no interest whatever in the foregoing claim.

(*Officer's Signature.*)

Surgeon's Affidavit.

It is hereby certified that —— formerly —— of Captain ——'s company, in the —— regiment of ——, who, it appears by the accompanying pension certificate, was placed on the pension roll at the rate of —— dollars per month, on account, as he states, of having received a [*Here give a particular description of the wound, injury or disease, and specify in what manner it has affected the applicant, so as to produce disability in the degree stated; and show its origin and progress*], while in the line of duty, and in the said service, on or about the —— day of ——, in the year ——, at a place called ——, in the State of ——, is not only still disabled in consequence of the said injury, but in the opinion of the undersigned, is entitled to [one fourth, one half, *or, as the case may be*], more than he already receives as a pensioner, being disabled to a degree amounting to [*this must be filled up with the degree of disability, as* one fourth, one third, one half, three fourths], a total disability. (*Signatures of two Surgeons.*)

Sworn to and subscribed before me, the day and year aforesaid; and I certify that I am acquainted with —— and —— and know them to be respectable surgeons, in good standing in their profession; and that I have no interest whatever in the above claim. (*Officer's Signature.*)

To these must be appended the certificate of the Clerk of the proper Court, under its seal, as to the official character of the magistrate administering the oaths.

The foregoing papers, and the certificate of pension,

must be sent to the Pension Agent, at the agency where the pensioner has been paid.

Application for Increase of Navy Invalid Pensions.

STATE OF —— }
County of —— } *ss.*

On this —— day of ——, 18—, before me, ——, a ——, personally appeared, —— a resident of ——, who being duly sworn, declareth that he is the same person in whose favor a certificate of pension was issued on the —— day of —— 18—, under the signature and seal of the Secretary of the Interior, at the rate of —— dollars, —— cents, per month, from the —— day ——, 18—, and which pension has been paid him to the —— day of ——, 18—, inclusive, at the Navy Pension Agency.

That the disability for which the said pension was allowed was caused by —— in the line of his duty, while attached to the United States [*here insert class and name of vessel*], and holding the rank of ——, in the year 18—, and was graduated for [*state degree of disability mentioned in certificate*] disability from manual labor; but that such disability having since increased, the said ——, for the purpose of obtaining a corresponding increase of his pension, requests that a Board of Survey may be ordered in his case, to be held at the United States Naval Station at ——.

(*Claimant's Signature.*)

Sworn and subscribed to before me, the day and year aforesaid; and I certify that I have no interest in the above claim.

(*Officer's Signature.*)

The Clerk's certificate and seal must be attached, as in other cases.

This declaration must be accompanied by the affidavit of two witnesses, who can swear to the claimant's identity.

CHAPTER XX.

PENSION CERTIFICATES LOST OR ILLEGALLY WITHHELD.

REGULATIONS IN CASES OF LOST CERTIFICATES.

THE oath to be taken before a duly qualified magistrate, whose official character and signature must be properly authenticated.

If the pensioner has never received a formal certificate, but has drawn his pension on a mere notification, as was the case in a few instances many years ago, he should insert "*but has never received a formal certificate, and now wishes to obtain one.*"

The pensioner's oath must be supported by the evidence of another person as to identity. The person must swear that he well knows him to be the same person described in the affidavit. The magistrate must certify that the deponent is a person of veracity. This oath must also be authenticated by the certificate of the proper officer, under his seal of office, setting forth that the officer before whom the affidavit may be made is a justice of the peace, judge or notary public, as the case may be.

When a person, acting as an agent or attorney for a pensioner, loses the certificate, the affidavit of that person is also required, which must be authenticated as above.

In every case where the clerk of the court or other certifying officer has no public seal of office, the certificate of a member of Congress, proving the official character and signature of the certifying officer, should be sent with the papers.

Mode of authenticating papers.—In every instance where the certificate of the certifying officer who authenticates the papers is not written on the same sheet which contains the affidavit or other paper authenticated, the certificate must be attached thereto by a piece of tape or small ribbon, the ends of which must pass under the seal of office of the certifying officer, so as to prevent any paper from being improperly attached to the certificate.

No attention will be given to applications from persons who act as agents, unless they are known at the War Department, or are vouched for as respectable persons by some one who is known to the Department. J. L. EDWARDS.

Application for Renewal of Lost Certificate.

STATE OF —— }
County of —— } *ss.*

On this —— day of ——, 18—, before the subscriber, a —— for said county, personally appeared ——, who, on his oath, declares that he is the same person who formerly belonged to the company commanded by Captain ——, in the regiment commanded by Colonel ——, in the service of the United States; that his name was placed on the pension roll of the State of ——; that he received a certificate of that fact under the signature and seal of the Secretary of ——; which certificate, on or about the —— day of ——, 18—, at or near [*here state particulars of loss or destruction of certificate.*] (*Claimant's Signature.*)

Sworn and subscribed to before me, the day and year aforesaid; and I certify that I have no interest in the above claim.

(*Officer's Signature.*)

Affidavit of Witness.

STATE OF —— }
County of —— } *ss.*

On this —— day of ——, 18—, before the subscriber, a —— for said county, personally appeared ——, who, on his oath, declares that he well knows ——, who has executed the foregoing affidavit, to be the identical pensioner named therein. He further says that he has no interest in the above claim. (*Signature of Witness.*)

Sworn and subscribed to before me, the day and year aforesaid; and I certify that the said —— is to me well known to be a person of veracity.

(*Officer's Signature.*)

Append certificate of Clerk, under seal, as in other cases.

REGULATIONS WHERE PENSION CERTIFICATES ARE ILLEGALLY WITHHELD.

The pensioner must state, in its place in the affidavit here appended, the amount of pension to which he is now entitled, which, in some cases, varies from that in the original certificate; and he must sign and make oath to the affidavit.

The oath may be administered by any officer properly qualified to take an affidavit.

Such officer will state, in the place indicated in his certificate below, the evidence of identity of the affiant or pensioner—whether personal knowledge or the affidavits of respectable persons—giving their names.

Affidavit.

STATE OF —— } ss.
County of —— }

Be it known, that before me, ——, a justice of the peace, in and for the county aforesaid, personally appeared ——, and made oath, in due form of law, that he is the identical —— named in an original pension certificate now illegally withheld by —— [*here state the facts respecting the detentiou of the certificate*]; that he is entitled to a pension of —— dollars per month, on account of the wounds and disabilities received [*or*, of services rendered the United States] during the —— war; that he served in the company of Captain ——, in the —— regiment; that he now resides in ——, and has there resided for the space of —— years past; and that, previous thereto, he resided in ——. (*Claimant's Signature.*)

Sworn to and subscribed before me, the day and year aforesaid.

(*Officer's Signature.*)

Officer's Certificate.

STATE OF —— } ss.
County of —— }

Conformably to the regulations of the War Department of the 27th October, 1832, I, ——, a magistrate in the county above-named, do hereby certify that I have the most satisfactory evidence, viz: personal knowledge [*or*, the affidavit of —— and ——, two respectable witnesses of said county] that ——, who this day appeared before me to take the oath of identity, is the identical pensioner he declares himself to be in the annexed affidavit; and I am also satisfied that the statement made by him in relation to the pension certificate is true. I further certify that I have no interest in the claim of said ——.

Given under my hand this —— day of ——, A. D. 18—.

(*Officer's Signature.*)

STATE OF —— } ss.
County of —— }

I, ——, clerk of the —— court, in the county and State aforesaid, do hereby certify that ——, before whom the foregoing papers were executed, was at the date of the same a justice of the peace in and for said county, duly authorized by law to administer oaths; and his name thereunto subscribed is his signature.

[L. S.] In testimony whereof, I have hereunto subscribed my name and affixed my official seal, this —— day of ——, A. D. 18—.

(*Clerk.*)

CHAPTER XXI.

TRANSFER OF PAY AGENCY.

PENSION OFFICE, [*No. Date.*]

A PENSIONER desirous of having his pension transferred to another agency, must make his application according to the subjoined form.

The oath of the applicant must be taken before a duly qualified magistrate, whose official character and signature must be certified by the proper officer. The county clerk, Secretary of State, or some other officer, will certify under his seal of office, that the officer who administered the oath is a justice of the peace, judge, mayor, alderman or notary public (as the case may be), and that the signature purporting to be his is genuine.

The oath must be supported by the testimony of some respectable person, as to the pensioner's identity. He must swear that the person who has taken the oath is the person described in the affidavit. The magistrate must certify that the witness is a person of veracity, and the affidavit must also be authenticated in the manner above directed.

In every case where the clerk of the court, or other certifying officer, has no public seal of office, the certificate of a member of Congress, proving the official character and signature of the certifying officer, should be sent with the papers.

Form of Application for a Transfer of Pension to another Pay Agency.

STATE OF —— }
County of —— } *ss.*

On this —— day of ——, 18—, before me, the subscriber, a justice of the peace for the said county of ——, personally appeared ——, who, on his oath, declares that he is the same person who formerly belonged to the company commanded by Captain ——, in the regiment commanded by Colonel ——, in the service of the United States; that his name was placed on the pension roll of the State of ——, from whence he has lately removed; that he now resides in the State of ——, where he intends to remain, and wishes his pension to be there payable in future. The following are his reasons for removing from —— to ——. (*Claimant's Signature.*)

Sworn and subscribed to before me, the day and year aforesaid.

(*J. P.*)

STATE OF —— } ss.
County of —— }

On this —— day of ——, A. D. 18 —, before me, the subscriber, a —— in and for said county, duly authorized to administer oaths, personally came —— and ——, whom I know to be residents of the county and State aforesaid, and persons whom I certify to be respectable and entitled to credit, and who being duly sworn, say that they were present and saw —— sign and make oath to the foregoing affidavit. They further say that they are acquainted with the said ——, and know him to be the identical person he represents himself to be, and who made oath as aforesaid.

(*Signatures of Witnesses.*)

Sworn to and subscribed before me, this —— day of ——, A. D. 18—, and I certify that I have no interest in this case, nor am I concerned in its prosecution. (*J. P.*)

The Clerk of the proper Court must certify, under seal to the official character of the Magistrate.

CHAPTER XXII.

PAYMENT OF PENSIONS.

OFFICIAL INSTRUCTIONS AND FORMS OF APPLICATION FOR PAYMENT OF PENSIONS.[1]

In case a pension has remained unclaimed by any pensioner for the term of *fourteen* months after the same has become due and payable, it can not be paid by the Pension Agent, but application therefor must be made to the Treasury Department: if the certificate issued through the War or Interior Departments (on account of military service), to the Third Auditor; if through the Navy Department, to the Fourth Auditor of the Treasury.

I. When application is made for the payment of a pension, the first thing that seems necessary is, that the identity of the person in whose behalf the pension is claimed should be established.

II. Under the provisions of the acts of 6th April, 1838, and 23d August, 1842, where a pension has remained unclaimed by any pensioner for the term of fourteen months after the same became due and payable, it can not be paid by the Pension Agent, but application therefor must be made to the Treasury of the United States through the Third Auditor, if the pension certificate issued from the War Department; and through the Fourth Auditor, if it issued from the Navy Department. Each Pension Agent, immediately on the expiration of fourteen months, subsequent to each semi-annual payment, will certify to the office of the Second Comptroller a correct list, containing the name, rank, rate of pension, amount due, and time of last payment of each pensioner remaining unpaid on the roll of his agency, whose pension has been due and payable for the term of fourteen months prior to the date of such certificate. When, however, a new pensioner is placed on the roll, or an old pension is renewed, the fourteen months commence running from the semi-annual payment next after the date of his, or her, pension certificate, and not from the commencement or renewal of the pension.

III. When an attorney shall make application for a pension, (be the rank of the pensioner what it may), he must deposit with you a

[1] These regulations and forms apply to the payment of pensions, both army and naval.

power of attorney in his favor, duly acknowledged, and dated on, or subsequent to, the day on which the pension claimed became due, and within ninety days of the time of his applying for payment, and also his own affidavit that said power was not given to him by reason of any sale, transfer or mortgage of said pension; and the execution of the power must be in the presence of at least one witness, other than the magistrate before whom it is acknowledged.

IV. In all cases of payments upon a power of attorney, the justice of the peace or magistrate before whom the power is executed, must have lodged with the agent the certificate of the clerk of some court of record, under seal of the court, that he is legally authorized to act as such, and also a paper bearing his proper signature, certified to be such by the clerk of some court of record.

V. It is advisable, and is so recommended, that Pension Agents procure and place in a book the signature and seals of clerks of the different courts within their agency, who may be authorized to certify as to powers, the better to detect, by comparison of the signatures and seals, impositions that may be attempted.

VI. Under the provisions of the act of 2d March, 1829, and 29th June, 1840, in case of the death of any pensioner, the arrears of pension due to him at the time of his death must be paid—

1. "To the widow of the deceased pensioner, or to her attorney," proving herself to be such before a court of record.

2. If there be no widow, then to the executor or administrator on the estate of such pensioner, for the sole and exclusive benefit of the children, to be by him distributed among them in equal shares; and the law of 1840 declares that the arrears of pension "shall not be considered a part of the assets of said estate, nor liable to be applied to the payment of the debts of said estate in any case whatever."

3. In case of the death of any pensioner who is a widow leaving children, the amount of pension due at the time of her death must be paid to the executor or administrator for the benefit of her children, as directed in the foregoing paragraph.

4. In case of the death of any pensioner, whether male or female, leaving children, the amount of pension may be paid to any one or each of them, as they may prefer, without the intervention of an administrator. If one of the children is selected to receive the amount due, he, or she, must produce a power of attorney from the others for that purpose, duly authenticated.

5. If there be no widow, child or children, then the amount due

such pensioner at the time of his death must be paid to the legal representative of the decedent.

6. When an executor or an administrator shall apply for the pension due to a deceased person, he must deposit with you a certificate of the clerk of the court, judge of probate, register of wills, ordinary or surrogate (as the case may be), stating that he is duly authorized to act in that capacity on the estate of the deceased pensioner, and, if a male, that it has been proved to his satisfaction that there is no widow of the said pensioner living.

VII. In all cases of payments being made of moneys due a deceased pensioner, the original pension certificate must be surrendered, as evidence of the identity of the person to whom the pension claimed was due, or other substantial evidence of such identity must be produced in case such certificate can not be obtained for surrendry, and that due search and inquiry have been made for said certificate, and that it can not be found. The date of said pensioner's death must be proved before a court of record.

VIII. A certificate of the facts proved must be obtained from the clerk of the court. It is not necessary for the clerk to give the evidence in detail, but only to state the facts that have been proved, and certify under his seal of office that the testimony adduced was satisfactory to the court; and in case a pension certificate is illegally withheld from a pensioner, he (or she, as the case may be) must produce evidence of identity and the facts.

IX. When a pensioner is placed under guardianship, the guardian applying for a pension must, in addition to the evidence of the pensioner's identity, deposit with you a certificate, from the proper authority, that he is, at that time, acting in that capacity, and also satisfactory evidence that his ward was living at the date the pension claimed became due. The identity of the pensioner, in such cases, must be established.

X. For all payments made by you duplicate receipts must be taken, one of each you will forward, with your quarterly accounts, to the Third Auditor of the Treasury for pensions under the War Department, and to the Fourth Auditor for pensions under the Navy Department; and in all cases where a pensioner or attorney makes a mark from inability to write his name, there must be a witness thereto, otherwise such receipt or voucher will not be admitted at the Treasury.

(I.) *Application of Invalid Pensioner for Payment of Pension.*

STATE OF —— }
County of —— } *ss.*

Be it known, that before me ——, a justice of the peace, in and for the county and State aforesaid, duly authorized by law to administer oaths for general purposes, personally appeared ——, and made oath in due form of law that he is the identical person named in an original certificate in his possession, of which I certify the following is a true copy: (*Here insert a copy of his certificate of pension.*)

That the said —— now resides in ——, and has resided there for the space of — years past; and that previous thereto he resided in ——, and that he has not been employed, or paid in the army, navy or marine service of the United States from —— till ——, of the truth of which statement I am fully satisfied.

(*Two Witnesses.*) (*Signature of Claimant.*)

Sworn to and subscribed before me this —— day of ——, A D. 18—.

(*J. P.*)

Every two years an examination of the condition of the invalid is required, before payment will be made. See the act, regulations and forms in the latter part of this Chapter.[1]

(II.) *Power of Attorney.*

Know all men by these presents, that I,—, of ——, in the State of ——, do hereby constitute and appoint —— my true and lawful attorney, for me, and in my name, to receive from the agent of the United States for paying pensions in ——, State of ——, my pension from the —— day of ——, 18— to the —— day of ——, 18—.

Witness my hand and seal this —— day of ——, 18—.

Sealed and delivered in presence of, [L. S.]

(*Two Witnesses.*)

(III.) *Acknowledgment.*

STATE OF —— }
County of —— } *ss.*

Be it known, that on this —— day of ——, 18—, before me, ——, justice of the peace, in and for the county and State aforesaid, personally appeared —— above-named, and acknowledged the foregoing power of attorney to be his act and deed. In testimony whereof, I have hereunto set my hand the day and year last above-written. (*J. P.*)

[1] See also oath of allegiance, on p. 302.

(IV.) *Affidavit of Attorney.*

STATE OF —— } ss.
County of —— }

Be it known, that on the —— day of ——, 18—, before me a[1] ——, duly authorized by law to administer oaths for general purposes, personally appeared ——, the attorney named in the foregoing power of attorney, and made oath that he has no interest whatever in the money he is authorized to receive by virtue of the foregoing power of attorney, either by any pledge, mortgage, sale, assignment or transfer, and that he does not know or believe that the same has been so disposed of to any person whatever.

(*Signature of Attorney.*)

Sworn and subscribed, the day and year last above-mentioned, before me,

(*J. P.*)

(V.) *Clerk's Certificate.*

STATE OF —— } ss.
County of —— }

I, ——, clerk of the —— court, within and for said county, do hereby certify that ——, Esq, before whom the foregoing declaration and power of attorney were made, and who has thereunto subscribed his name, was at the time of so doing a justice of the peace, in and for the State and county aforesaid, duly commissioned and sworn, and that his signature thereto is genuine.

[L. S.] In testimony whereof, I have hereunto signed my name and affixed my official seal, this —— day of ——, 18—.

(*Clerk.*)

(VI.) *Widow's Application.*[2]

STATE OF —— } ss.
County of —— }

Be it known, that before me, ——, a justice of the peace, in and for the county aforesaid, duly authorized by law to administer oaths, personally appeared ——, widow of ——, and made oath in due form of law, that she is the identical person named in an original certificate in her possession, of which (I certify) the following is a true copy [*Here insert a copy of her certificate of pension*]: That she has not intermarried, but continues the widow of the above-mentioned ——, and that she now resides in ——, and has resided there for the space of —— years past; and that previous

[1] Pension agents are authorized to administer oaths in such cases.

[2] With slight variations, this form can be used for mother's applications.

thereto she resided in ——, of the truth of which statement I am fully satisfied.

(*Two Witnesses.*) (*Claimant's Signature.*)

Sworn and subscribed before me this —— day of ——, A. D. 18—.

(*J. P.*)

To this must be appended a power of attorney, acknowledgment, affidavit and Clerk's certificate, according to the foregoing forms, II, III, IV, V.

(VII.) *Guardian's Application.*[1]

STATE OF —— }
County of —— } *ss.*

Be it known, that before me ——, a justice of the peace, in and for the county aforesaid, duly authorized by law to administer oaths, personally appeared ——, guardian of ——, and made oath, in due form of law, that the said —— is still living, and is the identical person named in an original certificate in his possession, of which (I certify) the following is a true copy [*Here insert a copy of the certificate*]: That —— now resides in —— and has resided there for the space of —— years past; and that previous thereto —— resided in ——; of the truth of which statement I am fully satisfied.

(*Two Witnesses.*) (*Guardian.*)

Sworn to and subscribed before me, this —— day of ——, A. D. 18—.

(*J. P.*)

Here must follow a power of attorney, acknowledgment, affidavit, and Clerk's certificate, according to the foregoing forms II, III, IV, V. A copy of the letters of guardianship, with the certificate of the proper Court (under seal) that the guardian is still acting as such, must also accompany this affidavit.

Where payment of a pension is claimed, under a certificate which is illegally withheld from the pensioner, he must make application in accordance with the Regulations and Forms, Chapter XX.

For Regulations and Forms to be observed in applying for the payment of arrears of pensions, see Chapter XVII.

[1] This form is applicable to guardians of minor sisters also.

INSTRUCTIONS AND FORMS TO BE OBSERVED IN PAYING AND IN APPLYING FOR THE PAYMENT OF NAVY AND PRIVATEER PENSIONS.

PENSION OFFICE, May, 1840.

The agents for paying navy pensions are directed to observe the following rules:

1. The identity of the pensioner must be proved by the exhibition of his certificate, and by his oath and signature, before a justice of the peace, or other officer duly qualified to administer oaths, in accordance with the subjoined form, marked "A."

2. If application be made by, or on behalf of a widow, proof of her identity that she is still living, and has not intermarried, must be furnished according to the form herewith, marked "B."

3. Payments to a guardian will be made on evidence that the child or children are living, and that they are not over sixteen years of age; and a certificate from the proper authority that he is, *at the time*, acting in that capacity, agreeably to the annexed form, marked "C."

4. All pensions unclaimed for two years and upwards will previous to the payment, be referred by the agent, with all the documents, to the Fourth Auditor of the Treasury for investigation; and, if found correct by the accounting officers, they will be returned to the agent for payment.

5. No payment of pensions will be made for a less period than six months, either by the agents or the Fourth Auditor, except in the first payments becoming due to pensioners, or where they shall die, or the pension expires, previous to the time for the regular semi-annual payments. J. L. EDWARDS.

"A."

Application of Invalid Naval Pensioner.

STATE OF —— }
County of —— } *ss.*

Be it known, that before me, a ——, in and for the county aforesaid, personally appeared ——, an invalid pensioner, and made oath, in due form of law, that he is the identical —— named in an original certificate of pension, bearing date at the —— Department, on the —— day of ——, and signed by ——, Secretary of the ——; which certificate he exhibited to me, and by which it appears that he is entitled to a pension of —— dollars per month. (*Claimant's Signature.*)

Sworn to and subscribed before me, this —— day of —— A. D. 18—.

(*Officer's Signature.*)

To this must be added a power of attorney, acknowlment, affidavit, and Clerk's certificate, as in army applications. See Forms II, III, IV, V, pages 290–3, of this Chapter. Every two years, an examination of the invalid must be had, according to the act of March 3, 1859, see page 300. See also oath of allegiance, on p. 302.

"B."

Application of Widow Pensioner.

STATE OF —— }
County of —— } *ss.*

Be it known, that before me, a —— in and for the county aforesaid, personally appeared ——, widow of ——, and made oath in due form of law, that she is the identical —— named in an original certificate of pension, bearing date at the —— Department, on the —— day of ——, and signed by the Secretary of the ——; which certificate she exhibited to me, and by which it appears she is entitled to a pension of —— dollars per month, and that she has not intermarried, but continues the widow of the said ——. (*Claimant's Signature.*)

Sworn to and subscribed before me, this —— day of ——, A. D., 18—.
(*Officer's Signature.*)

Should the claimant not make application for payment in person, a power of attorney, etc., according to Forms II, III, IV, V, in the former part of the chapter, must accompany his affidavit. See also Form VI, which may be substituted for the form of affidavit just given.

"C."

Application of Guardian of Minor Children.

STATE OF —— }
County of —— } *ss.*

Be it known, that before me, a —— in and for the county aforesaid, personally appeared ——, guardian of ——, orphan child [*or* children] of——, and made oath in due form of law, that he is the guardian named in the accompanying certificate of guardianship; that his wards are the children of ——, referred to in an original certificate of pension, bearing date at the —— Department, on the —— day of ——, and signed by ——, Secretary of the ——; by which it appears that they are entitled to a pension of ——

dollars per month; and that said children are still living, and not over sixteen years of age.

(*Claimant's Signature.*)

Sworn to and subscribed before me, this —— day of ——, A. D., 18—.

(*Officer's Signature.*)

Claimants may use Form No. VII, page 297, instead of this, if desired. A copy of the letters of guardianship with the certificate of the proper Court that the party is still acting as guardian, must accompany this affidavit. Should the guardian desire to draw the money due at the semi-annual payment by attorney, he must execute the necessary papers, according to Forms II, III, IV, V, pages 290–3.

By the second section of an act approved March 3, 1859, entitled "an act making appropriation for the payment of invalid and other pensions of the United States, for the year ending the thirtieth of June, eighteen hundred and sixty,"[1] it is provided:

SEC. 2. That in all cases of application for the payment of pensions to invalids, under the several laws of Congress granting pensions to invalids, the affidavit of two surgeons or physicians, whose credibility as such shall be certified by the magistrate before whom the affidavit is made, stating the continuance of the disability for which the pension was originally granted (describing it), and the rate of such disability at the time of making the affidavit, shall accompany the application of the first payment, which shall fall due upon a day in the fiscal year for which provision is made herein, to be declared by the Secretary of the Interior, and at the end of every two years thereafter; and if, in a case of continued disability, it shall be stated at a rate below that for which the pension was originally granted, the applicant shall only be paid at the rate stated in the affidavit: *Provided*, That where the pension shall have been originally granted for a total disability, in consequence of the loss of a limb or other cause, which can not, either in whole or in part, be removed, the

[1] U. S. Statutes at Large, vol. xi, 439.

above affidavit shall not be necessary to entitle the applicant to payment.

REGULATIONS.

PENSION OFFICE, *July* 1, 1859.

Invalid pensioners of the Army and Navy, who are, by the above enactment, subjected to biennial examinations, will be required to present, with their usual vouchers, on the 4th day of September and 1st day of January next, respectively, the certificate as to the state of their disability, in accordance with the form hereto appended.

The operation of this act of Congress virtually suspends the semi-annual payments of invalid pensions at the commencement of each biennial period, until the certificate of two physicians or surgeons has been presented. Pension agents will pay each pensioner according to the ratio of disability certified to, but in no case for a greater sum per month than the rate expressed in the pension certificate.

The semi-annual reports of pension agents to this office must show the rate of pension expressed in the pension certificate, as well as the rate at which the pension has been paid under this law; and the word "exempt," written opposite the names of all those whose disability is of an incurable character. Whenever there is more than one pensioner on the roll of the same name, great care should be observed to perpetuate the identity of each.

GEO. C. WHITING, *Commissioner.*

The eighth section of "an act to grant pensions," approved July 14, 1862, is as follows:

SEC. 8. *And be it further enacted*, That the Commissioner of Pensions be, and he is hereby, empowered to appoint, at his discretion, civil surgeons to make the biennial examinations of pensioners which are or may be required to be made by law, and to examine applicants for invalid pensions, where he shall deem an examination by a surgeon to be appointed by him necessary; and the fees for each of such examinations, and the requisite certificate thereof, shall be one dollar and fifty cents, which fees shall be paid to the surgeon by the person examined, for which he shall take a receipt and forward the same to the Pension Office; and upon the allowance of the claim of the person examined, the Commissioner of Pensions shall furnish to such person an order on the pension agent of his State for the amount of the surgeon's fees.

Surgeon's Affidavit.

We, the subscribers, practicing physicians [*or* surgeons] in the town of ——, county of ——, and State of ——, do hereby certify, that we have carefully examined ——, who is now on the invalid pension roll of the agency at ——, in the State of ——, and find that [*Here describe his present physical condition and disability*]. And further, that his present disability for obtaining subsistence by manual labor amounts to [one fourth, one third, one half, two thirds, three fourths, *or* total, *as the case may be.*]

} (*Physicians or Surgeons.*)

Sworn to and subscribed before me, this —— day of ——, A. D., 18—; and I certify that I am acquainted with the said —— and ——, and know them to be physicians [*or* surgeons] in good standing in said town of ——, as to skill and integrity. (*Officer's Signature.*)

This must be followed by the certificate of the Clerk of the proper Court, under its seal, as to the official character of the person by whom the oath is administered.

Since the commencement of the war of 1861, all pensioners, before receiving their semi-annual payments, are required to make the following affidavit:

Oath of Allegiance.

STATE OF ——
County of —— } *ss.*

I, ——, a pensioner of the United States, do solemnly —— that I will support, protect and defend the Constitution and Government of the United States, against all enemies, whether domestic or foreign, and that I will bear true faith, allegiance and loyalty to the same, any ordinance, resolution or law of any State Convention or Legislature to the contrary notwithstanding; and, further, that I do this with a full determination, pledge and purpose, without any mental reservation or evasion whatsoever; and, further, that I will well and faithfully perform all the duties which may be required of me by law. So help me God. (*Pensioner's Signature.*)

Subscribed and sworn to before me, this —— day of ——, 18—.

(*Officer's Signature.*)

STATE OF ——
County of —— } *ss.*

I, ——, clerk of the —— court, within and for said county, do hereby certify that ——, Esq., before whom the foregoing declaration and power of attorney were made, and who has thereunto subscribed his name, was at the time of so doing a justice of the peace, in and for the State and county aforesaid, duly commissioned and sworn, and that his signature thereto is genuine.

[L. S.] In testimony whereof, I have hereunto signed my name and affixed my official seal, this —— day of —— 18—.

(*Clerk.*)

DECISIONS OF THE SECOND COMPTROLLER OF THE TREASURY RELATIVE TO THE PAYMENT OF PENSIONS, BY "AGENTS FOR PAYING PENSIONS."

The references are to the volume and books in the Comptroller's Office containing the *decisions.*

1. The Second Comptroller has no authority to decide on pension claims; that belongs exclusively to the Commissioner of Pensions. *Vol.* x, *p.* 353.

3. Pensions are payable to the persons named in the certificate, if living, and to the legal representatives of such as may have died. *Vol.* xiv, *p.* 21.

4. No deduction is to be made from the amount of pension due a deceased pensioner, on account of his indebtedness to the United States which accrued before the granting of the pension. *Capt. Angus' case, May,* 1837.

5. If once placed on the pension roll, and thus having acquired a legal claim to a semi-annual payment of a certain sum of money, the pensioner shall fail to assert this claim for six years, he can not have his account audited without the authority of Congress. *Vol.* xi, *pp.* 107, 160.

6. When the War Department has given special directions as to the payment of a pension, it is the duty of the pension agents to follow the directions; and if payment be made, not in accordance with such directions, it can not be admitted at the treasury to the credit of the agent. *Vol.* xi, *p.* 403.

7. An invalid pensioner is legally entitled to his pension, although employed on hire in the service of the United States. *Vol.* xiv, *p.* 68.

8. The conviction and imprisonment of a pensioner for crime does not disqualify him from taking the usual oath of identity; nor does it deprive him of his right to draw his pension, or to appoint an agent to draw it for him. *Decisions, March* 20, 1852.

9. When an act of Congress directs the Secretary of War to make payment of a pension to the heirs of a deceased person, and that officer has issued the certificate in conformity to the law, the pension agent can not pay over the money to any other person than the heirs, as expressly directed in the act. *Vol.* xiii, *p.* 30; *vol.* xii, *p.* 376.

10. The amount of pension due a pensioner under several acts of Congress, can be properly paid without a separate power of attorney under each act. One power of attorney will be sufficient, if it covers all the time for which the pension is due under all the acts. *Vol.* xiv, *p.* 141.

11. A pensioner may at any time revoke a power of attorney, which he

has given for the collection of his pension, and demand payment to himself at the agency. *Vol.* xiv, *p.* 464.

12. By the fourth section of the act of July 4, 1836, the attorney of a pensioner is required to make oath, not only that he has no interest in the money by any pledge, etc., but also that "he does not know or believe that the same has been so disposed of to any other person whatever." *Vol.* viii, *p.* 43.

13. The oath to be taken by the attorney of a pensioner claiming under the act of July 4, 1836, must be administered and certified by the agent who makes the payment, or an accounting officer of the Treasury. *Vol.* vi, *p.* 195.

14. When a simple power of attorney is given to draw the money due a pensioner at a certain date, and the pensioner dies before the pension becomes due, the power of attorney is a nullity. *Vol.* ix, *p.* 541.

15. The attorneys of commissioned officers who are pensioners, and of widows pensioned under the navy pension laws, are required to make oath that they have no interest in the money they are authorized to receive, "by any pledge, mortgage, sale or transfer." *Vol.* xi, *p.* 356.

16. An attorney of a pensioner may take the required oath before a notary, when the notary is by law authorized to administer oaths in other cases. *Vol.* xiv, *p.* 2.

17. The term "legal representatives" of a deceased pensioner, as used in the act of March 2, 1829, means the executor of the last will and testament of the deceased pensioner, or the administrator on his estate. *Vol.* x, *p*, 428.

18. Arrears due a deceased pensioner may be paid to the administrator, unless some one or more of the heirs entitled, make known to the pension agent a preference that their shares should be paid without the intervention of an administrator. *Vol.* viii, *p.* 359.

19. The pension act of 19th of June, 1840, was not designed to repeal the act of March 2, 1829, but it does authorize payment to an administrator, notwithstanding there are children living. Where there are no children living, the law does not apply. — *Vol.* xiii, *p.* 28.

20. The pension act of June 19, 1840, provides that the pension shall not be considered as part of the assets of the deceased pensioner's estate, nor liable to be applied to the payment of the debts of said estate; therefore the amount of pension due at the time of the death of a female pensioner may be paid to her children, or to the administrator, for the sole and exclusive benefit of her children, to be distributed among them in equal shares. *Vol.* xii, *p.* 160.

21. When the executor or administrator of a deceased pensioner claims payment of the balance of pension due at the time of the death of a pensioner, the certificate of the proper court to the fact of the death will be sufficient, without certifying that there are children living. In the case of

a male pensioner, it should appear by the certificate that there is no widow; as, in case of a widow surviving the deceased pensioner, she and not the executor or administrator, is entitled to the balance. *Vol.* xiv, *p.* 22.

22. On the death of a pensioner having neither wife nor child, the balance of pension due at the time of his death, is not payable to his half-sister, but to the executor or administrator on his estate. *Vol.* ix, *p.* 637.

23. The balance of pension due a deceased pensioner at the time of his decease, is payable to the widow only, if she remain unmarried. The children have no legal claim to it, except in case of the death or intermarriage of the widow. *Vol.* ix, *p.* 26.

24. A widow claiming arrears of pension due her deceased husband, must prove herself before a court of record, to be the widow of the deceased pensioner, and also take the oath that she is the identical person thus proved to be the widow. *Vol.* xiv, *p.* 19.

25. Where a widow, pensioned under the act of July 21, 1848, contracts another marriage, the agent must require her pension certificate to be surrendered, on paying her pension to the date of such intermarriage. If she has a child entitled to the reversion of the pension, application must be made with proper proof to the Commissioner of Pensions, for a new certificate in the name of the child. *Vol.* xiii, *p.* 193.

26. By the acts of March 2, 1829, and June 19, 1840, the balance due a deceased revolutionary pensioner, leaving children, but no widow, belongs to the children, and can be paid only to them, or to the executor or administrator, on the estate of the deceased pensioner for their benefit. *Vol.* xi, *pp.* 16, 244, 190.

27. A widow pensioner, under the law of July 4, 1836, or July 21, 1848, is entitled to her pension up to the date of her death or intermarriage, if either occur within the five years for which the pension runs; and for the remainder of the time, if any, the pension inures to the child or children under sixteen years of age. *Vol.* xii, *p.* 344.

28. On the death of a female pensioner, the balance of pension due at the time of her death is, by law, payable to her children then living. *Vol.* x, *p.* 5.

29. The share due each of the surviving children of a pensioner may be paid to his or her attorney, without the production of the original certificate, or a compliance with the regulation of Sept. 1, 1846. *Vol.* xiii, *p.* 25.

30. When a pensioner, who is a widow, dies, leaving children, the amount of pension due at the time of her death belongs not to the executor or administrator, but to her surviving children, to be distributed among them in equal shares. *Vol.* xiv, *p.* 38; *Vol.* xi, *p.* 104.

31. Payment of arrears due a deceased pensioner, who left no widow, must always be made to surviving children, if any, and not to representatives of children, who died during the lifetime of the pensioner. *Vol.* xv, *p.* 426.

32. Children not being entitled to the pension, except upon the marriage of their mother, proof of her marriage and its date must be filed with their claim. *Vol.* xiii, *p.* 341.

33. When a child is by law entitled to the balance of pension due a deceased parent, the receipt of the child to the pension agent, is deemed sufficient, notwithstanding said child be a *femme covert* at the time of signing the receipt. *Vol.* xi, *p.* 65.

34. Where one of the children named in a pension certificate dies unmarried, before the certificate is received, leaving brothers and sisters, the share of pension due him may be paid to the surviving children, without taking out letters of administration. *Vol.* xii, *p.* 147.

35. Where one of two or more children named in a pension certificate can not be found, and a certificate from the proper court, if offered as a voucher by the attorney of the other children, affirming that satisfactory evidence has been produced of the death of such child, or that he has been so long absent without having heard from, as to be considered legally deceased by the laws of the State where he had lived, it will be considered sufficient proof of the right of the surviving children to draw the balance of the pension due. *Vol.* xii, *pp.* 134, 146.

36. When several children are embraced in the pension certificate, the oath of identity is not required from all, but only from the one who may be authorized by regular power of attorney from the others to receive the pension money due. *Vol.* xii, *p.* 87.

37. A grandchild of a deceased pensioner can not, in any case, claim to receive the arrears of pension due the pensioner at the time of his death. If no widow or children survive the pensioner, payment must be made to the executor or administrator. *Vol.* xiv, *pp.* 44, 344.

38. At the death of the ward, the powers of the guardian cease. The balance of pension, therefore, due a pensioner who was under guardianship at the time of his decease, is not payable to the guardian. *Vol.* viii, *p.* 65.

39. Whenever a navy pension has been unclaimed for two years, the application of the pensioner, and all the documents in support of his claims must be referred to the Fourth Auditor of the Treasury for investigation. *Vol.* viii, *p.* 22.

40. Where an invalid pensioner's name has been continued on the rolls, and for a series of years he has not claimed the pension at the agency by producing the required proof of continued disability, and afterwards produces that proof and claims under the original certificate, payment should be made at the Treasury. But if his name was stricken from the rolls of the agency so that he could not obtain his pension by applying there with the proper proof, and is to receive it by virtue of a new order from the Department, he should be paid at the agency. *Vol.* xiv, *p.* 63.

41. The pension agent may, if he thinks proper, require the attorney

to receive the money at the office of the agency, though if it were paid on receipts executed elsewhere, the voucher would not be objectionable on that account. *Vol.* xiv, *p.* 221.

42. The regulations for paying pensions require that the certificate shall be set out in the application, and that the applicant shall make oath that he is the identical person named in that certificate. *Vol.* xiii, *p.* 123.

43. In cases where there is no county court seal, the pension agent will not reject vouchers for lack of the seal alone, but he will require the certificate of the clerk that there is no seal. *Decisions, September,* 1846.

44. A pensioner residing in Canada may execute his papers before a justice of the peace in the vicinity of his residence, if he is too feeble to cross over to the United States to have his papers authenticated. *Vol.* xiv, *p.* 125.

45. Where a pensioner neither signs nor makes his mark to vouchers requiring his signature, the pension agent is not authorized to pay the money. *Vol.* xii, *p.* 509.

46. Pension agents may administer all the necessary oaths in the preparation of papers for the payment of pensions. By the act of February 19, 1849, section two, the deputies and clerks of pension agents have the same power as the agents to administer oaths. *Vol.* xii, *p.* 219.

47. Notaries public are not considered as authorized *ex officio,* to administer oaths in the preparation of pension papers, but if the general authority to administer oaths has been conferred upon them by the statute laws of the particular State in which they reside and are commissioned, the oaths taken before them would be valid and of course respected by the pension agents. It should, however, be shown that such authority exists under the law of the State. *Vol.* xii, *pp.* 1, 83. *September* 9, 1847.

48. It is required by the proviso in the first section of the act of September 16, 1850, chapter 52, that the official character of a notary shall be established by other evidence than his seal and signature. The proviso in the first section applies only to cases where the notary has certified that oaths or affirmations were taken before him, and not to certificates of acknowledgment of instruments. *Vol.* xiv, *p.* 111.

49. A pension agent must require that the certificates should be set out in the oath of identity. *Vol.* xiii, *p.* 21.

50. The omission of the words "duly authorized by law to administer oaths" from the oath of identity or acknowledgment of the power of attorney in the pension papers, is not so important as to render it necessary to reject the papers on that account. *Vol.* xi, *pp.* 404, 423, 437.

51. By the act of the General Assembly of the State of Ohio, passed March 22, 1849, notaries are authorized to administer oaths in all cases where an oath is required in the execution of papers to draw pensions at the pension agencies or at the Treasury of the United States. *Vol.* xiv, *p.* 62.

52. That section of the pension instructions which requires a witness to pension vouchers where the pensioner or attorney of a pensioner subscribes by a mark in consequence of inability to write, applies to the oath of identity as well as to every other necessary voucher. In all cases, therefore, a witness is required, other than, and in addition to the magistrate before whom the affidavit is made. *Vol.* xii, *p.* 85.

53. A power of attorney to draw a pension must be dated and acknowledged on, or subsequent to the day on which the pension becomes due. *Vol.* xiv, *pp.* 228, 430; xiii, *pp.* 123, 287, 291.

54. When interlineations and additions are made in a power of attorney to draw a pension, they must be noted by the magistrate. *Vol.* vi, *p.* 44.

55. When a pensioner receives from the pension agent a greater sum than was his due, the excess should stand to his debit, and be considered as so much paid, and no further payment should be made until something shall become due, after deducting the sum so overpaid. *Vol.* viii, *pp.* 222, 421.

56. A power of attorney to draw a pension is not vitiated in consequence of its giving authority to draw for a time antecedent to that from which the pension is due. *Vol.* xiv, *p.* 88.

57. If the pension agent pay to the attorney more money than the pensioner authorized the attorney to receive, the pensioner is not legally accountable for the excess, unless it be shown that he received such excess, or sanctioned the act of the attorney in so receiving it. *Vol.* viii, *p.* 438.

58. On the application of a guardian for the payment of a pension due his wards, he must furnish proof that they are still living, are under twenty-one years of age, and that he still continues to be their guardian. *Vol.* viii, *p.* 25.

CHAPTER XXIII.

BOUNTY LANDS AND LAND WARRANTS.

SECTION I.

LAWS RELATING TO BOUNTY LANDS.[1]

BY an act of February 11, 1847, entitled "an act to raise for a limited time an additional military force, and for other purposes,"[2] bounty land is granted to the surviving soldiers of the war with Mexico, and to the widows and children of those who died in the service, as follows:

SEC. 9. *And be it further enacted*, That each non-commissioned officer, musician or private,[3] enlisted or to be enlisted in the regular army, or regularly enlisted in any volunteer company for a period of not less than twelve months, who has served or may serve[4] during the present war with Mexico,[5] and who shall receive an honora-

1 See LAWS RELATING EXCLUSIVELY TO LAND WARRANTS, in the after part of this section, page 325.

2 U. S. Statutes at Large, vol. ix, 124.

3 An act of May 27, 1848 (U. S. Statutes at Large, vol. ix, 232), directs that the benefits of this act shall not be withheld from non-commissioned officers or privates who were promoted to commissioned officers during the war.

Clerks in the Quartermaster's Department are not entitled to bounty land, unless regularly enlisted in the service. *August* 13, 1853.

4 A soldier on furlough is considered in the service, and his claim for bounty land should not be curtailed by deducting the time spent on furlough. *Secretary Stuart, January* 27, 1852.

5 A soldier honorably discharged before the expiration of twelve months, without having been sick or wounded, is not entitled to bounty land under this act. *Attorney-General Clifford, March* 17, 1848.

This act embraces regular soldiers enlisted for twelve months or longer, who served in the war with Mexico. *Attorney-General Johnson, July* 27, 1849.

Where a soldier was not mustered into service when his company was,

ble discharge, or who shall have been killed, or died of wounds received or sickness incurred in the course of such service, or who shall have been discharged before the expiration of his term of service in consequence of wounds received or sickness incurred in the course of such service, shall be entitled to receive a certificate or warrant from the War Department for the quantity of one hundred and sixty acres, and which may be located by the warrantee, or his heirs-at-law, at any Land Office of the United States, in one body, and in conformity to the legal subdivisions of the public lands, upon any of the public lands in such district then subject to private entry;[1] and upon the return of such certificate or warrant, with evidence of the location thereof having been legally made, to the General Land Office, a patent shall be issued therefor. That in the event of the death of any such non-commissioned officer, musician or private, during service, or after his discharge, and before the issuing of a certificate or warrant as aforesaid, the said certificate or warrant shall be issued in favor, and inure to the benefit of his family

but was borne on the rolls, and finally regularly mustered out of service, he is entitled to bounty land under this act. *Secretary Ewing, November* 12, 1849.

The death of a soldier after the expiration of the term of service, but before receiving his discharge, does not bar his heirs from claiming bounty land under this act—even though he was killed in an affray. *Secretary Ewing, February* 28, 1850.

Where a soldier was discharged before the expiration of his term of service, and the cause of discharge was not mentioned in his certificate, it was held that he might prove that he was discharged on account of sickness, by credible persons cognizant of the fact. *Secretary Ewing, March* 9, 1850.

A private soldier who enlisted for five years, but during the term of service was promoted to a commissioned office, in which he served to the end of the war, is entitled to bounty land. *Secretary Ewing, March* 28, 1850. See also note 3, preceding page.

Sickness or other unavoidable cause preventing a soldier from being mustered into service, does not bar him of his right to bounty land. *Secretary Ewing, July* 1, 1850.

Enlistments after the close of the Mexican war do not entitle the parties to bounty land for service in said war. *Commissioner Waldo, August* 18, 1853.

1 This refers to land subject to entry at the minimum price, and not such lands as are held by statute at two dollars per acre. *Attorney-General Clifford, January* 18, 1848.

or relatives, according to the following rules: first, to the widow and to his children; second, his father; third, his mother.[1] And in the event of his children being minors, then the legally constituted guardian of such minor children shall, in conjunction with such of the children, if any, as may be of full age, upon being duly authorized by the orphans' or other court having probate jurisdiction, have power to sell and dispose of such certificate or warrant for the benefit of those interested. And all sales, mortgages, powers or other instruments of writing,[2] going to affect the title to any such bounty right, made or executed prior to the issue of such warrant or certificate, shall be null and void to all intents and purposes, whatsoever, nor shall such claim to bounty right be in any wise affected by, or charged with, or subject to, the payment of any debt or claim incurred by the soldier prior to the issuing of such certificate or warrant; *Provided*, That no land warrant issued under the provisions of this act shall be laid upon any lands of the United States to which there shall be a pre-emption right, or upon which there shall be an actual settlement or cultivation: *Provided further*, That every such non-commissioned officer, musician and private, who may be entitled, under the provisions of this act, to receive a certificate or warrant for one hundred and sixty acres of land, shall be allowed the option to receive such certificate or warrant, or a Treasury scrip[3] for one hundred dollars; and such scrip, whenever it is preferred, shall be

---

1 By act of May 27, 1848, this was extended to brothers and sisters, on failure of the other "relatives" designated. U. S. Statutes at Large, vol. ix, 232. Under this act it was held that sisters of the half-blood are entitled. *Attorney-General Toucey, September* 7, 1848. Also, that illegitimate sisters of an illegitimate brother who leaves no other relatives, are entitled. *Commissioner Waldo, December* 15, 1853.

2 The claim to bounty land can not be devised by will. *Attorney-General Johnson, June* 28, 1850.

These warrants were afterwards made assignable. See act of March 22, 1852, page 325.

3 Having elected to take this scrip, and having received the necessary certificate, the soldier is concluded by it, and can not afterwards surrender it and take land. *Attorney-General Clifford, October* 30, 1847.

Widows and children must furnish proof of identity before payment of this scrip will be made to them. *Comptroller Whittlesey, September* 10, 1849.

issued by the Secretary of the Treasury to such person or persons as would be authorized to receive such certificates or warrants for lands; said scrip to bear an interest of six per cent. per annum, payable semi-annually, redeemable at the pleasure of the government. And that each private, non-commissioned officer and musician, who shall have been received into the service of the United States, since the commencement of the war with Mexico, for less than twelve months, and shall have served for such term, or until honorably discharged, shall be entitled to receive a warrant for forty acres of land, which may be subject to private entry, or twenty-five dollars in scrip, if preferred: and in the event of the death of such volunteer during his term of service, or after an honorable discharge, but before the passage of this act, then the warrant for such land or scrip shall issue to the wife, child or children, if there be any, and, if none, then to the father, and, if there be no father, then to the mother of such deceased volunteer: *Provided*, That nothing contained in this section shall be construed to give bounty land to such volunteers as were accepted into service, and discharged without being marched to the seat of war. [1]

A joint resolution of March 24, 1848,[2] establishes the following rule of evidence in cases arising under the act of February 11, 1847.

JOINT RESOLUTION *relative to the Evidence which shall be considered satisfactory in Applications for Bounty Lands.*

Be it Resolved by the Senate and House of Representatives of the United States of America in Congress assembled, That in all cases of application for bounty land warrants, under the act approved February eleventh, eighteen hundred and forty-seven, the honorable discharge of the applicant, showing the same was predicated on a surgeon's certificate of disability, shall be considered as satisfactory evidence to the Commissioner of Pensions that the disability was incurred in the course of service.

[1] This proviso is repealed by act of March 22, 1852. U. S. Statutes at Large, vol. x, iii.

[2] U. S. Statutes at Large, vol. ix, 334.

By a joint resolution of August 10, 1848,[1] the benefits of the act of February 11, 1848, were extended to the marine and ordnance corps, as follows:

JOINT RESOLUTION *concerning certain Portions of the Marine and Ordnance Corps.*

Resolved by the Senate and House of Representatives of the United States of America in Congress assembled, That the officers, non-commissioned officers, privates and musicians of the marine corps,[2] who have served with the army in the war with Mexico, and also the artificers and laborers of the ordnance corps serving in said war, be placed in all respects, as to bounty land and other remuneration, in addition to ordinary pay, on a footing with the officers, non-commissioned officers, privates and musicians of the army: *Provided,* That this remuneration shall be in lieu of prize money and all other extra allowances.

"A resolution relative to the payment of dividends or interest on war bounty scrip," approved August 10, 1850,[3] is as follows:

Resolved by the Senate and House of Representatives of the United States of America in Congress assembled, That the Secretary of the Treasury be, and he is, hereby directed, in redeeming and discharging the obligations of the Government for war bounty scrip, which are made assignable, to pay to the assignee and holder of such obligations, all dividends or interest which have been or shall be declared and set apart, and passed to the credit of the obligee upon the books of the Treasury, subsequent to the date of the assignment, unless such dividends or interest has been paid to the obligee before the transfer of the scrip upon the books in the office of the Register of the Treasury, or the presentation thereof for final payment.

The bounty of the Government was greatly enlarged by an act approved September 28, 1850, entitled "an act

1 U. S. Statutes at Large, vol. ix, 340.

2 Such portions of the marine corps as served in Mexico, whether on ship-board or land, are entitled to the benefits of the act of February 11, 1847. *Attorney-General Johnson, Sept.* 17, 1849.

3 U. S. Statutes at Large, vol. ix, 562.

granting bounty land to certain officers and soldiers who have been engaged in the military service of the United States."[1] This act is as follows:

Be it enacted by the Senate and House of Representatives of the United States of America in Congress assembled, That each of the surviving, or the widow,[2] or minor children[3] of deceased commissioned and non-commissioned officers, musicians or privates, whether of regulars,[4] volunteers, rangers or militia,[5] who performed military service in any regiment, company or detachment, in the service of the United States,[6] in the war with Great Britain, declared by the United States on the eighteenth day of June, eighteen hundred and twelve, or in any of the Indian wars since seventeen hundred and ninety,[7]

---

1 U. S. Statutes at Large, vol. ix, 520.

2 An act of August 5, 1854 (U. S. Statutes at Large, vol. x, 581), directs that this shall be construed to embrace widows who married again, in case they are again widows at the time of making the application. (See last note, this section of the act.)

3 The guardian for such children must be appointed in the county and State where they reside. *Secretary Graham, Oct.* 15, 1850.

The widow being married or dead, minor children are entitled. *Secretary Graham, Oct.* 26, 1850.

Minors must be such at the issuance of a warrant, to enable them to take under the act of September 28, 1850. *Comm'r Waldo, May* 30, 1853.

4 Regular soldiers are entitled to bounty land only for services in some recognized war. *Comm'r Waldo, Feb.* 28, 1854.

Such of the marine corps as served in any of the wars referred to in this act are entitled to land bounty. *Secretary Stuart, Oct.* 12, 1850. But midshipmen in the Mexican war are not entitled. *Comm'r Waldo, November* 2, 1853.

5 Teamsters, as such, are not entitled to bounty land under this act. *Comm'r Waldo, Septr.* 3, 1853. But are under act of 1855. See page 318.

6 The provisions of this act were extended to State troops called into the military service, and who were paid by the United States, subsequent to June 18, 1812, by the fourth section of "an act making land warrants assignable, and for other purposes," approved March 22, 1852. U. S. Statutes at Large, vol. x, page 3. See this act, page 325.

7 The "Creek disturbances" in 1836 was a war within the meaning of this act. *Secretary Stuart, Feb.* 26, 1851.

Land bounty is not granted by this act to volunteers engaged in remov-

and each of the commissioned officers[1] who were engaged in the military service of the United States in the late war with Mexico, shall be entitled to land as follows: Those who engaged to serve twelve months, or during the war, and actually served nine months,[2] shall receive one hundred and sixty acres, and those who engaged to serve six months, and actually served four months, shall receive eighty acres, and those who engaged to serve for any or an indefinite period,[3] and actually served one month, shall receive forty acres: *Provided*, That whenever any officer or soldier was honorably discharged in consequence of disability in the service, before the expiration of his period of service, he shall receive the amount to which he would have been entitled if he had served the full period for which he had engaged to serve: *Provided*, The person so having been in service shall not receive said land, or any part thereof, if it shall appear, by the muster rolls of his regiment or corps, that he deserted,[4] or was dishonorably discharged from the service, or if he has received, or is entitled to, any military land bounty under any act of Congress heretofore passed.[5]

ing the Indians from North Carolina, in 1838 or 1839. *Secretary Stuart, March*, 19, 1851.

Nor were the Winnebago disturbances in 1827, such war. *Comm'r Waldo, May* 23, 1853.

1 The mother of a commissioned officer is not entitled to bounty land under this act. *Comm'r Waldo, Nov.* 14, 1853.

Midshipmen in the Mexican war are not entitled under this act. *Comm'r Waldo, Nov.* 21, 1853.

2 Several terms of service may be united, and a warrant claimed for the aggregate time, but not more than one warrant will issue to the same person. *Secretary Stuart, Jan.* 22, 1851, *and Oct.* 12, 1850.

Calendar months govern in the computation of time. *Comm'r Waldo, Oct.* 26, 1853. (See also section 2 of this act and notes.)

By an act of March 22, 1852, it is provided that in computing the length of service, one day shall be allowed for every twenty miles traveled from the place of enlisting or volunteering to the place of mustering in. See this act, page 325. Mileage is to be ascertained by the table of distance published by the Post-Office Department. *Comm'r Waldo, Sept.* 18, 1854.

3 Minute men who served but twenty-two days, are not entitled to bounty land under this act. *Comm'r Waldo, June* 10, 1853.

4 Desertion appearing upon the rolls can not be contradicted by parol evidence. *Comm'r Waldo.*

5 Widows of deceased soldiers in the war of 1812, who in their lifetime

SEC. 2. *And be it further enacted*, That the period during which any officer or soldier may have remained in captivity [1] with the enemy shall be estimated and added to the period of his actual service, and the person so detained in captivity shall receive land under the provisions of this act in the same manner that he would be entitled in case he entered the service for the whole term, made up by the addition of the time of his captivity, and had served during such time.

SEC. 3. *And be it further enacted*, That each commissioned and non-commissioned officer, musician or private, for whom provision is made by the first section hereof, shall receive a certificate or warrant from the Department of the Interior for the quantity of land to which he may be entitled, and which may be located by the warrantee or his heirs-at-law, at any Land Office of the United States, in one body and in conformity to the legal subdivisions of the public lands, upon any of the public lands in such district subject to private entry;[2] and upon return of such certificate or warrant, with evidence of the location thereof having been legally made to the General Land Office, a patent shall be issued therefor. In the event of the death of any commissioned or non-commissioned officer, musician or private, prior or subsequent to the passage of this act, who shall have served as aforesaid, and who shall not have received bounty land for such services, a like certificate or warrant shall be issued in favor, and inure to the benefit of his widow, who shall re-

---

received bounty land for their services in that war, can not claim under this act. *Comm'r Waldo, Oct.* 15, 1853.

[1] A soldier on parole is still in "captivity." *Secretary Graham, Oct.* 15, 1850.

Prisoners of war on parole are not entitled to bounty land. *Comm'r Waldo, March* 16, 1853.

Captivity entitles the soldier to bounty land, only for the time he remains a prisoner with the enemy. *Comm'r Waldo, April* 16, 1853. (These decisions are contradictory.)

[2] An act of March 3, 1851 (U. S. Stat. at Large, vol. ix, 598), provides that no land bounty under any act passed prior to that time "shall be satisfied out of any public lands not heretofore brought into market, and now subject to entry at private sale under existing laws." And it was held under this act that warrants could not be located upon lands in Oregon, because no lands in that territory (now State) were subject to entry at the passage of the act. *Secretary Crittenden, May* 2, 1851.

ceive one hundred and sixty acres of land in case her husband was killed in battle, but not to her heirs: *Provided*, She is unmarried at the date of her application:[1] *Provided further*, That no land warrant issued under the provisions of this act shall be laid upon any land of the United States to which there shall be a pre-emption right, or upon which there shall be an actual settlement and cultivation; except with the consent of such settler, to be satisfactorily proven to the proper land officer.

SEC. 4. *And be it further enacted*, That all sales, mortgages, letters of attorney, or other instruments of writing, going to affect the title or claim to any warrant or certificate issued, or to be issued, or to any land granted or to be granted, under the provisions of this act, made or executed prior to the issue, shall be null and void to all intents and purposes whatsoever; nor shall such certificate or warrant, or the land obtained thereby, be in any wise affected by, or charged with, or subject to, the payment of any debt or claim incurred by such officer or soldier, prior to the issuing of the patent: *Provided*, That the benefits of this act shall not accrue to any person who is a member of the present Congress:[2] *Provided further*, That it shall be the duty of the Commissioner of the General Land Office, under such regulations as may be prescribed by the Secretary of the Interior, to cause to be located, free of expense, any warrant which the holder may transmit to the General Land Office for that purpose, in such State and land district as the said holder or warrantee may designate, and upon good farming land, so far as the same can be ascertained from the maps, plats and field notes of the surveyor, or from any other information in the possession of the local office, and, upon the location being made as aforesaid, the Secretary shall cause a patent to be transmitted to such warrantee; *And provided further*, That no patent issued under this act shall be delivered upon any power of attorney or agreement dated before the passage of this act, and that all such powers of attorney or agreements be considered and treated as null and void.

---

1 The second marriage of the widow deprives her of the benefit of this act, unless she was a widow at the time of the passage of the law, and of her application for the land bounty. *Secretary Graham, Oct. 26, 1850.* This modified—see third note to the first section of this act.

2 This proviso was repealed by act of August 5, 1854. (U. S. Statutes at Large, vol. x, 589.)

By an act of March 3, 1855, entitled "an act in addition to certain acts granting bounty land to certain officers and soldiers who have been engaged in the military service of the United States,"[1] Congress seems to have endeavored to exhaust its power to grant bounty lands; as will be apparent from the act:

Be it enacted by the Senate and House of Representatives of the United States of America in Congress assembled, That each of the surviving commissioned and non-commissioned officers, musicians and privates, whether of regulars, volunteers, rangers or militia, who were regularly mustered into the service of the United States, and every officer, commissioned or non-commissioned, seaman, ordinary seaman, marine, clerk, and landsman in the navy, in any of the wars in which this country has been engaged since seventeen hundred and ninety, [2] and each of the survivors of the militia or volun-

---

1 U. S. Statutes at Large, vol. x, 701.

[See notes to act of September 28, 1850, for many decisions which will apply to this act.]

[See also the official construction given this act, under regulations for executing the same, page 330.]

2 This act is greatly extended by act of May 14, 1856, which immediately follows it.

Pursers, officers, etc., in the navy of the revolution, and sea-fencibles, are beneficiaries under it. Officers, etc., of private armed vessels, chaplains in the navy, and persons in the revenue cutter service are not beneficiaries, except when placed on the naval establishment, under the act of February 25, 1799. *Commissioner Waldo to Dr. Mayo, May* 19, 1855.

This act (in connection with the act of May 14, 1856), has been held to apply to the following wars:

Wayne's War, 1790 to 1794.
French War of 1799.
War of 1812. June 18, 1812, to February 17, 1815.
Seminole War, 1817 to 1818.
Black Hawk War of 1832.
Creek War of 1836-1837.
Florida War, 1835 to 1842.
Disturbances, Canada Frontier, 1838–1839.
Pennsylvania Whisky Insurrection.
Cherokee Removal of 1838.
Mexican War, 1846 to May 30, 1848.

teers, or State troops of any State or Territory, called into military service, and regularly mustered therein, and whose services have been paid by the United States, shall be entitled to receive a certificate or warrant from the Department of the Interior for one hundred and sixty acres of land; and where any of those who have been so mustered into service and paid shall have received a certificate or warrant, he shall be entitled to a certificate or warrant for such quantity of land as will make, in the whole, with what he may have heretofore received, one hundred and sixty acres to each such person having served as aforesaid: *Provided*, The person so having been in service shall not receive said land warrant if it shall appear by the muster rolls of his regiment or corps that he deserted, or was dishonorably discharged from service: *Provided further*, That the benefits of this section shall be held to extend to wagon-masters and teamsters who may have been employed, under the direction of competent authority, in time of war, in the transportation of military stores and supplies.

SEC. 2. *And be it further enacted*, That in case of the death of any person who, if living, would be entitled to a certificate or warrant, as aforesaid, under this act, leaving a widow, or, if no widow, a minor child or children, such widow, or, if no widow, such minor child or children, shall be entitled to receive a certificate or warrant for the same quantity of land that such deceased person would be entitled to receive under the provisions of this act, if now living: *Provided*, That a subsequent marriage shall not impair the right of any such

---

Texas Ranging Service, 1846 to 1855.
Apache War, since the Mexican War.
S. W. Arkansas Frontier Disturbances, 1836.
California War, 1850-1851.
Cayuse Digger Indian War, 1853.
Rogue River War, 1853.
Navajo and Apache War.
Revolutionary War.
Invasion of Plattsburg, September, 1814.
Battle of King's Mountain.
Battle of Nickojack.
Attack on Lewistown, war of 1812.
Patriot War.
Aristook War.

widow to such warrant, if she be a widow at the time of making her application: *And provided further*, That those shall be considered minors who are so at the time this act shall take effect.

SEC. 3. *And be it further enacted*, That in no case shall any such certificate or warrant be issued for any service less than fourteen days, except where the person shall actually have been engaged in battle, and unless the party claiming such certificate or warrant shall establish his or her right thereto by recorded evidence of said service.[1]

SEC. 4. *And be it further enacted*, That said certificates or warrants may be assigned, transferred and located by the warrantees, their assignees, or their heirs-at-law, according to the provisions of existing laws regulating the assignment, transfer and location of bounty land warrants.

SEC. 5. *And be it further enacted*, That no warrant issued under the provisions of this act shall be located on any public lands, except such as shall at the time be subject to sale at either the minimum or lower graduated prices.

SEC. 6. *And be it further enacted*, That the registers and receivers of the several land offices shall be severally authorized to charge and receive for their services in locating all warrants under the provisions of this act the same compensation or per centage to which they are entitled by law for sales of the public lands for cash, at the rate of one dollar and twenty-five cents per acre; the said compensation to be paid by the assignees or holders of such warrants.

SEC. 7. *And be it further enacted*, That the provisions of this act, and all the bounty land laws heretofore passed by Congress, shall be extended to Indians, in the same manner and to the same extent as if the said Indians had been white men.

SEC. 8. *And be it further enacted*, That the officers and soldiers of the revolutionary war, or their widows or minor children, shall be entitled to the benefits of this act.

SEC. 9. *And be it further enacted*, That the benefits of this act shall be applied to and embrace those who served as volunteers at the invasion of Plattsburgh, in September, eighteen hundred and fourteen; also at the battle of King's Mountain, in the revolution-

---

[1] The clause relating to record evidence is repealed. See act of May 14, 1856, page 322, sec. 3.

ary war, and the battle of Nickojack against the confederated savages of the south.

SEC. 10. *And be it further enacted*, That the provisions of this act shall apply to the chaplains who served with the army in the several wars of the country.

SEC. 11. *And be it further enacted*, That the provisions of this act be applied to flotilla-men, and to those who served as volunteers at the attack on Lewistown, in Delaware, by the British fleet, in the war of eighteen hundred and twelve–fifteen.

An act amendatory of the foregoing, approved May 14, 1856, is as follows:

AN ACT *to amend the act in addition to certain acts granting Bounty Land to certain Officers and Soldiers who have been engaged in the Military Service of the United States, approved March third, eighteen hundred and fifty-five.*

Be it enacted by the Senate and House of Representatives of the United States of America in Congress assembled, That in all cases where a certificate or warrant for bounty land for any less quantity than one hundred and sixty acres shall have been issued to any officer or soldier, or to the widow or minor child or children of any officer or soldier, under existing laws, the evidence upon which such certificate or warrant was issued shall be received to establish the service of such officer or soldier, in the application of himself, or of his widow or minor child or children, for a certificate or warrant for so much land as may be required to make up the full sum of one hundred and sixty acres, on proof of the identity of such officer or soldier, or, in case of his death, of the marriage and identity of his widow, or, in case of her death, of the identity of his minor child or children: *Provided nevertheless*, That if, upon a review of such evidence, the Commissioner of Pensions shall not be satisfied that the former certificate or warrant was properly granted, he may require additional evidence as well of the term as of the fact of service.

SEC. 2. *And be it further enacted*, That in all cases where a pension has been granted to any officer or soldier, the evidence upon which such pension was granted shall be received to establish the service of such officer or soldier in his application for bounty land under existing laws; and upon proof of his identity as such pensioner, a certificate or warrant may be issued to him for the quantity of land to which he shall be entitled· and in case of the death of such pensioned officer or soldier, his widow shall be entitled to a certificate or warrant for the same quantity of land to which her husband would have been entitled, if living, upon proof that she is such widow; and in case of the death of such officer or soldier, leaving a minor child or children and no widow, or where the widow may have deceased before the issuing of any certificate or warrant, such minor child or children shall be entitled to a certificate or warrant for the same quantity of land as the father would have been entitled to receive, if living, upon proof of the decease of father and mother: *Provided nevertheless*, That if, upon a review of such evidence, the Commissioner of Pensions shall not be satisfied that the pension was properly granted, he may require additional evidence as well of the term as of the fact of service.

SEC. 3. *And be it further enacted*, That so much of the third section of the "act in addition to certain acts granting bounty land to certain officers and soldiers who have been engaged in the military service of the United States," approved March third, eighteen hundred and fifty-five, as requires the party claiming a certificate of warrant under the provisions of said act, to establish his or her right thereto by record evidence of the service for which such certificate or warrant has been or may be claimed, be, and the same is hereby, repealed, and parol evidence, where no record evidence exists, may be admitted to prove the service performed, under such rules and regulations as the Commissioner of Pensions may prescribe.

SEC. 4. *And be it further enacted*, That the eighth section of the act above-mentioned, approved the third day of March, in the year eighteen hundred and fifty-five, shall be construed as embracing officers, marines, seamen, and other persons engaged in the naval service of the United States during the revolutionary war, and the widows and minor children of all such officers, marines, seamen and other persons engaged as aforesaid.

SEC. 5. *And be it further enacted*, That the provisions of the said act shall extend to all persons who have served as volunteers with the armed forces of the United States, subject to military orders, for the space of fourteen days, in any of the wars specified in the first section of the said act, whether such persons were or were not mustered into the service of the United States.

SEC. 6. *And be it further enacted*, That the widows and minor children of all such persons as are specified in the last preceding section of this act, and are now dead, shall be entitled to the same privileges, as the widows and minor children of the beneficiaries named in the act to which this is an amendment.

SEC. 7. *And be it further enacted*, That when any company, battalion or regiment, in an organized form, marched more than twenty miles to the place where they were mustered into the service of the United States, or were discharged more than twenty miles from the place where such company, battalion or regiment was organized; in all such cases, in computing the length of service of the officers and soldiers of any such company, battalion or regiment, there shall be allowed one day for every twenty miles from the place where the company, battalion or regiment was organized to the place where the same was mustered into the service of the United States; and also, one day for every twenty miles from the place where such company, battalion or regiment was discharged to the place where it was organized, and from whence it marched to enter the service: *Provided*, That such march was in obedience to the command or direction of the President of the United States, or some general officer of the United States commanding an army or department, or the chief executive officer of the State or Territory by which such company, battalion or regiment was called into service.

"An act to extend the provisions of the act entitled 'an act in addition to certain acts granting bounty land to certain officers and soldiers who have been engaged in the military services (*sic.*) of the United States' to the officers and soldiers of Major David Bailey's battalion of Cook county (Illinois) volunteers," approved March 3, 1857, provides as follows:

Be it enacted by the Senate and House of Representatives of the United States of America in Congress assembled, That all those officers and soldiers of Major David Bailey's battalion of Cook county (Illinois) volunteers stationed at Fort Dearborn, in the Black Hawk war of eighteen hundred and thirty-two, who have never received warrants for bounty land for services in said war, shall be entitled to receive a certificate or warrant from the Department of the Interior for one hundred and sixty acres of land, upon making proof by record evidence or such parol evidence as the Commissioner of Pensions may require of having served in said war for the term of at least fourteen days; the provisions of this act to extend to the widows and minor children of said officers and soldiers who have died or may die before receiving such warrant or certificate.

By "an act to secure homesteads to actual settlers on the public domain," approved May 20, 1862, the following provisions are made in favor of those who have performed or may perform service in the army or navy of the United States:

Be it enacted by the Senate and House of Representatives of the United States of America in Congress assembled, That any person who is the head of a family, or who has arrived at the age of twenty-one years, and is a citizen of the United States, or who shall have filed his declaration of intention to become such, as required by the naturalization laws of the United States, and who has never borne arms against the United States Government, or given aid and comfort to its enemies, shall from and after the first January, eighteen hundred and sixty-three, be entitled to enter one quarter section or a less quantity of unappropriated public lands, upon which said person may have filed a pre-emption claim, or which may, at the time the application is made, be subject to pre emption at one dollar and twenty-five cents, or less, per acre; or eighty acres or less of such unappropriated lands at two dollars and fifty cents per acre, to be located in a body, in conformity to the legal subdivisions of the public lands, and after the same shall have been surveyed: *Provided,* That any person owning and residing on land may, under the provisions of this act, enter other land lying contiguous to his or her said land, which shall not, with the land so already owned and occupied, exceed in the aggregate one hundred and sixty acres.

SEC. 2. *And be it further enacted,* That the person applying for the benefit of this act shall, upon application to the register of the land office in which he or she is about to make such entry, make affidavit before the said register or receiver that he or she is the head of a family, or is twenty-one or more years of age, or shall have performed service in the army or navy of the United States, and that he has never borne arms against the Government of the United States or given aid and comfort to its enemies, and that such application is made for his or her exclusive use and benefit, and that said entry is made for the purpose of actual settlement and cultivation, and not either directly or indirectly for the use or benefit of any other person or persons whomsoever; and upon filing the said affidavit with the register or receiver, and on payment of ten dollars, he or she shall thereupon be permitted to enter the quantity of land specified. . . .

SEC. 6. *And be it further enacted*, That . . . *Provided*, . . . *provided, further*, That no person who has served, or may hereafter serve, for a period of not less than fourteen days in the army or navy of the United States, either regular or volunteer, under the -laws thereof, during the existence of an actual war, domestic or foreign, shall be deprived of the benefits of this act on account of not having attained the age of twenty-one years.

LAWS RELATING EXCLUSIVELY TO LAND WARRANTS.[1]

AN ACT *in relation to Military Land Warrants*.[2]

Be it enacted by the Senate and House of Representatives of the United States of America in Congress assembled, That any non-commissioned officer, musician or private, or his widow or heirs, who shall receive and hold in his own right a land warrant, issued by the Government of the United States for military service, may locate the same in on [one] legal subdivision, on any public land subject to private entry, taking said land at the price at which the same is subject to private entry, and reckoning the warrant at one dollar and twenty-five cents per acre for the number of acres therein contained, and paying the balance, if any, in money; but no claim shall exist on the Government to pay for any balance on said warrant in money.

Approved, August 14, 1848.

AN ACT *to make Land Warrants assignable and for other purposes*.

Be it enacted by the Senate and House of Representatives of the United States of America in Congress assembled, That all warrants for military bounty land which have been or may hereafter be issued under any law of the United States, and all valid locations of the same which have been or may hereafter be made, are hereby de-

1 See pages 309–24, for several acts pertaining to the issue of land warrants.

2 U. S. Statutes at Large, vol. ix, 332.

clared to be assignable, by deed or instrument of writing made and executed after the taking effect of this act, according to such form and pursuant to such regulations as may be presented by the Commissioner of the General Land Office, so as to vest the assignee with all the rights of the original owner of the warrant or location: *Provided*, That any person entitled to pre-emption right to any land shall be entitled to use any such land warrant in payment of the same, at the rate of one dollar and twenty-five cents per acre, for the quantity of land therein specified: *Provided*, That the warrants which have been or may hereafter be issued, in pursuance of said laws or of this act, may be located according to the legal subdivisions of the public lands, in one body, upon any land of the United States subject to private entry at the time of such location at the minimum price: *Provided, further*, That when such warrant shall be located on lands which are subject to entry at a greater minimum than one dollar and twenty-five cents per acre, the locator of such warrants shall pay to the United States, in cash, the difference between the value of such warrants, at one dollar and twenty-five cents per acre, and the tract of land located on.

SEC. 2. *And be it further enacted*, That the registers and receivers of the land offices shall hereafter be severally authorized to charge and receive for their services in locating all military bounty land warrants issued since the eleventh day of February, eighteen hundred and forty-seven, the same compensation or per centage to which they are entitled by law for sales of the public lands for cash, at the rate of one dollar and twenty-five cents per acre; the said compensation to be hereafter paid by the assignees or holders of such warrants.

SEC. 3. *And be it further enacted*, That registers and receivers, whether in or out of office at the passage of this act, or their legal representatives in case of death, shall be entitled to receive from the Treasury of the United States, for services heretofore performed in locating military bounty land warrants, the same rate of compensation provided in the preceding section for services hereafter to be performed, after deducting the amount already received by such officers under the act entitled "an act to require the holders of military land warrants to compensate the land officers of the United States for services in relation to the location of these warrants," approved May seventeen, eighteen hundred and forty-eight: *Provided*,

That no register or receiver shall receive any compensation out of the treasury for past services who has charged and received illegal fees for the location of such warrants: *And provided further*, That no register or receiver shall receive for his services, during any year, a greater compensation than the maximum now allowed by law.

SEC. 4. *And be it further enacted*, That in all cases where the militia, or volunteers, or State troops, of any State or territory were called into military service, and whose services have been paid by the United States subsequent to the eighteenth of June, eighteen hundred and twelve, the officers and soldiers of such militia, volunteers or troops, shall be entitled to all the benefits of the act entitled "an act granting bounty land to certain officers and soldiers who have been engaged in the military service of the United States," approved September twenty-eight, eighteen hundred and fifty, and shall receive lands for their services according to the provisions of said act, upon proof of length of service as therein required; and that the last proviso of the ninth section of the act of the eleventh of February, eighteen hundred and forty-seven (see 9th section, 1847), be and the same is hereby repealed: *Provided*, That nothing herein contained shall authorize bounty land to those who have heretofore received or become entitled to the same.

SEC. 5. *And be it further enacted*, That where any company, battalion or regiment, in an organized form, marched more than twenty miles to the place where they were mustered into the service of the United States, or were discharged more than twenty miles from the place where such company, battalion or regiment was organized; in all such cases, in computing the length of service of the officers and soldiers of any such company, battalion or regiment, with a view to determine any quantity of land any officer or soldier is entitled to under said act, approved twenty-eighth of September, eighteen hundred and fifty, there shall be allowed one day for every twenty miles from the place where the company, battalion or regiment was organized to the place where the same was mustered into the service of the United States; and also one day for every twenty miles from the place where such company, battalion or regiment was discharged to the place where it was organized, and from whence it marched to enter the service.

[*Approved, March* 22, 1852.]

AN ACT *declaring the Title to Land Warrants in certain cases*

Be it enacted by the Senate and House of Representatives of the United of America in Congress assembled, That when proof has been or shall hereafter be filed in the Pension Office, during the lifetime of a claimant, establishing, to the satisfaction of that office, his or her right to a warrant for military services, and such warrant has not been or may not hereafter be issued until after the death of the claimant, and all such warrants as have been heretofore issued subsequent to the death of the claimant, the title to such warrants shall vest in the widow, if there be one, and if there be no widow, then in the heirs or legatees of the claimant; and all such warrants, and all other warrants issued pursuant to existing laws, shall be treated as personal chattels, and may be conveyed by assignment of such widow, heirs or legatees, or by the legal representatives of the deceased claimant, for the use of such heirs or legatees only.

SEC. 2. *And be it further enacted*, That the provisions of the first section of the act approved March twenty-two, eighteen hun dred and fifty-two, to make land warrants assignable, and for other purposes, shall be so extended as to embrace land warrants issued under the act of the third March, eighteen hundred and fifty-five.

[*Approved, June* 3, 1858.]

AN ACT *to authorize the re-issue of Land Warrants, in certain cases, and for other purposes.*

Be it enacted by the Senate and House of Representatives of the United States of America in Congress assembled, That whenever it shall appear that any certificate or warrant issued in pursuance of any law of the United States granting bounty land, has been lost or destroyed, whether the same had been sold or assigned by the warrantee or not, the Secretary of the Interior shall be, and is hereby authorized and required to cause a new certificate or warrant, of like tenor, to be issued in lieu thereof, which new certificate or warrant may be assigned, located and patented in like manner as other certificates or warrants for bounty land are now authorized by law, to be assigned, located and patented; and in all cases where warrants have been or may be re-issued, the original warrant, in whoseever hands it may be, shall be deemed and held to be null and void, and the assignment thereof, if any there be, fraudulent·

and no patent shall ever issue for any land located therewith, unless such presumption of fraud in the assignment be removed by due proof, that the same was executed by the warrantee in good faith and for a valuable consideration.

SEC. 2. *And be it further enacted*, That the Secretary of the Interior shall be, and is hereby authorized and required to prescribe such rules and regulations for carrying this act into effect as he may deem necessary and proper in order to protect the Government against imposition and fraud by persons claiming the benefits of this act, and all laws and parts of laws for the punishment of false swearing and frauds against the United States, are hereby made applicable to false swearing and fraud under this act.[1]

[*Approved*, *June* 23, 1860.]

SECTION II.

FORMS AND INSTRUCTIONS FOR OBTAINING BOUNTY LAND WARRANTS, DUPLICATE WARRANTS AND WAR SCRIP; AND ALSO FOR THE LOCATION AND ASSIGNMENT OF WARRANTS.

As the liberal provisions and unlimited application of the acts of March 3, 1855, and May 14, 1856, have, in effect, superseded all former laws granting bounty lands for military services, it would be but superfluous to insert

1 A practice has grown up of executing and acknowledging the assignment in writing by the warrantee in blank; leaving a blank for the name of the assignee. When the instrument by which the assignment purports to have been made, comes up for examination in the General Land Office, the question, Who is the assignee? is decided by inspection; parol evidence to contradict the record is rejected, and claimants of title who seek to show ownership of the warrant while the blank in the assignment remained open, are properly referred to the courts for a determination of the question of right. The General Land Office, when it finds by inspection, that a warrant was regularly assigned in writing for value to "A. B.," who has made the location, can not set aside that record, and declare that "C. D." is the true owner and holds the title. The only persons, therefore, who are "assignees" within the terms of the laws and the regulations of the General Land Office on that subject, are those whose names are found in the instrument of writing by which the last assignment was made. *Secretary Thompson, Sept.* 12, 1860.

here the regulations and forms prescribed for obtaining the benefits of such former acts.

In applying for war scrip, under the act of February 11, 1847, a declaration must be made as in applications for bounty land. To this must be appended a "request for money," according to the following form:

[*Residence and Date.*]

TO THE COMMISSIONER OF PENSIONS:

Sir:—I request that my claim to bounty land, under the ninth section of the act of the eleventh of February, 1847, entitled "an act to raise for a limited time an additional military force, and for other purposes," may be examined; and if I am entitled to land, I wish to relinquish, and do hereby relinquish, my right thereto, and in lieu thereof, to receive one hundred dollars [*or* twenty-five dollars, *as the case may be*].

(*Signature of Claimant.*)

In presence of —— Justice of the Peace.

The same proof in support of a claim for scrip is required from the party applying as in the case of applications for bounty land.

The following Instructions and Forms will be observed by persons applying to the Pension Office for bounty land under the act of March 3, 1855, and the act of May 14, 1856, in amendment thereof:

These acts entitle each of the surviving persons in the following classes to a certificate or warrant for such quantity of land as shall make, in the whole, with what he may have heretofore received, one hundred and sixty acres, provided he shall have served a period not less than fourteen days, to-wit:

1. Commissioned and non-commissioned officers, musicians and privates, whether of the regulars, volunteers, rangers or militia, who were regularly mustered into the service of the United States in any of the wars in which this country has been engaged since 1790.

2. Commissioned and non-commissioned officers, seamen, ordinary seamen, flotilla men, marines, clerks and landsmen in the navy in any of said wars.

3. Militia, volunteers and State troops of any State or Territory called into military service, and regularly mustered therein, and whose services have been paid by the United States.

4. Wagonmasters and teamsters who have been employed, under the direction of competent authority, in time of war, in the transportation of military stores and supplies.

5. Officers and soldiers of the revolutionary war, and marines, seamen and other persons in the naval service of the United States during that war.

6. Chaplains who served with the army in the several wars of this country.

7. Volunteers who served with the armed forces of the United States in any of the wars mentioned, subject to military orders, whether regularly mustered into the service of the United States or not.

Each of the surviving persons in the following classes are entitled to a like certificate for a like quantity of land, without regard to the length of service, provided he was regularly mustered into service, and shall establish the same by record evidence, to-wit:

1. Officers and soldiers who have been actually engaged in any battle in any of the wars in which this country has been engaged.

2. Those volunteers who served at the invasion of Plattsburg, in September, 1814.

3. The volunteers who served at the battle of King's Mountain in the revolutionary war.

4. The volunteers who served at the battle of Nickojack against the confederated savages of the South.

5. The volunteers who served at the attack on Lewistown, in Delaware, by the British fleet, in the war of 1812.

In addition to these classes, this act also extends to all Indians who have served the United States in any of their wars the provisions of this and all the bounty land laws heretofore passed, in the same manner, and to the same extent, as if said Indians had been white men.

Where the service has been rendered by a substitute, he is the person entitled to the benefit of this act, and not his employer.

In the event of the death of any person who, if living, would be entitled to a certificate or warrant as aforesaid, leaving a widow, or if no widow, a minor child or children, such widow, or if no widow, such minor child or children, is entitled to a certificate or warrant for the same quantity of land such deceased persons would be entitled to receive under the provisions of said acts if now living.

A subsequent marriage will not impair the right of any such widow to such warrants, if she be a widow at the time of her application. Persons within the age of twenty-one years on the 3d day of March, 1855, are deemed minors within the intent and meaning of said act.

To obtain the benefits of this act, the claimant must make a declaration, under oath, substantially according to the forms hereto annexed. The signature of the applicant must be attested, and his or her personal identity established by the affidavits of two witnesses, whose residences must be given, and whose credibility must be sustained by the certificate of the magistrate before whom the application is verified.

The best evidence of identity is the affidavit of the witnesses, or the certificate of the magistrate to the same, as a matter within their personal knowledge. Statements of *belief* merely will not be sufficient. If, however, the witnesses or magistrate can not state from personal knowledge, statements of belief, *with the grounds of such belief*, will be received. If from acquaintance, the particulars of the acquaintance should be stated, so that it may be seen how far they warrant the belief stated. So if from other grounds.

The accompanying form is the proper one where the identity of the applicant is within the personal knowledge of the magistrate. It can be varied according to the circumstances, but must be in conformity with the foregoing instructions.

No certificate will be deemed sufficient in any case, unless the facts are certified to be within the personal knowledge of the magistrate or other officer who shall sign the certificate, or the names and places of residence of the witnesses by whom the facts are established be given, or their affidavits, properly authenticated, be appended to the certificate.

All papers necessary to be verified by oath must be sworn to before, and certified and authenticated by, proper public officers who have no interest in the result of the case, and are not concerned in its prosecution; and every such public officer must set forth in his certificate that he is not so interested or concerned.

The official character and signature of the magistrate who may administer the oath must be certified by the clerk of the proper court of record of his county, under the seal of the court. Whenever the certificate of the officer who authenticates the signature of the magistrate is not written on the same sheet of paper which contains the signature to be authenticated, the certificate must be attached to said paper by a piece of tape or ribbon, the ends of which must pass under the official seal, so as to prevent any paper from being improperly attached to the certificate.

When the commission of a notary public, or a certified copy of his appointment, with his official seal and signature attached, and the certificate of the clerk of a court of the genuineness of his signature, is filed in this office, his own certificate, under his official seal, will be recognized thereafter during his term of office; but, in the absence of said commission or certified copy of his appointment, an affidavit taken before such officer will not be received in any case, unless it be accompanied by a certificate of the proper officer, showing his authority and the genuineness of his signature.

To all official certificates by a notary public of whose appointment general proof has been filed as above suggested, should be added a brief reference to such proof on file, so as to insure against its being overlooked.

Applications by widows must be supported by satisfactory proof of the marriage of the claimant to the soldier on account of whose services her claim is made; of his death; and that the claimant at the time of making her application was a widow—i. e., *unmarried.*

If the marriage was in any State or country where any public records of marriages are kept, it should be proved by a duly certified copy of the record; or, if there is no such record, by the testimony of credible witnesses who were present at the marriage; and where such testimony exists, and is not produced, satisfactory reasons must be stated, under oath, why it is not produced. If it is shown by affidavit *that no record evidence or testimony of eye-witnesses can be procured,* the claimant may then produce the best other evidence in her power; such as the testimony of witnesses who were acquainted with her and her husband during his lifetime; knew them to live together as man and wife, and that they were reputed so to be; and that the fact of their having been married was never called in question by their acquaintances.

In no case will the mere statement of the witnesses that the claimant *is the widow* of the deceased, be taken as evidence of the marriage; but the witnesses must state the facts and circumstances from which they derive their knowledge or opinion that she is the widow of the deceased.

Witnesses to prove the death of the soldier must state their means of knowledge concerning it, and, as nearly as they can, the time and place of its occurrence.

The evidence to prove the existing widowhood of the claimant must be direct, and the statement of witnesses that the claimant is the party she represents herself to be, will not be received as satisfactory proof of widowhood.

Applications in behalf of minors should be made in their names by their guardian or next friend. Where there are several minors entitled to the same gratuity, one may make the declaration. The warrant will be issued to all jointly. In addition to proof of service, as in other cases, applications by minors must be supported by satisfactory proof of their being the lawful children of the soldiers, on account of whose services their claim is made; of his death; of there being no widow surviving at the time of making their application; of their ages; and that they are the only surviving children of the deceased soldier, who were under the age of twenty-one years on the third day of March, 1855.

General reputation, among those acquainted with the family, without any question of being the lawful children of the deceased soldier, will be received as evidence of their being such.

The suggestions before made in relation to proof of the death of the soldier, in cases of application by widows, apply also to applications by minor children.

If there is any public record of the births of the children, a certificate of the same, properly authenticated, must be furnished. If there be none such, but a private or family record, it must be forwarded to this office for inspection, with proof of its authenticity. It will be duly returned to the parties, if desired. But if no public or private record of the births exist or can be produced, that fact must be shown by proper affidavit, and then other evidence will be received. Witnesses to prove the ages must state particularly their means of knowledge concerning them, and how they now fix the same. To avoid mistake, the names and ages of *all* the surviving children of the deceased soldier should be shown by proper proof, so that this office may determine who of them are entitled to the land.

If a party die before the issue of a warrant to which he would be entitled, if living, the right to said warrant dies with him. In such case, the warrant is void, and should be returned to this office to be canceled, and the party next entitled in right of the service claimed should make an application; and if there be no such party, the grant lapses under the limitation of the beneficiaries to the bounty. If the claimant die after the issue of the warrant, the title thereto vests in his heirs-at-law in the same manner as real estate in the place of the domicile of the deceased, and can only be assigned or located by said heirs.

Applications made by Indians must be authenticated according to the regulations to be prescribed by the Commissioner of Indian Affairs.

If record evidence of the service on account of which a claim is made exists, it must be produced. But if there be none, parol evidence will be received instead. In such cases the positive testimony of at least two witnesses who were in the same service, or in a situation to know the facts about which they testify, will be required to establish the service alleged. And the witnesses in their affidavits must state particularly the facts and circumstances of the service claimed, and their means of knowledge concerning the same.

In no case will parol evidence be admitted to vary or discredit the length of any service shown by the rolls.

When claim is made for any allowance on account of mileage not shown by the rolls, a declaration must be made, stating the place where the company or corps in which service is alleged was organized; where it was mustered into the service of the United States; the distance between those two places, and by whose order the march was made. Also, the place where it was discharged from service, and the distance from thence to the place where it was organized. This statement must be supported by testimony of witnesses or other proper proof.

In all claims under these acts, reference may be made to any evidence on file in this office, but in all such references, care must be taken to give a particular description of the case in which such evidence is offered:

All additional evidence should be distinctly noted as such, with a particular description of the claim to which it relates.

J. MINOT, *Commissioner.*

NOTE.—In all references to claims for bounty land under these or previous acts, and in all inquiries relative to the same, parties will be careful to state the name of the applicant; the number of the application, and the act under which it was made.

(1)

Form of a Declaration to be made by a Person who has never before had a Land Warrant, or made a Declaration therefor.

STATE OF —— } ss.
County of —— }

On this —— day of ——, A. D. one thousand eight hundred and ——, personally appeared before me, a justice of the peace [*or other officer authorized to administer oaths for general purposes*], within and for the county and State aforesaid, ——, aged —— years, a resident of ——, in the State of ——, who, being duly sworn according to law, declares that he is the identical ——, who was a —— in the company[1] commanded by Captain ——, in the —— regiment of ——, commanded by ——, in the war with Great Britain, declared by the United States, on the 18th day of June, 1812 [*or other war embraced in said act, describing what war*]; that he enlisted [*or volunteered, or was drafted*], at ——, on or about the —— day of ——, A. D. ——, for the term of ——, and continued in actual service in said war for the term of fourteen days, and was honorably discharged at ——, on the —— day of ——, A. D. ——.[2]

He makes this declaration for the purpose of obtaining the bounty land to which he may be entitled under the act approved March 3, 1855. He also declares that he has not received a warrant for bounty land under this or any other act of Congress, nor made any other application therefor.

(*Claimant's Signature.*)

We, —— and ——, residents of ——, in the State of ——, upon our oaths, declare that the foregoing declaration was signed and acknowledged by ——, in our presence, and that we believe, from the appearance and statements of the applicant, that he is the identical person he represents himself to be. (*Signatures of Witnesses.*)

The foregoing declaration and affidavit were sworn to and subscribed before me on the day and year above-written; and I certify that I know the affiants to be credible persons; that the claimant is the person he represents himself to be, and that I have no interest in this claim.

(*J. P.*)

---

[1] If the claimant was a regimental or staff officer, the declaration must be varied according to the facts of the case.

[2] If the claimant was discharged in consequence of disability incurred by the service, or if he was in captivity with the enemy, he must vary his declaration so as to set forth the facts of the case.

Here must follow the certificate of the Clerk, under the seal of the proper Court, of the official character of the magistrate administering the oaths.

(2)

Form of a Declaration to be made where the party has had a Warrant, and desires another.

STATE OF —— }
County of —— } *ss.*

On this —— day of ——, A. D. one thousand eight hundred and ——, personally appeared before me, a justice of the peace [*or other officer authorized to administer oaths for general purposes*], within and for the county and State aforesaid, ——, aged —— years, a resident of ——, in the State of ——, who, being by me duly sworn according to law, declares that he is the identical —— who was a —— in the company commanded by Captain ——, in the —— regiment of ——, commanded by ——, in the war with Great Britain, declared by the United States, on the 18th day of June, 1812 [*or other war, as the case may be*], for the term of ——, and continued in actual service in said war for fourteen days; that he has heretofore made application for bounty land, under the act of September 28, 1850 [*or other act, as the case may be*], and received a land warrant, No. ——, for —— acres, which he has since legally disposed of, and can not now return.

He makes this declaration for the purpose of obtaining the additional bounty land to which he may be entitled under the act approved the 3d day of March, 1855. He also declares, that he has never applied for nor received, under this act or any other act of Congress, any bounty land warrant, except the one above-mentioned. (*Signature of the Claimant.*)

We, —— and ——, residents of ——, in the State of ——, upon our oaths, declare that the foregoing declaration was signed and acknowledged by ——, in our presence, and that we believe, from the appearance and statements of the applicant, that he is the identical person he represents himself to be. (*Signatures of Witnesses.*)

The foregoing declaration and affidavit were sworn to and subscribed before me on the day and year above-written; and I certify that I know the affiants to be credible persons; that the claimant is the person he represents himself to be, and that I have no interest in this claim. (*J. P.*)

This must also be followed by the certificate of the Clerk, under the seal of the proper Court, attesting the official character of the magistrate.

(3)

Form of Declaration to be made by the Widow of a deceased Person who has not had a Land Warrant.

STATE OF —— }
County of —— } *ss.*

On this —— day of ——, A. D. one thousand eight hundred and ——, personally appeared before me, a justice of the peace [*or other officer authorized to administer oaths for general purposes*], within and for the county and State aforesaid, ——, aged —— years, a resident of ——, in the State of ——, who, being duly sworn according to law, declares that she is the widow of ——, deceased, who was a —— in the company commanded by Captain ——, in the —— regiment of ——, commanded by ——, in the war with Great Britain, declared by the United States, on the 18th day of June, 1812 [*or other war, as the case may be*]; that her said husband enlisted [*or volunteered, or was drafted*], at ——, on or about the —— day of ——, A. D. ——, for the term of —— and continued in actual service in said war for the term of ——, and was honorably discharged at ——, on the —— day of ——, A. D. ——.

She further states that she was married to the said ——, in ——, on the —— day of ——, A. D. ——, by one ——, a ——, and that her name before her said marriage was ——; that her said husband died at —— on the —— day of —— , A. D. ——, and that she is now a widow.[1]

---

[1] The notes to the preceding declaration (1) are also applicable to this. In some cases it will, perhaps, be impossible for the widow to state the facts in relation to her husband's services with the particulaity as to dates, etc., indicated by the above form. In such case she must state such facts as she can.

This declaration must be accompanied by satisfactory proof of the marriage, of the husband's death, and the present widowhood of the claimant. If there be a public record of the marriage, a duly certified copy of it should be forwarded, if possible. If there be none but a private or family record, such family record, or a certified copy of the same, should be forwarded, with the affidavit of some disinterested persons proving the genuineness of the original, and the correctness of the copy. If no public or private record of the marriage exist, or can be procured, that fact should be set forth in the declaration; and in such case, other evidence—such as the testimony of persons who knew the parties in the lifetime of the husband, and knew them to cohabit as husband and wife, and to be so reputed—will be admissible. [See forms under title, GRATUITOUS PENSIONS—WIDOWS AND ORPHANS, REVOLUTIONARY WAR, page 128.]

In no case, however, will the mere statement of witnesses that the

She makes this declaration for the purpose of obtaining the bounty land to which she may be entitled under the "act approved March 3, 1855;" and she further declares that she has not received or applied for bounty land under this or any other act of Congress.[1]

(*Claimant's Signature.*)

We, —— and ——, residents of ——, in the State of ——, upon our oaths declare that the foregoing declaration was signed and acknowledged by —— in our presence, and that we believe, from the appearance and statements of the applicant, that she is the identical person she represents herself to be. (*Signatures of Witnesses.*)

The foregoing declaration and affidavit were sworn to and subscribed before me on the day and year above-written; and I certify that I know the affiants to be credible persons; that the claimant is the person she represents herself to be, and that I have no interest in this claim. (*J. P.*)

[Add certificate of Clerk, under seal, as in other cases.]

(4)

Form of Declaration to be made by the Widow of a deceased Person who has had a Land Warrant, and desires another.

STATE OF —— } ss.
County of —— }

On this —— day of ——, A. D. one thousand eight hundred and ——, personally appeared before me, a justice of the peace [*or other officer authorized to administer oaths for general purposes*], within and for the county and State aforesaid, ——, aged —— years, a resident of ——, in the State of ——, who, being duly sworn according to law, declares that she is the widow of ——, deceased, who was a —— in the company commanded by Captain ——, in the —— regiment of ——, commanded by —— in the war with Great Britain, declared by the United States on the 18th day of June, 1812 [*or other war, as the case may be*]; that her said husband enlisted [*or volunteered, or was drafted*], at ——, on or about the —— day of ——, A. D. ——, for the term of ——, and continued in actual service in said war for the term of ——, and was honorably discharged at ——, on the —— day of ——, A. D. ——.

---

claimant *is the widow* of the deceased be taken as evidence of the marriage; but the witnesses must state *facts* and *circumstances* from which they derive their knowledge or opinion that she is the widow of the deceased.

[1] The preceding forms may be used for applications for minors, *mutatis mutandis.*

She further states that she was married to the said ——, in ——, on the —— day of ——, A. D. ——, by one ——, a ——, and that her name before her said marriage was ——; that her said husband died at —— on the —— day of ——, A. D. ——, for proof of which she refers to her former declaration; and that she is now a widow.

She further declares that she has heretofore made application for bounty land, under the act approved September 28, 1850 [*or other act, as the case may be*], and obtained a land warrant for —— acres, No. ——, which she has legally disposed of, and it can not now be returned.

She makes this declaration for the purpose of obtaining the bounty land to which she may be entitled under the "act approved March 3, 1855."

(*Claimant's Signature.*)

We, —— and ——, residents of ——, in the State of ——, upon our oaths declare that the foregoing declaration was signed and acknowledged by ——, in our presence; and that we believe, from the appearance and statements of the applicant, that she is the identical person she represents herself to be, and is still a widow. (*Signatures of Witnesses.*)

The foregoing declaration and affidavit were sworn to and subscribed before me on the day and year above-written; and I certify that I know the affiants to be credible persons; that the claimant is the person she represents herself to be, and is still a widow; and that I have no interest in this claim. (*J. P.*)

[Attach Clerk's certificate and seal, in the usual form.]

It is not necessary that proof of marriage and death should accompany the foregoing declaration; the only additional proof required being *continued widowhood.*

Claimants are referred to the notes to the Declaration (3).

PENSION OFFICE,
Washington, March 28, 1855.

The pressing requests from all parts of the country for information in regard to the construction and application of the bounty land act, passed March 3, 1855, as well as for information touching the instructions and forms recently issued by this office, have increased to such an extent that the issuing of a general circular has been rendered imperative, in order that all applicants may be apprised at an early day of the views of this office in regard to their stated cases:

1. Widows who have received forty acres of land, and who are

applying for the additional one hundred and twenty acres granted them under the late act, will not be required to furnish proof of their marriage and the death of their husbands, when that evidence has already been furnished, and is on file in this or any other department of the Government; but it will be necessary to furnish proof of continued widowhood. The number of the warrant previously granted should be stated in the new application, but it is not absolutely indispensable that it should appear.

2. The certificate of a notary public, with his official seal attached, is sufficient, provided he is not an agent for the claimant. Accompanying proof must be furnished of the genuineness of the signature, and the fact established that his commission had not expired at the time the application was made.

3. The form on page 7 of the "Instructions and Forms," [Declaration No. 1], can be used by persons making application for bounty land, under the late act, for services in the navy.

4. A case stated is not a case established, and this office will refrain from giving an opinion on suppositious cases, as the facts furnished seldom correspond with those which appear in the formal application.

L. P. WALDO, *Commissioner.*

PENSION OFFICE,
Washington, April, 1855.

With the view of meeting the most important of the almost numberless questions in regard to the interpretation and application of the bounty land act of March 3, 1855, the undersigned has deemed it necessary to issue the following general explanatory circular:

RECORD EVIDENCE.—The words "record evidence," which appear in the act, are not to be taken in their strict legal sense, but rather in their military acceptation. As a general rule, as applied to military service, any entry made by a person in the day and time said service was rendered, whose duty it was to notice and register the fact, will be regarded by this office as "record evidence." But there may be other record evidence of military service. The records of many towns show that certain individuals served as the *quota* for such towns in the revolutionary war. The historical societies in many of the States contain evidence of the military service of individuals whose names are not found on the muster or pay rolls of any corps. Many well-accredited histories furnish evidence of individual military service that can not be elsewhere found. It is not to be supposed that these and other like proofs of service are to be disregarded.

Distant and Pacific and Actual and Perilous Service during a time of War.—A distinction is recognized by this office between distant and pacific and actual and perilous service during a time of war. Were this distinction not to be made, all the officers and men who were engaged in the military or naval service of the country during any of the great or minor wars in which the United States has been involved, would receive the like liberal land bounty for the hardships and dangers encountered by only a portion of their number. The framers of the late act never contemplated to place the quiet occupants of barracks, hundreds if not thousands of miles distant from the seat of war, on an equal footing with those who were engaged in deadly strife in Florida or Mexico.

Applications for Bounty Land for Separate Services.—The design of the law is, that no one person shall receive more than one hundred and sixty acres of land, although he may have served in two or more wars. In the case of a woman marrying twice, and surviving both husbands, and both entitled to bounty land, she is only entitled to one bounty, but she may make her election under either husband. If there be minor children living of the non-elected husband, they are also entitled to land.

The Revenue Cutter Service.—Persons employed in the revenue cutter service do not belong to the navy. The fact that a revenue cutter, in a time of war, was employed to carry instructions, does not change her organic character. In this view of the question, the officers and crews of the revenue cutter service, no matter where or when employed, are not entitled to land bounty under the act of March 3, 1855.

Revolutionary Naval Service.—The officers and men (or their widows and minor children) who were engaged in the naval service of the country during the revolutionary war, are regarded as among the beneficiaries of the act of March 3, 1855.

Regularly Mustered into Service.—The fact that a person's name appears on the rolls of an organized military company, called into existence by lawful requisition for a specific object, and that the members of said company were paid by the government of the United States for their services while so organized, is regarded as sufficient evidence that he was regularly mustered into service.

THE PATRIOT AND AROSTOOK WARS.—The benefits of the act are extended to all officers and men, whether of the army or navy, who were engaged in any of the wars in which this country has been involved since 1790. In this broad and comprehensive scheme of national reward, those who were engaged in any of our Indian wars, as well as that portion of the militia of the States of New York and Maine who served during the so-called Patriot and Arostook wars, are included. In the last-named class of beneficiaries, this office does not recognize "the armed police" of Maine. This was not a voluntary but a hired civil force, commanded by a civil officer, and were called out for a civil service; and, while engaged in that service, were under the protection of State and federal troops.

THE INVASION OF PLATTSBURG.—Something more is necessary than the mere assertion or the actual proof of presence at the invasion of Plattsburg by the British army in September, 1814. Some might have been drawn there from idle curiosity, and others may have been there unwilling spectators. As the act reads, and it is only susceptible of one interpretation, it will not be sufficient if the applicant for bounty land proves that he was near Plattsburg, or that he was on his way to Plattsburg, at the time; but he must furnish satisfactory evidence that he was at the invasion of Plattsburg under some recognized military organization.

EVIDENCE ALREADY FURNISHED.—In the case of a person applying for additional land, under the new act, a repetition of evidence is not required. Where the necessary evidence is on file in this or any other executive office at the seat of Government, a reference in the application to such a state of facts will be sufficient.

L. P. WALDO, *Commissioner of Pensions.*

PENSION OFFICE, *January* 23, 1856.

Sir:—All applications by widows for bounty land, under the act of March 3, 1855, must be supported by satisfactory proof of the marriage of the claimant to the soldier on account of whose services her claim is made; of his death; and that the claimant, at the time of making her application, was a widow—i. e., *unmarried.*

If the marriage was in any State or country where any public records of marriages are kept, it should be proved by a duly certified copy of the record; or, if there is no such record, by the testimony of credible witnesses who were present at the marriage; and where such testimony exists and is not produced, satisfactory reasons must be stated, under oath, why it is not produced. If it is shown by affidavit *that no record evidence or testimony of eye-witnesses can be procured*, the claimant may then produce the best other evidence in her power; such as the testimony of witnesses who were acquainted with her and her husband during his lifetime; knew them to live together as man and wife, and that they were reputed so to be; and that the fact of their having been married was never called in question by their acquaintances.

In no case will the mere statement of the witnesses that the claimant *is the widow* of the deceased, be taken as evidence of the marriage; but the witnesses must state the facts and circumstances from which they derive their knowledge or opinion that she is the widow of the deceased.

Witnesses, to prove the death of the soldier, must state their means of knowledge concerning it, and, as nearly as they can, the time and place of its occurrence.

The evidence to prove the existing widowhood of the claimant must be direct, and the statement of witnesses that the claimant is the party she represents herself to be will not be received as satisfactory proof of widowhood.

J. MINOT, *Commissioner.*

REGULATIONS AND FORMS RELATING EXCLUSIVELY TO LAND WARRANTS.

GENERAL LAND OFFICE, *November* 1, 1858.

Annexed is a copy of the act of Congress approved June 3, 1858, "declaring the title of land warrants in certain cases."

In virtue of this act, the title to land warrants issued *after* the death of the warrantee vests in the "widow," if there be one, and if there be none, in the heirs and legatees of the claimant.

All such warrants are declared "personal chattels," and may be assigned by "such widows," "heirs" or "legatees," or by the "legal representatives of the deceased claimant, for the use of such heirs or legatees only." [1]

---

[1] The proceeds of the sale of a warrant, made by an administrator, is the absolute property of the widow herself, or legatees, without regard to any debt contracted by the warrantee; but the practice of this office has been to recognize assignments properly made by an administrator for dis-

To make a warrant, when issued to deceased persons, available, it should be accompanied by a certificate, under seal, from a court having jurisdiction of probate matters, giving the *date* of the *decease* of the claimant.

1. If he died *before* the date of the warrant, then the name of his "*widow*" should be stated in that certificate, if there be one, whose assignment will be sufficient in the ordinary form.

2. If no widow, that fact should appear in the certificate of the probate court, showing the names of the heirs, and only heirs-at-law, of the claimant, naming such as are *adults* and such as are *minors.* If all are adults, then their simple transfer is all that is required on the warrant, to which the certificate of the probate court must be appended; if some or all are minors, they may assign by their guardians, whose letter of guardianship should also be appended.

3. If the claimant died *after* the date of the warrant, then the title thereto descends according to the law of domicile.

In this class of cases, if the claimant died *intestate*, there should be a certificate from the probate court giving the names of the heirs, and only heirs-at-law, who, if adults, may assign, as in ordinary cases; and if minors, may assign by guardians, as aforesaid.

If the warrantee died *testate*, a certified transcript of the will should be annexed, with an assignment by the legatees or by the executors, where the will does not specifically dispose of the warrant; but in that case a transcript of the letters testamentary must accompany the transfer.

4. Or, in any of the foregoing cases of *intestacy*, the warrant may be assigned by the administrator of the decedent, as his legal representative, "for the use of the heirs only;" but the assignment must be accompanied by a certified copy of the letters of administration.

5. In virtue of the 2d section of said act of 3d June, 1858, warrants under the act of 1855, as well as those issued under previous laws, may be applied to lands "which are subject to entry at a greater minimum than" $1 25 per acre, by the locator paying, "in cash, the difference between the value of such warrants at one dollar and twenty-five cents per acre, and the tract of land located on."

tribution of the proceeds among the heirs-at-law, after payment of the funeral and proper court expenses. (Attorney's and administrator's fees not taxed by the court, are not regarded as proper court expenses.) *Extract from a letter of the Commissioner of the General Land Office.*

Thus, for example, one hundred and sixty-acre warrant may be located on one hundred and sixty acres at $2 50 per acre, and the difference, $200, paid in cash, or two warrants of eighty acres each, or four warrants of forty acres, may be applied to one hundred and sixty-acre tract, each, however, to be located on a specific legal subdivision of the one hundred and sixty acres, and the difference, $200, must in all cases be paid in cash.

6. In regard to all pre-emptions, at *one dollar and twenty-five cents* per acre, it is held, that a pre-emptor may use one, two or more warrants in locating the land pre-empted, each warrant to cover a specific subdivision of the land, that is, a forty-acre warrant must be located on a specific forty-acre tract, an eighty on an eighty-acre tract, and so on.

When a subdivision is fractional, and overruns the number of acres called for by the warrant, the fractional excess must be paid for in cash.

In all respects, except so far as qualified by the foregoing, the circular and its forms of 3d May, 1855, will govern in regard to bounty land warrants.

The following general sections are added for the information of parties interested.

7. Patents for bounty land locations are issued in the exact order of date of location; and are sent to the district land office for delivery, unless, before the transmission, a party files, in this office, the duplicate certificate, when the patent will be sent to such address as the owner may indicate.

8. When the duplicate certificate is lost, the patent will be delivered, upon the patentee filing in this office his affidavit, stating the fact of its loss, and that it was not assigned by him, and that he is the present *bona fide* owner of the land.

9. When an original warrant which had been assigned is lost, and a duplicate warrant is issued in lieu of it, a new assignment must be indorsed thereon from the warrantee, or in default of that, a decree of title must be obtained from a court of competent jurisdiction, and a transcript thereof appended to the duplicate warrant.

THOS. A. HENDRICKS, *Commissioner.*

Approved:

J. THOMPSON, *Secretary of the Interior.*

PENSION OFFICE, *Washington City, August* 15, 1860.

To carry into effect the law of June 23, 1860, authorizing the re-issue of land warrants in certain cases, the Secretary of the Interior has prescribed the following rules and regulations:

1. Whenever a warrant has failed to reach the hands of the party entitled to receive it, and to whom it was sent, or has been lost or destroyed after having been received, in order to prevent the issuing of a patent to a fraudulent holder of the same, the actual owner must at once file in the General Land Office a caveat in the form of an affidavit, duly authenticated, setting forth the nature of his title to the warrant, and the particulars as to its loss, and giving his post-office address.

2. He must give public notice of the facts in the case, at least once a week for six successive weeks, in some newspaper of general circulation published at or nearest the place to which the warrant was directed, or where the loss occurred. In such publication (a copy of which must be furnished to *this office*, with the affidavit of the publisher as to its due appearance) the intention must also be expressed of applying to the Commissioner of Pensions for a re-issue of the lost warrant, which must be minutely described.

3. The filing of the caveat in the General Land Office and the advertisement of the loss being only preliminary steps towards the observance of the regulations, the owner of the lost warrant must file in this office, as soon after the discovery of the loss as practicable, his declaration under oath, duly authenticated, setting forth fully and distinctly the time, place and circumstances of the loss, and, if he be the original warrantee, that he never sold, assigned, nor voluntarily parted with his right to the warrant in question.

4. In cases where a re-issue of a warrant is sought on the ground of the non-reception of the original warrant, the agent or person to whom it was sent must unite with the warrantee or make a separate affidavit as to its non-reception.

5. If the applicant for the re-issue be not the person to whom the warrant was issued, but claims to be the *bona fide* owner thereof by purchase, for a valuable consideration, he must give the name and residence of the warrantee, the name and residence of the person of whom he bought it, and, as far as he may know or can ascertain, the names and residences of each of the several parties through whom the title of the warrant descended to him from the original war-

rantee, and adduce satisfactory evidence in proof of each and all his statements in reference thereto.

6. The identity of the applicant must be satisfactorily established, and the credibility of each and every affiant must be duly certified by the magistrate administering the oaths, and his official character and signature must be verified by the proper officer under his seal of office.

7. This office will also, for the space of three months, advertise the alleged loss of the original warrant, and the pendency before it of the application for its re issue, in the "Constitution" newspaper, published at the seat of Government, and no warrant will be re-issued under the foregoing act until after the expiration of three months from the date of the filing of the petition in this office, and not then if it shall be ascertained that the original is in existence.

The foregoing regulations will be strictly enforced in every instance. GEO. C. WHITING, *Comm'r of Pensions.*

FORMS AND REGULATIONS FOR THE ASSIGNMENT OF LAND WARRANTS AND LOCATIONS.

By the first section of the act of Congress entitled "an act making land warrants assignable, and for other purposes," approved March 22, 1852, it is provided: "That all warrants for military bounty land which have been, or may hereafter be issued, under any law of the United States, and all valid locations of the same which have been, or may hereafter be made, are hereby declared to be assignable, by deed or instrument of writing, made and executed after the taking effect of this act, according to such form, and pursuant to such regulations as may be prescribed by the Commissioner of the General Land Office, so as to vest the assignee with all the rights of the original owners of the warrant or location."

In accordance with the provisions of this section, the following forms are prescribed for the assignment of the warrants and locations referred to, to-wit:

Form of Assignment.—No. 1.

For value received, I, ——, to whom the within warrant, No. ——, was issued, do hereby sell and assign unto ——, of ——, and to his heirs and assigns forever, the said warrant, and authorize him to locate the same, and receive a patent therefor. Witness my hand and seal, this —— day of ——, A.D. 18—.

Attest: [*Two Witnesses.*] [L. S.]

STATE OF —— }
County of —— } *ss.*

On this —— day of ——, in the year eighteen hundred and ——, before me, personally came ——, to me well known, and acknowledged the foregoing assignment to be his act and deed, and I certify that the said —— is the identical person to whom the within warrant issued, and who executed the foregoing assignment thereof. (*Officer's Signature.*)

Acknowledgment where the Vendor is not known to the Officer, and his Identity has to be proved.

STATE OF —— }
County of —— } *ss.*

On this —— day of ——, in the year ——, before me, personally came ——, and ——, and the said —— being well known to me as a credible and disinterested person, was duly sworn by me, and on his oath declared and said, that he well knows the said ——, and that he is the same person to whom the within warrant issued (*or was assigned*), and who executed the foregoing assignment, and his testimony being satisfactory evidence to me of that fact, the said —— thereupon acknowledged the said assignment to be his act and deed. (*Officer's Signature.*)

Form for the Assignment of the Location.—No. 2.

For value received, I, ——, to whom the within certificate of location was issued, do hereby sell and assign unto ——, and to his heirs and assigns forever, the said certificate of location, and the warrant and land therein described, and authorize him to receive the patent therefor.

Witness my hand and seal, this —— day of ——, 18—.

Attest: [*Two Witnesses.*] [L. S.]

Form of Acknowledgment where the Vendor is personally known to the Officer taking the same.

STATE OF —— }
County of —— } *ss.*

On this —— day of ——, in the year ——, personally appeared [*Here insert the name of the person to whom the certificate of location issued*] to me well known, and acknowledged the foregoing assignment to be his act and deed; and I certify, that the said [*Here insert the name of the person to whom the certificate of location issued*] is the identical person to whom the within certificate of location issued, and who executed the foregoing assignment thereof. (*Officer's Signature.*)

Form of Acknowledgment where the Vendor is not personally known to the Officer, and where his Identity has to be proven.

STATE OF —— } ss.
County of—— }

On this —— day of ——, in the year ——, before me personally came [*Here insert the name of the person to whom the certificate of location issued*], and [*Here insert the name and residence of a witness*], and the said [*Here insert the name of the witness*] being well known to me as a credible and disinterested person, was duly sworn by me, and on his oath declared and said that he well knows the said [*Here insert the name of the person to whom the certificate of location issued*], and that he is the same person to whom the within certificate of location issued, and who executed the foregoing assignment; and his testimony being satisfactory evidence to me of that fact, the said [*Here insert the name of the person to whom the certificate of location issued*] thereupon acknowledged the said assignment to be his act and deed. (*Officer's Signature.*)

Assignment No. 1 and acknowledgment must be indorsed upon the warrant, and No. 2 and acknowledgment upon the certificate of location; and must be attested by two witnesses, acknowledged before a register or receiver of a land office, a judge of a court of record, a justice of the peace, or a commissioner of deeds resident in the State from which he derives his appointment; and in every instance where the acknowledgment is made before any officer other than the register or receiver of a land office, it must be accompanied by a certificate, under seal of the proper authority, of the official character of the person before whom the acknowledgment was made, and also of the genuineness of his signature.

All assignments of bounty land warrants issued under the act of September 28, 1850, made before the date of this act, are invalid and void.

The same section provides, "That any person entitled to preemption right to any land, shall be entitled to use any such land warrant in payment of the same, at the rate of $1 25 per acre for the quantity of land therein specified."

By this provision, all persons entitled to pre-emption, whether on offered or unoffered lands, can use a military bounty land warrant in payment for the tract pre-empted, reckoning the said warrant at $1 25 per acre for the quantity therein specified, whether the land so claimed is at the usual or enhanced minimum.

Should the area of the tract claimed exceed the amount called for in the warrant, the pre-emptor will have to pay for the excess in cash, but if it should fall short, he is not entitled to a refunding of the excess.

It is further provided by the same section, "that the warrants which have been, or may hereafter be, issued in pursuance of said laws or of this act, may be located according to the legal subdivisions of the public lands, in one body, upon any lands of the United States subject to private entry at the time of such location, at the minimum price: *Provided, further*, That when said warrants shall be located on lands which are subject to entry at a greater minimum than $1 25 per acre, the locator of said warrant shall pay to the United States, in cash, the difference between the value of such warrants at $1 25 per acre, and the tract of land located on."

By these provisions, where the lands are subject to private entry at $1 25 per acre, the holder of an eighty-acre warrant can take any two forty-acre lots, forming a compact body of eighty acres; and the holder of a warrant for one hundred and sixty acres, can take two eighty-acre, or four forty-acre tracts, forming a compact body of one hundred and sixty acres.

Where the minimum price of the lands, subject to private entry proposed to be located is more than $1 25 per acre, the holder of the warrant can locate, in accordance with the instructions contained in the foregoing paragraph, the quantity specified in the warrant, by paying the difference in cash.

This act does not authorize the holder of an eighty-acre warrant to locate therewith a forty-acre tract of land at $2 50 per acre in full satisfaction thereof, but he must locate, by legal subdivisions, the compact body of eighty acres, as near as may be, and pay the difference in cash. So also of one hundred and sixty acre warrants, except in pre-emption cases as hereinbefore stated.

Each warrant is to be distinctly and separately located, so that it follows that no body of land can be located by an assignee of various warrantees, with a number of warrants; nor can a pre-emptor in any case use more than one warrant in the location of the land pre-empted by him, and the excess, if any, must be paid for by him in cash.

The second section of this act provides, "that the registers and receivers of the land offices shall hereafter be severally authorized to charge and receive for their services in locating all military bounty land warrants, issued since the 11th day of February, 1847, the same compensation or per-centage to which they are entitled by law for sales of the public lands for cash, at the rate of $1 25 per acre, the said compensation to be hereafter paid by the assignees or holders of such warrants."

The third section of this act provides, "that registers and receivers, whether in or out of office at the passage of this act, or their legal representatives in case of death, shall be entitled to receive from the treasury of the United States for services heretofore performed in locating military bounty land warrants, the same rate of compensation provided in the preceding section for services hereafter to be performed, after deducting the amount already received by such officers under the act entitled 'an act to require the holders of military land warrants to compensate the land officers of the United States for services in relation to the location of those warrants,' approved May 17, 1848: *Provided*, That no register or receiver shall receive any compensation out of the treasury for past services who has charged and received illegal fees for the location of such warrants: *And provided, further*, That no register or receiver shall receive for his services during any year a greater compensation than the maximum now allowed by law."

Where parties may desire to avail themselves of the privilege of having their warrants located through the General Land Office, as provided for by the act of 28th September, 1850, they must take the necessary steps to pay to the register and receiver the fees to which they are entitled. The same course must be observed by persons remote from the district land offices in making applications by letter to these officers. Without the payment of those fees the warrants can not be located.

By the terms of this law the fees are as follows:

For a 40-acre warrant, fifty cents each to register or receiver—total $1 00.

For an 80-acre warrant, one dollar each to register and receiver—total $2 00.

For a 160-acre warrant, two dollars each to register and receiver—total $4 00.

P. S.—Numerous applications having been made for authority to sell warrants and locations under powers of attorney, the following forms are prescribed for that purpose, which, however, must invariably be indorsed on the warrant, or they will not be recognized.

Form of a Power of Attorney—No. 3.

Know all men by these presents, that I [*here insert the name of warrantee*], of the county of ——, and State of ——, do hereby constitute and appoint ——, of ——, my true and lawful attorney, for me, and in my name, to sell and convey the within land warrant, No. ——, for —— acres of land, which issued under the act of September, 1850.

Signed in presence of
(*Witnesses.*)
(*Warrantee's Signature.*)

The acknowledgment of this power of attorney must be taken and certified in the same manner as the acknowledgments of the sales of the warrant or certificate of location hereinbefore prescribed, and must also be indorsed on the warrant.

J. BUTTERFIELD, *Commissioner.*

Power of Attorney to locate Warrant

Know all men by these presents, that I, ——, of the county of ——, and State of ——, do hereby constitute and appoint ——, of ——, my true and lawful attorney, for me, and in my name, to locate land warrant, No. ——, for —— acres of land, which issued under the act of September, 1850 (*or other act, as the case may be*).

Witness my hand and seal, this —— day of ——, A. D., 18—.

Executed in presence of
(*Witnesses.*)
[L. S.]

STATE OF ——
County of —— } ss.

On this ——day of ——, in the year 18—, personally appeared ——, before the undersigned authority within and for said county, and acknowledged the foregoing power of attorney to be his act and deed; and I certify that I am acquainted with the said ——, and know him to be the same person who is described in said power, and who executed the same.

(*Officer's Signature.*)

[Here must follow the certificate of the Clerk, under seal, as in other cases.]

CHAPTER XXIV.

BOUNTY MONEY—ARMY AND NAVY.

LAWS, REGULATIONS AND FORMS.

By an act of July 5, 1838,[1] it was provided that every able-bodied non-commissioned officer, musician or private soldier, who should re-enlist into his company or regiment within two months before, or one month after the expiration of his term of service, should receive three months' extra pay as a bounty for such re-enlistment.[2] This act was repealed by act of August 3, 1861;[3] but not to the prejudice of rights acquired under it.

An act of June 17, 1850,[4] granted a bounty to persons enlisting at distant military posts and stations, equal to the expense of transporting and subsisting the soldier from the harbor of New York to the place of service; to be paid in unequal installments, at the end of each year's service, in such manner that the amounts should annually increase, and the largest be paid at the expiration of the term of service. This act was also repealed by the act of August 3, 1861.

There is now no bounty allowed by law for enlistments or re-enlistments in the army—the only bounty being for length of service.

The third section of "an act to provide a more efficient

---

1 U. S. Statutes at Large, vol. v, 560.

2 This provision was extended to the marine corps, by act of August 5, 1854.

3 U. S. Statutes at Large, vol. xii, 288.

4 *Ibid*, vol. ix, 439.

discipline for the navy," approved March 2, 1855,[1] contains the following provisions:

SEC. 3. *And be it further enacted*, That if any seaman, ordinary seaman, landsman or boy, shall re-enlist for three years, within three months after his discharge, he shall, on presenting his honorable discharge, or on accounting in a satisfactory manner for its loss, be entitled to pay during the said three months, equal to that to which he would have been entitled if he had been employed in actual service.

An act of February 11, 1847, making provision for prosecuting the war with Mexico, grants bounty land to those who serve to the end of the war, or to the heirs of those killed during its progress, and authorizes the parties entitled to such land to accept, in lieu thereof, war scrip for an amount of money, in the nature of a bounty. This law, with the amendments thereto, and the regulations and forms for obtaining such scrip, may be found in Chapter XXIII.

The fifth and sixth sections of "an act to authorize the employment of volunteers to aid in enforcing the laws and protecting public property," approved July 22, 1861,[2] are as follows:

SEC. 5. *And be it further enacted*, That the officers, non-commissioned officers and privates, organized as above set forth, shall, in all respects, be placed on the footing, as to pay and allowances, of similar corps of the regular army. *Provided*, That the allowances of non-commissioned officers and privates for clothing, when not furnished in kind, shall be three dollars and fifty cents per month, and that each company officer, non-commissioned officer, private, musician and artificer of cavalry shall furnish his own horse and horse equipments, and shall receive forty cents per day for their use and risk, except that in case the horse shall become disabled or shall

1 U. S. Statutes at Large, vol. x, 627.

2 *Ibid*, vol. xii, 268.

die, the allowance shall cease until the disability be removed or another horse be supplied. Every volunteer, non-commissioned officer, private, musician and artificer who enters the service of the United States under this act, shall be paid at the rate of fifty cents in lieu of subsistence, and if a cavalry volunteer, twenty-five cents additional in lieu of forage, for every twenty miles of travel from his place of enrollment to the place of muster, the distance to be measured by the shortest usually traveled route; and when honorably discharged, an allowance, at the same rate from the place of his discharge to his place of enrollment, and, in addition thereto, if he shall have served for a period of two years, or during the war, if sooner ended, the sum of one hundred dollars: *Provided*, That such of the companies of cavalry herein provided for as may require it, may be furnished with horses and horse equipments in the same manner as in the United States army.

SEC. 6. *And be it further enacted*, That any volunteer who may be received into the service of the United States under this act, and who may be wounded or otherwise disabled in the service, shall be entitled to the benefits which have been or may be conferred on persons disabled in the regular service; and the widow, if there be one, and if not, the legal heirs of such as die, or may be killed in service, in addition to all arrears of pay and allowances, shall receive the sum of one hundred dollars.

The fifth section of "an act to increase the present military establishment of the United States," approved July 29, 1861, extends the benefits of the foregoing act to certain soldiers of the regular army, as follows:

SEC. 5. *And be it further enacted*, That the term of enlistments made and to be made in the years eighteen hundred and sixty-one and eighteen hundred and sixty-two, in the regular army, including the force authorized by this act, shall be for the period of three years, and those to be made after January one, eighteen hundred and sixty-three, shall be for the term of five years, as at present authorized, and that the men enlisted in the regular forces, after the first day of July, eighteen hundred and sixty-one, shall be entitled to the same bounties, in every respect, as those allowed or to be allowed to the men of the volunteer forces.

An army appropriation bill of July 5, 1862, makes the following amendments to the acts of July 22, 1861, and July 29, 1861:

SEC. 6. *And be it further enacted,* That section five of the act "to authorize the employment of volunteers to aid in enforcing the laws and protecting public property," approved July twenty-second, eighteen hundred and sixty-one, and section five of the act "to increase the present military establishment of the United States," approved July twenty-nine, eighteen hundred and sixty-one, shall be so construed as to allow twenty-five dollars of the bounty of one hundred dollars therein provided to be paid immediately after enlistment to every soldier of the regular and volunteer forces hereafter enlisted during the continuance of the existing war, and the sum of seven millions five hundred thousand dollars is hereby appropriated for such payment.

An act of July 11, 1862, grants to the widows and heirs of regulars the same bounty, as to the widows and heirs of volunteers, under the act of July 22, 1861. It also gives a construction to the word "heirs," in the sixth section of the last-named act. This act, July 11, 1862, is as follows:

AN ACT *making Appropriations for the Payment of the Bounty authorized by the sixth section of an act entitled "an act to authorize the employment of Volunteers to aid in enforcing the Laws, and protecting Public Property," approved July twenty-second, eighteen hundred and sixty-one, and for other purposes.*

Be it enacted by the Senate and House of Representatives of the United States of America in Congress assembled, That the following sums be and the same are hereby appropriated, out of any money in the Treasury not otherwise appropriated, for the objects hereinafter expressed, viz:

For payment of the bounty to widows, children, fathers, mothers, brothers and sisters of such volunteers as may have died or been killed, or may die or be killed, in service, authorized by the sixth section of an act entitled "an act to authorize the employment of volunteers to aid in enforcing the laws and protecting public property," approved July twenty-second, eighteen hundred and sixty-one, five millions of dollars, or so much thereof as may be found necessary: *Provided*, That said bounty shall be paid to the following persons, and in the order following, and to no other person, to-wit: First, to the widow of such deceased soldier, if there be one. Second, if there be no widow then to the children of such deceased soldier, share and share alike. Third, if such soldier left neither a widow or child or children, then, and in that case, such bounty shall be paid to the following persons, provided they be residents of the United States, to-wit: First, to his father, or if he shall not be living, or has abandoned the support of his family, then to the mother of such soldier; and if there be neither father nor mother as aforesaid, then such bounty shall be paid to the brothers and sisters of the deceased soldier, resident as aforesaid.

SEC. 2. *And be it further enacted*, That the sum of three thousand dollars, or so much thereof as may be found necessary, be and the same is hereby appropriated for the expenses of the committee on disloyal employees of the Government, appointed by resolution of the House of Representatives, July eight, eighteen hundred and sixty-one.

SEC. 3. *And be it further enacted*, That that part of the sixth section of the act "to authorize the employment of volunteers to aid in enforcing the laws and protecting public property," approved July twenty-second, eighteen hundred and sixty-one, which secured to the widow, if there be one, and if not to the legal heirs of such volunteers as die or may be killed in service, in addition to all arrears of pay and allowances, a bounty of one hundred dollars, shall be held to apply to those persons who have enlisted in the regular forces since the first day of July, eighteen hundred and sixty-one, or shall enlist in the regular forces during the year eighteen hundred and sixty-two, and be paid to the heirs named in this act, and that the bounties herein provided for shall be paid out of any money unappropriated for bounty to volunteers.

Approved, July 11, 1862.

The third and fourth sections of "a bill to amend the act calling forth the militia to execute the laws of the Union, suppress insurrections, and repel invasions, approved, February 28, 1795, and the acts amendatory thereof, and for other purposes," approved July 16, 1862, provide:

SEC. 3. *And be it further enacted*, That the President be, and he is hereby authorized, in addition to the volunteer forces which he is now authorized by law to raise, to accept the services of any number of volunteers, not exceeding one hundred thousand as infantry, for a period of nine months, unless sooner discharged. And every soldier who shall enlist under the provisions of this section shall receive his first month's pay, and also $25 as bounty, upon the mustering of his company or regiment into the service of the United States. And all provisions of law relating to volunteers enlisted in the service of the United States for three years, or during the war, except in relation to bounty, shall be, and the same are extended to, and are hereby declared to embrace the volunteers to be raised under the provisions of this section.

SEC. 4. *And be it further enacted*, That, for the purpose of filling up the regiments of infantry now in the United States service, the President be, and he hereby is, authorized to accept the services of volunteers in such numbers as may be presented for that purpose, for twelve months, if not sooner discharged. And such volunteers, when mustered into the service, shall be in all respects upon a footing with similar troops in the United States service, except as to service bounty, which shall be fifty dollars, one half of which to be paid upon their joining their regiments, and the other half at the expiration of their enlistment.

An act of July 17, 1862, "for the better government of the navy of the United States," contains the following:

SEC. 4. *And be it further enacted*, That a bounty shall be paid by the United States for each person on board any ship or vessel-of-war belonging to any enemy at the commencement of an engagement which shall be sunk or otherwise destroyed in such engagement, by any ship or vessel belonging to the United States, or which it may be necessary to destroy in consequence of injuries sustained in action, of one hundred dollars, if the enemy's vessel was of inferior force; and of two hundred dollars, if of equal or superior force; to be divided among the officers and crew in the same manner as prize money; and when the actual number of men on board any such vessel can not be satisfactorily ascertained, it shall be estimated according to the complement allowed to vessels of their class in the navy of the United States; and there shall be paid as bounty to the captors of any vessel-of-war captured from an enemy, which they may be instructed to destroy, or which shall be immediately destroyed for the public interest, but not in consequence of injuries received in action, fifty dollars for every person who shall be on board at the time of such capture.

INSTRUCTIONS IN PREPARING CLAIMS FOR BOUNTY MONEY.

The following instructions and forms are extracted from a circular of the Second Auditor of the Treasury, relating to claims for pay and bounty. The residue of the circular will be found under PAY—next Chapter.

OF BOUNTY.—The act, approved July 11, 1862, provides, "that said bounty shall be paid to the following persons, and in the order following, and to no other person, to-wit: First, to the widow of such deceased soldier, if there be one. Second, if there be no widow, then to the children of such deceased soldier, share and share alike. Third, if such soldier left neither widow, nor child, nor children, then, and in that case, such bounty shall be paid to the following persons, provided they be residents of the United States, to-wit: First, to his father, or if he shall not be living, or has abandoned the support of his family, then to the mother of such soldier; and if there be neither father nor mother, as aforesaid, then such bounty shall be paid to the brothers and sisters of the deceased soldier, resident as aforesaid."

By the same act, the bounty of one hundred dollars to widows, etc., of volunteers is also given to the widows, etc., of those persons who have enlisted in the regular forces since the first day of July, 1861, or shall enlist in the regular forces during 1862, to be paid to the heirs named in this act. Widows of commissioned officers, and of soldiers dying after being discharged, are not entitled to bounty, nor are the widows of deceased three months' volunteers.

DISLOYALTY.—In section four of "an act to grant pensions," approved July 24, 1862, it is provided, "that no moneys shall be paid to the widow, or children, or any heirs of any deceased soldier, on account of bounty, back pay or pension, who have in any way been engaged in, or who have aided or abetted the existing rebellion in the United States; but the right of such disloyal widow or children, heir or heirs, of such soldier shall be vested in the loyal heir or heirs of the deceased, if any there be."

Information in regard to such cases will receive the attention of the accounting officers.

APPLICATION.—The claimant or claimants must make a written application, under oath, and over his, her or their own signature, stating his, her or their name, age, residence, connection to the deceased, with the letter or name of the captain of the company and regiment to which he belonged; time of his death and the nature of the pay claim—whether "arrears of pay," etc.; and the "$100 bounty," under act of July 22, 1861.

An application by a guardian should give the name and age of the ward or wards, and should be accompanied by letters of guardianship, or an authenticated copy thereof. In the application of a mother, claiming bounty, her husband being alive, the facts upon which the claim is made should be clearly stated and proved. If the soldier died unmarried, leaving no child, it must be stated by the applicant, and also by the disinterested witnesses.

PROOF.—To satisfy the accounting officers that the person or persons thus claiming is or are entitled to the money in the character he, she or they claim, the depositions of two credible witnesses will be required, stating that they are acquainted with the claimant or claimants, the connection held to the deceased, and that they (the deponents) are disinterested. Proof of marriage (record evidence, if possible) must always accompany the applications of those claiming to be widows. If the soldier died unmarried, it must be so stated by the applicant, and also by the disinterested witnesses.

AUTHENTICATION.—The application and depositions, above required, to be subscribed and sworn to before a judge, commissioner, notary public or justice of the peace, duly authorized to administer oaths, accompanied by the certificate and seal of a court of record as to the fact of the said judge, etc., being duly commissioned and acting in his official capacity at the time of the execution of the foregoing papers.

BOUNTY.—No discharged soldier can, under any circumstances, receive the bounty provided by the act of July 22, 1861, unless "he shall have served for a period of two years, or during the war, if sooner ended;" but "the widow, if there be one, and if not, the legal heirs of such as die, or may be killed in the service, in addition to all arrears of pay and allowances, shall receive the sum of one hundred dollars."

MODE OF PRESENTING CLAIMS.—All claims for arrears of pay and bounty money may be sent directly to this office. When received, they are entered upon the register; as soon as practicable they will be examined, and if found correct in form, they are placed upon the files for settlement, and their receipt acknowledged. If incorrect, the party sending it is immediately notified. No "special cases" will be made at the solicitation of attorneys, but when evidence can be obtained, cases will be audited in the order in which they are received. The only exception to this rule is when, in settling a case in its order, evidence is found upon the same rolls by which to settle other claims of soldiers deceased in the same company. Letters of inquiry in relation to a claim, should specify the name of the deceased, and the company, regiment and State to which he belonged, and in all cases, to secure an answer, the name, post-office and State of the writer should be distinctly written.

FORMS.—The form accompanying this circular is intended only as a guide, and must be varied to suit special cases. No claim is rejected on account of the form in which it is presented, if it substantially complies with the instructions.

TO CORRESPONDENTS.—Letters of inquiry relating to the pay of soldiers in hospital or on furlough, should be addressed to the paymaster-general. Inquiries relating to the pay of deceased teamsters or other employees of the quartermaster's department, or for the pay of horses killed or lost in the service, to the third auditor; and relating to the pay and bounty of persons in the marine or naval service, to the fourth auditor.

POSTAGE.—The Government pays all postages on such business communications, whether received or transmitted by this office.

EZRA B. FRENCH,

Second Auditor of the Treasury Department, Washington City, D. C.

Form of Application for Arrears of Pay and Bounty.

I, ——, of ——, in the county of ——, and State of ——, on oath, say that my age is —— years, and that I am the —— of ——, late of ——, in the State of ——, who was a —— in company ——, of the —— regiment of ——, and died in the service of the United States at ——, on the —— day of ——, 18—. [*If the soldier died unmarried, leaving no child, it should be here stated. If the application is by the mother, she should also state the name of the father of the deceased, his death, or abandonment of the support of his family, giving the date and all facts necessary to a proper understanding of the case. If the application is by the widow of the deceased, she should here state her maiden name; when, where and by whom she was married to him, and whether or not there is record evidence of such marriage.*]

I make this application to recover all arrears of pay or other allowances due to the deceased from the United States, and the bounty provided by the sixth section of the act of July 22, 1861.

(*Signature of Claimant.*)

STATE OF —— }
County of —— } *ss.*

Personally appeared the above-named ——, to me well known, and subscribed and made oath to the foregoing statement, on this —— day of ——, 18—, before me. (*Name and Official Title.*]

Form of Affidavit.

We, —— and ——, of ——, in the county of ——, and State of ——, on oath, say that we are and have been for —— years well acquainted with ——, the applicant, and with the said ——, deceased, who was a —— in company ——, of the —— regiment ——, and know —— to be the —— of the said deceased [*if he died unmarried, leaving no child, it should be here stated; and if the application is by the mother, the fact of her widowhood, or the abandonment of her husband, should be stated as in the application*]; and that we have no interest whatever in this application. (*Signatures.*)

Certificate of the magistrate, the same as above.[1]

Here should follow the certificate of the Clerk of the Court, under seal, in the usual form.

This application must be accompanied by the following proof:

IN THE CASE OF A WIDOW:

1. Her marriage with the deceased. This proof must be made in the same manner as in applications for pensions. See "WIDOWS AND ORPHANS — REVOLUTIONARY WAR," page 158.

2. Widowhood and identity. These may be proved by the affidavit of the witnesses above given.

1 It should also state that the witnesses are credible.

IN THE CASE OF CHILDREN:

1. The marriage of the parents. This must be proved in like manner as in applications by widows.

2. Death of widow.

3. That they are the children, and *all* the children, of the deceased.

Items two and three may be proved by the affidavit of two witnesses, according to the form furnished by the Second Auditor.

If the application is made by the guardian of minors, a certified copy of his letters of guardianship must be sent, and a certificate from the proper Court that he is still acting as guardian.

IN THE CASE OF A FATHER:

1. That he is the father of the deceased.

2. That the deceased left neither widow nor child.

These facts may be proved by the affidavit of witnesses, according to the form.

IN THE CASE OF A MOTHER:

1. The death of her husband, the father of the deceased.

2. That she was the mother of the deceased.

3. That he left neither widow nor child.

4. In the case of abandonment by her husband, he being still living, that fact must also be proved.

These items of testimony may all be proved by the affidavit of two witnesses, as above.

IN THE CASE OF BROTHERS AND SISTERS:

1. The marriage and death of their parents. This must be proved as in the case of widows.

2. That they are the brothers and sisters of the deceased.

3. That he left neither widow nor child.

These latter items may be proved by the affidavits of witnesses.

In the case of children, fathers, and brothers and sisters, positive proof of relationship to the deceased will not be required. General reputation and undisputed relationship will suffice.

OTHER FORMS IN ILLUSTRATION.

Widow's Declaration for Bounty Money and Arrears.

STATE OF —— } ss.
County of —— }

On this —— day of ——, 18—, before me, a ——, in and for the county and State above named, personally appeared ——, who, after being duly sworn according to law, declares and says ——, that she is aged —— years; that she is a resident of ——, county of ——, State of ——; and that she is the widow of ——, who was a —— in company ——, commanded by Captain ——, of the —— regiment of —— volunteers, commanded by Colonel ——, and who [was killed *or* died] at ——, on or about the —— day of ——, 18—, while in the service of the United States.

That she was married to the said —— on the —— day of ——, 18—, at ——, by one ——, a ——; that her name before her said marriage was ——; and that she has remained a widow since the death of her said husband. And she further states that she believes there is —— public record of her said marriage[1] ——.

She makes this declaration for the purpose of obtaining the bounty money, arrears of pay, and all other arrearages or sums of money due her by reason of the services of the soldier above named, under and by virtue of an act of Congress, passed July 22, A. D. 1861; also of all other acts

[1] Should there be a public record, and a copy thereof filed with the declaration, this clause may be omitted. Should there be no public but a private record, the declaration should so state. If neither public nor private record, this should be stated; and so also if neither public nor private record, nor witnesses living (or, if living, their place of residence unknown) who were present at the marriage. These statements are necessary in order to admit the class of evidence which the claimant is able to furnish.

now in force upon this subject. And she hereby constitutes and appoints ——, her attorney in fact, to prosecute this claim, and authorizes him to receive and receipt for a draft or certificate, for the amount that may be allowed her. *(Claimant's Signature.)*

Attest: *(Two Witnesses.)*

Sworn to, subscribed and acknowledged, before me, the day and year first above written; and on the same day personally came —— and ——, residents of ——, in the county of ——, State aforesaid, who, being duly sworn according to law, declare that they are personally acquainted with Mrs.——, widow of ——, who has made and subscribed the foregoing declaration, and were acquainted with her and her said husband before he entered the service, and know that they lived together as man and wife, and were so reputed; that she is the widow of the identical —— who performed the military service mentioned in said declaration, and has remained a widow since his death; that their knowledge of the identity of her husband with the soldier is derived from ——.

And they further testify that they reside as above stated, and are disinterested in this claim. *(Witnesses' Signatures.)*

Sworn to and subscribed before me, and I certify that I am not interested in this claim, or concerned in its prosecution; that I believe the affiants to be credible persons, and the declarant the person she represents herself to be. *(Magistrate's Signature.)*

STATE OF —— }
County of —— } *ss.*

I, ——, clerk of the —— court in and for the county and State above named, do hereby certify that ——, Esq., before whom the foregoing declaration and affidavits were made, and who has thereunto signed his name, was at the time of so doing, an acting ——, in and for said county, duly commissioned and sworn; that all of his official acts, as such, are entitled to full faith and credit, and that his signature thereto is genuine.

In testimony whereof, I have hereunto set my hand and affixed [L. S.] the seal of said court, at ——, in said county, this —— day of ——, A. D. 18—. *(Clerk.)*

For instructions relative to the proof necessary to support the foregoing declaration, see remarks immediately preceding the declaration.

Claim of Heirs for Arrears, Bounty Money, etc., of Deceased Officer or Soldier.

STATE OF —— }
County of —— } *ss.*

On this —— day of ——, 18—, before me, a ——, in and for the county and State above named, personally appeared ——, aged —— years, a resident of ——, county of ——, State of ——, who, being duly sworn according to law, declare that they are the children and heirs of ——, who was a —— of company ——, commanded by Captain ——, in the —— regiment of —— volunteers; that the said —— volunteered at ——, on or about the —— day of ——, 18—, for ——, and [died *or* was killed] at ——, on or about the —— day of ——, 18—, while in said service; that the said —— left surviving him no widow, nor child or children, other than these claimants.

This declaration is made for the purpose of obtaining the arrears of pay, bounty money, extra pay, and all other arrearages or sums of money due by reason of the services of the soldier above named; and —— is hereby constituted —— attorney to prosecute this claim, and is authorized to receive and receipt for a draft payable to the order of this declarant or declarants for whatever sum may be allowed on the same, and to assign and convert the same into current funds.

Attest: (*Two Witnesses.*) (*Signature of Heirs.*)

Sworn to, subscribed and acknowledged before me the day and year first above written, and on the same day personally appeared ——, and ——, residents of ——, who being duly sworn according to law, declare that they are personally acquainted with ——, and ——, who have made and subscribed the foregoing declaration, and know that they are the children and heirs-at-law of ——, who was a —— in Captain —— company —— of the —— regiment of —— volunteers, and who died or was killed while in the service of the United States, as stated in said declaration. That the said ——, left surviving him no widow, or child or children, other than the said —— and ——. That their knowledge of their identity as heirs of the soldier named is derived from personal acquaintance. That they reside as above stated, and are disinterested in this claim. (*Witnesses' Signatures.*)

Sworn to and subscribed before me, and I certify that I am not interested in this claim, or concerned in its prosecution; and I believe the affiants to be credible persons, and the declarants the persons they represent themselves to be. (*Officer's Signature.*)

Here must follow the certificate of the Clerk, as in the preceding case.

When there are several heirs, and it will be difficult to have them unite in a declaration, one of them should take out letters of administration, and make the claim as administrator.

The foregoing several declarations may readily be

altered to suit the cases of father, mother, brothers or sisters of deceased soldiers.

Application of Soldier for Arrears of Pay, or for Arrears of Pay and Bounty.

STATE OF —— } ss.
County of —— }

On this —— day of ——, 18—, before me, a ——, in and for the county and State above named, and by law duly authorized to administer oaths for general purposes, personally appeared ——, aged —— years, who being duly sworn according to law, declares that he is not indebted or accountable to the United States on any account whatever; and he further states that he is the identical ——, who was a —— in company ——, commanded by Captain ——, in the —— regiment of —— volunteers, commanded by Colonel ——; that he enlisted at ——, in the State of ——, on or about the —— day of ——, 18—, for the term of ——, and was honorably discharged at ——, on or about the —— day of ——, 18—, by reason of the expiration of his term of service;[1] and that he claims there is due him from the United States, for pay and allowances, as follows:——

He makes this declaration to obtain the arrears of pay, bounty money, extra pay, and all other arrearages or sums of money due him by reason of the services above named; and he hereby constitutes and appoints ——, his attorney, to prosecute this claim, and authorizes him to receive and receipt for a certificate for whatever sum may be allowed on the same, and to attend to and procure the settlement of such business as deponent may have with the United States, in any office or department of the same, and to receive and receipt for all sums of money that may be found due deponent, upon any account or claim now unsettled.

Attest: (*Two Witnesses.*) (*Signature of Claimant.*)

Sworn to, and subscribed and acknowledged before me, the day and year first above mentioned, and on the same day personally came before me —— and ——, residents of ——, to me known as credible witnesses, who being duly sworn according to law, declare that they are personally acquainted with ——, who has made and subscribed the foregoing declaration, and know that he is the identical person who performed the service therein named; that their knowledge of his identity is derived from ——. That they are disinterested in the claim, and reside at the place above named. (*Signatures of Witnesses.*)

---

[1] Bounty money can only be claimed at the expiration of two years from the time of enlistment, or at the end of the war. Should the foregoing form be used for obtaining arrears of pay only, the reason of discharge may be given according to the fact.

Sworn to and subscribed before me; and I certify that I am not interested in the claim or concerned in its prosecution; and I further certify that I know the affiants to be credible witnesses, and the declarant is the person he represents himself to be.

(*Officer's Signature.*)

This must be followed by the certificate of the Clerk of the proper Court, under seal, in the usual form.

Power of Attorney for Drawing Bounty or Pay.

Know all men by these presents: That I, ——, a —— in company — —, commanded by Captain ——, of the —— regiment of —— volunteers, commanded by Colonel ——, do hereby make, constitute and appoint ——, of ——, my true and lawful attorney, for me and in my name, place and stead, to ask, demand, receive and receipt for any and all bounty, pay or other money due me from the United States Government, for services in said company. And I do hereby authorize my said attorney, for me, to sign the pay roll of said regiment and perform any and all other acts necessary to be done in the premises as fully, to all intents and purposes, as I, myself, if personally present, could do, hereby ratifying all that my said attorney shall or may do in the premises.

In testimony whereof I hereto set my hand and seal, this —— day of ——, A. D., 18—.

Executed in presence of } [L. S.]
(*Witnesses.*)

STATE OF —— } ss.
County of ——

On this —— day of ——, A. D., 18—, before me, a —— within and for said county, personally came ——, to me well known to be the identical person he represents himself to be, and acknowledged the signing and sealing of the foregoing power of attorney, for the purposes therein expressed.

And I certify that I have no interest whatsoever in the claim of the said ——.

(*Officer's Signature.*)

Add certificate and seal as in other cases.

CHAPTER XXV.

PAY—ARMY AND NAVY.[1]

THE following Tables of Pay are inserted for the convenience of claimants. In pension cases the monthly rates are governed by the monthly pay proper, exclusive of subsistence, forage, etc. In applications for pay, claimants will include commutation of rations, forage, servants, etc.

I.

ARMY PAY AT THE CLOSE OF THE REVOLUTION.[2]

RANK OR GRADE.	PER MO.
Major-General	$166
Aid-de-Camp	50
Brigadier-General of Cavalry	156¼
Brigadier-General	125
Aid-de-Camp	50
Brigadier-Major of Cavalry, Artillery or Infantry	50
Brigade-Quartermaster	15*
Brigade-Chaplain	50
Quartermaster-General	166⅔
Deputy Quartermaster-General with Southern Army	125
Same, with Main Army	75
Assistants, each	30
Commissary of Forage for Main Army	60
Same, for Southern Army	60
Wagonmaster	60
Deputy Wagonmaster for Southern Army	50
Wagon Conductor	20
Director of Artificers	40
Sub do do	26⅔
Adjutant-General	125
Deputy do	75
Ass't. do	50
Ass't. Deputy do	50
Clerk to Adjutant-General	40
Inspector-General	300
His Secretary	$50
Inspector for separate army	30*
Assistant do	10*
Paymaster-General	150
Deputy do, and Ass't Deputy 8-10ths per cent. on money disbursed.	
Deputy Paymaster-General for Southern Army	75
Do for Main Army	75
Assistant Paymaster-General	70
Director of Hospital	102
Deputy do, and Physician	100
Surgeon	90
Apothecary and Purveyor	92
Deputy do	59
Mates, each	42
Stewards, each	31
Wardmasters, each	21
Commissary-General of Military Stores, per annum	1000
Assistants or Superintendents, pay in the line only.	
Field Commissary of Military Stores	50
Deputy do	40
Conductor or Clerk	30
Commissary of Prisoners for Army	75

[1] For extra pay, see that title, Chapter XXVI, page 423.

[2] This is pay proper, and does not include rations, forage, or other emoluments.

* In addition to pay in the line.

TABLES OF PAY—ARMY.

RANK OR GRADE.	PER MO.
Assistant Com. Pris. of Army	$40
Commissary of Marine Prisoners, alias, *Deputy*, with separate Army, per annum	1200
Geographer to Main Army	60
Do Southern Army	60
Assistant Geographer - -	30
Chain Bearer - - -	15
Judge-Advocate - - -	75
Deputy do, for Southern Army, from the line -	60
Deputy do, in same army with Judge-Advocate - -	15*
Clothier-General, per annum	5000
Deputies—pay fixed by the Clothier-General.	
Surveyor of Ordnance -	40*
Inspector of Rations, etc., for Southern Army - -	166⅔
Do for Main Army -	166⅔
Captain of Engineers -	50
Lieutenant - - -	33⅓
Sergeant - - -	10
Corporal - - - -	9
Private - - -	8⅓
Colonel of Infantry - -	100
Lieutenant-Col. do - -	95
Major - - - -	62⅓
Captain - - - -	50
Captain Lieutenant - -	33⅓
First do - - -	33⅓
Second do - - -	33⅓
Paymaster and Clothier -	30*
Adjutant - - - -	16*
Quartermaster - - -	16*
Surgeon - - - -	59
Surgeon's-Mate - -	42
Sergeant-Major - - -	11¼
Quartermaster-Sergeant -	11¼
Fife-Major - - - -	10⅓
Drum do - - - -	10⅓
Sergeant - - - -	10
Bombardier - - -	9
Corporal - - - -	9
Gunner - - - -	8⅔
Drummer - - - -	8⅔
Fifer - - - -	8⅔
Matross - - - -	8⅓
Colonel of Cavalry - -	93¾

RANK OR GRADE.	PER MO.
Lieutenant-Colonel Cavalry	$75
Major - - - -	60
Captain - - - - -	50
Lieutenant - - -	33⅓
Cornet - - - - -	26⅔
Ridingmaster - -	33⅓
Paymaster of Battalion -	25*
Adjutant of do -	15*
Quartermaster of do - -	15*
Surgeon of do -	60
Surgeon's-Mate - - -	40
Quartermaster-Sergeant -	15
Sergeant - - - -	15
Trumpet-Major - -	11
Trumpeter - - - -	10
Saddler - - - - -	10
Farrier - - - - -	10
Corporal - - -	10
Dragoon - - - - -	8⅓
Colonel of Infantry -	75
Lieutenant-Colonel - -	60
Major - - - - -	50
Captain - - - - -	40
Captain Lieutenant - -	26⅔
Lieutenant - - -	26⅔
Ensign - - - -	20
Paymaster and Clothier -	30
Adjutant - - -	13
Quartermaster - - -	13*
Surgeon - - - -	59
Surgeon's-Mate - - -	40
Sergeant-Major - -	10
Quartermaster-Sergeant -	10
Sergeant - - -	10
Drum-Major - - -	9
Fife-Major - - -	9
Drummer - - - - -	7⅓
Fifer - - - - -	7⅓
Corporal - - - - -	7⅓
Private - - - - -	6⅔
Captain of Provosts - -	50
Lieutenant - - -	33⅓
Clerk - - - - -	33⅓
Quartermaster-Sergeant -	15
Sergeants - - - - -	15
Trumpeters - - -	10
Corporals - - - -	10
Executioners - - -	10
Provosts or Privates - -	8⅓

* In addition to pay in the line.

II.

PAY PROPER OF THE ARMY AT THE CLOSE OF THE WAR OF 1812.

RANK OR GRADE.	PER MO.	RANK OR GRADE.	PER MO.
Major-General	$200	Assistant Com. Mil. Sup.	$60
Secretary to General commanding Army	24*	Superintendent of Artificers	45
Aid-de-Camp to Major-Gen.	24*	Assistant do	30
Brigadier-General	104	Master Workman of Artificers	30
Aid to do	20*	Under do do	16
Brigade Major	24*	Colonel of Ordnance	90
Do Chaplain	50	Lieutenant do	75
Judge-Advocate	50	Major do	60
Adjutant and Inspector-General	104	Captain do	50
Adjutant-General	90	1st Lieutenant do	33⅓
Inspector do	90	2d do do	33⅓
Assistant do	60	3d do do	30
Topographical Engineers	60	Master Armorer of Ordnance	30
Assistant do	40	Master Carriagemaker do	30
Paymaster-General	166⅔	Master Blacksmith do	30
Deputy do	50*	Armorer of Ordnance	16
Assistant do	30*	Carriagemaker do	16
District Paymaster	50	Blacksmith do	16
Assistant do	40	Artificer do	13
Quartermaster-General	104	Laborer do	9
Same	75	Physician and Surgeon-Gen'l	208⅓
Deputy Quartermaster-Gen.	60	Apothecary-General	150
Assistant do do	40	Assistant Apothecary	45
Principal Wagonmaster	40	Hospital Surgeon	75
Wagonmaster	30	Hospital Mate	40
Assistant Foragemaster	30	Steward of Hospital	20
Conductor of Artillery	33⅓	Wardmaster do	16
Principal Barrackmaster	40	Garrison Surgeon	45
Deputy do	30	Garrison Mate	30
Commissary-General of Purchases	250	Professor of Natural and Experimental Philosophy	60
Deputy Commissary-General of Purchases, 2½ per cent. on disbursements.		Assistant do do	40
Superintendent-Gen'l of Military Supplies	250	Professor of Mathematics	50
Special Commissary of Military Supplies	60	Assistant do	40
		Professor of the Art of Engineering	50
		Assistant do do	40
		Teacher of the French Language	40
		Teacher of Drawing	40

* In addition to pay in the line.

TABLES OF PAY—ARMY.

RANK AND GRADE.	ENGINEERS.	LIGHT INFANTRY	ARTILLERY.	LIGHT DRAG'NS.	INFANTRY AND RIFLEMEN.	RANGERS.	SEA-FENCIBLES.
Colonel - - - - - - -	$75	$90	$90	$90	$75		
Lieutenant-Colonel - - -	60	75	75	75	60		
Major - - - - - - -	50	60	60	60	50		
Adjutant and Paymaster, each -	10*	10*	10*	10*	10*		
Quartermaster - - - - -		10*	10*	10*	10*		
Surgeon - - - - - -		60		60	60		
Surgeon's-Mate - - - - -		45		45	45		
Sergeant-Major - - - - -		12		12	12		
Quartermaster-Sergeant - - -		12		12	12		
Principal Musician - - -	11	11		11	11		
Captain - - - - - - -	40	50	50	50	40	50	40
1st Lieutenant - - - - -	30	33⅓	33⅓	33⅓	30	33⅓	30
2d Lieutenant - - - - -	25	33⅓	33⅓	33⅓	25	33⅓	25
2d Lieut. and Conductor of Artillery		33⅓					
3d do do do		30	30	30	23	30	23
Cornet - - - - - -				26⅔			
Ensign - - - - - - -					20	26⅔	
Ridingmaster - - - - -			56⅔				
Master of the Sword - - - -			26⅔				
Cadet of Military Academy -	16						
Sergeant - - - - - -	11	11	11	11	11		
Corporal - - - - - -	10	10	10	10	10		
Musician - - - - - - -	9	9	9	9	9		
Private - - - - - -	8	8	8	8	8		
Boatswain of Fencibles - - -							20
Gunner do - -							20
Quartergunner do - - -							18
Men of Quartergunner of Fencibles							12
Driver of Artillery - - - - -		8					
Artificer - - - - - -	13	13					
Saddler - - - - - - -		13		13			
Farrier - - - - - -		13		13			
Blacksmith - - - - - -				13			

* In addition to pay in the line.

† Officers of rangers when *mounted* receive the same pay, etc., as dragoon officers; when *not* mounted, the same pay as infantry officers.

III.

PAY OF THE ARMY PRIOR TO JANUARY 1, 1855.

RANK AND CLASSIFICATION OF OFFICERS.	PAY.	SUBSISTENCE. 20 cts. for each ration.		FORAGE $8 per month each horse.		SERVANTS. Pay, etc., of a private.		TOTAL MONTHLY PAY.
	PER MONTH.	NO. OF RATIONS.	MONTHLY COMMUTATION VAL.	NO. OF HORSES.	MONTHLY COMMUTATION VAL.	NO. OF SERV'TS.	MONTHLY COMMUTATION VAL.	
Major-General - - - - -	$200	15	$90	3	$24	4	$62.00	376.00
Senior Aid to General-in-Chief	60	4	24	3	24	2	33.00	141.00
Aid-de-Camp - - - - -	24*	1	6	1	8			38.00
Brigadier-General - - -	104	12	72	3	24	3	46.50	246.50
Aid-de-Camp - - - - -	20*			1	8			28.00
Adjutant-General (Col.) - -	90	6	36	3	24	2	33.00	183.00
Assistant Adjutant-General (Col.)	75	5	30	3	24	2	33.00	162.00
do do do (Major)	60	4	24	3	24	2	33.00	141.00
do do do (Capt.)	50	4	24	1	8	1	16.50	98.50
Judge Advocate (Major) - -	60	4	24	3	24	2	33.00	141.00
Inspector-General (Colonel) - -	90	6	36	3	24	2	33.00	183.90
Quartermaster-General (Brig.-Gen.)	104	12	72	3	24	3	46.50	246.50
Assistant Q. M. General (Col.) -	90	6	36	3	24	2	33.00	183.00
Deputy Q. M. General (Lieut.-Col.)	75	5	30	3	24	2	33.00	162.00
Quartermaster (Major) - -	60	4	24	3	24	2	33.00	141.00
Assistant Quartermaster (Captain)	50	4	24	1	8	1	16.50	98.50
Com.-Gen. of Subsistence (Col.) -	90	6	36	3	24	2	33.00	183.00
Assist. Com.-Gen. Sub. (Lieut.-Col.)	75	5	30	3	24	2	33.00	162.00
Commissary of Subsistence (Major)	60	4	24	3	24	2	33.00	141.00
do do (Captain)	50	4	24	1	8	1	16.50	98.50
Assistant Commissary of Subsistence	20*							20.00
Paymaster-General, $2,500 per an.								208.33
Deputy Paymaster-General - -	75	5	30	3	24	2	33.00	162.00
Paymaster - - - - -	60	4	24	3	24	2	33.00	141.00
Surgeon-General, $2,500 per annum								208.33
Surgeons, 10 years' service - -	60	8	48	3	24	2	33.00	165.00
Surgeons, less than 10 years' service	60	4	24	3	24	2	33.00	141.00
Assist. Surg., 10 years' service -	50	8	48	1	8	1	16.50	122.50
do do 5 years' service	50	4	24	1	8	1	16.50	98.50
do do less than 5 y'rs serv.	33⅓	4	24	1	8	1	16.50	81.83
ENGINEERS, TOPOGRAPHICAL ENGINEERS AND ORDNANCE:								
Colonel - - - - - -	90	6	36	3	24	2	33.00	183.00

* In addition to pay in the line.

PAY OF THE ARMY PRIOR TO JANUARY 1, 1855.—*Continued.*

RANK AND CLASSIFICATION OF OFFICERS.	PAY.	SUBSISTENCE. 20 cts. for each ration.		FORAGE $8 per month each horse.		SERVANTS. Pay, etc., of a private.		TOTAL MONTHLY PAY.
	PER MONTH.	NO. OF RATIONS.	MONTHLY COMMUTATION VAL.	NO. OF HORSES.	MONTHLY COMMUTATION VAL.	NO. OF SERV'TS.	MONTHLY COMMUTATION VAL.	
Lieutenant-Colonel - - -	$75	5	$30	3	$24	2	$33.00	162.00
Major - - - - - - -	60	4	24	3	24	2	33.00	141.00
Captain - - - - - -	50	4	24	1	8	1	16.50	98.50
1st Lieutenant - - - - -	33⅓	4	24	1	8	1	16.50	81.83
2d do (brevet same) -	33⅓	4	24	1	8	1	16.50	81.83
MOUNTED DRAGOONS AND RIFLEMEN:								
Colonel - - - - - -	90	6	36	3	24	2	33.00	183.00
Lieutenant-Colonel - - -	75	5	30	3	24	2	33.00	162.00
Major - - - - - - -	60	4	24	3	24	2	33.00	141.00
Captain - - - - - -	50	4	24	2	16	1	16.50	106.50
1st Lieutenant - - - - -	33⅓	4	24	2	16	1	16.50	89.83
2d do (brevet same) -	33⅓	4	24	2	16	1	16.50	89.83
Adj't and Reg. Quartermaster -	10*							10.00
ARTILLERY AND INFANTRY:								
Colonel - - - - - -	75	6	36	3	24	2	31.00	166.00
Lieutenant-Colonel - - -	60	5	30	3	24	2	31.00	145.00
Major - - - - - - -	50	4	24	3	24	2	31.00	129.00
Captain - - - - - -	40	4	24			1	15.50	79.50
1st Lieutenant - - - - -	30	4	24			1	15.50	69.50
2d do (brevet same) -	25	4	24			1	15.50	64.50
Adj't and Reg. Quartermaster -	10*			1	8			18.00

Prof. of Natural and Experimental Philosophy - -	$75
Assistant Prof. do - -	50
Prof. of Mathematics - -	60
Assistant do - -	50
Commander Corps Cadets -	60
Prof. of Engineering -	60
Asssistant do - -	50
Inst. of Practical Engineering	50
Prof. of Chemistry, Mineralogy and Geology - -	60
Assistant do do - -	50
Chaplain and Prof. of Ethics	60
Assistant Prof. do -	50
Teacher of French Language [1]	50
Teacher of Drawing [2] - -	50

* In addition to pay in the line.

1-2 These were changed to professorships, with the same pay as other professors, by act of March 3, 1855. (U. S. Statutes at Large, vol. x, 703.)

TABLES OF PAY—ARMY.

Master of the Sword [1] -	46⅔
Military Storekeeper, Clothing Depot, $1250 per annum.	
Storekeeper of Ordnance at Arsenals of Construction, $1250 per annum.	
Storekeeper of Ordnance, $800 per annum.	
Chaplain, not to exceed -	40
Sergeant-Major of Dragoons or Mounted Riflemen -	17
Quartermaster Sergeant do do	17
Chief Bugler do do	17
First Sergeant do do	16
Sergeant do do	13
Corporal do do	10
Bugler do do	9
Far. and Blacksmiths do do	11
Private do do	8
Master Armorer, Ordnance [2] -	30
Master Carriagemaker, do [3]	30
Master Blacksmith, do [4]	30
Armorer, do [5]	16
Blacksmith, do [6]	16
Carriage Maker, do [7]	16
Artificer [8] - - - - -	13
Laborer - - - - -	9
Hospital Steward, at a post of more than four companies, pay of Ordnance Sergeant -	18
Hospital Steward (first Sergeant)	16
Matron - - - - -	6
ARTILLERY AND INFANTRY:	
Cadet [9] - - - - -	24
Sergeant-Major - -	17
Quartermaster-Sergeant -	17
Principal Musician, Infantry	17
First Sergeant - - -	16
Ordnance Sergeant, in addition to pay of Sergeant -	5
Sergeant - - - - -	12
Corporal - - - -	9
Artificer of Artillery - -	11
Musician - - - - -	8
Private - - - - -	7
SAPPERS, MINERS AND PONTONIERS:	
Sergeant - - - -	30
Corporal - - - - -	16
Musician - - - -	8
Private, first class - -	13
Private, second do - -	9

The pay of the army has been increased, and additional officers have been created, by sundry acts, which will be found after these tables.

1 By act of May 10, 1854 (U. S. Statutes at Large, vol. x, 277), this was changed to $1200 per annum; and by act of February 16, 1857 (U. S. Statutes at Large, vol. xi, 161), was increased to $1500 per annum, with fuel and quarters.

2-8 An appropriation act of July 5, 1862, contains the following section:

SEC. 3. *And be it further enacted,* That the enlisted men of the Ordnance Department now designated as master-workmen shall hereafter be designated and mustered as sergeants; those now designated as armorers, carriage makers and blacksmiths shall be designated and mustered as corporals; those now designated as artificers shall be designated and mustered as privates of the first class, and those now designated as laborers shall be designated and mustered as privates of the second class: *Provided,* That the pay, rations and clothing now authorized by law to the respective grades of enlisted ordnance men shall not be changed.

9 This was increased to $30 per month, by act of March 3, 1857 (U. S. Statutes at Large vol. xi, 252.)

TABLES OF NAVY PAY.

IV.

PAY OF THE NAVY IN THE REVOLUTION.

GRADE.	PAY.	VESSEL OF 20 GUNS.	VESSEL OF 10 TO 20 GUNS.	VESSEL UNDER 10 GUNS.
Captain	$32 00	$60 00	$48 00	$48 00
Lieutenants Commanding				30 00
Lieutenants	20 00	34 00	24 00	24 00
Surgeon	21 33	25 00	21 33	21 33
Surgeon's Mate	13 33	15 00	13 33	13 33
Purser	21 33	34 00	24 00	24 00
Chaplain	20 00			
Master	20 00	30 00	24 00	24 00
Mate	15 00			
Midshipmen	12 00			
Boatswain	15 00	15 00	13 00	12 00
Gunner	15 00	15 00	13 00	12 00
Carpenter	15 00	15 00	13 00	12 00
Sailmaker	10 00			
Captain's Clerk	15 00	15 00	12 00	12 00
Boatswain's Mates, first	9 50			
Do do second	8 00	9 50	9 00	9 00
Carpenter's Mates	10 66	9 50	9 00	9 00
Coxswains	9 00			
Gunner's Mates	10 66	9 50	9 00	9 00
Quartergunners	8 00			
Master-at-Arms		10 00	9 80	9 00
Armorer	9 00			
Steward	10 00			
Cooper	9 00			
Cook	12 00	9 00	8 50	8 50
Quartermaster	9 00	9 00	8 50	8 50
Sailor's Mate	8 33			
Yeoman	9 00	9 60	9 00	9 00
Seaman	8 00			
Pilot (usual rate)				

V.

PAY OF THE NAVY IN 1813.

GRADE.	MONTHLY PAY.
Captain of a vessel of 32 guns and upwards	$100
Captain of a vessel of 20 guns or under 32 guns	75
Master commandant	60
Lieutenant	40
Lieutenant Commanding	50
Chaplain	40
Surgeon	50
Surgeon's Mate	30

TABLES OF NAVY PAY.

GRADE.	MONTHLY PAY.	GRADE.	MONTHLY PAY.
Master - - - - -	$40	Yeoman of the Gun-room -	$18
Purser - - - - -	40	Quartergunner - - -	18
Boatswain - - - - -	20	Quartermaster - -	18
Gunner - - - - -	20	Carpenter 's Mate - -	19
Sailmaker - - - - -	20	Armorer - - -	18
Carpenter - - -	20	Steward - - - - -	18
Midshipman - - -	19	Cooper - - - - -	18
Master's Mate - - -	20	Master-at-Arms - - -	18
Captain's Clerk - -	25	Cook - - - - -	18
Boatswain's Mate - -	19	Seaman - - - -	12
Cockswain - - -	18	Ordinary Seaman - -	10

VI.

PAY OF THE NAVY, JANUARY 1, 1835.

GRADE.	HALF OF MONTHLY PAY.	GRADE.	HALF OF MONTHLY PAY.
Captain - - - - -	$50	Sailmaker - - -	$10
Commander or Master Commandant, and Lieutenant Commanding - - -	30	Sailmaker's Mate - -	9½
Lieutenant - - -	25	Master-at-Arms - -	9
Sailing Master or Master -	20	Armorer - - - - -	9
Passed Midshipman -	12½	Cook - - - - -	9
Midshipman - - -	9½	Cockswain - - - -	9
Surgeon, $35, or $30, or $27½, or $25, according to length of service.		Stewards, all kinds - -	9
Passed Assistant Surgeon, $22½ or $17½, according to length of service.		Captain of main or fore top, or forecastle - -	7½
Assistant Surgeon - -	15	Captain's Clerk - - -	12½
Purser - - - - -	20	Purser's Clerk - -	12½
Chaplain - - - - -	20	Ship's Corporal - - -	7
Pilot - - - - -	20	Seaman - - -	6
Master's Mate - - -	10	Ordinary Seaman - -	5
Gunner - - -	10	Landsman - - -	4
Gunner's Mate - - -	9½	Boy - - - - - -	3
Boatswain - - -	10	ENGINEERS.	
Boatswain's Mate - -	9½	Engineer-in-Chief - -	—
Carpenter - - -	10	Chief Engineer - -	25
Carpenter's Mate - -	9½	First Assistant Engineer -	15
		Second do do -	10
		Third do do - -	10
		Fireman, first and second class	6
		Coal-Heavers - - -	6

VII.

NAVY PAY UNDER THE ACT OF MARCH 2, 1835.

RADE.	ON LEAVE OR WAITING ORDERS. PER ANNUM.	NAVY YARDS OR OTHER DUTY, PER ANNUM.	SEA SERVICE, PER ANNUM.	OF THE FLEET, PER ANNUM.
Captains—Senior in Service	$3500	$4500	$4500	
of Squadrons			4000	
others	2500	3500	3500	
Commanders.	1800	2100	2500	
Lieutenants—commanding			1800	
others	1200	1500	1500	
Surgeons—1st five years of commission	1000	1250	1333	1500
2d " " "	1250	1500	1600	1800
3d " " "	1400	1750	1866	2100
4th " " "	1600	2000	2133	2400
20 years and upwards	1800	2250	2400	2700
Passed Assistant Surgeons	859	1150	1260	
Assistant Surgeons	650	950	950	
Pursers—of Ships of the Line			3500	
of Frigates or Razees			3000	
of Sloops or Steamers, 1st class			2000	
of Brigs, Schooners and Steamers, less than first class			1500	
of Naval Station, California[1]		3000		
of Navy Yards and Receiving Ships at Boston, New York and Norfolk, and Navy Yard at Pensacola		2500		
of Navy Yards at Portsmouth, Philadelphia and Washington		2000		
of Naval Stations within the U. S. and at other places		1500		
1st five years of commission	1000			
2d " " " "	1200			
3d " " " "	1600			
Twenty years and upwards	1800			
Chaplains	800	1200	1200	
Professors of Mathematics	800	1500	1500	
Passed Midshipmen	600	750	750	
Midshipmen	300	350	400	
Masters—Ships of the Line			1100	
others	750	1000	1000	
Masters' Mates—warranted	300	450	450	

1 This was increased to $4000, by act of March 3, 1853. (U. S. Statutes at Large, vol. x, 616.)

TABLES OF NAVY PAY.

GRADE.	ON LEAVE OR WAITING ORDERS, PER ANNUM.	NAVY YARDS OR OTHER DUTY, PER ANNUM.	SEA SERVICE, PER ANNUM.	OF THE FLEET, PER ANNUM.
Boatswains—Ships of the Line - -			800	
of Navy Yards at Boston, New York, Norfolk and Pensacola		800		
on other duty - - -		700	700	
1st Ten Years' Service -	500			
after " " - -	600			
Gunners, Carpenters and Sailmakers, same as Boatswains - - - - - -				
Chief Engineers—1st Five Years - -	1200	1500	1500	
after - - -	1400	2000	2000	
First Assistant Engineers - - -	850	1000	1000	
Second " " - - -	600	800	800	
Third - - - - - - - -	400	600	600	

GRADE.	PAY PER ANN.
Navy Agents, commission not to exceed - - - -	$2000
Temporary Navy Agents -	
Naval Storekeepers - -	
Officers of Navy on Foreign Stations - - - -	1500
Engineer-in-chief - -	3000
Naval Constructors - -	2300
Agents for inspection, etc. of Hemp - - - -	1000
Agents for preservation of Live Oak Timber - - -	1000
Secretaries to Commanders of Squadrons when commanding-in-chief - - -	1000
Agents do. not com.-in-chief	900
Clerks of Yards or Com. of Yards second to Commanders of Yards	750
Clerks to Commanders of Squadrons - - - - -	500
Clerks to Captains of Fleets and Commanders of Vessels	500
Clerks or Assistants to Pursers in Ships-of-the-Line -	700
Clerks in Frigates and Navy Yards at Boston, New York and Norfolk - - -	500

GRADE.	PAY PER MO.
Yeoman—Ships of the Line	$40
Yeoman—Frigate - - -	35
Yeoman—Sloop - - -	28
Yeoman—Smaller Vessel -	18
Armorer—Ships of the Line	25
Armorer—Frigate - - -	$20
Armorer—Sloop - - -	15
Mates, Master's, not warranted	25
Mates—Boatswain's - -	19
Mates, Gunner's - - -	19
Mates, Carpenter's - -	19
Mates, Sailmaker's - -	15
Mates, Armorer's - -	15
Master-at-Arms - - -	19
Ship's Corporal - - -	15
Coxswains - - - -	18
Quartermasters - - -	15
Quartergunners - - -	15
Captains of Forecastle - -	18
Captains of Tops - -	15
Captains of Afterguard -	15
Captains of Hold - -	15
Coopers - - - - -	15
Painters - - - - -	15
Stewards, Ship's - - -	24
Stewards, Officer's - -	18
Stewards, Surgeon's - -	18
Cooks, Ship's - - -	18
Cooks, Officer's - - -	15
Masters of the Band - -	18
Musicians, first class - -	12
Musicians, second class -	10
Seamen - - - -	12
Ordinary Seamen - -	10
Landsmen - - - -	9
Boys - - - - -	6 to 8
Firemen, first class - -	30
Firemen, second class -	20
Coal-heavers - - -	15

One ration only, per day, is allowed to each officer attached to vessels for sea service, since the passage of the act of March 3, 1835.

For the changes in the rates of pay which have been made since the passage of the act of March 3, 1835, see sundry acts in the latter portion of this Chapter.

VIII.

PAY OF THE MARINE CORPS—REVOLUTION.

GRADE.	PAY PER MO.	GRADE.	PAY PER MO.
Captain - - - -	$30 00	Drummer - - - -	$7 33
Lieutenant - - -	18 00	Fifer - - - - -	7 33
Sergeant - - - -	8 00	Marine - - - -	6 66
Corporal - - -	7 33		

IX.

PAY OF MARINES, MARCH 3, 1835.

GRADE.	PER MO.	GRADE.	PER MO.
Colonel - - - -	$	Orderly Sergeant - -	$8
Lieutenant-Colonel - -	30	Sergeant - - - - -	6½
Major - - - - - -	25	Corporal - - - - -	4½
Captain - - - - -	20	Private - - - - -	3½
Lieutenant—1st and 2d - -	15	Musician - - - - -	4

X.

PAY OF MARINE CORPS PRIOR TO AUGUST, 1854.

GRADE.	PER MO.
Colonel Commandant - -	$75
Lieutenant-Colonel, at sea or on leave - - - - -	60
Lieutenant-Colonel commanding	60
Majors, at sea or on leave -	50
Majors, commanding - -	50
Staff Captains - - -	
Staff Adjutant and Inspector	60
Staff Pay and Quartermasters, each - - - - - -	60
Staff Lieutenants - -	
Staff Assistant Quartermasters	50
Captains, at sea or on leave, 30 years' service - - -	40
Captains, do 25 years' service	40
Captains, do 20 " "	40
Captains, on shore duty, 30 yrs' service - - - - -	40
Captains, on shore duty, 25 years' service - - - - -	40
Captains, on shore duty, 20 years' service - - - -	40
Captains, commanding guard in receiving ship or squadron, 30, 25 or 20 years' service -	40
First Lieutenants, at sea or on leave, 20, 15 or 10 years' service - - - - - - -	30
First Lieutenants, on shore duty, 20, 15 or 10 years' service -	30
First Lieutenants, commanding guard in receiving ship or squadron, 15 or 10 years' service - - - - - -	30
Second Lieutenants, at sea or on leave, 10, 5 or less than 5 yrs' service - - - - -	25
Second Lieutenants, on shore duty, 10, 5 or less than 5 yrs' service - - - - -	25
Second Lieutenants, commanding guard in receiving ship or squadron - - - - -	25

LAWS, GENERAL AND SPECIAL, RELATING TO ARMY PAY.

By acts of May, 13, 1846,[1] and June 18, 1846,[2] the pay of volunteers and militia in the war with Mexico is fixed at the same rates as in the case of regulars of the various grades. In addition, the last-named act allows fifty cents, in lieu of subsistence, and twenty-five cents in lieu of forage to mounted soldiers, for every twenty miles travel, by the most direct route, from their places of residence to the place of rendezvous or discharge.

JOINT RESOLUTION *directing the payment of certain Volunteers and Militia, under the Limitations therein prescribed.*[3]

Resolved by the Senate and House of Representatives of the United States of America in Congress assembled, That the Secretary of War be, and he is hereby, authorized and required to cause to be paid, out of the appropriation made by the act providing for the prosecution of the existing war between the United States of America and the Republic of Mexico, approved the thirteenth day of May, one thousand eight hundred and forty-six, to the volunteers and militia, called and actually received, by virtue of the orders of General E. P. Gaines, into the service of the United States, during the present year, and discharged before joining the army, and such companies as were actually organized and rendezvoused under said call, including the two companies of Major Gally's command, and the company at Baton Rouge arsenal; and also the company of Mississippi volunteers (Natchez Fencibles), and also the company of Mississippi volunteers (Pontotoc Rovers), organized and assembled at Vicksburg, and afterwards disbanded or discharged, and the companies of Ohio volunteers assembled at Camp Washington, near Cincinnati, and who claim to have been mustered into service, one day's pay and allowances for every day detained in service, and the usual traveling allowances, and no more. And further, that where States or individuals have paid the expenses or provided the means of

1 U. S. Statutes at Large, vol. ix, 9.

2 *Ibid*, vol. ix, 17.

3 *Ibid*, vol. ix, 115.

transportation of volunteers to the place of rendezvous, and furnished subsistence or clothing, the proportional amount thus furnished to each man, not exceeding the legal allowance to each, may be charged on the pay rolls, and withheld, and paid to the State or individual who actually provided the same. And further, that when surgeons and assistant surgeons have attended regiments of volunteers to the time when medical officers duly appointed by the United States entered upon their duties with said regiments, they may receive the same rate of compensation, and to a like number, as provided for by law; and persons doing the duties of assistant quartermasters and assistant commissaries, under like circumstances, may in like manner receive the same rate of compensation, and to a like number, as authorized by existing law.

Approved August 8, 1846.

AN ACT *to authorize the Secretary of War to settle and adjust the Expenses of the Rogue River Indian War.*

Be it enacted by the Senate and House of Representatives of the United States of America in Congress assembled, That the Secretary of War be, and he is hereby, authorized and directed to adjust and settle, on just and equitable principles, all claims for services rendered in the late war with the Rogue River Indians, in Oregon—known as the Rogue River war—according to the muster-rolls of the same; also for subsistence, forage, medical stores and expenditures, as well as for any other necessary and proper supplies furnished for the prosecution of said war; and that, on such adjustment [the same shall] be paid out of any moneys in the Treasury not otherwise appropriated.

Approved, July 17, 1854.

AN ACT *to increase the Pay of the Rank and File of the Army, and to encourage Enlistments.*[1]

Be it enacted by the Senate and House of Representatives of the United of America in Congress assembled, That the pay of the non-commissioned officers, musicians and privates[2] of the army of the United States, shall be increased at the rate of four dollars per month, and

1 U. S. Statutes at Large, vol. x, 575.

2 These words were by act of March 3, 1857 (U. S. Statutes at Large, vol. xi, 200), construed to include all enlisted men in the army.

to continue for the term of three years from and after the first day of January next, and until otherwise fixed by law.

SEC. 2. *And be it further enacted*, That every soldier, who, being honorably discharged from the service of the United States, shall, within one month thereafter, re-enlist, shall be entitled to two dollars per month, in addition to the ordinary pay of his grade, for the first period of five years after the expiration of his previous enlistment, and a further sum of one dollar per month for each successive period of five years, so long as he shall remain continually in the army; and that soldiers now in the army, who have served one or more enlistments, and been honorably discharged, shall be entitled to the benefits herein provided for a second enlistment.

SEC. 6. *And be it further enacted*, That the allowance to soldiers employed at work on fortifications, in surveys, in cutting roads, and other constant labor, of not less than ten days, authorized by the act approved March second, eighteen hundred and nineteen, entitled "an act to regulate the pay of the army when employed on fatigue duty," be increased to twenty-five cents per day for men employed as laborers and teamsters, and forty cents per day when employed as mechanics, at all stations east of the Rocky Mountains, and to thirty-five cents and fifty cents per day, respectively, when the men are employed at stations west of those mountains.[1]

Approved, August 4, 1854.

An act making appropriations for the support of the Military Academy, approved April 23, 1856,[2] allows additional compensation to certain persons in that institution, as follows:

Librarian and assistant librarian, not exceeding one hundred and twenty dollars each per annum; the non-commissioned officer in charge of mechanics' and other labor, the soldier acting as clerk in the adjutant's office, and the four enlisted men in the philosophical and chemical departments, not exceeding fifty dollars each per annum.

---

[1] U. S. Statutes at Large, vol. xi, 51. By act of August 5, 1854, these provisions are extended to the marine corps.

[2] *Ibid*, vol. xi, 5.

AN ACT *making Appropriations for the Support of the Military Academy for the Year ending the thirtieth of June, eighteen hundred and fifty-eight.*[1]

SEC. 2. *And be it further enacted*, That there shall be appointed at the military academy, in addition to the professors authorized by the existing laws, a professor of Spanish, at a salary of two thousand dollars per annum.

Approved, February 16, 1857.

AN ACT *to increase the Pay of the Officers of the Army.*

Be it enacted by the Senate and House of Representatives of the United States of America in Congress assembled, That from and after the commencement of the present fiscal year, the pay of each commissioned officer of the army, including military storekeepers, shall be increased twenty dollars per month, and that the commutation price of officers' subsistence shall be thirty cents per ration.

SEC. 2. *And be it further enacted*, That the Secretary of War be authorized, on the recommendation of the council of administration, to extend the additional pay herein provided to any person serving as a chaplain, at any post of the army.

Approved, February 21, 1857.

It is provided by "an act making appropriations for the support of the army for the year ending the thirtieth June, eighteen hundred and fifty-nine," approved June 12, 1858,[2] that "the superintendent of the military academy, while serving as such by appointment of the President, shall have the local rank, the pay and allowances of a colonel of engineers; that the commandant of the corps of cadets at the military academy while serving as such by appointment of the President, shall have the local rank, the pay and allowances of a lieutenant-colonel of engineers, and besides his other duties, shall be charged with the duty of instructor in the tactics of the

1 U. S. Statutes at Large, vol. xi, 160.

2 *Ibid*, vol. xi, 332.

three arms at said academy; and that the senior assistant instructor in each of the arms of service, viz: of artillery, cavalry and infantry, shall severally receive the pay and allowances of the assistant professor of mathematics."

AN ACT *to authorize the employment of Volunteers to aid in enforcing the Laws and protecting Public Property.*[1]

SEC. 5. *And be it further enacted*, That the officers, non-commissioned officers and privates, organized as above set forth, shall, in all respects, be placed on the footing, as to pay and allowances, of similar corps of the regular army: *Provided*, That the allowances of non-commissioned officers and privates for clothing, when not furnished in kind, shall be three dollars and fifty cents per month, and that each company officer, non-commissioned officer, private, musician and artificer of cavalry shall furnish his own horse and horse equipments, and shall receive forty cents per day for their use and risk, except that in case the horse shall become disabled, or shall die, the allowance shall cease until the disability be removed or another horse be supplied.[2] Every volunteer non-commissioned officer, private, musician and artificer, who enters the service of the United States under this act, shall be paid at the rate of fifty cents in lieu of subsistence, and if a cavalry volunteer, twenty-five cents additional, in lieu of forage, for every twenty miles of travel from his place of enrollment to the place of muster—the distance to be measured by the shortest usually traveled route; and when honorably discharged an allowance at the same rate, from the place of his discharge to his place of enrollment, and, in addition thereto, if he shall have served for a period of two years, or during the war if sooner ended, the sum of one hundred dollars: *Provided*, That such of the companies of cavalry herein provided for, as may require it, may be furnished with horses and horse equipments in the same manner as in the United States army.

SEC. 7. *And be it further enacted*, That the bands of the regi-

1 U. S. Statutes at Large, vol. xii, 268.

2 This allowance of forty cents per day for the risk and use of horses was repealed by an act of July 17, 1862.

ments of infantry and of the regiments of cavalry shall be paid as follows: one fourth of each shall receive the pay and allowances of sergeants of engineer soldiers; one fourth those of corporals of engineer soldiers; and the remaining half those of privates of engineer soldiers of the first class; and the leaders of the band shall receive the same pay and emoluments as second lieutenants of infantry.[1]

SEC. 8. *And be it further enacted*, That the wagoners and saddlers shall receive the pay and allowances of corporals of cavalry. The regimental commissary-sergeant shall receive the pay and allowances of regimental sergeant-major, and the regimental quartermaster-sergeant shall receive the pay and allowances of a sergeant of cavalry.

SEC. 9. *And be it further enacted*, That there shall be allowed to each regiment one chaplain, who shall be appointed by the regimental commander on the vote of the field officers and company commanders on duty with the regiment at the time the appointment shall be made. The chaplain so appointed must be a regular ordained minister of a Christain denomination, and shall receive the pay and allowances of a captain of cavalry, and shall be required to report to the colonel commanding the regiment to which he is attached, at the end of each quarter, the moral and religious condition of the regiment, and such suggestions as may conduce to the social happiness and moral improvement of the troops.[2]

Approved, July 22, 1861.

An Act for the Relief of the Ohio and other Volunteers.

Whereas, the War Department has decided that the term of service of the ninety days' volunteers, called out under the act of seventeen hundred and ninety-five, commenced only on the day when they where actually sworn into the service of the United States; and whereas, the troops now in service of the United States from the State of Ohio were not sworn into said service until some days after their organization and acceptance as companies by the governor of said State, and that for such period, under existing laws, no payment can be made: Therefore,

1 This section is repealed by act of July 17, 1862, and other provision is made for the employment of bands.

2 This section amended by act of July 17, 1862.

Be it enacted by the Senate and House of Representatives of the United States of America in Congress assembled, That the proper disbursing officer compute and pay to the said volunteers compensation from the day of their organization and acceptance as companies by the governor of the State of Ohio, as aforesaid, until the expiration of their term of service.

SEC. 2. *And be it further enacted,* That where the militia of other States are situated similarly with those of Ohio, the War Department pay them according to the provisions of the foregoing section.

Approved, July 24, 1861.

AN ACT *in addition to the "act to authorize the employment of Volunteers to aid in enforcing the Laws and protecting Public Property," approved July twenty-second, eighteen hundred and sixty-one.*[1]

Be it enacted by the Senate and House of Representatives of the United States of America in Congress assembled, That the President of the United States be, and he is hereby, authorized to accept the services of volunteers, either as cavalry, infantry or artillery, in such numbers as the exigencies of the public service may, in his opinion, demand, to be organized as authorized by the act of the twenty-second of July, eighteen hundred and sixty-one: *Provided,* That the number of troops hereby authorized shall not exceed five hundred thousand.

SEC. 2. *And be it further enacted,* That the volunteers authorized by this act shall be armed as the President may direct; they shall be subject to the rules and articles of war, and shall be upon the footing, in all respects, with similar corps of the United States army, and shall be mustered into the service for "during the war."

Approved, July 25, 1861.

AN ACT *to increase the present Military Establishment of the United States.*[2]

SEC. 4. *And be it further enacted,* That the officers and enlisted men raised in pursuance of the foregoing sections shall receive the same pay, emoluments and allowances, and be on the same footing, in every respect, with those of corresponding grades and corps now in the regular service. The regimental bands will be paid as fol-

[1] U. S. Statutes at Large, vol. xii, 274.

[2] *Ibid,* vol. xii, 279.

lows: one fourth of each, the pay and allowances of sergeants of engineer soldiers; one fourth, those of corporals of engineer soldiers; and one half, those of engineer soldiers of the first class.[1] The drum-major, or leader of the band, the pay and emoluments of a second lieutenant of infantry. The saddler, sergeants, veterinary sergeants, company quartermaster-sergeants and drum majors, will receive the pay and allowances of sergeants of cavalry. The battalion adjutant and battalion quartermasters and commissaries will receive the emoluments now provided by law for regimental adjutants.

Approved, July 29, 1861.

AN ACT *to provide for the Suppression of Rebellion against and Resistance to the Laws of the United States, and to amend the act entitled "an act to provide for calling forth the Militia to execute the Laws of the Union," etc., passed February twenty-eight, seventeen hundred and ninety-five.*

SEC. 3. *And be it further enacted,* That the militia so called into the service of the United States shall be subject to the same rules and articles of war as the troops of the United States, and be continued in the service of the United States until discharged by proclamation of the President: *Provided,* That such continuance in service shall not extend beyond sixty days after the commencement of the next regular session of Congress, unless Congress shall expressly provide by law therefor: *And provided, further,* That the militia so called into the service of the United States shall, during their time of service, be entitled to the same pay, rations and allowances for clothing as are or may be established by law for the army of the United States.

Approved, July 29, 1861.

AN ACT *providing for the better Organization of the Military Establishment.*[2]

SEC. 2. *And be it further enacted,* That the President be, and he is hereby, authorized to appoint, by and with the advice and consent of the Senate, in addition to the number authorized by existing laws and in accordance with existing regulations, five assistant inspector-generals, with the rank and pay of majors of cavalry; ten surgeons, and

1 Repealed as to bands, July 17, 1862.

2 U. S. Statutes at Large, vol. xii, 287.

twenty assistant surgeons, to have the pay, rank and allowances, and perform the duties of similiar officers in the present military establishment. That, hereafter, the adjutant-general's department shall consist of the following officers, namely: One adjutant-general, with the rank, pay and emoluments of a brigadier-general; one assistant adjutant-general, with the rank, pay and emoluments of a colonel of cavalry; two assistant adjutant-generals, with the rank, pay and emoluments each of a lieutenant-colonel of cavalry: four assistant adjutant-generals, with the rank, pay and emoluments each of a major of cavalry; and twelve assistant adjutant-generals, with the rank, pay and emoluments each of a captain of cavalry; and that there shall be added to the subsistence department, four commissaries of subsistence, each with the rank, pay and emoluments of a major of cavalry; and eight commissaries of subsistence, with the rank, pay and emoluments each of a captain of cavalry, and to be taken from the line of the army, either of the volunteers or regular army.

SEC. 3. *And be it further enacted*, That there shall be added to each of the corps of engineers and topographical engineers three first and three second lieutenants, to be promoted thereto in accordance with the existing laws and regulations. And there shall be added to the quartermaster's department one colonel, two lieutenant-colonels, four majors, and twenty captains, with the rank, pay and allowances of officers of cavalry; and whenever any army captain of the quartermaster's department shall have served fourteen years' continuous service he shall be promoted to the rank of major; and that there shall be added to the quartermaster's department as many master wagoners, with the rank, pay and allowances of sergeants of cavalry, and as many wagoners, with the pay and allowances of corporals of cavalry as the military service, in the judgment of the President, may render necessary. And there shall be added to the ordnance department of the United States army, as now organized, one chief of ordnance, with the rank, pay and emoluments of the quartermaster general of the army; one colonel, one lieutenant-colonel, and six second lieutenants; the field officers to be appointed by selection from the officers of the army; and the second lieutenants from the graduates of the United States military academy, by transfers from the engineers, or the topographical engineers, or the artillery.

SEC. 4. *And be it further enacted*, That there shall be added to the corps of engineers three companies of engineer soldiers, to be commanded by appropriate officers of said corps, to have the same pay and rations, clothing and other allowances, and be entitled to the same benefits, in every respect, as the company created by the act for the organization of a company of sappers and miners and pontoniers, approved May sixteen, eighteen hundred and forty-six. . . .

SEC. 5. *And be it further enacted*, That there be added to the medical staff of the army a corps of medical cadets, whose duty it shall be to act as dressers in the general hospitals and as ambulance attendants in the field, under the direction and control of the medical officers alone. They shall have the same rank and pay as the military cadets at West Point. . . .

SEC. 6. *And be it further enacted*, That in general or permanent hospitals female nurses may be substituted for soldiers, when, in the opinion of the surgeon-general or medical officer in charge, it is expedient to do so; the number of female nurses to be indicated by the surgeon-general or surgeon in charge of the hospital. The nurses so employed to receive forty cents a day and one ration in kind, or by commutation, in lieu of all emoluments except transportation in kind.

SEC. 15. *And be it further enacted*, That any commissioned officer of the army, or of the marine corps, who shall have served as such for forty consecutive years, may, upon his own application to the President of the United States, be placed upon the list of retired officers, with the pay and emoluments allowed by this act.

SEC. 16. *And be it further enacted*, That if any commissioned officer of the army, or of the marine corps, shall have become, or shall hereafter become, incapable of performing the duties of his office, he shall be placed upon the retired list and withdrawn from active service and command and from the line of promotion, with the following pay and emoluments, namely: the pay proper of the highest rank held by him at the time of his retirement, whether by staff or regimental commission, and four rations per day, and without any other pay, emoluments, or allowances; and the next officer in rank shall be promoted to the place of the retired officer, according to the established rules of the service. And the same rule of promotion shall be applied successively to the vacancies consequent upon the retirement of an officer: *Provided,* That should the brevet lieutenant-general be retired under this act, it shall be without reduction in his current pay, subsistence, or allowances: *And provided further,* That there shall not be on the retired list at any one time more than seven per centum of the whole number of officers of the army, as fixed by law.

Approved, August 3, 1861.

AN ACT *to increase the Pay of the Privates in the Regular Army and in the Volunteers in the service of the United States, and for other Purposes.*[1]

Be it enacted by the Senate and House of Representatives of the United States of America in Congress assembled, That the pay of the privates in the regular army and volunteers in the service of the United States be thirteen dollars per month for three years from and after the passage of this act and until otherwise fixed by law.[2]

SEC. 2. *And be it further enacted,* That the provisions of the act entitled "an act for the relief of the Ohio and other volunteers," approved July twenty-fourth, eighteen hundred and sixty-one, be and the same are hereby extended to all volunteers mustered into the service of the United States, whether for one, two or three years, or for and during the war.

Approved, August 6, 1861.

AN ACT *to reorganize and increase the efficiency of the Medical Department of the Army.*

Be it enacted by the Senate and House of Representatives of the United States of America in Congress assembled, That there shall be added to the present medical corps of the army ten surgeons and ten assistant surgeons, to be promoted and appointed under existing laws; twenty medical cadets, and as many hospital-stewards as the surgeon-general may consider necessary for the public ser-

---

1 U. S. Statutes at Large, vol. xii, 326.

2 By the act of July 17, 1862, it is prescribed that this shall not apply to commissioned officers. An important decision has just been made by the Secretary of War and Paymaster-General. The decision is in effect, that a soldier is entitled to pay from the day he enlists, and that he is not to wait until his company is full, or the formal muster of the regiment into government service.

vice, and that their pay and that of all hospital-stewards in the volunteer as well as the regular service shall be thirty dollars per month, to be computed from the passage of this act. And all medical cadets in the service shall, in addition to their pay, receive one ration per day either in kind or commutation.

SEC. 2. *And be it further enacted*, That the surgeon-general to be appointed under this act shall have the rank, pay and emoluments of a brigadier-general. There shall be one assistant surgeon-general, and one medical inspector-general of hospitals, each with the rank, pay and emoluments of a colonel of cavalry, and the medical inspector-general shall have, under the direction of the surgeon-general, the supervision of all that relates to the sanitary condition of the army, whether in transports, quarters or camps, and of the hygiene, police, discipline and efficiency of field and general hospitals, under such regulations as may hereafter be established.

SEC. 3. *And be it further enacted*, That there shall be eight medical inspectors, with the rank, pay and emoluments each of a lieutenant-colonel of cavalry, and who shall be charged with the duty of inspecting the sanitary condition of transports, quarters and camps, of field and general hospitals, and who shall report to the medical inspector-general, under such regulations as may be hereafter established, all circumstances relating to the sanitary condition and wants of troops and of hospitals, and to the skill, efficiency and good conduct of the officers and attendants connected with the medical department.

Approved, April 16, 1862.

AN ACT *to define the Pay and Emoluments of certain Officers of the Army, and for other purposes.*

Be it enacted by the Senate and House of Representatives of the United States of America in Congress assembled, That officers of the army entitled to forage for horses shall not be allowed to commute it, but may draw forage in kind for each horse actually kept by them when and at the place where they are on duty, not exceeding the number authorized by law: *Provided however*, That when forage in kind can not be furnished by the proper department, then, and in all such cases, officers entitled to forage may commute the same according to existing regulations: *And provided, further*, That officers of the army and of volunteers assigned to duty which requires them to be mounted, shall, during the time they are employed on such duty, receive the pay, emoluments and allowances of cavalry officers of the same grade respectively.

SEC. 2. *And be it further enacted*, That major-generals shall be entitled to draw forage in kind for five horses; brigadier-generals for four horses; colonels, lieutenant-colonels and majors for two horses each; captains and lieutenants of cavalry and artillery, or having the cavalry allowance, for two horses each; and chaplains for one horse only.

SEC. 3. *And be it further enacted*, That whenever an officer of the army shall employ a soldier as his servant he shall, for each and every month during which said soldier shall be so employed, deduct from his own monthly pay the full amount paid to or expended by the Government per month on account of said soldier; and every officer of the army, who shall fail to make such deduction, shall, on conviction thereof before a general court martial, be cashiered.

SEC. 4. *And be it further enacted*, That the first section of the act approved August six, eighteen hundred and sixty-one, entitled "an act to increase the pay of privates in the regular army and in the volunteers, in the service of the United States, and for other purposes," shall not be so construed, after the passage of this act, as to increase the emoluments of the commissioned officers of the army And the eighth section of the act of twenty-second July, eighteen hundred and sixty-one, entitled "an act to authorize the employment of volunteers to aid in enforcing the laws and protecting public property," shall be so construed as to give to quartermaster-sergeants the same compensation as to regimental commissary-sergeants.

SEC. 6. *And be it further enacted*, That each brigade in the volunteer service may have sixteen musicians as a band, who shall receive the pay and allowances now provided by law for regimental bands, except the leader of the band, who shall receive forty-five dollars per month, with the emoluments and allowances of a quartermaster-sergeant.

SEC. 7. *And be it further enacted*, That, in lieu of the present rate of mileage allowed to officers of the army when traveling on public duty, where transportation in kind is not furnished to them by the

Government, not more than six cents per mile shall hereafter be allowed, unless where an officer is ordered from a station east of the Rocky Mountains to one west of the same mountains, or vice versa, when ten cents per mile shall be allowed to him; and no officer of the army or navy of the United States shall be paid mileage, except for travel actually performed at his own expense, and in obedience to orders.

SEC. 9. *And be it further enacted,* That hereafter the compensation of all chaplains in the regular or volunteer service or army hospitals shall be one hundred dollars per month and two rations a day when on duty: . . . .

SEC. 20. *And be it further enacted,* That the different regiments and independent companies heretofore mustered into the service of the United States as volunteer engineers, pioneers, or sappers and miners, under the orders of the President or Secretary of War, or by authority of the commanding general of any military department of the United States, or which having been mustered into the service as infantry shall have been reorganized and employed as engineers, pioneers, or sappers and miners, shall be and the same are hereby recognized and accepted as volunteer engineers, on the same footing in all respects in regard to their organization, pay and emoluments as the corps of engineers of the regular army of the United States, and they shall be paid for their services already performed as is now provided by law for the payment of officers, non-commissioned officers, and privates of the engineer corps of the regular army.

Approved, July 17, 1862.

The new militia law of July, 1862, contains the following provisions:

SEC. 5. *And be it further enacted,* That the President shall appoint, by and with the advice and consent of the Senate, a judge-advocate general, with the rank, pay and emoluments of a colonel of cavalry . . .

SEC. 6 *And be it further enacted,* That there may be appointed by the President, by and with the advice and consent of the Senate, for each army in the field, a judge-advocate, with the rank, pay and emoluments, each, of a major of cavalry, who shall perform the duties of judge-advocate for the army to which they respectively belong, under the direction of the judge-advocate general.

LAWS RELATING EXCLUSIVELY TO PAY OF THE NAVY AND MARINE CORPS.

AN ACT *making Appropriations for the Naval Service for the Year ending the thirtieth of June, one thousand eight hundred and fifty-five.*[1]

SEC. 5. *And be it further enacted*, That the pay of the boatswains, gunners, carpenters and sailmakers of the navy, shall be as follows: On leave, or waiting orders, per annum, six hundred dollars; shore duty, seven hundred dollars; sea service, nine hundred dollars. An addition of two per centum on the foregoing rates for every year's sea service, and an addition upon sea pay of ten per centum, when serving in ships with four hundred men, and twenty per centum, when serving in ships with nine hundred men.[2]

Approved, August 5, 1854.

GENERAL ORDER.—From and after this date the monthly pay of the petty officers, seamen, ordinary seamen, landsmen, boys, etc., in the Navy, will be increased as follows:

Yeoman in ships-of-the-line, to - - - - - -	$45 00
Do. " frigates-of-the-line, to - - - - - -	40 00
Do. " sloops-of-the-line, to - - - - - -	30 00
Do. " vessels smaller than sloops, to - - -	24 00
Armorers in ships-of-the-line, to - - - - - - -	30 00
Do. " frigates-of-the-line, to - - - - -	25 00
Do. " sloops-of-the-line, to - - - - - -	20 00
Ship's steward, to - - - - - - - - - -	30 00
Boatswain's, gunner's, and carpenter's mates, and mates-at-arms, to - - - - - - - - - - -	25 00
Ship's cook, coxswain, quartermasters, captains of forecastle, and surgeon's steward, to - - - - - - -	24 00
Sailmaker's mates, quarter-gunners, captains of tops, captains of afterguards, captains of holds, cooper, painters, armorer's mate, ship's corporal, master of band, cabin steward, ward-room steward, cabin cook, and ward-room cook, to - - - - - - - - - -	20 00
Seamen, to - - - - - - - - - - - -	18 00

1 U. S. Statutes at Large, vol. x, 583.

2 This section is superseded by the act of June 1, 1860.

Musicians, 1st class, to - - - - - - - - -	$15 00
Ordinary seamen, to - - - - - - - - - -	14 00
Landsmen and musicians of 2d class, to - - -	12 00
Boys, to - - - - - - - - - -	8, 9 and 10 00

This increase will not apply to those enlisted for receiving-ships, and shore stations. Those now in the service who have received a bounty under the General Order of May 23, 1853, will be charged with such part of the bounty as is proportioned to the unexpired term of their enlistment.

An advance of two months' pay only will be made when the recruit shall be received and duly entered on the books of some receiving-ship. The other existing regulations, with regard to enlistments, will continue in force.

J. C. DOBBIN, *Sec'y of the Navy.*

Navy Department, August 11, 1854.

CIRCULAR.

TREASURY DEPARTMENT, FOURTH AUDITOR'S OFFICE, *Oct.* 16, '54.

The act making appropriations for the naval service, approved August 5, 1854, provides, "That the non-commissioned officers, musicians and privates of the United States Marine Corps shall be entitled to and receive the same pay and bounty for re-enlisting as are now, or may hereafter be allowed to the non-commissioned officers, musicians and privates in the infantry of the army.

This extends the provisions of "an act to increase the pay of the rank and file of the army, and to encourage enlistments," approved August 4, 1854, in respect to pay, and of the 29th section of the act of July 5, 1838, as to bounty (three months' extra pay), for re-enlisting, to the non-commissioned officers, musicians and privates of the marine corps, from the date of the act, viz., August 5, 1854.[1]

1. The pay of the non-commissioned officers, musicians and privates of the marine corps is, therefore, increased at the rate of four dollars per month. The retention of one dollar per month, however, from the pay of the musicians and privates of the marine corps, directed by the act of March 2, 1833, and extended to the whole term of their enlistment by the 5th section of the act of March 3, 1849, is to be continued.

---

[1] U. S. Statutes at Large, vol. x, 587.

2. Every non-commissioned officer, musician and private of the marine corps, who, having been honorably discharged from the service of the United States, shall, within one month thereafter, re-enlist, is entitled to two dollars per month in addition to the ordinary pay of his grade, for the first period of five years after the expiration of his previous enlistment, and a further sum of one dollar per month for each successive period of five years, so long as he shall remain continuously in the marine corps.

3. Every marine who was in service at the date of the passage of the act, who had served one or more enlistments and been honorably discharged, is entitled to the above additional pay provided for a second enlistment, viz.: two dollars per month for the first five years from the date of the act.

4. Every marine, honorably discharged before the passage of the act, but who re-entered service within one month after his discharge, and subsequently to the date of the act, is entitled, from the date of such re-entry, to two dollars per month in addition to the ordinary pay of his grade.

5. Every able-bodied non-commissioned officer, musician or private soldier of the marine corps, who has re-enlisted since the fifth of August, 1854, or who may hereafter re-enlist into the corps "within two months before or one month after the expiration of his term of service," is entitled to receive three months' extra pay,[1] as provided for like grades in the army, by the 29th section of the act approved July 5, 1838. The "three months' extra pay" (bounty) thus allowed (together with the increase of four dollars per month) is included in the ordinary pay of the grade in which the marine may be serving when discharged.

6. The allowance to marines employed at work on fortifications, in surveys, in cutting roads, and other constant labor, of not less than ten days, authorized by the act approved March 2, 1819, entitled "an act to regulate the pay of the army when employed on fatigue duty, is increased to twenty-five cents per day for men employed as laborers and teamsters, and forty cents per day for men employed as mechanics, at all stations east of the Rocky Mountains, and thirty-five cents and fifty cents per day, respectively, when the men are employed at stations west of those mountains. The allow-

---

[1] This provision in favor of soldiers is repealed by act of August 3, 1861.

ance of "whisky or spirits," or commutation therefor, is discontinued from and after August 5, 1854.

7. The necessary data to enable the paymasters and pursers to calculate the additional pay and bounty should be entered upon the transfer and pay-rolls. The dates of the several re-enlistments, and whether the marine had been honorably discharged, should be entered opposite the name in each case, or the certificate of the adjutant and inspector, to that effect, should accompany the pay-rolls.

A. J. O'BANNON, *Acting Fourth Auditor.*

Approved: JOHN M. BRODHEAD, *Second Comptroller.*

[NOTE.—This circular is inserted here because it fully sets forth the law in several respects, and, in addition, gives a construction to the law, which has all the force of a statutory provision.]

"An act to promote the efficiency of the Navy," approved February 28, 1855,[1] provides for the appointment of naval officers to examine into the efficiency of the captains, commanders, lieutenants, masters and passed midshipmen in the navy, and directs:

SEC. 2. *And be it further enacted,* That all officers who shall be found by the said board incapable of performing the duties of their respective offices, ranks or grades, shall, if such finding be approved by the President, be dropped from the rolls, or placed in the order of their rank or seniority at the time, upon a list in the Navy Register, to be entitled the reserved list; and those so placed on the reserved list shall receive the leave of absence pay, or the furlough pay, to which they may be entitled when so placed, according to the report of the board and approval of the President, and shall be ineligible to further promotion, but shall be subject to the orders of the Navy Department at all times for duty; and vacancies created in the active service list by placing officers on the reserved list, shall be filled by regular promotion in the order of rank or seniority. And officers who may be promoted to fill the vacancies created by the reserved list shall, while unemployed, receive only the "leave of absence" or "waiting orders" pay to which they would have been entitled if such promotion had not been made; but when employed at sea, or on other duty, they shall receive, in addition to such

[1] U. S. Statutes at Large, vol. x, 617.

"leave of absence" or "waiting orders" pay, the difference between the "waiting orders" or "leave of absence" pay and the lowest sea-service pay of the grade to which they may be so promoted.[1] . . .

AN ACT *to increase and regulate the Pay of the Navy of the United States.*

Be it enacted by the Senate and House of Representatives of the United States of America in Congress assembled, That from and after the passage of this act the annual pay of the officers of the navy, on the active list, hereinafter named, shall be as follows:[2]

CAPTAINS.—The senior flag-officer, created under and by virtue of an act of Congress approved March second, eighteen hundred and fifty-seven, shall receive four thousand five hundred dollars.

Captains, when commanding squadron, five thousand dollars.

All other captains on duty at sea, four thousand two hundred dollars.

Captains on other duty, three thousand six hundred dollars.

When on leave or waiting orders, three thousand dollars.

COMMANDERS.—Every commander on duty at sea, for the first five years after the date of his commission, two thousand eight hundred and twenty-five dollars.

For the second five years after the date of his commission, three thousand one hundred and fifty dollars.

---

1 This act was so amended by act of January 16, 1857 (U. S. Statutes at Large, vol. xi, 153), as to authorize an officer placed on the retired or dropped list to demand a court of inquiry, which shall determine whether such officer shall be restored to the active list, or whether he shall remain on the retired list, on leave of absence or furlough pay. And officers not thus restored, within one year from the passage of the amendatory act, are entitled to receive one year's duty pay of their respective grades.

By an act of February 21, 1861 (U. S. Statutes at Large, vol. xii, 133), the President was authorized to place on the retired list any medical officer who was or might become, from physical or mental infirmity, incapable of further service at sea; and the pay of such officers to be the leave of absence pay of their several grades, as it existed prior to the act of June 1, 1860.

The act of February 28, 1855, was also amended by an act of August 3, 1861, "for the better organization of the navy;" which see, page 407. By the last named act, the pay of retired officers is fixed at specific rates.

2 The pay of some of the officers in this list is altered by the act of July 16, 1862, page 408.

Every commander on other duty, for the first five years after the date of his commission, two thousand six hundred and sixty-two dollars.

For the second five years after the date of his commission, two thousand eight hundred and twenty-five dollars.

All other commanders, two thousand two hundred and fifty dollars.

Lieutenants commanding at sea, two thousand five hundred and fifty dollars.

LIEUTENANTS.—Every lieutenant on duty at sea, one thousand five hundred dollars.

After he shall have seen seven years' sea-service in the navy, one thousand seven hundred dollars.

After he shall have seen nine years' sea service, one thousand nine hundred dollars.

After he shall have seen eleven years' sea-service, two thousand one hundred dollars.

After he shall have seen thirteen years' sea-service, two thousand two hundred and fifty dollars.

Every lieutenant on other duty shall receive one thousand five hundred dollars.

After he shall have seen seven years' sea-service in the navy, one thousand six hundred dollars.

After he shall have seen nine years' sea-service, one thousand seven hundred dollars.

After he shall have seen eleven years' sea-service, one thousand eight hundred dollars.

After he shall have seen thirteen years' sea-service, one thousand eight hundred and seventy-five dollars.

Every lieutenant on leave or waiting orders, one thousand two hundred dollars.

After he shall have seen seven years' sea-service in the navy, one thousand two hundred and sixty-six dollars.

After he shall have seen nine years' sea-service, one thousand three hundred and thirty-three dollars.

After he shall have seen eleven years' sea-service, one thousand four hundred dollars.

After he shall have seen thirteen years' sea-service, one thousand four hundred and fifty dollars.

CHAPLAINS.—Chaplains shall be paid as lieutenants.

Every chaplain shall be permitted to conduct public worship according to the manner and forms of the church of which he may be a member.

Every chaplain retained in the service shall be required to report annually, to the Secretary of the Navy, the official services performed by him.

MASTERS.—Every master in the line of promotion, when on duty as such at sea, one thousand two hundred dollars.

When on other duty, one thousand one hundred dollars.

When on leave or waiting orders, eight hundred and twenty-five dollars.

PASSED MIDSHIPMEN.—Every passed midshipman, when on duty as such at sea, one thousand dollars.

When on other duty, eight hundred dollars.

When on leave or waiting orders, six hundred and fifty dollars.

MIDSHIPMEN.—Every midshipman at sea, five hundred and fifty dollars.

When on other duty, five hundred dollars.

When on leave of absence or waiting orders, four hundred and fifty dollars.

SURGEONS.—Every surgeon on duty at sea, for the first five years after the date of his commission as surgeon, two thousand two hundred dollars.

For the second five years after the date of his commission as surgeon, two thousand four hundred dollars.

For the third five years after the date of his commission as surgeon, two thousand six hundred dollars.

For the fourth five years after the date of his commission as surgeon, two thousand eight hundred dollars.

For twenty years and upwards after the date of his commission as surgeon, three thousand dollars.

Fleet surgeons, three thousand three hundred dollars.

Every surgeon on other duty, for the first five years after the date of his commission as surgeon, two thousand dollars.

For the second five years after the date of his commission as surgeon, two thousand two hundred dollars.

For the third five years after the date of his commission as surgeon, two thousand four hundred dollars.

For the fourth five years after the date of his commission as surgeon, two thousand six hundred dollars.

For twenty years after the date of his commission as surgeon, two thousand eight hundred dollars.

Every surgeon on leave or waiting orders, for the first five years after the date of his commission as surgeon, one thousand six hundred dollars.

For the second five years after the date of his commission as surgeon, one thousand eight hundred dollars.

For the third five years after the date of his commission as surgeon, one thousand nine hundred dollars.

For the fourth five years after the date of his commission as surgeon, two thousand one hundred dollars.

For twenty years and upwards after the date of his commission as surgeon, two thousand three hundred dollars.

PASSED ASSISTANT SURGEONS.—Every passed assistant surgeon on duty at sea, one thousand five hundred dollars.

When on other duty, one thousand four hundred dollars.

When on leave or waiting orders, eleven hundred dollars.

ASSISTANT SURGEONS.—Every assistant surgeon on duty at sea, one thousand two hundred and fifty dollars.

When on other duty, one thousand and fifty dollars.

When on leave or waiting orders, eight hundred dollars.

PURSERS.—Every purser on duty at sea, for the first five years after the date of his commission, two thousand dollars.

For the second five years after the date of his commission, two thousand four hundred dollars.

For the third five years after the date of his commission, two thousand six hundred dollars.

For the fourth five years after the date of his commission, two thousand nine hundred dollars.

For twenty years and upwards after the date of his commission, three thousand one hundred dollars.

Every purser on other duty, for the first five years after the date of his commission, one thousand eight hundred dollars.

For the second five years after the date of his commission, two thousand one hundred dollars.

For the third five years after the date of his commission, two thousand four hundred dollars.

For the fourth five years after the date of his commission, two thousand six hundred dollars.

For twenty years and upwards after the date of his commission, two thousand eight hundred dollars.

Every purser on leave or waiting orders, for the first five years after the date of his commission, one thousand four hundred dollars.

For the second five years after the date of his commission, one thousand six hundred dollars.

For the third five years after the date of his commission, one thousand eight hundred dollars.

For the fourth five years after the date of his commission, two thousand dollars.

For twenty years and upwards after the date of his commission, two thousand two hundred and fifty dollars.

PROFESSORS OF MATHEMATICS.—Every professor of mathematics on duty, one thousand eight hundred dollars.

When on leave or waiting orders, nine hundred and sixty dollars.

ENGINEERS.—Every chief engineer on duty, for the first five years after the date of his commission, one thousand eight hundred dollars.

For the second five years after the date of his commission, two thousand two hundred dollars.

For the third five years after the date of his commission, two thousand four hundred and fifty dollars.

After fifteen years after the date of his commission, two thousand six hundred dollars.

Every chief engineer on leave or waiting orders, for the first five years after the date of his commission, one thousand two hundred dollars.

For the second five years after the date of his commission, one thousand three hundred dollars.

For the third five years after the date of his commission, one thousand four hundred dollars.

After fifteen years after the date of his commission, one thousand five hundred dollars.

Every first assistant engineer on duty, one thousand two hundred and fifty dollars.

While on leave or waiting orders, nine hundred dollars.

Every second assistant engineer on duty, one thousand dollars.

While on leave or waiting orders, seven hundred and fifty dollars.

Every third assistant engineer on duty, seven hundred and fifty dollars.

While on leave or waiting orders, six hundred dollars.

WARRANTED OFFICERS.—Every boatswain, gunner carpenter and sailmaker on duty at sea, for the first three years' sea service after the date of his warrant, one thousand dollars.

For the second three years' sea service after the date of his warrant, one thousand one hundred and fifty dollars.

For the third three years' sea service after the date of his warrant, one thousand two hundred and fifty dollars.

For the fourth three years' sea service after the date of his warrant, one thousand three hundred and fifty dollars.

For twelve years' sea service and upwards, one thousand four hundred and fifty dollars.

WHEN ON OTHER DUTY.

For the first three years of sea service after the date of warrant, eight hundred dollars.

For the second three years' sea service after the date of his warrant, nine hundred dollars.

For the third three years' sea service after the date of his warrant, one thousand dollars.

For the fourth three years' sea service after the date of his warrant one thousand one hundred dollars.

For twelve years' sea service and upwards, one thousand two hundred dollars.

WHEN ON LEAVE OR WAITING ORDERS.

For the first three years' sea service after the date of his warrant, six hundred dollars.

For the second three years' sea service after the date of his warrant, seven hundred dollars.

For the third three years' sea service after the date of his warrant eight hundred dollars.

For the fourth three years' sea service after the date of his warrant, nine hundred dollars.

For twelve years' sea service and upwards, one thousand dollars.

SEC. 2. *And be it further enacted*, That nothing in this act contained shall be so construed as to increase or modify the present pay of chiefs of bureaus in the Navy Department, with whom shall be classed the present superintendent of the naval observatory: *Provided*, That the officer now charged with experiments in gunnery at the navy yard, Washington, shall receive the sea service pay of the grade now next above him.

SEC. 3. *And be it further enacted*, That hereafter no service shall be regarded as sea service but such as shall be performed at sea under the orders of a department, and in vessels employed by authority of law.

SEC. 4. *And be it further enacted*, That nothing in this act contained shall be held to modify or affect the existing power of the Secretary of the Navy to furlough officers or to affect the furlough pay.

SEC. 5. *And be it further enacted*, That the increased pay hereinbefore provided for masters shall attach to masters not in the line of promotion, whether on the active or reserved list; and officers on the reserved list, when called into active service, shall receive the pay of their respective grades as herein provided during the term of such service: *Provided*, That nothing herein contained shall be construed to change or modify the present pay of officers on the reserved list, either on leave or furlough.

Approved, June 1, 1860.

"An act to provide for the appointment of assistant paymasters," approved July 17, 1861,[1] establishes the office of assistant paymaster, and provides:

SEC. 3. *And be it further enacted*, That the annual pay of assistant paymasters shall be as follows, viz:

On duty at sea, for the first five years after date of commission, one thousand three hundred dollars: after five years from date of commission, one thousand five hundred dollars.

On other duty, for the first five years after date of commission, one thousand dollars; after five years from date of commission, one thousand two hundred dollars.

On leave of absence or waiting orders, for the first five years after date of commission, eight hundred dollars; after five years from date of commission, one thousand dollars; and when attached to vessels for sea service, each assistant paymaster shall be entitled to one ration per day.

"An act providing for the better organization of the military establishment,"[2] provides as follows:

---

1 U. S. Statutes at Large, vol. xii, 258.

2 *Ibid*, vol. xii, 287.

SEC. 21. *And be it further enacted*, That any officer of the navy who has been forty years in the service of the United States may, upon his own application to the President of the United States, be placed upon the list of retired officers of the navy, and shall receive the pay and emoluments allowed by this act.

SEC. 22. *And be it further enacted*, That if any officer of the navy shall have become, or shall hereafter become, incapable of performing the duties of his office, he shall be placed upon the retired list and withdrawn from active service and command and from the line of promotion, with the following pay and emoluments, viz.: [1]

Captains in the navy, thirteen hundred dollars.

Commanders in the navy, eleven hundred dollars.

Lieutenants in the navy, one thousand dollars.

Surgeons ranking with captains, thirteen hundred dollars.

Surgeons ranking with commanders, eleven hundred dollars.

Surgeons ranking with lieutenants, one thousand dollars.

Paymasters ranking with captains, thirteen hundred dollars.

Paymasters ranking with commanders, eleven hundred dollars.

Paymasters ranking with lieutenants, one thousand dollars.

Chief engineers, one thousand dollars.

First assistant engineers, seven hundred dollars.

Second assistant engineers, five hundred dollars.

Third assistant engineers, four hundred dollars.

Masters, four hundred dollars.

Passed midshipmen, three hundred and fifty dollars; and with four rations per day to each of the above-named officers of the navy, to be commuted at thirty cents, each ration, and without any other pay or allowances. Captains, commanders and lieutenants now on the retired list of the navy shall receive the same compensation and no greater than is allowed to retired officers of the same rank by the provisions of this act. The next officer in rank shall be promoted to the place of the retired officer, according to the established rules of the service. And the same rule of promotion shall be applied successively to the vacancies consequent upon the retirement of an officer.

SEC. 23. *And be it further enacted*, That whenever any officer of

[1] These rates of pay altered by act of July 16, 1862, page 408, this Chapter.

the navy, on being ordered to perform the duties appropriate to his commission, shall report himself unable to comply with such order, or whenever, in the judgment of the President of the United States, an officer of the navy shall be in any way incapacitated from performing the duties of his office, the President, at his discretion, shall direct the Secretary of the Navy to refer the case of such officer to a board of not more than nine, and not less than five commissioned officers, two fifths of whom shall be members of the medical bureau of the navy; the board, except those taken from the medical bureau, to be composed, if possible (as far as may be), of his seniors in rank. The determination of the board in each case shall, with a record of its proceedings, be transmitted to the Secretary of the Navy, to be laid before the President for his approval or disapproval, and orders in the case. The board, whenever it finds an officer incapacitated for active service, will report, whether, in its judgment, the incapacity result from long and faithful service, from wounds or injury received in the line of duty, from sickness or exposure therein, or from any other incident of service; if so, and the President approve of such judgment, the disabled officer shall thereupon be placed upon the list of retired officers, according to the provisions of this act. But if such disability or incompetency proceeded from other causes, and the President concur in opinion with the board, the officer may be retired upon furlough pay, or he shall be wholly retired from the service, with one year's pay, at the discretion of the President; and in this last case his name shall be wholly omitted from the navy register. The members of the board shall, in every case, be sworn to an honest and impartial discharge of their duties, and no officer of the navy shall be retired, either partially or wholly, from the service without having had a fair and full hearing before the board, if he shall demand it.

Approved, August 3, 1861.

Sections 15 and 16 of the foregoing act provide for the retirement of officers of the marine corps. These sections may be found in the former part of this Chapter, page 391.

AN ACT *to establish and equalize the Grades of Line Officers of the United States Navy.*

SEC. 15. *And be it further enacted,* That from and after the passage of this act, the annual pay of the several ranks and grades of officers of the navy on the active list hereinafter named shall be as follows, viz:

Rear Admirals, when at sea, shall receive five thousand dollars;

When on shore duty, four thousand dollars;

When on leave of absence, or waiting orders, three thousand dollars.

Commodores, when at sea, shall receive four thousand dollars;

When on shore duty, three thousand two hundred dollars;

When on leave of absence, or waiting orders, two thousand four hundred dollars.

Captains, when at sea, shall receive three thousand five hundred dollars;

When on shore duty, two thousand eight hundred dollars;

When on leave of absence, or waiting orders, two thousand one hundred dollars.

Commanders, when at sea, shall receive two thousand eight hundred dollars;

When on shore duty, two thousand two hundred and forty dollars;

When on leave of absence, or waiting orders, one thousand six hundred and eighty dollars.

Lieutenant Commanders, when at sea, shall receive two thousand three hundred and forty-three dollars;

When on shore duty, one thousand eight hundred and seventy-five dollars;

When on leave of absence, or waiting orders, one thousand five hundred dollars.

Lieutenants, when at sea, shall receive one thousand eight hundred and seventy-five dollars;

When on shore duty, one thousand five hundred dollars;

When on leave of absence, or waiting orders, one thousand two hundred dollars.

Masters, when at sea, shall receive one thousand five hundred dollars.

When on shore duty, one thousand two hundred dollars;

When on leave of absence, or waiting orders, nine hundred and sixty dollars.

Ensigns, when at sea, shall receive one thousand two hundred dollars;

When on shore duty, nine hundred and sixty dollars;

When on leave of absence, or waiting orders, seven hundred and sixty eight dollars.

Midshipmen shall receive five hundred dollars.

SEC. 16. *And be it further enacted,* That whenever any officer of the navy, of a class subject by law or regulation to examination before promotion to a higher grade, shall have been absent on duty at the time when he should have been examined, and shall have been found qualified at a subsequent examination, the increased rate of pay to which he may be entitled shall be allowed to him from the date when he would have received it, had he been found qualified at the time when his examination should have taken place.

SEC. 17. *And be it further enacted,* That in calculating the graduated pay of boatswains, gunners, carpenters and sailmakers in the navy, as established by the law, the sea service shall be computed from the dates of their appointments or entry into the service in their respective grades, in lieu of the dates of their warrants.

SEC. 18. *And be it further enacted,* That the Secretary of the Navy be and he is hereby authorized to assign clerks and laborers attached to one bureau to duty in another, and also to detail a surgeon or assistant surgeon, or passed assistant surgeon, as assistant to the Bureau of Medicine and Surgery, who shall receive the highest shore pay of his grade.

SEC. 19. *And be it further enacted,* That all officers, while at sea or attached to a sea-going vessel, shall be allowed one ration.

SEC. 20. *And be it further enacted,* That the relative rank between officers of the navy and army on the retired list shall be the same as on the active list, and the annual pay of retired naval officers shall be as follows, viz:

Admirals, two thousand dollars.

Commodores, eighteen hundred dollars.

Captains, sixteen hundred dollars.

Commanders, fourteen hundred dollars.

Lieutenant Commanders, thirteen hundred dollars.

Lieutenants, one thousand dollars

Masters, eight hundred dollars.

Ensigns, five hundred dollars.

And no rations shall be allowed to any officers of the navy on the retired list. And the pay of all naval officers appointed by virtue of an act entitled "an act to provide for the temporary increase o the navy," approved July twenty-fourth, eighteen hundred and sixty-one, shall be the same as that of officers of a like grade in the regular navy.

Approved, July 16, 1862.

FORMS AND REGULATIONS.

Claims for pay, extra pay, allowances and bounties, for services in the army, during the war of 1812, should be presented to the Third Auditor; for services rendered since that time to the Second Auditor; and for services in the navy or marine corps, whether in the war of 1812 or since that time, to the Fourth Auditor of the Treasury.

A volunteer or soldier should receive at the time of his discharge a regular discharge, and two duplicate pay certificates.

With these papers he can be paid by any paymaster of the army on their presentation. If the discharged volunteer or soldier has failed on obtain such certificates, and the regiment to which he belonged is disbanded or beyond his reach, or if he has obtained such certificates, and payment has for any reason been refused upon their presentation to a paymaster of the army, he should make a declaration over his signature according to Form on page 415, and forward said declaration, together with his pay certificates and discharge (if he has them, if not, their absence must be accounted for in said declaration) to the Second Auditor of the Treasury Department, at Washington. Such claim will be audited by the Department, and the result communicated to claimant or his attorney.

Soldiers not entitled to pay.

The 1638th section of the United States Army Regulations provides as follows: "In case any individual shall be discharged within three months after entering the service, for a disability which ex isted at that time, he shall receive neither pay nor allowances, except subsistence and transportation to his home."

Soldiers not discharged.

A volunteer or soldier at home on a furlough, or for any other cause, absent from his regiment on pay day, should send power of attorney to some member of his regiment (captain preferred), authorizing such person to draw his pay; said power of attorney should be as near as can be, according to Form on page 416.

OFFICIAL INSTRUCTIONS OF THE SECOND AUDITOR OF THE TREASURY DEPARTMENT IN PREPARING CLAIMS FOR SOLDIER'S PAY AND BOUNTY.

To enable those who may have claims upon the United States, for money due deceased officers and soldiers, on account of services rendered, whether in the regular or volunteer service, to obtain the same, with the least delay, the following information is furnished:

Order of payment.

ORDER FIRST.—If the deceased was married, payment will be made—first, to the widow; second, if no widow, to his child or children (if minors, to the guardian).

ORDER SECOND.—If he died unmarried—first, to the father; second, if the father is dead, to the mother; third, if both parents are dead, to the brothers and sisters collectively; lastly, to the heirs general (to be distributed in accordance with the laws of the State in which the deceased had his domicile.)

Application, proof and authentication.

APPLICATION.—The claimant or claimants must make a written application, under oath, and over his, her or their own signature, stating his, her or their name, age, residence, connection to the deceased, with the letter or name of the captain of the company and regiment to which he belonged; time of his death and the nature of the pay claimed—whether "arrears of pay," etc.; and the "$100 bounty," under act of July 22, 1861.

An application by a guardian should give the name and age of the ward or wards, and should be accompanied by letters of guardianship, or an authenticated copy thereof. In the application of a mother, claiming bounty, her husband being alive, the facts upon which the claim is made should be clearly stated and proved. If the soldier die unmarried, leaving no child, it must be stated by the applicant, and also by the disinterested witnesses.

PROOF.—To satisfy the accounting officers that the person or persons thus claiming is or are entitled to the money in the character he, she or they claim, the depositions of two credible witnesses will be required, stating that they are acquainted with the claimant or claimants, the connection held to the deceased, and that they (the deponents) are disinterested.

AUTHENTICATION.—The application and depositions above required, to be subscribed and sworn to before a judge, commissioner, notary public or justice of the peace, duly authorized to administer oaths, accompanied by the certificate and seal of a court of record as to the fact of the said judge, etc., being duly commissioned and acting in his official capacity at the time of the execution of the foregoing papers.

If the soldier died unmarried, it must be so stated in the application of those claiming to be his father, mother, brothers or sisters, as well as by the witnesses.

Proof of marriage (record evidence, if possible), must always accompany the applications of those claiming to be the widows.

Administration.

As the taking out of "letters of administration" is attended with considerable expense (often unnecessary), it is suggested that it be done only when required by the Auditor.

Discharged soldiers.

When a soldier (or volunteer) is discharged, he is (or should be) furnished with a regular "discharge," and two (duplicate) "pay certificates," and one or more disability certificates if discharged on account of disability. Upon these papers he can be paid by a paymaster of the army upon their presentation. Should he fail to present them for payment to a paymaster, or, having presented them, and payment refused, and they are sent to this office, the applicant must state the reasons for such refusal, accompanied by proof of identity and authentication, as in the case of deceased soldiers. In no case should the "oath of identity," on the back of the "discharge," be filled up, as the "discharge" is returned to the soldier after his claim has been acted upon. Where "pay certificates" and certificates of disability have been withheld, he must send all other papers given to him at the time of his discharge, together with the certificate of his captain that no such certificates were given to him, and the reasons for withholding them. In case the certificates are claimed to have been lost, an affidavit of such loss must be furnished, stating the circumstances under which it occurred; that he had diligently searched for them without success, and that he has not received pay thereon, nor assigned them to any person.

MODE OF PAYMENT.—Payments will be made by an order from the

accounting officers on any paymaster of the army. Such order will require the signature on the claimant on its face before it will be paid.

Mode of presenting claims.

All claims of arrears of pay and bounty may be sent directly to this office. When received they are entered upon the register; as soon as practicable they will be examined, and if found correct in form, they are placed upon the files for settlement, and their receipt acknowledged. If incorrect, the party sending it is immediately notified. No "special cases" will be made at the solicitation of attorneys, but when evidence can be obtained, cases will be audited in the order in which they are received. The only exception to this rule is when, in settling a case in its order, evidence is found upon the same rolls by which to settle other claims of soldiers deceased in the same company. Letters of inquiry in relation to a claim, should specify the name of the deceased, and the company, regiment and State to which he belonged; and in all cases, to secure an answer, the name, post-office and State of the writer should be distinctly written.

FORMS.—The form accompanying this circular is intended only as a guide, and must be varied to suit special cases. No claim is rejected on account of the form in which it is presented, if it substantially complies with the instructions.

TO CORRESPONDENTS.—Letters of inquiry, relating to the pay of soldiers in hospital or on furlough, should be addressed to the Paymaster-General. Inquiries relating to the pay of deceased teamsters or other employees of the Quartermaster's Department, or for horses killed in the service, to the Third Auditor; and relating to the pay and bounty of persons in the marine or naval service to the Fourth Auditor.

All claimants wishing to obtain information or to present claims, can communicate with this office by mail, and will receive as speedy reply as the business of the office will allow.

POSTAGE.—All communications to and from this Department will be sent free of postage. Address,

EZRA B. FRENCH,
Second Auditor of the Treas. Dept. Washington, D. C.

The foregoing is a portion of a circular issued by the

Second Auditor, relating to pay and bounty. The residue of the circular may be found under BOUNTY MONEY, Chapter XXIV.

The following are the forms appended to the foregoing circular:

Form of Application for Arrears of Pay and Bounty.

I, ——, of ——, in the county of ——, and State of ——, on oath, say, that my age is —— years, and that I am the identical ——, late of ——, in the State of ——, who was a —— in company ——, of the —— regiment of ——, and died in the service of the United States at ——, on the —— day of ——, 18—. [*If the soldier died unmarried, leaving no child, it should be here stated. If the application is by the mother, she should also state the name of the father of the deceased, his death, or abandonment of the support of his family, giving the date and all the facts necessary to a proper understanding of the case. If the application is by the widow of the deceased, she should here state her maiden name; when, where and by whom she was married to him, and whether or not there is record evidence of such marriage.*]

I make this application to recover all arrears of pay, or other allowances due to the deceased from the United States, and the bounty provided by the sixth section of the act of July 22, 1861. (*Signature of Claimant.*)

STATE OF —— }
County of —— } *ss.*

Personally appeared the above-named ——, to me well known, and subscribed and made oath to the foregoing statement, on this —— day of ——, 18—, before me. (*Officer's Signature.*)

Form of Affidavit.

We, —— and ——, of ——, in the county of —— and State of ——, on oath, say, that we are, and for —— years have been, well acquainted with ——, the applicant, and with the said ——, deceased, who was a ——, in company ——, of the —— regiment of ——, and know —— to be the —— of the deceased. [*If he died unmarried, leaving no child, it should be here stated; and if the application is by the mother, the fact of her widowhood, or the abandonment of her husband, should be stated in the application*], and that we have no interest whatever in this application.

(*Signatures of two Witnesses.*)

Here must follow the certificate of the magistrate, as above;[1] and the certificate of the Clerk of the proper

1 The certificate also should state that the witnesses are credible.

Court, under its seal, attesting the official character of the magistrate, must also be appended.

The foregoing application must, when not made by the person by whom the service was performed, be accompanied by proof, in addition to the above affidavit. The character of this proof may be ascertained by referring to the forms given in the preceding Chapter, relating to BOUNTY MONEY.

Reference is also here made to the last-mentioned Chapter, for many forms that apply to claims for arrears of pay. In the war of 1861, claims for bounty money and arrears of pay are adjusted at the same office, and application for both may be joined. Forms for these joint applications, as well as a form of power of attorney, may be found in said Chapter on BOUNTY MONEY.

Application of Soldier for Arrears of Pay.

STATE OF —— }
County of —— } *ss.*

On this —— day of ——, A. D. 18—, personally appeared before me, a ——, in and for said county,——, a resident of said county, and made oath in due form of law, that he is the identical ——, who was a —— in company ——, commanded by Captain ——, in the —— regiment of——, commanded by Colonel ——, in the war with ——. That he volunteered [*or* enlisted, *or* was drafted], at ——, on the —— day of —— 18—; and remained in actual service until the —— day of —— 18—, when he was honorably discharged, at ——, on account of the expiration of his term of service [*or other reason*]. That he claims there is due him from the United States, for pay and allowances, as follows: [*Here specify items of claims*]. The same having never been paid him by the United States, or any of its officers. [*Should any portion of the amount have been paid, or should the claimant be indebted to the United States for clothing, or otherwise, it should be stated.*] And he hereby appoints ——, his attorney, and authorizes him to receive and receiptfor the certificate which may issue upon his foregoing application, and to do any and all acts necessary to effect the purpose of his said appointment. [*A separate power of attorney may be executed according to the form in the preceding chapter, in lieu of this.*]

(*Two Witnesses, if Attorney appointed.*) (*Claimant's Signature.*)

And I hereby certify, that at the same time personally appeared before me, —— and ——, to me well known to be credible witnesses, and who, being duly sworn, depose and say, that the above named ——, now present, is, to their knowledge, the identical person named in the above deposition, and that the said affidavit is correct, as they verily believe; that they are well acquainted with the said claimant, and are wholly disinterested.

(*Signatures of Witnesses.*)

Sworn to, subscribed and acknowledged by the said —— [*the claimant*], and by the said —— and —— [*witnesses*], before me, the day and year aforesaid. (*Officer's Signature.*)

This must be followed by the certificate of the Clerk, under seal, as in other cases.

Form of Application for Arrears of Pay due a deceased Officer or Soldier, by Widow, Heirs or Administrator.

STATE OF —— } ss.
County of —— }

On this —— day of ——, A. D., 18—, before me, a ——, in and for said county, personally appeared ——, to me well known, and made oath in due form of law that —— is the —— of ——, deceased, who was a —— in company ——, commanded by Captain ——, in the —— regiment of ——, commanded by Colonel——, in the war with ——; that said ——, volunteered [*or was drafted, or enlisted*] at ——, on the —— day of ——, A. D., 18—, and was honorably discharged [*or was killed at* ——] on the —— day of——, A. D., 18—, on account of the expiration of his term of service [*or other reason.*] (*Officer's Signature.*)

[Conclude as in preceding applications, and add a like affidavit.]

In addition to the affidavit of the witnesses, other proof is necessary in certain cases. The nature of this proof may be ascertained by referring to the forms and regulations under BOUNTY MONEY, page 361, preceding Chapter.

In applications for mileage, in going from the place of enlistment to the place of rendezvous, or from the place of discharge to the place of residence, or when traveling under orders, an account should be made out, according to the rates prescribed in the seventh section of the act of July 17, 1862, on page 394, and an application be made in the same manner as for arrears of pay, and with the same accompanying proof.

Officers claiming mileage while traveling under orders, should annex to the account the order under which the journey was performed.

Payment of prisoners of war.

The following general order will be found important to those families whose husbands are now or may become prisoners of war.

[General Order, No. 22.]

WAR DEPARTMENT, ADJUTANT-GENERAL'S OFFICE,
Washington, Oct. 23, 1861.

The following plan for paying to the families of officers and soldiers in the service of the United States who are or may become prisoners of war, sums due them by Government, having been approved by the President, it is published for the benefit of all concerned:

Payment will be made to persons presenting a written authority from a prisoner to draw his pay; or, without such authority, to his wife, the guardian of his minor children, or his widowed mother in the order named.

Application for such payment to be made to the senior paymaster of the district in which the prisoner is serving, and must be accompanied by the certificate of a judge of a court of the United States, or of some other party, under the seal of a court of record of the State in which the applicant is a resident, setting forth that the applicant is the wife of the prisoner, the guardian of his children, or his widowed mother, and if occupying either of the last two relationships towards him, that there is no one in existence who is more nearly related according to the above classification.

Payments will be made to parties thus authorized and identified, or their receipts made out in the manner that would be recognized by the prisoner himself, at least one month's pay being in all cases retained by the United States. The officer making the payment will see that it is entered on the last previous muster-roll for the payment of the prisoner's company, or will report it, if those rolls are not in his possession, to the senior paymaster of the district, who will either attend to the entry or give notice of the payment to the Paymaster-General, if the rolls have been forwarded to his office.

RULES OBSERVED AT THE OFFICE OF THE FOURTH AUDITOR IN THE SETTLEMENT OF CLAIMS TO BALANCES DUE TO DECEASED SEAMEN OR MARINES AT THE TIME OF THEIR DEATH.

1. Payment of balances due deceased seamen or marines will not be made except to administrators, *who are heirs*, or appointed *with the consent of heirs*, or to creditors to the amount of their respective claims. But no payment shall be made to a creditor, until the balance due to the deceased person shall have remained in the Treasury, uncalled for by an administrator appointed as aforesaid, for six weeks after information of the death of such person shall have been received at the Department; and where the balance exceeds the sum of twenty dollars, no claim of a creditor will be paid, until an advertisement shall have been inserted for three successive days, in the newspaper employed to publish the laws in the city of Washington, calling upon other claimants to present their claims at the office of the Fourth Auditor within two months; at the end of which term, if the balance shall not have been demanded by an administrator appointed as aforesaid, the claims which shall have been presented and proved before the accounting officers will be paid in equal proportion, the expense of the advertisement having been first defrayed out of the sum due to the deceased person at the time of his death.

2. Payment of arrearages claimed under a will, will only be made after satisfactory proof of the will is adduced to the accounting officers. Wills of persons in actual service must be in writing, and attested by an officer, if the testator were not himself an officer. The executor will be required to produce the original will, or a copy duly authenticated.

3. Heirship, or consent of heirs, may be shown by the fact being inserted in the letters of administration, or must be proved by the affidavit of two disinterested persons, taken before an officer empowered to administer oaths.

4. Payment may be made immediately to the heirs of the deceased, when it shall be shown that the cost of obtaining administration at the proper place would exceed one third part of the balance due.

5. The penalty of the administration bond should be shown by the certificate of administration, or otherwise.

DECISIONS OF SECOND COMPTROLLER.

SOLDIER'S PAY.

[The references are to volumes in the Comptroller's office.]

No crime except desertion forfeits the pay of a soldier, except upon sentence of a court-martial, unless, in consequence of the crime, the soldier is withdrawn from service. *Vol.* xv, *p.* 448.

When a soldier, who was discharged on the expiration of his term of service, claims pay and clothing, his name not appearing on the regimental pay-roll for the time embraced in his claim, the accounting officers will require the production of the descriptive certificate of his discharge, as the surest evidence that the claim has not been paid by the paymaster.

When the witnesses required by the regulations, to payments made to soldiers can not be had, other satisfactory proof of the signature may be received. *Vol.* xiv, *p.* 50.

A receipt by mark, witnessed by two paymaster's clerks, is a substantial compliance with the regulation. *Vol.* xiv, *p.* 75.

When a soldier is discharged, and his account settled and paid by a paymaster, the payment purporting to be in full, that payment is to be considered final, unless shown by conclusive testimony to have been erroneous. *John A. Powell's case, January*, 1848.

When, from the situation of his company, or the nature of the service, a soldier can not receive his discharge, when his term expires, and is from necessity retained in service, he is to be paid up to the time of his actual discharge. *Vol.* vi, *p.* 149.

A soldier discharged on habeas corpus as a minor, forfeits all pay and allowances previously due, both by the regulations of the army, and general principles. *Vol.* xv, *p.* 38.

When an officer or soldier is furloughed, in anticipation of his discharge or the expiration of his term of service, he can not claim for the balance of his term both his travel pay and his pay as in service. *Lieut. Fellnagle's case, and W. S. Thompson's case, Oct.* 19, 1848.

A soldier, who is taken prisoner by the enemy, is entitled to his pay and allowance during the time he is detained, and to traveling allowance from the place where he is released to his home. Volunteers, however, are not, under such circumstances, entitled to compensation for use and risk of horses. *Vol.* xii, *p.* 429.

A private soldier of militia or volunteers, who is illegally and against his will discharged from service, is entitled to his pay up to the time of the discharge of the company to which he belonged, or to the expiration of his term of enlistment. *W. C. Hayse's case, June* 16, 1849.

A soldier under arrest by the civil authority on a criminal charge, will be entitled to his pay for the time he was in custody, provided he is tried and acquitted, or discharged without trial. *Case of Dennes Clary, January* 8, 1844.

DECEASED CLAIMANTS.

In order to show that the person claiming money due a deceased person from the United States, has a legal right to receive it, he should produce and file with the disbursing officer making the payments, the original letter of administration, or a copy thereof duly certified, or an official certificate from the clerk of the court from which it issued, that it appears by the records of said court that he has been duly appointed, and is legally empowered to act as administrator on the deceased person's estate. *Vol.* xii, *p.* 184.

Where the balance due a deceased person is paid to an administrator deriving his authority from a court of competent jurisdiction, though obtained by fraudulent means, payment will not be made again when claimed by the true representative of the deceased. But where payment is made to an administrator whose authority is derived from a court possessing no power to grant administration, the legal representatives of the deceased have a valid claim on the government for the money. When the jurisdiction of the court granting the power is denied, and the question is one of fact merely, such as the residence of the deceased, etc., the most conclusive evidence of the want of jurisdiction will be required. *Philip Robinson's case, April* 10, 1851.

In the case of a gratuity granted by act of Congress to the relatives of deceased persons, the collateral relatives, whether of the whole or half blood, should participate equally, in the order pointed out in the act. *Dec. Sec. Compt. Nov.* 19, 1830.

When the amount due from the United States to a deceased person has been paid to one claiming to be the only brother of the deceased, upon proof that was then deemed satisfactory that he was the only brother, and that there was no widow, and other claim for the money is presented by a person claiming to be the widow, the clearest evidence should be required of the fraud and perjury of the proof on which payment was made, of the absence of all knowledge of it on the part of the second claimant, and of her right as the widow, before the money is paid again. *Vol.* xv, *pp.* 11, 173.

Questions as to the right of the whole or half blood to inherit balances due deceased persons, will be determined in conformity with the law of the State of which the deceased was a citizen. *Sergeant W. C. Baker's case, September* 22, 1849.

The government do not recognize an administrator appointed without the consent of the heirs of the deceased. *Vol.* iii, *p.* 37.

Where arrearages are claimed by an executor, for the benefit of others, either the will should be probated in the county where the deceased lived, or those interested in the trust should signify their assent that the amount should be paid to the executor without probate of the will. *Vol.* xv, *p.* 73.

Payment of an amount due a deceased person for articles purchased by the Navy Department, may be made to the guardian of the children of the deceased, where it appears by the certificate of the probate court that the wards of the guardian are the sole heirs, and also that the debts of the deceased have been paid, and the estate closed by a settlement of the administrator's account; otherwise, payment should be made to the administrator. *Vol.* xiv, *p.* 206.

Arrears due a deceased soldier may be paid without administration to the widow, child, father, mother, brothers and sisters, but not to more remote heirs; and no after application for the benefit of creditors will be recognized.

Arrears of pay may be legally paid to the mother of a deceased soldier, he being an illegitimate son, leaving neither wife nor child.

A soldier can not, by a will, transfer his right to extra pay or land; but *can* his arrears of pay.

CHAPTER XXVI.

EXTRA PAY—ARMY AND NAVY.

"AN act to amend an act entitled 'an act supplemental to an act entitled 'an act providing for the prosecution of the existing war between the United States and Mexico, and for other purposes,'" approved July 19, 1848,[1] contains the following section:

SEC. 5. *And be it further enacted*, That the officers, non-commissioned officers, musicians and privates engaged in the military service of the United States in the war with Mexico, and who served out the term of their engagement, or have been or may be honorably discharged—and first, to the widows; second, to the children; third, to the parents; and fourth, to the brothers and sisters of such who have been killed in battle, or who died in service, or who, having been honorably discharged, have since died, or may hereafter die, without receiving the three months' pay herein provided for—shall be entitled to receive three months' extra pay: *Provided*, That this provision of this fifth section shall only apply to those who have been in actual service during the war.

AN ACT *for the Relief of the Widows and Orphans of the Officers, Seamen and Marines of the Brig-of-war Somers.*[2]

Whereas the United States brig-of-war Somers was foundered at sea, in the offing of the harbor of Vera Cruz, while engaged, under very hazardous circumstances, in the prosecution of hostilities against an enemy of this republic; therefore,

Be it enacted by the Senate and House of Representatives of the United States of America in Congress assembled, That the widows, if any such there be, and, in case there be no widow, the child or children, and if there be no child, then the parent or parents, and if there are no

---

[1] U. S. Statutes at Large, vol. ix, 247.

[2] *Ibid*, vol. ix, 331.

parents, to the brothers and sisters who were minors and under the age of eighteen at the time of such loss of the officers, seamen and marines who were in the service of the United States, and lost in the United States brig-of-war Somers, shall be entitled to and receive, out of any money in the treasury not otherwise appropriated, a sum equal to twelve months' pay of their respective deceased relations aforesaid, in addition to the pay due to the said deceased at the date of the loss of said vessel.

Approved, August 14, 1848.

By a joint resolution of June 16, 1848,[1] the Secretary of War was directed to pay the regiment of mounted troops which was mustered into the service by Colonel Curtis, in 1847, and discharged before joining the army, the pay and allowances (including traveling allowances) of mounted men, from the time when the several companies reached San Antonio until they were mustered out, and pay and traveling allowances on their return home; also, to the companies of Captains Smith and Hill, until they refused to be mustered out or were disbanded; also, to pay said regiment for horses lost for want of forage.

A general appropriation act of September 30, 1850,[2] makes additional provision for the payment of Texas mounted rangers, and directs that the accounts of the companies commanded by Captains Hill, Smith, Roberts, Sutton, Ross, McCulloch, Johnson and Blackwell, who were retained in or called into the service by the Governor of the State, should be audited and settled by the accounting officers of the treasury.

By the first section of "an act making appropriations for the support of the army for the year ending the thirtieth of June, one thousand eight hundred and fifty-one,"

1 U. S. Statutes at Large, vol. ix, 335.

2 *Ibid*, vol. ix, 559.

approved September 28, 1850,[1] it is, among other things, provided as follows:

Be it enacted by the Senate and House of Representatives of the United States of America in Congress assembled, That the following sums be and the same are hereby appropriated, out of any money in the treasury not otherwise appropriated, for the support of the army for the year ending the thirtieth of June, one thousand eight hundred and fifty-one: . . .

For extra pay to the commissioned officers and enlisted men of the army of the United States, serving in Oregon or California, three hundred and twenty-five thousand eight hundred and fifty-four dollars, on the following basis, to-wit: That there shall be allowed to each commissioned officer as aforesaid, while serving as aforesaid, a per diem, in addition to their regular pay and allowances, of two dollars each; and to each enlisted man as aforesaid, while serving as aforesaid, a per diem, in addition to their present pay and allowances, equal to the pay proper of each as established by existing laws; said extra pay of the enlisted men to be retained until honorably discharged. This additional pay to continue until the first of March, eighteen hundred and fifty-two,[2] or until otherwise provided.

By the first section of an appropriation act of August 31, 1852,[3] the foregoing provisions were extended to the officers, petty officers, seamen and marines of the United States navy, and to the officers and men of the revenue service, who served in the Pacific Ocean, on the coast of California and Mexico, since the 28th day of September, 1850. By an appropriation act of August 31, 1852,[4] the same provisions (except that the extra allowance was but half the regular pay) were extended to officers and men serving in New Mexico, for one year, from March 1, 1852.

---

1 U. S. Statutes at Large, vol. ix, 504.

2 Time extended one year, by act of August 31, 1852. (U. S. Statutes at Large, vol. x, 105.

3 U. S. Statutes at Large, vol. x, 100.

4 *Ibid*, vol. x, 105.

By an appropriation act of March 3, 1853,[1] the provisions of the act of September 28, 1850, were extended to the two companies of the regiment of mounted riflemen, which garrisoned Fort Laramie, while they occupied that post; and by a like act of March 3, 1853,[2] the same provisions were granted to the officers, petty officers and seamen of the United States navy; to the officers, non-commissioned officers, musicians and privates of the marine corps; and to the officers and men of the revenue service, who served in the Pacific Ocean, on the coast of California and Mexico, during the late war with Mexico, and since the conclusion of the war up to the twenty-eighth of September, eighteen hundred and fifty; . . . and that this provision, allowing extra pay, as well as that contained in the navy appropriation act of August thirty-first, eighteen hundred and fifty-two, shall extend to and include all naval storekeepers who were stationed on the Pacific coast; and the additional compensation authorized by the foregoing provision, and by the navy appropriation act of eighteen hundred and fifty-two, shall be paid to the legal representatives of all deceased persons who would have been entitled to receive the same if living.

AN ACT *for the relief of the United States Troops who were Sufferers by the recent Disaster to the Steamship San Francisco.*

Be it enacted by the Senate and House of Representatives of the United States of America in Congress assembled, That there shall be paid, under the direction of the President, to each of the officers, non-commissioned officers, musicians and privates,[3] who, on the twenty-first day of December, eighteen hundred and fifty-three,

1 U. S. Statutes at Large, vol. x, 214.

2 *Ibid,* vol. x, 220.

3 For a partial list of these, see note on page 191.

embarked at New York, under orders for California, on the steamship San Francisco, and who was on board that vessel on the occasion of her recent disaster at sea, and to Lieutenant Francis Key Murray, and any other officer or seaman of the United States navy, who was on board the said steamship, under orders, a sum equal in amount to his pay and allowances for eight months.

SEC. 2. *And be it further enacted*, That if any such officer, noncommissioned officer, musician or private shall have died before receiving such payment, from any cause consequent upon said disaster, his widow, if one survive him, and if not, then his minor children, if any there be, shall be paid a sum equal in amount to six months' pay and allowances of the deceased. . . .

An act of August 1, 1856,[1] allows the widows, or children, or parents, or brothers and sisters (in the order named) of the officers, seamen, marines, captain's clerk, assistant draughtsman, and others in service, who were lost in the sloop-of-war Albany, on the 18th day of April, 1855, and in the brig Porpoise, on the 29th day of June, 1855, twelve months' pay, in addition to the pay due at the time those vessels were lost.

By the twelfth section of a naval appropriation bill of March 3, 1857,[2] it is provided that the surviving officers of the navy of the Republic of Texas, who were commissioned at the time of annexation, shall be entitled to the pay of officers of like grades, waiting orders, in the navy of the United States, for five years from the time of annexation.

AN ACT *for the Relief of the Widows and Orphans of the Officers, Seamen and Marines of the United States Sloop-of-war Levant, and for other purposes.*[3]

Be it enacted by the Senate and House of Representatives of the United States of America in Congress assembled, That for the purpose of fixing the time at which shall commence the pensions, under

1 U. S. Statutes at Large, vol. xi, 29.

2 *Ibid*, vol. xi, 243.

3 *Ibid*, vol. xii, 273.

the existing laws, of the widows and orphan children of the officers, seamen, marines and others in service, who were lost in the United States sloop-of-war Levant, as well as the time to which the pay of said officers, seamen, marines and others in the service shall be allowed, the thirtieth day of June, one thousand eight hundred and sixty-one, shall be deemed and taken to be the day on which the said sloop-of-war Levant foundered at sea.

SEC. 2. *And be it further enacted*, That the widow or child or children, and in case there shall be no widow or child or children (as aforesaid), then the parent or parents, and if there be no parents, the brothers and sisters of the officers, seamen, marines and others in service, who were lost in said sloop-of-war Levant, including captain's clerk and assistant draughtsman, shall be entitled to and receive, out of any money in the treasury not otherwise appropriated, a sum equal to twelve months' pay of their respective deceased relations aforesaid, in addition to the pay due to the said deceased at the date of the loss of said vessel.

Approved, July 24, 1861.

Form of Claim for Three Months' extra Pay for an Officer or Soldier.

STATE OF —— }
County of —— } *ss.*

On this —— day of ——, A.D. 18—, before me, a —— within and for said county, personally appeared ——, and made oath in due form of law that he is the identical —— who was a ——, in the company commanded by Captain ——, in the —— regiment of ——, commanded by Colonel ——, in the war between the United States and Mexico; that he volunteered [*or* enlisted] at ——, on the —— day of ——, 18—; and was honorably discharged at ——, on the —— day of ——, 18—, on account of the expiration of his term of service [*or other cause*]. He makes this declaration to obtain the extra pay to which he is entitled by the act of July 18, 1848; and says that he has never received said extra pay, nor made application therefor until the present time.

He hereby appoints —— his attorney, and authorizes him to receive and receipt for any certificate or draft which may issue upon his aforesaid claim, and to do and perform any and all acts, necessary to effect the object of his said appointment. (*Signature of Claimant.*)

(*Two Witnesses.*)

And I hereby certify, that at the same time personally appeared before me, —— and ——, well known by me to be credible witnesses, who, being first duly sworn, say that they are well acquainted with ——, who signed the foregoing affidavit in their presence; that he is the identical person he represents himself to be; that said affidavit is correct, as they verily believe; and that they have no interest whatsoever in his said claim.

(*Signature of Witnesses.*

Subscribed, sworn to, and acknowledged by the said [*the claimant*], and by the said [*the witnesses*], the day and year aforesaid.

(*Officer's Signature.*)

To this must be appended the usual certificate of the Clerk, under seal.

Claim for Three Months' extra Pay by Widows.

STATE OF —— }
County of —— } *ss.*

On this —— day of ——, A.D. 18—, before me a —— within and for said county, personally appeared ——, and made oath, in due form of law, that she is the widow of ——, deceased, who was a —— in the company commanded by Captain ——, in the —— regiment of ——, commanded by Colonel ——, in the war between the United States and Mexico. That the said —— volunteered [*or* enlisted] at —— [*conclude as in preceding form*].

(*Two Witnesses.*) (*Signature of Claimant.*)

And I hereby certify that at the same time personally appeared before me —— and ——, to me well known to be credible witnesses, who, being sworn, say that they are well acquainted with the above-named ——, and know her to be the widow of ——, deceased, who was a —— in the company commanded by Captain ——, in the regiment of —— commanded by Colonel ——, in the war between the United States and Mexico. That they were acquainted with the said —— in his lifetime, and know that he and the said —— lived together as husband and wife, and were reputed to be such, and affiants have never heard their marriage doubted or called in question: That the said —— died on the —— day of ——, 18--; That the said [*the widow*], who signed the above affidavit in their presence is the identical person named therein: That they believe the statements of said affidavit to be correct; and that they have no interest in her said claim.

(*Signatures of Witnesses.*)

Sworn to, subscribed and acknowledged by the said [*the widow*], and also by the said [*the witnesses*], the day and year aforesaid.

(*Officer's Signature.*)

Here will follow the certificate and seal of Clerk, as in other cases.

The foregoing forms may be varied to suit the cases of heirs, administrators, etc.

Claims for extra pay for services in the navy and marine corps, on the coast of California and Mexico, are adjusted by the Navy Agent at Washington City, D. C., under the following regulations prescribed by the Comptroller of the Treasury:

TREASURY DEPARTMENT, SECOND COMPTROLLER'S OFFICE, *March* 1, '54.

To ALBERT G. ALLEN, ESQ., *Navy Agent, Washington, D. C.:*

Sir: In addition to the present regulations on the subject of "extra pay," granted by the acts of August 31, 1852, and March 3, 1853, to the officers and men of the navy, who served in the Pacific, on the coast of California and Mexico, during the late war with Mexico, the following are made necessary by the increasing number of spurious claims. You will enforce them in all cases, in which the papers shall be executed after the 20th instant, except in California and Oregon, where the time may be extended to the 15th of April, next; and when the new regulations and forms have been sent to individual agents or claimants, *their* applications must comply with such regulations, if the papers were executed after the date at which, in due course of mail, the regulations were received.

1. The claimant will add to his oath of identity that he has not previously applied for payment of his extra pay; or, if he has applied, he will state the circumstances, the time and the name of his attorney or assignee, if he employed any.

2. In case the claim purports to have been assigned, or the power of attorney recites a valuable consideration, the amount of the consideration of such power of attorney or assignment, must be stated in dollars and cents, by words written at length in the body of the instrument, and not at the top, or beginning of the power. When a consideration is subsequently denied by the original claimant, the onus of proof will be placed upon the attorney or assignee.

3. The magistrate or notary, before whom the power of attorney or assignment may be executed, must add to his certificate, that no blanks, interlineations nor erasures, were in the instrument at the date of his authentication thereof, or if there were any, he must

describe them according to facts. He must also name the papers accompanying said instrument.

4. There having been instances in which genuine official seals, cut from authentic official documents, have been pasted upon forged papers, it will be required that official seals be not merely pasted upon the instrument, but they must be impressed upon the paper attested.

5. Whenever the signature to any voucher is made by an X mark, a witness thereto, other than the magistrate or notary acting in the case, will be required.

6. Claimants not having convenient personal access to the Navy Agent's office, and who are ignorant of the sum allowed them, will be furnished with a statement of the sum, *only* upon their first filing their oath of identity with their discharge annexed; or if the claimant has lost his certificate of discharge, let him account for its absence.

7. When payment is claimed by an administrator, the right of the person to administer according to the laws of the state in which the letters of administration were granted, must appear in the papers from the proper court; and if the right vested previously in others, it must be shown that they have renounced, or the reason of their non-appointment must be stated. As letters of administration appear to be obtained with extreme facility, and as administrators are applying as legal representatives of persons who are alive and are applying for themselves, great caution should be exercised in administration cases; and if need be, additional proof of death, etc., should be required, though the letters of administration may be granted in due form. The amount of the penalty of the administrator's bond should be stated, and payment should not be made unless it is double the amount of the claim. The administrator in his oath of identity should be required to describe the person of the decedent he represents—that is, his age, height, complexion, color of eyes and hair, stating whether his knowledge was derived from personal acquaintance or from the information of others.

J. M. BRODHEAD, *Comptroller.*

Form of an Oath of Indentity for a Person claiming as a Petty Officer, Seaman, Ordinary Seaman, Landsman or Boy.

I, ——, do solemnly swear that I am the identical —— who served by that name as a ——, on board the United States ship ——, in the Pacific, on the coast of California and Mexico, from —— to ——, 18—, and who is named in the certificate of discharge, dated ——, 18—, signed by——, which is herewith presented and surrendered [*or if his discharge is sold, lost or otherwise disposed of, the facts and circumstances accounting for it must be sworn to*]. I also solemnly swear that I am now —— years of age, am a native of ——, that I enlisted at [*name the place or port, rendezvous, or vessel*], on or about the —— day of ——, 18—, into the grade of ——; that my ship's nnmber was ——, and that I performed duty on board of [*name in succession each vessel on which service was performed, during the whole enlistment or enlistments, places and dates of transfer*]. I also solemnly swear that I have not made any previous or other application for the extra pay now claimed by me [*or if he has, state where, when and how*], and further, that I now reside at, and am employed as ——.

(*Two Witnesses:*) (*Signature of Claimant.*)

Sworn to and subscribed before me, this —— day of ——, A. D. 18—. And I certify that to my knowledge the statement of deponent in regard to his residence and employment is true; my knowledge of deponent being derived from [*here the magistrate will state whether from personal acquaintance or otherwise*]. And I also certify that the above-named deponent appears to be about the age stated by him; that he is about ——feet —— inches in height; of —— complexion, ——hair, and —— eyes.

(*Signature of Officer.*)

[Here will follow certificate and seal of Clerk.]

Form of Receipt of Claimant.

Received this —— day of ——, 18—, of ——, Navy Agent at Washington, D. C., the sum of —— dollars and —— cents, in full for services rendered by me on board the United States ship ——, in the Pacific, on the coast of Mexico, in the years ——, for which services extra pay is granted by the act of Congress, entitled "an act making appropriations for the naval service for the year ending June 30, 18—."

(*To be signed in duplicate by Claimant.*)

Form of acknowledgment of Receipt.

STATE OF —— }
County of —— } ss.

On this —— day of ——, A. D. 18—, before me ——, a —— in and for the county and State aforesaid, personally appeared ——, who signed the foregoing receipt in duplicate, in my presence; and I certify that he is the same —— who claims to have served on board the United States ship ——, in the Pacific, on the coast of Mexico and California, in the years ——.

(*Signature of Officer.*)

[Here will follow certificate and seal of Clerk.]

Duplicate receipts in the foregoing form are required for each vessel, and for each act, when payment is claimed under more than one, to be signed by the claimant or his attorney in his name. When he is to be paid through a third party, in lieu of his receipts, he must execute, substantially in the following form, a power of attorney, in which, if there be a valuable consideration named, it must not be recited at the commencement, as is often done, or over the top, but as prescribed in the body of the power.

Form of Power of Attorney.

Know all men by these presents, that I, —— being entitled to extra pay, under the act of Congress, entitled "an act making appropriations for the naval service for the year ending June 30, 18—," approved —— 18—, amounting to —— dollars and —— cents, as a —— from ——, 18—, to ——, 18—, on board the United States ship ——, which served in the Pacific Ocean, on the coast of California and Mexico, since May 13, 1846, for and in consideration of the sum of —— dollars to me in hand paid, do hereby appoint —— my attorney, for me and in my name to demand and receive from the Navy Agent at Washington, D. C., or other proper officers of the United States, the amount of extra pay hereinbefore recited, and to receipt therefor, hereby confirming all that my said attorney may lawfully do in the premises, as fully as if done by myself.

Signed and sealed in our presence, } [SEAL.]
this —— day of —— 18—. }
(*Two Witnesses:*)

STATE OF —— } *ss.*
County of —— }

On this —— day of ——, A. D. 18—, before the undersigned authority, within and for the county and State aforesaid, personally appeared ——, to whom I read and fully explained the foregoing power of attorney, and who signed and acknowledged the same in my presence to be his free act and deed; and I further certify that at the time of taking such acknowledgment, the power or warrant of attorney aforesaid, contained neither a blank, an interlineation, nor an alteration [*or, if it did, describe the same according to the facts*], and that I have annexed hereto [*specifying the papers he may affix*]. (*Officer's Signature.*)

[Certificate of the Clerk of the Court under seal.]

A certificate of identity from a commissioned or warrant officer of the navy will be required in all cases where the discharge is lost or mislaid, in the following form:

I certify that the signature to the [within, foregoing, *or* annexed receipt, in duplicate, *or* power of attorney, *as the case may be*], is witnessed by me; that it was signed in my presence by ——, who is well known to me as the identical person who served by that name on board the United States ship ——, in the Pacific, as a ——, in the year ——, and who is named in the discharge herewith annexed. [*If the discharge be not produced, the officer will so vary the certificate as to suit other facts within his knowledge in reference to his discharge or service.*]

(*To be dated and signed by the officer, subjoining his rank.*)

If the discharge or a certified copy thereof be furnished, and the certificate of some commissioned or warrant officer can not be obtained, the claimant will so state on oath, giving the reasons, and the affidavit of two credible and disinterested witnesses, will be required instead, viz:

Form of Affidavit of Witnesses.

STATE OF —— }
County of —— } *ss.*

On this —— day of ——, 18—, before me, a ——, in and for the State and county aforesaid, duly qualified to administer oaths, personally appeared ——, residing at ——, and employed as ——, and also ——, residing at ——, and employed as ——, who are known to me as credible witnesses, residing and employed as stated, and who, being duly sworn, depose and say, that they reside and are employed as aforesaid; that they have a personal knowledge of ——, who signed the foregoing receipts [*or* power of attorney, *as the case may be*], in their presence, and that he is the identical ——, who served on board the United States ship ——, as a ——, from —— to ——, and who is named in the discharge, dated ——, and signed by ——, which he affixed in their presence to this original receipt; that their knowledge of him was obtained [*Here state fully how obtained. If they served on the ship at the same time, they will give their rate, ship's number, and, if more than one of the same name was on the ship, their numerical designation, as John Smith, first*]. And they further depose, that they have no interest in the claim of the said —— for extra pay.

(*Signatures of Witnesses.*)

Sworn to and subscribed, the day and year above-written, before me.

(*Signature of Officer.*)

[Here will follow certificate and seal of Clerk.]

If the claimant be, at the time of making his application, in the naval service of the United States, he will make the statement required in the foregoing oath of identity, in the form of a declaration, simply substituting the word "declare," for "swear," wherever it occurs; and sign the same before a commissioned officer of his vessel or station, who will certify to the fact, and also to the personal description of the claimant, as required from a civil authenticating officer. This declaration must be accompanied by the same proofs of identity, in every respect, as the oath of identity of a claimant not in service.

Extra pay due a deceased person may be paid to his legal representatives, made such by letters testamentary, if his will expressly recites it, or to a residuary legatee. The executor or legatee must furnish an authenticated copy of the will, from the court which admitted it to probate, together with his oath of identity, receipts or power of attorney, etc. It may also be paid on letters of administration, which letters of administration must recite the names of *all* the heirs, and there must be indisputable evidence presented of the death of the person on account of whose service the claim is made, provided such letters show that the bond is double the amount due, and that such letters were granted to the only heir, or to the heir having the first right to administer, or at the request of all the other heirs, or to a creditor, and, in the latter case, only to the amount of such claim against the deceased as may be approved by the court granting such letters.

Form of Oath of Identity by Executor or Administrator.

I, ——, of ——, in the county of ——, State of ——, depose and say that I am the identical —— named in the accompanying letters of administration [*or letters testamentary, or copy of letters, etc., as the case may be*], on the estate of ——, deceased, and that said letters are unrevoked and now in full force and effect; that the said —— was at the time of his death a legal resident of ——, county of ——, State of ——, and that he was the identical person who served by that name on board the United States ship ——, on the coast of California, in the years ——, who is named in the certificate of discharge herewith surrendered, and who died [*state where he died, and whether he was in the service of the United States or not at the time of his death*], on or about the —— day of ——, 18—, and to whose estate extra pay is due under the provisions of the act of Congress of March 3, 1853, and for which extra pay I now apply as his legal representative. And I further swear that the said ——, was a native of ——, was —— years of age; that he was about —— feet —— inches in height, of —— complexion, —— eyes and —— hair, and that he entered the naval service at ——, on or about the —— day of ——, 18—. [*State whether these facts were matters of personal knowledge to the deponent, or were derived from others. If the discharge be not produced, he must depose to having made due search for it among the effects of the decedent, and to any facts in reference to the disposition of it within his knowledge.* (*Signature of Claimant.*)

STATE OF —— }
County of —— } ss.

Personally appeared before me, a —— in and for the county and State aforesaid, duly qualified to administer oaths, ——, who signed the foregoing deposition in my presence, and made oath to the truth of the same.

And I certify that I know the deponent to be the administrator named in the accompanying letters of administration.

Witness my hand, this —— day of ——, A. D., 18—.

(*Officer's Signature.*)

[Here will follow the certificate and seal of Clerk.]

If an executor or administrator desires to be paid through a third party, he will execute a power of attorney and acknowledgment of the same according to the forms heretofore prescribed, making the necessary changes.

CHAPTER XXVII.

CLAIMS FOR HORSES OR OTHER PROPERTY LOST OR DESTROYED.

LAWS, REGULATIONS AND FORMS.

SUNDRY acts have been passed making compensation for the loss or destruction of horses or other property in battle or otherwise, in the service; but the act of March 3, 1849, is so broad in its provisions, that it practically supersedes all other acts, and renders their insertion here unnecessary.

AN ACT *to provide for the payment of Horses and other Property lost or destroyed in the Military Service of the United States, approved March* 3, 1849.

Be it enacted by the Senate and House of Representatives of the United States of America in Congress assembled, That any field, or staff, or other officer, mounted militiaman, volunteer, ranger or cavalry, engaged in the military service of the United States since the 18th of June, 1812, or who shall hereafter be in said service, and has sustained, or shall sustain damage without any fault or negligence on his part, while in said service, by the loss of a horse in battle, or by the loss of a horse wounded in battle, and which has died, or shall die of said wound, or, being so wounded, shall be abandoned by order of his officer and lost, or shall sustain damage by the loss of any horse by death or abandonment, because of the unavoidable dangers of the sea when on board a United States transport vessel, or because the United States failed to supply transportation for the horse, and the owner was compelled by the order of his commanding officer to embark and leave him, or in consequence of the United States failing to supply sufficient forage, or because the rider was dismounted and separated from his horse, and ordered to do duty on foot, at a station detached from his horse, and when the officer in the immediate command ordered or shall order the horse turned out to graze in the woods, prairies or commons, because the United States failed or shall fail to supply sufficient forage, and the loss was or shall be consequent thereof, or for the loss of necessary equipage in consequence of the loss of his horse as aforesaid, shall be allowed and paid the value thereof, not to exceed two hundred dollars, provided, that if any payment has been or shall be made to any one aforesaid for the use and risk, or for forage after the death, loss or abandonment of his horse, and payment shall be deducted from the value thereof, unless he satisfied or shall satisfy the paymaster at the time he made or shall make the payment, or thereafter show by proof that he was remounted, in which case, the deduction shall only extend to the time he was on foot; and provided, also, if any payment shall have been or shall hereafter be made to any person above mentioned on account of clothing, to which he was not entitled by law, such payment shall be deducted from the value of his horse or accoutrements.

SEC. 2. *And be it further enacted*, That any person who has sustained or shall sustain damage by the capture or destruction by an enemy, or by the abandonment or destruction, by the order of the commanding-general, the commanding officer or quartermaster of any horse, mule ox, wagon, cart, boat, sleigh or harness, while such property was in the military service of the United States, either by impressment or contract, except in cases where the risk to which the property would be exposed was agreed to be incurred by the owner, and any person who has sustained or shall sustain damage by the death or abandonment and loss of any such horse, mule or ox, while in the service aforesaid, in consequence of the failure on the part of the United States to furnish the same with sufficient forage; and any person who has lost, or shall lose, or has had or shall have destroyed by unavoidable accident any horse, mule, ox, wagon, cart, boat, sleigh or harness, while such property was in the service aforesaid, shall be allowed and paid the value thereof at the time he entered the service: *Provided*, it shall appear that such loss, capture, abandonment, destruction or death was without any fault or negligence on the part of the owner of the property, and while it was actually employed in the service of the United States.

SEC 3. *And be it further enacted*, That the claims provided for under this act shall be adjusted by the third auditor, under such rules as shall be prescribed by the Secretary of War, under the direction or with the assent of the President of the United States, as well in regard to the receipt of applications of claimants as the species and degree of evidence, the manner in which such evidence shall be taken and authenticated, which rules shall be such as, in the opinion of the President, shall be best calculated to obtain the object of this act, paying a due regard as well to the claims of individual justice as to the interest of the United States; which rules and regulations shall be published for four weeks in such newspapers, in which the laws of the United States are published, as the Secretary of War shall direct.

SEC 4. *And be it further enacted,* That in all adjudications of said auditor upon the claims above-mentioned, whether such judgments be in favor of or adverse to the claim, shall be entered in a book provided by him for that purpose, and under his direction; and when such judgments shall be in favor of such claim, the claimant or his legal representative shall be entitled to the amount thereof, certified by said auditor, at the Treasury of the United States.

SEC. 5. *And be it further enacted,* That in all instances where any minor has been or shall be engaged in the military service of the United States, and was or shall be provided with a horse or equipments, or military accouterments, by his parent or guardian, and has died or shall die without paying for said property, and the same has been or shall be lost, captured, destroyed or abandoned, in the manner before mentioned, said parent or guardian shall be allowed pay therefor, on making satisfactory proof, as in other cases, and the further proof that he is entitled thereto, by having furnished the same.

SEC. 6. *And be it further enacted,* That in all instances where any person, other than a minor, has been or shall be engaged in the military service aforesaid, and has been or shall be provided with a horse or equipments, or with military accouterments, by any person, the owner thereof, who has risked or shall take the risk of such horse, equipments or military accouterments on himself, and the same has been or shall be lost, captured, destroyed or abandoned, in the manner before mentioned, such owner shall be allowed pay therefor, on making proof, as in other cases, and the further proof that he is entitled thereto, by having furnished the same and having taken the risk on himself.

SEC. 7. *And be it further enacted,* That in all cases where horses have been condemned by a board of officers on account of their unfitness for service, in consequence of the Government failing to supply forage, all such horses and their equipage shall be allowed and paid for, whenever the facts shall be proven, by legal and satisfactory evidence, whether oral or written, that such condemned horse and the equipage was turned over to a quartermaster of the army, whether any receipt therefor was given and produced or not.

AN ACT *to provide for the Equitable Settlement of the Accounts of the Officers and Crews of the Frigate Congress and other Vessels.*

Be it enacted by the Senate and House of Representatives of the United States of America in Congress assembled, That the proper accounting officers of the treasury be and they hereby are authorized and directed to settle, upon the principles of justice and equity, the accounts of the officers, sailors, marines and crews of the United States frigate Congress, the sloop Cumberland, and of any other vessel or vessels-of-war, the books of which were lost or destroyed in consequence of the naval engagements at Hampton Roads, on the eighth and ninth of March, Anno Domini one thousand eight hundred and sixty-two.

SEC. 2. *And be it further enacted*, That the Secretary of the Navy be and he is hereby authorized to furnish to the sailors, marines and crews of any of the vessels engaged in the naval actions in the foregoing section mentioned, whose bedding, clothing or other property was lost or destroyed therein, *with* an amount sufficient to cover their losses, and not exceeding sixty dollars to each man, to be paid in kind or in money, at the discretion of the flag-officer of the North Atlantic Squadron.

Approved, April 2, 1862.

A RESOLUTION *for the Relief of the Officers, Non-commissioned Officers and Privates of the Battalion of Marines on Board the Transport Governor, on the third of November*, 1861.

Resolved by the Senate and House of Representatives of the United States of America in Congress assembled, That the sum of seven thousand one hundred and sixty-three dollars and fifty-one cents be and the same is hereby appropriated, out of any money in the treasury not otherwise appropriated, to compensate the officers, non-commissioned officers and privates who composed the marine battalion attached to the Port Royal naval expedition, under Flag-officer Dupont, for the losses of their personal effects by the foundering of the steamer Governor, in which they were embarked, on the third of November last; and that the Secretary of the Navy cause the said sum, or so much thereof as may be necessary, to be paid to them according to the estimated value of their personal effects lost in the manner aforesaid.

Approved July 11, 1862.

A RESOLUTION *to Compensate the Crew of the United States Steamer Varuna, for Clothing and other Property Lost in the Public Service.*

Resolved by the Senate and House of Representatives of the United States of America in Congress assembled, That the proper accounting officers of the treasury be and they are hereby authorized, in settling the accounts of the petty officers, seamen and others of the crew of the United States steamer Varuna, which was sunk during the engagement near New Orleans, on or about the twenty-fourth day of April, eighteen hundred and sixty-two, to credit each of them with the amount of sixty dollars, to cover their losses of bedding, clothing and other property, occasioned by the sinking of the said steamer.

Approved, July 11, 1862.

RULES AND REGULATIONS.

Under the third section of the act of March 3, 1849, the Secretary of War, with the approval of the President, on the 26th of March, 1849, prescribed certain rules and regulations under which the claims were to be adjusted by the third auditor. They are substantially as follows:

Claims under the act are divided into *three* classes, viz:

Those under the first section being the *first* class.

Those under the second, fifth and sixth sections being the *second* class.

Those under the seventh section being the *third* class.

All claims to be presented to the office of the third auditor of the treasury, and substantiated by such evidence as is hereinafter designated, with respect to cases of the class under which it falls.

First class of cases.

To establish a claim under the provision of the first section of the act, the claimant must adduce the evidence of the officer under whose command he served when the loss occurred, if alive; or, if dead, then of the next surviving officer, describing the property; the value thereof at the time of entering the service; the time and manner in which the loss happened; and whether or not it was sustained without any fault or negligence on the claimant's part. The evidence should also, in case the claimant was remounted after the loss, state when remounted, how long he continued so, and explain whether the horse whereon he was remounted had not been furnished by the United States, or been owned by another mounted militiaman or volunteer, to whom payment for the use and risk thereof, or for its forage, while in the possession of the claimant, may have been made; and if it had been thus owned, should name the person and the command to which he belonged. And in every instance in which the claim may extend to equipage, the several articles of which the same consisted, and separate value of each should be specified.

Second class of cases.

To establish a claim under the provisions of the second, fifth, and sixth sections of the act, it will, in addition to the testimony required under the head of first class of cases, be necessary, in cases where the property lost was in the service by contract or impressment, to produce the testimony of the officer or agent of the United States who impressed or contracted for the service of the property mentioned in such claim, and also of the officer under whose command the same was employed at the time of the capture, destruction, loss or abandonment, declaring in what way the property was taken into the service of the United States, the value thereof, whether or not the risk to which it would be exposed was agreed to be incurred by the owner; and whether or not, as regarded horses, mules, oxen, he engaged to supply the same with sufficient forage, in what manner the loss happened, and whether or not it was sustained without any fault or negligence on his part.

A parent or guardian of a deceased minor will, in addition to such testimony applicable to his claim as is previously described, have to furnish proof, that he provided the minor with the property therein mentioned, that the minor died without paying for such property, and that he, the parent or guardian is entitled to payment for it by his having furnished the same.

SEC. 6. Besides the testimony in support of his claim hereinbefore required, every such owner thereof will have to prove that he did provide the horse, equipments or military accoutrements therein mentioned, and took the risk thereof on himself, and that he is entitled to pay therefor, by having furnished the same and taking the risk thereof on himself, and this proof should be contained in a deposition of the person who had been so provided by him with such horse, equipments or military accouterments.

Third class of cases.

To establish a claim under the provisions of the seventh section of the act, the claimant must adduce the evidence of the witnesses mentioned under the head of first class of cases, satisfactorily proving that the property therein described was, while in the military service of the United States, condemned by a board of officers on account of their being rendered unfit for service in consequence of the Government failing to supply forage, and that such property was turned over to a quartermaster of the United States army, explaining when the claimant was remounted, etc., as required in said first class of cases.

In no case can the production of evidence previously described be dispensed with, unless the impracticability of producing it be clearly proved, and then the nearest and best other evidence of which the case is susceptible, must be furnished in lieu thereof.

Every claim must be accompanied by a deposition of the claimant "declaring that he has not received from any officer or agent of the United States any horse or horses, equipage, accouterments, mule, wagon, cart, boat, sleigh or harness (as the case may be), in lieu of the property lost, nor any compensation for the same," and be supported, if practicable, by the original valuation list, if made by the appraisers of the property at the time the same was taken into the United States service, and in cases where the loss is alleged to have occurred because the United States failed to supply transportation for the horse, and the owner was compelled, by the order of his commanding officer, to embark and leave him, as provided for in the first section of the law; the affidavit of the claimant must, in addition to the declaration above-mentioned, declare "that he did, in obedience to the order of his officer, leave said horse or equipage, and that he never sold or otherwise disposed of said horse or equipage, and never received any compensation for said horse or equipage from any person whatever."

All evidence, other than the certificates of officers who at the time of giving them were in the military service of the United States, must be sworn to before some judge, justice of the peace, or other person duly authorized to administer oaths, and of which au thority proof should accompany the evidence.

Form of Application.

STATE OF ——
County of —— } *ss.*

On this —— day of ——, A. D. 18—, personally appeared before me, a —— within and for said county, duly authorized to administer oaths, ——, a resident of said county, to me well known, who being by me first duly sworn, deposes and says, that [1] he is the identical —— who was a ——, in the company, commanded by ——, in the regiment of ——, commanded by ——, that he entered the service of the United States on or about the ——, day of ——, A. D. 18—, and was regularly mustered into said service, and mounted upon a horse of the following description, viz : ——, which said horse was appraised in due form of the value of $——, that he continued mounted upon the said horse until the —— day of ——, 18—, when the said horse was lost in consequence of, and in the manner following, viz: ——. That at the time of the loss aforesaid he was under the immediate command of ——, that he was remounted on the —— day of ——, A. D. 18—, on a horse valued at $——, which he obtained of ——, who was ——, and continued so remounted until the —— day of 18—, when he was regularly and honorably mustered out of the service by ——.

And further, that he has not received from any officer or agent of the United States any horse, or other property in lieu of the horse lost as aforesaid, nor has he received any compensation for the same; the same having been lost without any fault or negligence on his part.

(*Claimant's Signature.*)

Sworn to and subscribed, before me,
this —— day of ——, A. D. 18—. }
(*Officer's Signature.*)

---

[1] This affidavit must be varied to suit the facts : if the property was *hired* to the Government, say: In accordance with the terms of a contract by him executed with [*name the person who made the contract, and his official rank and position, etc.,*] on said —— day of —— 18—, he did furnish to the United States [*here describe particularly the property lost, and give the value of each item thereof at the time the contract was made.*]

If, however, the property was taken for the use of the army by *impressment*, say : ["*First, give the name and official rank and position of the person who seized the property*], did without his consent seize and impress into the service of the United States, of the property of him the said [*name of claimant*], one [*here describe particularly the property, and give the value of each item at the time it was seized.*"]

STATE OF —— }
County of—— } *ss.*

On this —— day of ——, A. D., 18—, before me a —— within and for said county, duly authorized by law to administer oaths, personally came ——, a resident of said county, to me well known to be a credible witness, who, being by me duly sworn, deposes and says, that he is the identical ——, who was the *Captain* commanding a company of ——, in the regiment commanded by Colonel ——, in the service of the United States, in the war with ——, that —— was a ——, in the said company, having been regularly enrolled and mustered into the service, that at the time of his muster he was mounted on a horse of the following description, viz: ——, which said horse was duly appraised and valued at the sum of $——, that the horse above described was lost, on the —— day of ——, in consequence of ——, in the manner following, viz: ——, which said loss was sustained without any fault or negligence on the part of the claimant.

And deponent further states, that the said —— was remounted after said loss, on the —— day of ——, A. D., 18—, and continued so remounted until the —— day of ——, A. D., 18—.

And deponent further states, that the horse upon which the said —— was remounted as aforesaid, was not furnished by the United States or any of their officers or agents, or been owned by another mounted militiaman or volunteer, to whom payment for the loss and risk thereof, or for its forage, while in possession of the said ——, could have been made, *except* ——.

And deponent further states, that the horse upon which the said —— was remounted, was purchased by him of one ——, and the sum of $——, paid for the same.

And deponent further states, that the said —— was honorably discharged on the —— day of ——, A. D., 18—.

Subscribed and sworn to, before me, the day and year aforesaid.

(*Officer's Signature.*)

[Add certificate and seal of Clerk of Court.]

Power of Attorney.

Know all men by these presents, that I, ——, of ——, named in the foregoing declaration and affidavit, do hereby constitute and appoint ——, my true and lawful attorney, authorizing him to file this my claim for payment for —— in the military service of the United States, and to do all acts necessary and proper in the premises; to receive and receipt for a draft payable to my order for such sum as may be found due upon examination and settlement of my claim.

Witness my hand and seal this —— day of ——, A. D., 18—.

Signed, sealed in presence of }
(*Two Witnesses.*) } [L. S.]

STATE OF —— } ss.
County of—— }

On this —— day of ——, 18—, personally appeared before me the above named ——, to me known, and acknowledged the foregoing power of attorney to be his act and deed for the purpose therein mentioned.

(*Officer's Signature.*)

[Add certificate and seal of Clerk.]

CHAPTER XXVIII.

SUNDRY MATTERS RELATING TO ARMY AND NAVY.

By a resolution of March 3, 1847,[1] it is provided:

Resolved by the Senate and House of Representatives of the United States of America in Congress assembled, That the Secretary of War be, and he is hereby authorized and required to cause to be refunded to the several States, or to individuals for services rendered acting under the authority of any State, the amount of expenses incurred by them in organizing, subsisting and transporting volunteers previous to their being mustered and received into the service of the United States for the present war,[2] and for subsisting troops in the service of the United States, without waiting for deductions to be made from the pay of said volunteers.

The benefits of this resolution were, by an act of June 2, 1848,[3] extended "so as to embrace all cases of expenses heretofore incurred in organizing, subsisting and transporting volunteers, previous to their being mustered and received into the service of the United States for the present war,[2] whether by States, counties, corporations or individuals, either acting with or without authority of any States," provided the Secretary of War should be satisfied, by proof of the necessity of such expenditures. Interest was allowed upon moneys thus advanced, at six per centum per annum, where claimants paid or lost the interest upon advances, or were liable to pay it.

Claims under the foregoing resolution and act must be presented to the Second and Third Auditors of the Treas-

1 U. S. Statutes at Large, vol. ix, 206.

2 The war with Mexico.

3 U. S. Statutes at Large, vol. ix, 236.

ury, for examination. An abstract of the claim should be made out, and an affidavit of its correctness attached. With this should be filed such evidence in connection with the expenditure as the claimant may possess. Vouchers, showing the expenditures, with dates, items and amounts paid, must also be filed in support of the claim.[1]

EFFECTS OF DECEASED OFFICERS AND SOLDIERS.

Whenever an officer dies or is killed at any military post or station,

---

1 The Secretary of War has made the following decisions upon claims filed under the above provisions:

No allowance will be sanctioned for expenses of volunteers, whether officers or men, not afterwards mustered into the service; and there must be evidence that the persons supplied were mustered in.

Personal expenses of officers (except as to board and lodging) recruiting their companies prior to muster into service are not allowable; but the expenses of recognized agents of a State, when shown by bills and vouchers, will be refunded.

It is not sufficient to show that a gross amount was expended; still less, that sums were given to individuals to expend, without evidence by bills and vouchers that it was expended.

No more than fifty cents per day, per man, for subsistence, nor more than seventy-five cents for subsistence and quarters will be sanctioned, the rate to depend upon the price paid for complete rations at the nearest recruiting station or military post.

Purchases of subsistence in bulk, will be paid for at the current rates at the place of purchase, provided the quantities are in reasonable proportion to the number of men.

The articles of subsistence must be such as are recognized in the regular service; or if others are substituted, the cost of the whole must not exceed the price of regular supplies. This will also apply to forage for mounted volunteers. Spiritous liquors will not be paid for.

Transportation is restricted to the usual routes and modes of conveyance. Troops moving by land will not be allowed more than two four-horse wagons, and teams for the transportation of baggage and provisions for a company of from fifty to seventy-five men. Wagon hire for the transportation of men will not be refunded.

Bounties paid men to induce them to volunteer, will not be refunded.

As the law has made the payment of interest conditional upon certain contingencies, the facts should be fully stated from which the department can infer that the contingency has occurred.

or in the vicinity of the same, it will be the duty of the commanding officer to report the fact direct to the adjutant general, with the date and any other information proper to be communicated. If an officer die at a distance from a military post, any officer having intelligence of the same will, in like manner, communicate it, specifying the day of his decease; a duplicate of the report will be sent to department headquarters.

Inventories of the effects of deceased officers, required by the ninety-fourth article of war, will be transmitted to the adjutant-general. If a legal administrator or family connection be present, and take charge of the effects, it will be so stated to the adjutant-general.

Inventories of the effects of deceased non-commissioned officers and soldiers, required by the ninety-fifth article of war, will be forwarded to the adjutant-general, by the commander of the company to which the deceased belonged, and a duplicate of the same to the colonel of the regiment. Final statements of pay, clothing, etc., will be sent with the inventories. When a soldier dies at a post or station, absent from his company, it will be the duty of his immediate commander to furnish the required inventory, and at the same time to forward to the commanding officer of the company to which the soldier belonged a report of his death, specifying the date, place and cause; to what time he was last paid; and the money or other effects in his possession at the time of his decease; which report will be noted on the next muster roll of the company to which the man belonged. Each inventory will be indorsed: "Inventory of the effects of ——, late of —— company, —— regiment of ——, who died at ——, the —— day of ——, 18—."

If a legal representative receive the effects, it will be stated in the report. If the soldier leave no effects, the fact will be reported.

Should the effects of a deceased non-commissioned officer or soldier not be administered upon within a short period after his decease, they shall be disposed of by a council of administration, under the authority of the commanding officer of the post, and the proceeds deposited with the paymaster, to the credit of the United States, until they shall be claimed by the legal representatives of the deceased.

In all such cases of sales by the council of administration, a statement in detail, or account of the proceeds, duly certified by the council and commanding officer, accompanied by the paymaster's receipt for the proceeds, will be forwarded by the commanding officer to the adjutant-general. The statement will be indorsed: "Report of the proceeds of the effects of ——, late of —— company, —— regiment of ——, who died at ——, the —— day of ——, 18—."

MUSTER AND PAY ROLLS OF THE ARMY, NAVY AND MARINE CORPS.

Such of these rolls as were not destroyed in the burning of the War Department, in 1814, and the Treasury Department, in 1833, are located as follows:

In the Adjutant-General's Office.—1. All commissioned officers in the regular army, except rolls burned in 1814.

2. All enlisted men in the regular army since the peace of February 17, 1815.

3. Muster rolls and inspection returns of volunteers and militia called out, in the war of 1812, for the States of Vermont, New York, Pennsylvania, New Jersey, Delaware, North Carolina, and South Carolina (imperfect).

4. Muster rolls of volunteers and militia in the Florida war, from 1835 to 1842, and the Creek war in 1836—partially incomplete—the deficiencies supposed to be in the Second Auditor's office.

5. Muster rolls of volunteers and militia for the Mexican war, from April 24, 1846.

6. All enlisted men of the ten additional regiments of the army (say 3d dragoons or voltigeurs, and 9th to 16th infantry), raised by act of February 15, 1847; and partially in the Pension Office.

In the Second Auditor's Office.—Rolls of volunteers and militia in the Seminole wars of 1817; the Black Hawk war of 1832; the Florida wars from 1835 to 1842; and the Creek war in 1836.

In the Third Auditor's Office.—All enlisted men in the regular army *prior* to the peace of February 17, 1815;

and all volunteers and militia *prior* to and during the war of 1812, to the peace of February 17, 1815.

In the Fourth Auditor's Office.—Rolls of seamen, flotillamen and marines in all wars.

In the Pension Office.—1. All commissioned officers in the regular army—rolls partially in this office.

2. Muster rolls for volunteers of the Mexican war, from August 24, 1846.

3. Enlisted men of the ten additional regiments of the army (say 3d dragoons or voltigeurs, and 9th to 16th infantry), raised by act of February 10, 1847—partially in this office.

APPENDIX.

FOR the purpose of correcting certain erroneous views which prevail relative to the object of the appointment of Examining Surgeons, and their duties, under the eighth section of the act of July 14, 1862,[1] the following statement is made.

Original examinations of applicants for invalid pensions may be made by army surgeons, or by two private physicians or surgeons in each case, as heretofore. These examinations *may* be made by surgeons appointed by the Commissioner of Pensions; but it is not indispensable that they should be so made. Where the examination of the private physicians or surgeons appears by their affidavit, to have been complete, and a satisfactory case for an invalid pension has been made out, a further examination by a surgeon of the Cŏmmissioner will not be required; but the Commissioner reserves to himself, under the obvious intent of the law, the right of referring to a surgeon of his own appointment, for special examination and report, any case not satisfactorily established by the proof filed with the declaration of the applicant; and to secure uniformity in the method of making such special examinations, the present able and efficient commissioner, Hon. Joseph H. Barrett, has prepared a circular containing a schedule of private instructions for their guidance. From this circular he has kindly permitted the publication of the following extracts, which are deemed to be of a *public* character:

[1] See page 32, *ante*.

I. Your primary duty, as contemplated by law, is to examine applicants for invalid pensions when specially referred to you by this office, and enrolled invalid pensioners as biennially required. When requested to examine original applicants, you can do so, on satisfactory evidence of the applicant's identity, and that he has been regularly discharged from the military or naval service of the United States.

II. The points to be determined by your examination are—

1. The degree, if any, to which the applicant is disabled, by the particular injury or disease alleged, from obtaining his subsistence by manual labor.

2. The origin of the alleged disability, whether after entering the service, and in the line of duty, or not, so far as discoverable from its nature and the facts before you.

3. Its probable duration; whether permanent or temporary.

III. In estimating the degree of disability resulting from *wounds*, you will rate the loss of a limb, or of a hand or a foot, as total. The loss of one eye, the sight of the other being unimpaired, may be reckoned as one-half disability. Injuries causing great and incurable deformity, though not directly disqualifying for manual labor, should be regarded as tending to exclude the applicant from obtaining employment, and liberally estimated. In cases of disease, more specific directions can not be given as to the rate, but each case must be left to the judgment of the medical examiner. The former occupation of the applicant is not to be taken as the basis for reckoning the degree. Any cause other than that alleged, operating to increase the disability, should be noted, but not taken into account in this estimate.

VI. The fees for all original examinations, made at the request of the applicants, must be paid by them, and will not be refunded. In all special and biennial examinations, a receipt for the legal fee paid must be given to the person examined, who, if already a pensioner, or when he becomes such, will be entitled to repayment on forwarding his receipt to this office.

As before remarked, the instructions to examining surgeons are, in the main, private. Their relations to the Commissioner are confidential; and to him their reports are made, directly. The reasons for this, as well as for a special examination in many cases, are plain. The affidavit of the two physicians or surgeons which by the regulations is required to accompany every application for an invalid pension (except where the examination of the physicial condition of the claimant is made by an army surgeon, or a surgeon appointed under the eighth section), is entirely *ex parte.* The affiants are witnesses for the claimant; there is no cross-examination by the government or its agents; and no attempt is made, by counter testimony taken at the same time, to contradict the statements contained in the affidavit. This, as will readily be perceived, leaves the way open for the perpetration of serious frauds upon the government. The physicians or surgeons who testify, are, in many instances, friends of the claimants, in sympathy with them, easily persuaded into making an affidavit; and, not unfrequently, conceal facts, which if known, would defeat the application. To protect government against the wrong thus made possible, the law for the appointment of special examining surgeons was enacted. These surgeons are witnesses for the government; as its agents they make their examinations: and their testimony is also *ex parte.* To disclose to claimants or their attorneys the result of these examinations would be to render them almost useless, as well as to subject examining surgeons and the Commissioner to endless discussion, attempted explanations, complaints, fault-finding, abuse and other annoyances. These surgeons are selected for their professional ability and integrity; they are sworn to a faithful discharge of their duties; they have no personal interests at stake to warp their judgment. There is, therefore, every reasonable assurance, that claimants will be justly and impartially dealt with.

INDEX.

PAY.

www.ingramcontent.com/pod-product-compliance
Lightning Source LLC
LaVergne TN
LVHW020917110826
845150LV00004B/701

9781425555856